Cape May County,
New Jersey

Cape May County, New Jersey

The Making of an American Resort Community

Jeffery M. Dorwart

Rutgers University Press

New Brunswick, New Jersey

Third paperback printing, 1996

Library of Congress Cataloging-in-Publication Data

Dorwart, Jeffery M., 1944–
    Cape May County, New Jersey : the making of an American resort
community / by Jeffery M. Dorwart.
        p.   cm.
    Includes bibliographical references and index.
    ISBN 0-8135-1783-4
    ISBN 0-8135-1784-2 (pbk.)
    1. Cape May County (N.J.)—History.   I. Title.
F142.C2D67   1992
974.9'98—dc20   91-29058
                                              CIP

British Cataloging-in-Publication information available

The publication of this volume has been sponsored by the Cape May
County Board of Chosen Freeholders and has been supported by the
New Jersey Historical Commission.

This book is dedicated
in memory of
James S. Kilpatrick, Jr.

Contents

Foreword

With 1992 marking the three hundredth anniversary of the incorporation of Cape May County, the county's board of chosen freeholders determined that a scholarly history of the county should be prepared as part of the anniversary observance. In 1988 the board of freeholders officially appointed a Tercentennial Committee, consisting of ten community leaders, to facilitate the anniversary projects. The freeholders hired a Rutgers University historian to research and recount the three-hundred-year story.

The freeholder director at that time was James S. Kilpatrick, Jr., well known as an advocate of cultural and historic projects. He was the freeholder advisor to historical and cultural agencies, including the county museum and Historic Cold Spring Village. It was through his efforts that the county Cultural and Heritage Commission, which supports the local historical societies, was created. As a result of his vision, an accurate story of our county's history will be preserved for future generations.

It was with great pleasure that the Tercentennial Committee worked for and with Mr. Kilpatrick to finalize these projects to celebrate with pride the anniversary of the County of Cape May.

Jenny Ayres-Snyder, Director
Cape May County Cultural and Heritage Commission

Preface

This book originated with the decision by the Cape May County Board of Chosen Freeholders and the Cape May County Cultural and Heritage Commission to celebrate the three hundredth anniversary of the founding of Cape May County government with the publication of the first comprehensive history of the county. The board of freeholders and the Cultural and Heritage Commission recognized that although Cape May County's historic character had become one of its major attractions as a resort community, no one had compiled a complete history since 1897. County officials believed the tercentennial history should combine the latest research methods and scholarship with a popular narrative approach in order to appeal to both students of history and the general public interested in Cape May County's historic past. To further its goal of making the book accessible to a general audience, the board of freeholders arranged for publication of the book by Rutgers University Press.

The investigation of Cape May County history provided an opportunity to examine an American seashore community from its earliest roots as a pioneering maritime and farming colony to its evolution into a modern resort community. Study of this once-isolated New Jersey oceanfront region from its first recorded discovery by Henry Hudson in 1609 to its emergence as a twentieth-century vacationland revealed complex social and economic forces at work. From the beginning of its history, Cape May County was an area of cultural ferment where Native Americans confronted Europeans, African-Americans were held in slavery, and a socioeconomic type that this study defines as a whaler yeoman dominated the community. Through an extremely high rate of intermarriage among the original whaler yeoman families and their accumulation of a large share of scarce farmland on the wet, marshy peninsula, these families exerted tremendous political, social, and economic control over their county. They guided development and determined the direction and rate of change for over two hundred years.

Gradually, technological innovation, such as the railroad, and the introduction of a new immigrant population accelerated the pace of change. The founding of a unique Jewish-American settlement at Woodbine, the African-American town of Whitesboro, and Italian-American and Scandinavian-American enclaves along the once-uninhabited oceanfront barrier islands all pointed to the emergence of a multiethnic, multicultural community that threatened the domination of the older whaler yeoman families on the mainland. How Cape May County responded to these new forces, and to change, not only illuminates the evolution over an extended period of time of a southern New Jersey community but also enhances our understanding of the larger American experience within a changing community.

This book is in part the product of two years of conversations with many Cape May County residents, including a Goshen librarian, a Rio Grande genealogist, an Ocean City fisherman, a retired Italian-American baker from Philadelphia, a former editor of a Cape May City newspaper, and an African-American jazz pianist from Wildwood, among many others. I cannot acknowledge all individually, but I thank everyone who showed an interest in discussing with me the story of their county's past.

Special thanks go to those whose continuing support made this work possible. The late James S. Kilpatrick, Jr., especially, and Herbert Frederick, Ralph W. Evans, Daniel Beyel, and William E. Sturm of the Cape May County Board of Chosen Freeholders endorsed this project from the outset. A subcommittee of the Cape May County Tercentennial Committee reviewed the first draft of the manuscript. This committee included Raymond McCullough; Jennie Ayres-Snyder, the executive director of the commission; Thomas Leonard, the county librarian; Donald Pettifer, the director of Historic Cold Spring Village; Dr. Patricia Horton, county superintendent of schools; and Somers Corson, curator of the Cape May County Historical Society museum and library. Corson, whose roots trace back to the earliest whaler yeoman families, taught me more about Cape May County's tradition, heritage, and landscape than anyone else. More important, he shared his wisdom and friendship with me as we toured ancient Cape May

County cemeteries, remote woodland roads, and long-lost historic sites.

For their assistance in this project, I wish to thank the staff of Cape May County Clerk Angela Pulvino, particularly Rita Fulginiti and Diana Hevener; Barbara Sittineri of the Cultural and Heritage Commission staff; and the staff of the clerk's office of the board of freeholders. Thanks also go to H. Gerald MacDonald of Wildwood Crest for preparing the photographs for this book, Charles W. Snyder for drawing the maps, and especially to Loretta Carlisle of Rutgers University for typing the final draft of the manuscript.

Grants from the New Jersey Historical Commission and from the Rutgers University Research Council helped to fund the research, writing, and publication of this history.

Although many people and organizations assisted in the preparation of this book, the author alone assumes responsibility for the accuracy of the facts and for the interpretations presented in the following history of Cape May County, New Jersey, 1609–1992.

Jeffery M. Dorwart

Glossary of Place Names

Early Place Names	Present-Day Names (1992)
Anglesea	North Wildwood
Beesleys	Marmora
Belle Plain	Belleplain
Bennetts	Erma
Cape Island	City of Cape May
Cedar Grove	South Seaville
Cedar Hammocks	Goshen
Centerville	Cold Spring
Corson's Inlet	Strathmere
Corsonville	Palermo
Crandol Town	Rio Grande
Cressetown	Clermont
Dennis Creek	Dennisville
Dennis Inlet	Townsend's Inlet
Dennistown	Dennisville
Diamond Beach	Higbee's Beach
Dyer's Creek	Dias Creek
East Creek	Eldora
Eldredges	West Cape May
Falmouth	Town Bank
Foster Town	South Dennis
Gandytown	Ocean View
Goldin's Point	Beesley's Point
Gracetown	South Seaville
Gravelly Run	Burleigh
Hildreth	Rio Grande
Holly Beach	Wildwood
Kate's Corner	Clermont

Little Mill	Dennisville
Littleworth	Petersburg
New England Town	Town Bank
Nummytown	Rio Grande
Oceanville	Swainton
Ottens	North Wildwood
Peck's Beach	Ocean City
Peermont	Avalon
Portsmouth	Town Bank
Poverty Beach	U.S. Coast Guard Training Base, Cape May City
Pynes Lake	Lake Lily (Cape May Point)
Romney Marsh	Cape May Court House
Sacktown	Greenfield
Sea Grove	Cape May Point
Sig(g)town	Swainton
Skillinger's Creek	Cape Island Creek
Stipson's Island	Eldora
Stites Beach	Cape May Point
Swaintown	Erma
Teal Town	Fishing Creek
Townsend's Inlet	Clermont, Ocean View
West Creek	Eldora
Whale Beach	Strathmere
Willet's Point	Beesley's Point
Williamsburg	Tuckahoe
Wills Creek	Bidwell's Ditch (Creek)

Cape May County,
New Jersey

CHAPTER ONE

Founding a Community of Whaler Yeomen, 1609–1699

Henry Hudson, captain of the tiny sailing yacht *Half Moon*, first spied the peninsula that would become known as Cape May on a humid day in late August of 1609. Hudson sailed on a voyage financed by the Dutch East India Company to discover a water passage through North America to the East Indies. His explorations in 1609 took the veteran English navigator along the shore of what appeared to be a great bay and several miles up the coast of an unexplored cape. Hudson encountered the natural obstacles that later forced settlers to seek more accessible spots along the bay and great river—the Delaware—that flowed from its head. Strong tides pulled the *Half Moon* over dangerous shoals and sandbars, and the 122-ton boat struck bottom, forcing Hudson and his nervous crew to drop down the bay and ride out the night of August 28 at anchor. The next morning violent thunderstorms and a brisk northwesterly wind drove the *Half Moon* around the point of the uncharted cape and north along a string of heavily wooded coastal barrier islands.[1]

Hudson's senior officer, Robert Juet, thus recorded this first documented observation of the Delaware Bay and Atlantic Ocean shorelines of what would become the seashore resort community of Cape May County, New Jersey. Juet claimed in 1609 that the tides and shoals discouraged Captain Hudson from penetrating farther up the bay. Apparently Hudson decided that the waterway was not the fabled Northwest Passage that would give the Dutch East India Company a shortcut to the riches of the Far East. Nor did Hudson land on the Cape May peninsula. Nowhere in his account did Juet suggest that the captain or eighteen Dutch and English crewmen put ashore until they reached Sandy Hook, on the northern coast of what is now New Jersey.

1

Henry Hudson's contact with the Cape May peninsula in 1609 was only a brief interlude in his years of exploration. Nevertheless, news of his discovery of what is now the Delaware Bay and stretch of land that defined its northeastern boundary soon reached the Dutch and English, and probably the rival Spanish empire as well. Hudson's visit drew attention to a region that lay strategically between Spain's American holdings to the south and the French claims to the north and between the newly planted English colony of Virginia and the uninhabited New England tract, soon to fill with English Puritan colonists. Hudson's visit placed the Delaware Valley in the middle of the great commercial and imperial rivalries and migrations of population that dominated the seventeenth-century Atlantic world.

Shortly after Henry Hudson sounded the Delaware Bay, Samuel Argall, another English navigator, entered the bay. Assuming that it defined the northern boundary of a vague Virginia patent, he named the bay after the colony's new governor, Lord De La Warre. The Dutch cashed in first on their investment in hiring Hudson. Cornelis Hendrickson, Adriaen Block, Cornelis Jacobsen Mey (soon spelled May on charts and maps), and other Dutch sea captains sailed to the new lands to report on potential trading ventures for syndicates of Amsterdam merchants and entrepreneurs. Captain May's visits to the Delaware Valley between 1616 and 1624 led to the peninsula on the northeast side of the bay being named Cape May.[2]

The Cape May peninsula played a minor role in the larger commercial endeavors that marked Dutch domination of the Delaware Valley during the next forty years. Initially, the directors of the Dutch West India Company envisioned the region, which they called the South River to differentiate it from the North or Hudson River, as the center of their business enterprises in the New Netherlands. The Dutch built a series of small wooden forts and trading posts between 1624 and 1630, including one located one hundred miles up the Delaware River on Burlington Island, another at Fort Nassau near present-day Gloucester City, New Jersey, and one at Swanendael, on the Lewes Creek in the present state of Delaware.[3]

The Dutch searched for commercial opportunities around the Delaware Valley. Trade, barter, fishing, and fur trapping, not farming and settlement, drove the Dutch along the rivers and bay. Social and political divisions in the Netherlands prevented a unified colonial policy. Although this was not critical at first, it eventually meant that the Dutch could not prevent the Swedes and English from entering the region. Squabbles among Dutch West India Company merchant directors divided policy. Some pressed for development of the North River, with its town of New Amsterdam (now New York City) as the great fur entrepôt and administrative center; others hoped to develop the South River as the nexus of Dutch power and authority in the New World. A patroonship system whereby company directors received tracts of land in return for bringing settlers and developing commerce under license from the company added another limiting factor to the tenuous Dutch hold over the Delaware Valley. A patroon held authority that approximated that of a feudal lord with tithing, gaming, and magistracy rights and privileges. Few colonists considered this Old World relic as an incentive to settle in the New Netherlands.

The Dutch managed the Delaware Valley until the middle of the seventeenth century. Samuel Godyn, Samuel Blommaert, and Albert Conraets Burgh, West India Company directors, showed considerable interest during 1629–1630 in securing title to the Cape May peninsula. Burgh declared that he would establish a patroonship there. In 1630 the directors formed a syndicate with Kiliaen van Rensselaer, David Pietersen DeVries, and others to develop the South Bay. Navigator DeVries had earlier visited the bay and had reported sighting whales that came close to the shore, where they could be hunted by small whaling boats launched from the beach. Director Samuel Godyn determined that whale fishing provided the type of economic activity needed to develop South Bay commerce, similar to what the fur trade had done for the North Bay, or what tobacco had given the English in their Virginia colony.[4]

Plans for a Delaware Bay whale factory drove Godyn, DeVries, and their syndicate. Between 1630 and 1631 they developed a whaling station at Swanendael directly across the bay from Cape May, even though a Native American raiding party had earlier massacred the entire Dutch settlement on the Lewes Creek. The Dutch West India Company considered a whaling station for Cape May as well. Company agents Peter Heyssen and Gillis Hosset bought land during 1631 from several Native American tribal representatives who apparently resided on Cape May. A few weeks later, Peter Minuit, the director-general of New Netherlands, confirmed the first recorded patent for European ownership of Cape May property. This patent gave Samuel Godyn and Samuel Blommaert title to "the eastside of Godyn's Bay or Cape de May, reaching four miles from the said Cape towards the bay and four miles along the coast southward and another four miles inland, being sixteen square miles."[5]

The ten Native American signatories of the Cape May land patent of 1631 attested to a permanent native population on the peninsula. The simple act of trading the tip of the Cape May peninsula for some goods did not necessarily mean that these natives, who held a far different concept of property and title to the land than did the Europeans, sold the lands upon which they lived. But in their visit to Cape May, Heyssen and Hossett had found ten heads of households or possibly subchiefs to place their marks on the patent, suggesting that a sizable Native American settlement existed on the peninsula. Perhaps the large number of natives discouraged further Dutch development of the Cape May whalery. Observing other Native Americans along the New Jersey coast, Robert Juet noted that "we durst not trust them." Wary of a recurrence of the Swanendael massacre, the Dutch never attempted to build a trading post or whaling factory on their sixteen-square-mile Cape May tract.[6]

The Dutch whaling business in the South Bay faded. DeVries reported that his whalers had killed only seven small creatures in the bay and that they had yielded a few barrels of oil. He withdrew from the project. Samuel Godyn and other shareholders became discouraged and in 1635 transferred their Cape May land rights to the West India Company. The lure of whale fishing continued, however, and eventually became a primary motive for the founding of an English whaling community on the peninsula in the 1680s.[7]

What happened on the Cape May peninsula between the Dutch patent of 1631 and the first recorded permanent settlement of English whalers from New England and Long Island in the 1680s remains a mystery. Speculation about this gap in the historical record has become part of a Cape May County folklore and tradition and a significant aspect of the maritime region's character and self-image. Over the years, tradition has merged with documentary evidence and historical records, making difficult the separation of fact and folklore. As a remote maritime region and frontier community of independent seafaring people and isolated farmers, Cape May County remained outside the mainstream of both New Jersey and Philadelphia life. Consequently, Cape May's people developed their own cultural identity and interpretation of their history.[8]

The missing interval between 1631 and 1685, when the first records of settlement and government appear, fits into this rich tradition. Thus a memorial stone at Town Bank on the bayside in Lower Township marks the reputed site of Portsmouth Town, the first settlement founded by Long Island and New England whalers in 1640. No real documentary evidence exists to support this claim. The original site of the first town now lies under water nearly half a mile into the Delaware Bay, washed away by centuries of tidal action and violent storms that carried off hundreds of feet of bank and shoreline at Town Bank. No archaeological evidence remains to substantiate tradition or substitute for the absence of historical records.

Nevertheless, Cape May tradition repeated in all the standard histories of the county placed the earliest European settlement on Cape May high on the banks overlooking the Delaware Bay a few miles up the coast from the tip of the cape (now Cape May Point). The bank jutted into the bay at this spot in the seventeenth century and protected a deep tidal creek called New England Creek, forming a natural anchorage. Early maps of the bay showed an anchor symbol just off the Cape May bayshore at approximately the entrance to the old New England Creek and current Cape May Canal. If New England and Long Island whalers, traders, or travelers sought refuge, they must have entered here and perhaps, as Cape May County tradition relates, built a dozen log houses along the top of the bank overlooking the bay.[9]

A persistent story placed Puritan colonists from New Haven, Connecticut, at this spot on the Cape May peninsula in the 1640s. New Haven town voters had backed a scheme in 1641 to settle farms, advance trade, and spread the teachings of the Congregational church in the Delaware Valley. Fifty New Haven colonists led by George Lamberton and Nathaniel Turner settled temporarily seventy miles up the bay from Cape May Point at Varens Kill (now Salem Creek) and planted tobacco. Most of the colonists returned to New Haven, and other attempts by the New Haven Puritans to expand into the Delaware Valley in the 1650s met resistance from Peter Stuyvesant, the governor of New Netherlands. Possibly some of these New Englanders relocated during this period on the wild Cape May peninsula. One-third of the family names that appeared in the first Cape May County records of the 1680s and 1690s were identical to those of the New Haven families that appeared in the New Haven town records of the 1640s. Some of these names—most notably Osborne, Mason, Badcock, and Godfrey—were involved in the Delaware River settlement. Other families listed in the New Haven records whose names were similar to the first Cape May settlers included Dayton, Davis, Parsons, Raynor, Johnson, Smith, Swain, Willets, and Peck. The latter was most intriguing because a Peck left his name to Peck's Beach, now the site of Cape May County's northernmost seaside community of Ocean City.[10]

Smith, Johnson, and Davis were common colonial American family names, and establishing direct genealogical links between New Haven and Cape May has proved elusive. Many of the same names appear on Long Island, in the town records of East Jersey (the northern half of colonial New Jersey), and on Cape May. If New Haven colonists did not reside on the Cape May peninsula in the 1640s, perhaps their children or family members familiar with the earlier Delaware River adventure of planting a tobacco colony at Varens Kill (Salem Creek) sought out the region for settlement as part of a larger migration that brought pioneering families from New England to Long Island, then to East Jersey, and finally to the Cape May peninsula.

English adventurer Robert Evelyn and part of an expedition to the Delaware Bay under his uncle, Thomas Young, rather than New Haven Congregationalists, probably were the first Europeans to have ventured across the Cape May peninsula. Evelyn's narrative described conditions and details so thoroughly and accurately that undoubtedly he explored the wild cedar swamps, pine and oak forests, and swollen tidal creeks on Cape May. Caution needs to be exercised in reading his account, however: it served as a promotional tract for Sir Edmund Plowden in his abortive plan in the 1640s to establish a colony of New Albion in the region. Evelyn described giant turkeys, huge bison, and other marvelous wildlife on Cape May. Perhaps he derived his account from Native American tales rather than through actual observations.[11]

Evelyn encountered the Kechemeches, a subdivision of the Algonkin language group of Lenape Native Americans who resided on the lower part of the Cape. Evelyn described the Kechemeches as war weary from years of fighting against more powerful tribes to the northwest. The Kechemeches showed evidence of earlier contacts with white men, or at least with the white men's firearms—Evelyn's muskets frightened a fifty-man Lenape party, allowing a few men to force these natives to parley. "I had some bickering with them," he wrote, "and they are of so little esteem that I durst with fifteen men sit down or trade in despite of them." Evelyn displayed a typical seventeenth-century European perception of these Native Americans along the Delaware as timid but devious and dangerous savages who were overawed by the power of the musket. Evelyn established a stereotype of the Cape May Native American that remained for years. Presbyterian historian Edward S. Wheeler wrote two centuries later that the new religious retreat of Sea Grove lay on Cape May Point, where once reverberated the "war-whoop of the exultant savage."[12]

The Lenape developed an elaborate and sophisticated network of paths, trails, and creek crossings that undoubtedly facilitated Evelyn's progress around the Cape. Paths connected the "fast land" (dry, high ground), from Great Egg Harbor to the north down the seaside to the peninsula tip that was later called Cape Island. Another trail skirted the bay from Town Bank to the Dennis Creek (the largest bayside creek) and on through the Cedar Swamp. Two cape-length systems—the Tuckahoe and Cohansey trails—connected with cross-trails that linked bay to ocean. On his travels Evelyn spied cornfields, which suggested permanent, year-around settlement, although he never identified the location of any specific Native American village.

There is evidence that the Lenape lived permanently on the Cape May peninsula. An American Museum of Natural History survey of artifacts, skeletal remains, and shell piles throughout the peninsula made in 1913 suggested substantial Native American activity and village life. Dr. Julius Way, an amateur Cape May County archaeologist and historian, collected and studied flint arrowheads, shell piles, and skeletal remains during the 1920s and concluded that a major Lenape burial ground and main trail once existed in the Fishing Creek area. In 1933 Charles Cresse plowed up the remains of three Native Americans buried with flint implements and pottery pieces on his farm near the present town of Rio Grande. Construction workers uncovered similar burial sites in West Cape May and near Beesley's Point during the 1930s.[13]

The first European settlements were located on the exact spots where a 1913 geological survey map pinpointed Native American village sites. This suggests that the white settlers moved to lands that were burned clear of forest and brush by the Lenape in order to cultivate corn and vegetable plots or erect villages. Other evidence indicates that in addition to farming and village life, during the seventeenth century the Cape May Lenape carried on a vigorous wampum industry, gathered shellfish, and hunted the whale. The Burlington Court record noted that a Cape May Native American sold a whale to early settlers in 1685.[14]

Ancient Cape May deeds listed a number of "Indian Sachim-achers," including a Panktoe, Sakamoy, Tamahack, Squehon, and Tom Nummi. Somehow, Nummi (Nummy), who placed his mark on a 1688 document, emerged as the great Cape May native king or sachem. Dr. Maurice Beesley, who wrote the first county history in 1857, observed that King Nummy had become "a tradition related by oldest inhabitants." Early Cape May County land transfers spoke about property around "Nummies" at Fishing Creek or referred to large tracts as "Nummy's lands." According to tradition, King Nummy remained on the Cape May peninsula when the rest of his people migrated to the West so that he could care for the children of his sister, Princess Snow Flower, and her husband, the English missionary Benijah Thompson. This Nummy-Snow Flower story arose coinciden-tally with similar traditions about Native American princesses such as the legendary Pocahantas of the Virgina colony, and these may have inspired the Cape May tradition. Intermarriage between the Native Americans and both English and African-Americans on the peninsula undoubtedly occured, and the Snow Flower marriage symbolized this relationship. Designation of Nummy as the king who dominated Lenape council organization also may have received inspiration from surrounding colonial conditions. Trenton boasted the great Native American King Teddyuscung, Hackensack had King Oratam, and across the river King Tamany ruled his Pennsylvania tribes. Thus Cape May County identified its own King Nummy.[15]

Lenape sociopolitical organization and relations with European society, like much else of the formative period of Cape May County's history, remain part of the region's folklore and tradition. Archaeologi-cal evidence and documentary records are too sparse and fragmentary to draw firm historical conclusions. The records needed to recon-struct Cape May County's earliest history began to appear during the late seventeenth century as British officials replaced Dutch administra-tors in the Delaware Valley. British colonists, anxious to define their property lines and to record their business and governmental transac-tions, kept extensive court records, wills, deeds, and even cattle ear-mark books in each of their newly acquired provinces.

British expansion into the Delaware Valley accompanied the res-toration of Charles II to the throne in 1664 following the violent period of Oliver Cromwell's Puritan Commonwealth. Charles II pro-moted overseas empire, including seizure of the New Netherlands from the Dutch. He gave his brother James, the Duke of York, a patent to the territories that encompassed these Dutch holdings between the Hudson and Delaware rivers. The Duke of York, in turn, rewarded John Berkeley and George Carteret, loyal court allies, with a patent for lands west of Long Island, "extending South to Cape May and North as far as the Northernmost branch of the Hudson River." They named this province New Jersey after the Isle of Jersey, where Carteret had provided refuge for the exiled Stuarts during the recent English civil war.[16]

The New Jersey proprietors, Berkeley and Carteret, promoted economic development and settlement in the northern half of their province by granting political concessions, religious toleration, and relatively liberal property-owning arrangements. They stimulated movement of English population from New England, where the first settlements had been founded in the 1620s and 1630s, and from Long Island to East Jersey. Elizabethtown, Woodbridge, Shrewsbury, and Newark developed along the lines of the New England town, with village greens and a central square. Farmers, tradesmen, mariners, and religious separatists filled these East Jersey communities. Many became involved in disputes over customs duties, land titles, proprietary rights, and quitrents (rent paid by landowners in lieu of feudal or other services and obligations). Social and political tension and conflict attended the founding of East Jersey and contributed to the relocation of some families to West Jersey.[17]

East Jersey families involved in whale fishing moved to the Cape May peninsula in the 1680s, completing a migration that had taken them during the course of the seventeenth century from the British Isles to New England, to Long Island, and to East and West Jersey. Those families who bought land or resided temporarily in East Jersey under the Monmouth Patent of 1665 and other grants settled later on the Jersey Cape and became part of the original community. This connection included Hewitt, Leonard, Edwards, Davis, Spicer, Townsend, Whitlock, Richardson, Crawford, Dennis, Stillwell, and possibly Taylor.[18]

Development of the southern half of the Berkeley-Carteret patent, called West Jersey and including the Cape May peninsula, proceeded more slowly than that of East Jersey. Quick profits from the sale of land and trade eluded the opportunistic Berkeley, who in 1674 sold his proprietary right to this sparsely populated land to two members of the Society of Friends, John Fenwick and Edward Byllynge, the latter a prominent but financially troubled London brewer. Fenwick, ostensibly Byllynge's land agent and representative in the New World, founded a Quaker colony along Salem Creek on the Delaware River seventy miles north of the tip of the Cape May peninsula. Problems plagued Fenwick. He quarreled with Byllynge over his share of the property and with Edmund Andros, the governor of New York, over governing authority, land titles, and charter rights. Finally William Penn and several other Quakers intervened to protect Fenwick's settlement and to promote new communities in West Jersey as business enterprises and religious refuges.[19]

More noted for founding the Quaker colony of Pennsylvania and city of Philadelphia across the Delaware River, William Penn also helped to bring stability and order to West Jersey. He defended Quaker interests among top British officials in London, arbitrated disputes between Friends in America, and helped to separate the Jerseys into two provinces, East and West, to secure a Quaker proprietorship for the southern half. Penn contributed as well to the framing of "The Laws, Concessions and Agreements of 1677," most likely drawn up first by Edward Byllynge. This document gave West New Jersey one of the most liberal constitutions in the British Empire. It ensured freedom of religion, trial by jury, representative government, and other rights and privileges for English freeholders; a freeholder was defined as one who held office or landed estate free from any limitations as to inheritance rights or social class.[20]

During his involvement in New Jersey's affairs, William Penn may have shown some interest in the establishment of a whalery and a town on the Cape May peninsula, somewhat along the lines of that created later in Philadelphia. According to one account, Penn directed the construction of a large manor house on a piece of Cape May bayshore property and placed his land agent, a man named Forrest, there to develop a town. Another account has Penn visiting Jacob Spicer, an early Quaker landowner at Cold Spring in the lower part of the Cape May peninsula. Penn may have visited Cape May during tours of nearby New Castle and Lewes, Delaware, just across the bay, where he personally presented his frame of government to the local inhabitants. However, no evidence exists of a large house on the Jersey Cape before that built by Dr. Daniel Coxe's carpenters between 1687 and 1691. Penn's correspondence mentions no visit to Cape May, and early wills place the Forrests on Salem Creek in the 1680s, not on Cape May. Penn's interest in Cape May as a proposed site for a whale fishery or as the initial site for Philadelphia are, perhaps, another aspect of Cape May County folklore and tradition.[21]

Nevertheless, William Penn and the Quakers played an important part in the early development of Cape May peninsular society,
law, and economy. Thomas Budd, a Penn associate, published a pamphlet that sought to attract immigrants to Cape May, where he held
title to several thousand acres of land. "The lands from the Capes, to
about six miles above New Castle," the Quaker land promoter wrote
in 1685, "is for the most part very rich, there being very many naviga-
ble cricks on both sides of the River, and on the River and cricks are
great quantities of rich fat Marsh Land," which, if banked and drained,
could be planted "some years with corn and then with English hay-
seed." Budd explained that the Jersey Cape offered both good farmlands and employment for shipwrights, coopers, carpenters, smiths,
mariners, weavers, and other craftsmen. Cape May County's original
community reflected precisely this blend of maritime and farming
enterprise described by Budd in 1685.[22]

With validation of a patent from the Duke of York, the large
Quaker community at Burlington, one hundred miles up the Delaware River from the tip of Cape May, became in 1681 the administrative and judicial center for West Jersey. Here a Quaker-dominated
court dispensed justice, passed local laws, and provided moral and
economic guidelines for this wilderness province. Quaker justices
divided the land into Tenths, ordering Daniel Leeds, a Burlington
surveyor, to lay out ten equal parts along the Delaware from the Falls
(Trenton) to Cape May. Leeds never completed the survey for the
lower five tenths below the Salem Tenth, but the Burlington Court
applied its laws to the unsurveyed portion as well. Thus, in 1684, the
court ordered fines of twenty shillings for anyone living in the
"Lower Tenths" who failed to appear in Burlington Court when summoned by the justices.[23]

The records of the Burlington Court reveal that an active community and government existed on the Cape May peninsula between
1685 and 1688. The court records for this period mentioned at least
thirty different Cape May residents who were involved in court cases.
At the same time, the Burlington Court appointed a company or body
of officers for Cape May, one of the first steps in the definition of
county government. The Quaker justices in Burlington named Alexander Humphreys as undersheriff, Jonathan Pine and Samuel Matthews as town constables, and Caleb Carman as a justice of the peace
for Cape May. No record remains, however, of any town meeting or
county court session on Cape May between 1685 and 1688.[24]

The first Cape May officials executed the laws and orders emanating from Burlington. These laws showed the domination of Quaker justice and moral order. The Burlington Court ordered Alexander Humphreys to bring to Burlington from Cape May Abraham Weston, his wife, and their servant girl to testify about accusations that they had abused their children. In another case, the Burlington Court ordered a fine levied on Evan Davis for stealing a whale carcass from the Carman Whaling Company. In this same vein, Thomas Matthews, the ranger and timber warden, granted the Carmans permission to recover all dead whales and wrecked ships along the coast of the Cape May peninsula.[25]

Quaker influence appeared in other areas of Cape May's earliest society. The Burlington Court tried to stop the sale of rum to Native Americans, and Cape May officials enforced this measure by publicly revealing offenders. "The Deponant attesteth yt severall days After the above said Lawes were Published at Cape May he Came Into ye house of ye said [John] Jarvis & found Indians Drinking Rum, & one of ye Indians gave of ye said Rum to ye said Johnson & he Drank of it with ym," the first Cape May town book recorded. Punishment for crimes such as this or other minor violations reflected the tone of Quaker law, with those found guilty paying a small fine or working off the debt. The Quakers, including the Cape May authorities, treated fornication or adultery more harshly. These acts might lead to public whipping of both male and female parties, or the payment of a stiff fine. Compared to other colonial American communities, though, the Cape May peninsula and neighboring West Jersey, which lay within the province of the Quaker justices and legal and moral codes, experienced a stable, moderate, and equitable system. No witchcraft hysteria like that of New England in the 1690s or violent rioting like that in New York or East Jersey convulsed the Jersey Cape during the late seventeenth century.[26]

Despite a strong Quaker influence, non-Quakers founded the original Cape May community. Quaker legal and moral order remained strong, but economic and political power on the Jersey Cape fell to a group identified with an anti-Quaker faction in Burlington. Jeremiah Basse, an Anabaptist politician, and Dr. Daniel Coxe, an absentee Anglican landowner and real estate speculator, shaped the earliest socioeconomic and political fabric of Cape May peninsular society.

Dr. Daniel Coxe never set foot on the Jersey Cape or ventured to the New World, but this English court physician did more to establish the pattern of colonial settlement and the character of Cape May society than did anyone else. Coxe's interest in the Cape May peninsula was more than simple land speculation. A member of the Royal Society, Coxe fit the mold of John Locke and other late-seventeenth-century British social and constitutional architects who sought to rationalize their world, create an orderly society, and experiment with their environment. Among other things, Coxe dabbled with the effect of tobacco on animals and searched for ways to extract salts from vegetables and seawater. He held ideas about community planning, including the protection of the Cornwall Cape in Britain against beach erosion. He sought to blend the remnants of feudal organization with that of a vigorous landowning, merchant society free from feudal restrictions as part of what he called a "New Empire in America."[27]

Coxe accumulated twenty-two shares of the West Jersey proprietorship by 1687, some purchased from the estate of Edward Byllynge. This gave Coxe title to the lands and the right of government claimed by Byllynge. Coxe's West Jersey holdings assumed a central role in his proposed New Empire. Already this region had attracted British freeholders who provided a backbone for his socioeconomic experiment. "Greate Numbers come yearely from Bermudas, New England, New Yorke, Long Island, Pensilvania and other parts of America to purchase lands," Coxe explained, "and many hundred familyes from the before menconed places are there already seated." Coxe offered land to many more freeholders, leasing hundred-acre tracts and giving the leaseholder an option in three years to buy "fee simple" and thus obtain absolute possession of the land without any limit to the class of heirs.[28]

Daniel Coxe hired Adlord Bowde, a Hertford draper, as his land agent for New Jersey to clear titles, reaffirm earlier deeds, and negotiate with the Native Americans. Bowde concluded a purchase with them for land along the Delaware River from modern Salem County's Cohansey Creek to the tip of the Cape May peninsula. Bowde bought one tract for Coxe in 1688 from Sakamoy, Tamahack, Tom Nummi, and other Native American "Sachimachers." This tract extended from roughly the Maurice River in present-day Cumberland County around the entire Cape May peninsula. A later survey defined this tract with boundaries beginning at the Cedar Hammocks (now Goshen), proceeding northeast through present-day Mt. Pleasant and Petersburg, along the Tuckahoe River to the sea, where it ran down the seaside, around the point, and up the bay back to the Cedar Hammocks. Coxe had secured title from the Lenape to ninety-five thousand acres of the Cape May peninsula for which he paid sixteen gallons of rum, thirty-two knives, some tobacco boxes, looking glasses, flints, combs, clothing articles, and "six Jews harps."[29]

The previous year, John Dennis and several New England and Long Island whalers had already purchased the lower part of this same tract of land from the native sachem, Panktoe. Dennis was either the Irish Quaker shareholder of the West Jersey proprietorship who settled on Timber Creek in Gloucester County or one of the East Jersey Dennises who had speculated in Delaware Valley land since the 1670s. Charles Dennis, a member of the latter family, later married a daughter of the Ludlam family, the first known settlers on the large tidal stream called Dennis Creek. There was also a Dennis Inlet on the Cape May seaside marked on early maps, but Dennis Lynch, an early Cape May shipbuilder and landowner near present-day Townsend's Inlet, probably left his name to this inlet. In any case, John Dennis's associates in the purchase of 1687 can be identified with certainty as leading members of the first permanent community on Cape May that settled along New England Creek and the bayshore settlement of New England Town (Town Bank). Signatories of the deed with Panktoe included Samuel Matthews, Ezekiel Eldredge, Joseph Whilldin, Samuel Crow(ell), and John Carman. All founded their family lines in Cape May County, and Whilldin established, through marriage to Hannah Gorham of Plymouth, Massachusetts, the much-revered local connection to Mayflower ancestry.[30]

Daniel Coxe's purchase overlapped the claim made by John Dennis and his partners, but the latter's deeds were not recorded until 1695 by Jeremiah Basse and Thomas Revell in Burlington. Consequently, Matthews, Carman, Eldredge, and the others probably leased land from Coxe between 1688 and the early 1690s. They joined William Jacocks, Humphrey Hughes, Randall Hewitt, and other whalers from Long Island who signed leases with Coxe's representatives for tracts of land in the lower part of the peninsula. Coxe reported that he had received over one hundred pounds annual income from his Cape May leaseholders. He expected them to become landowning freeholders, explaining that they had "planted and built" on his property.[31]

Coxe involved the earliest settlers in a whaling enterprise on the Jersey Cape. "I have at the Expence of above three thousand pounds settled a Towne and Established a fishing for Whales which are very numerous about Cape May both within the Bay and without all along the sea coast which I am assured if well managed will bring in above 4000£ per Annum all charges Defrayed," Coxe wrote. Whaling already existed on the Cape. Matthews, Hughes, Hewitt, and Carman headed their own whaling companies, some originally organized on Long Island in the 1670s. Hand, Leonard, Pine, Osborne, Foreman, Raynor, and many other early settlers held shares in these whaling companies. Leaming, Taylor, Johnson, Parsons, Eldredge, and others worked as coopers, cordwainers, carpenters, or blacksmiths, trades that were tied to the whaling business.[32]

The Carman family linked Daniel Coxe to the Cape May whalers. Caleb Carman signed Coxe's deed in 1688 with the Native Americans as a witness, and undoubtedly the Carman Whaling Company became involved from the beginning in Coxe's enterprises. The Carmans had traded, whaled, and lived along the Delaware Bay and River for over a decade. They owned a house and a bayside town lot on the northern bank of New England Creek. They had built a tidal-powered grist- and sawmill and other buildings at the head of Cold Spring Creek by 1685. When Coxe ordered the first ship constructed on the Jersey Cape in 1688, Carman's sawmill most likely provided planks. The keel of Coxe's forty-ton vessel probably lay next to the Carman's mill at the head of Cold Spring Creek, rather than on the bayside near Town Bank as traditionally supposed.[33]

Daniel Coxe brought a number of new families to the Jersey Cape. Oliver Johnson, a cooper, built 140 barrels for Coxe during the winter of 1688. Johnson eventually acquired seaside property above Turtle Gut Inlet and settled permanently. Coxe hired Benjamin Godfrey, a merchant, to manage his proposed storehouse and shipping business. Godfrey may have resided in Coxe Hall, a two-story manor house constructed bayside on the northern bank of the next creek above New England Creek, later named Coxe Hall Creek. The first recorded Cape May County court session in May 1692 was held at "Godfrey's House." Godfrey purchased land on the seaside, became a permanent resident, and founded one of Cape May County's original family lines. Coxe appointed George Taylor in 1689 or 1690 as his land agent on the Jersey Cape with power of attorney. According to some accounts, Taylor had lived on Cape May since 1675, when he held the first religious service on the peninsula. More likely, Coxe recruited the well-educated Baptist minister and skilled carpenter to construct the manor house and build his ship. Either way, Taylor received the best plot of land near Turtle Gut Inlet and became the wealthiest property holder on the peninsula before 1700. When county government came to Cape May in 1692, Taylor served as the first clerk of the county.[34]

Dr. Coxe sent French Huguenots to Cape May in 1688 to develop salt-making, whale-fishing, and wine industries. Driven from Catholic France by the revocation in 1685 of the Edict of Nantes, which earlier had assured religious toleration for these French Protestants, many Huguenots fled to Holland, England, and America. These industrious craftsmen, merchants, and gardeners impressed Coxe, who directed a project in England to colonize Huguenots in Virginia and the Carolinas. Those sent to Cape May in 1688 resided in Gravesend, Long Island, and included John DuBrois, Andrew Lawrance, and Nicholas Martine. Coxe dispatched others from England. "Wee have lately sent over diverse Frenchmen skillful in makeing salt by the sun in pitts or pans," Coxe explained. The Huguenots developed the vineyards and gardens as well. "I have a plantacon att Cape May made by a very skilfull French Gardiner who is there resident," Coxe wrote. "Hee hath planted some thousand fruit Trees of divers and ye best sorts could be procured." Few of the more than twenty Huguenot families remained on the Jersey Cape. Only Nicholas Martine, among those hired by Coxe, purchased land and joined the Huets (Hewitt) and probably the Cresses as the original Huguenot settlers in Cape May County.[35]

Coxe introduced the first African-Americans to the Cape May peninsula in 1688. "I have either att Cape May or Burlington," he explained, "four stout Negroes." George Taylor, Coxe's official representative, owned four slaves, probably the four mentioned by Coxe. Taylor's slave Peter married Elizabeth Donkon (Duncan) in 1697, in the first African-American marriage ceremony recorded in Cape May County. The terms of their marriage contract required that "in case they should have aney Children, [they must] serve until they were 31 years of age or as the Law Derects &c." Joseph Holdin, Taylor's closest neighbor and probably kin, the second-largest property owner on the Jersey Cape before 1700, also owned one "Negro sarvant."[36]

The character of Cape May society took shape under Dr. Daniel Coxe's proprietorship between 1688 and 1692. Perhaps two hundred British, Dutch, French, Swedish, and African-American people lived on the Jersey Cape during this period. Of these, at least forty-seven held land for which they would later obtain title as freeholders, giving them absolute possession without restrictions on inheritance. A small Native American population stayed on the Jersey Cape as well, although Panktoe, Sakamoy, Tom Nummi, and others rapidly sold off their best land to Daniel Coxe's agents and to the New England and Long Island families.

Despite the growing population, Coxe's dream of creating a model mercantile and agricultural community on the Cape May peninsula as part of his New Empire faded by 1691, partly because the political climate in Britain remained unfavorable. King James II invalidated the charters for East and West New Jersey, and for a short period in 1688 and 1689 New Jersey came under control of Edmund Andros, governor of the Dominion of New England. This directly challenged Daniel Coxe's claims as the governor of New Jersey. Moreover, Coxe left affairs in America to a deputy-governor and agents who for various reasons proved unreliable. Adlord Bowde died a few months after negotiating property sales with the natives for Coxe. Someone poisoned Coxe's most competent and loyal land agent, James Budd, a Quaker merchant. Budd had enemies in Edmund Randall, Coxe's pottery chief in Burlington, and John Tatham, another land agent and a murky figure said to be a ruthless Catholic intriguer. Nicholas Martine, a Cape May resident, and others testified in a defamation suit brought by Tatham against the Budd family that Budd's enemies had murdered him.[37]

In the end, Daniel Coxe's business plans for the Cape May peninsula did not succeed. His agents never built "a Magazine or Storehouse in [the] Delaware River for European Commodities" or developed an entrepôt for shipment of Cape May fish, timber, and wines to Europe and the West Indies. Coxe's carpenters probably completed Coxe Hall, but labor problems slowed work on other buildings. Elizabeth Ramé complained that carpenters had not yet constructed the house promised to her husband by Dr. Coxe. French workers failed to receive promised tools. Food shortages occurred. Benjamin Godfrey sued Dr. Coxe for back wages. One of Coxe's ships foundered, and John DuBrois sailed off with another right at the peak of the whaling season, leaving the Cape May whalers without a whaling boat. Coxe's shipbuilding project remained unfinished. "There is a vessel on the stocks at Cape May that was begun in James Budd's tyme," George Taylor explained, "but since James' death nothing more is done to it."

Taylor "further saith that Mr. Dubrois spake to the whalemen to sawe Plank, at odde tymes, which they promised to doe, but did not."[38]

Finally Coxe sold his Cape May properties in early 1692 to a group of forty-eight London proprietors known as the West New Jersey Society. The sale marked a new epoch in Cape May's development, one that led to formation of county boundaries and government. The West Jersey Society divided its new lands, including the Cape May peninsula, into sixteen hundred shares, and a few months later the General Assembly of the Province of West New Jersey laid out four counties—Burlington, Gloucester, Salem, and Cape May. The assembly act of 12 November 1692 formally created Cape May County, although some type of administrative and governing structure had existed on the peninsula since 1685. Between 1687 and 1691, George Taylor conducted business for Coxe much as a county clerk would, and in early 1692 Taylor held a county court session on Cape May. Nevertheless, the assembly determined in November "that from henceforth Cape May shall be, and is hereby appointed a county."[39]

The first county boundary of 1692 encompassed the entire peninsula and included a huge wilderness tract of land between the Maurice River in present-day Cumberland County and West Creek, the current boundary between Cape May and Cumberland counties. It also defined a strip of land north of Great Egg Harbor and the Tuckahoe River as part of Cape May County. Boundary revision in 1694 placed this tract in Gloucester County and further revision in 1710 gave the territory from West Creek to the Maurice River to then Salem County. Other adjustments to the county boundaries occurred over the next two hundred years, mostly around the northwest corner of the county near the head of the Tuckahoe River, but by 1710 Cape May County's boundary had received its essential definition.[40]

The legislative act that established Cape May County also provided for the appointment of a body of justices and officials necessary to maintain peace and order. Criminal cases that involved over forty shillings in damages had to be heard at the Salem Court, which lay seventy miles up the bay. The General Assembly permitted Cape May County to hold its own court in 1693, with quarterly sessions on the third Tuesdays of December, March, June, and September. These court sessions still could not hear larger cases but became the primary place of assembly for local inhabitants to meet for legal as well as legislative and administrative purposes. The West Jersey assembly authorized in May 1694 that the "Freeholders" of the county should meet once a year at "the Town of Cape May" to chose five "good and sufficient men" to represent the county in Burlington. George Taylor, Jacob Dayton, John Shaw, Timothy Brandreth, and John Crawford represented the county in 1697 when they signed an agreement to support King William against "Papists, and other wicked and Traitorous persons."[41]

These five Cape May County representatives to the General Assembly in 1697 apparently held some influence: that year the assembly passed an act that enlarged the powers and privileges of Cape May County's court to cover all civil and criminal cases of any value and enacted another law for the construction of a road from Cape May to Burlington to permit county representatives "to attend publick service." The West Jersey assembly appointed George Taylor and John Crawford, two of the county's five representatives in 1697, as road commissioners to lay out what became the old Cape Road through the Cedar Swamp.[42]

Cape May County representatives joined a non-Quaker faction in Burlington that supported efforts by Jeremiah Basse in 1697 to become the governor of the province of West New Jersey. Jeremiah Basse was a vain, ambitious, and gluttonous man. "He is the most Cormorant in eating and drinking that I ever knew and greatest Lover of his belly," the Earl of Bellomont observed. William Penn mistrusted both Basse and Basse's stepbrother (brother-in-law), Joshua Barkstead, a wealthy Cohansey merchant and land speculator. "Colonel Basse and Colonel Barkstead are Alsatians [criminals or debtors], wooden colonels, little witt &c, ingrate, to the last my Enemies," Penn wrote. Basse in turn despised Penn and the Quakers who blocked his ambitions to accumulate land and dominate West Jersey politics. Basse coveted the governorship. "I never was so sick of a man's Company since I was born as of his," the Earl of Bellomont wrote Penn. "His head was so full of the Governour, and his mind so puff'd up and exalted with vanity, that he was insupportable to every body."[43]

Jeremiah Basse's anti-Quaker sentiments and ambitions promoted settlement and development of distant Cape May County as a stronghold for pro-Basse supporters. Basse, Barkstead, and an anti-Quaker faction in Burlington had helped to create a separate county on the Cape May peninsula so that it could serve as a political base. Members of an anti-Quaker faction, including John Tatham and John Worlidge, attended early sessions of the Cape May County court and controlled the earliest county proceedings. In order to facilitate travel for the corpulent Basse between Joshua Barkstead's Cohansey house in Salem County and the Cape May County court meetings, the justices decided on 19 June 1694 "to make & compleat ye road between Cape May & Cohansey so far as ye County of Cape May reaches, fitt for Man & horse to pass."[44]

The Quaker faction in West Jersey challenged Jeremiah Basse's domination over Cape May County. Several Cape May County Friends, led by Joseph Badcock, a shoemaker residing in the upper part of the county near the seaside, sought in 1693 and 1694 to remove Basse's ally, George Taylor, as the county clerk. The local Quakers testified against Taylor, claiming that he had falsified county court documents and altered the minutes of the court sessions. Basse rushed to the Jersey Cape to defend his man Taylor. Justices Joseph Holdin, John Jarvis, and Samuel Crowell, Taylor's closest allies and neighbors, considered the opposing testimony. Predictably they echoed Basse's arguments on behalf of Taylor. Joshua Barkstead sat as foreman of the Petty Jury at the hearings, and leading jury members included Basse deedholders Hewitt, Cresse, Mason, Hughes, Richardson, Fish, Osborne, and Raynor. Basse had given them choice waterfront properties despite earlier West Jersey Society instructions against such sales. Barkstead had surveyed these properties for them, and Basse brought their titles to Burlington, where anti-Quaker ally Thomas Revell recorded their deeds. This jury acquitted Taylor "by Procklymation."[45]

After George Taylor's acquittal, the county clerk received additional authority from Jeremiah Basse to act on his behalf with power of attorney to carry on all business when Basse was absent from the peninsula. Basse rewarded Joseph Holdin for defending Taylor by appointing Holdin as his personal representative to collect debts due Basse from county residents. Taylor's main opponent, Joseph Badcock, meantime, quietly left Cape May County.[46]

Jeremiah Basse retained political and economic control over Cape May County until the late 1690s, during which time he eagerly sought the governorship of the province. His land sales on the peninsula, ostensibly for the West Jersey Society, which earlier had hired Basse as its representative and land agent, created what might be called a community of whaler yeomen. The society instructed Basse not to sell its waterfront properties "convenient for whale fishing." Robert Hackshaw, the West Jersey Society correspondent with Basse, wrote in 1692 that "we mean ye land upon Cape May lying next to ye bay or upon ye sea coast, for that we will not yet sell." Basse ignored this instruction and sold the best locations along the creeks, sounds, and bay to his potential political allies among the whalers who had come to the Cape May peninsula from New England and Long Island. Basse's deeds gave these whalers immediate access to the sea, allowing their seasonal pursuit of the whale in the Delaware Bay or along the Atlantic coast.[47]

At the same time, Basse sold the whalers tracts of land that had been cleared or burned over already by the Lenape to plant corn. These plots were larger than those the whalers had held on Long Island but small enough to preclude the development of a tidewater planter gentry. Christopher Leaming thus owned 12 acres on Long Island and over 200 acres on Cape May, Arthur Cresse held 30 acres on Long Island and 350 acres on the Jersey Cape, and Shamgar Hand enlarged his holdings from 48 acres on Long Island to over 500 acres in Cape May County. The Cape May whaling families became owners of modest plantations, most between 200 and 500 acres, where they raised small herds of cattle and planted fields of corn and wheat (see Appendix A). The first landowners embodied the English concept of a yeoman as an owner of a small landed estate who cultivated his own land and held a respectable standing in the community below the rank of gentleman. Indeed, they referred to themselves in wills and other documents as yeomen.

The concept of the whaler yeoman described the occupational and social status of the pioneering families who founded Cape May County in the late seventeenth century. Jeremiah Basse made certain through his distribution of land titles that these families held the property and social standing necessary to make them freeholders who could vote to support his political ambitions. He confirmed their earlier titles to land purchased from the natives or leased from Daniel Coxe in what by the 1690s had become a complex fabric of irregularly shaped tracts of land along meandering creeks and around marshes and wetlands. These whaler yeoman families established control over Cape May County's political and economic development. Through intermarriage and raising large families they increased that domination. "They are none of them childless and some of them have proved very prolific," observed Aaron Leaming, Jr., the most prominent member of one of the original whaler yeoman families.[48]

The ascendancy of these original whaler yeoman families, more than any other factor, explains how Cape May County developed during the following century.

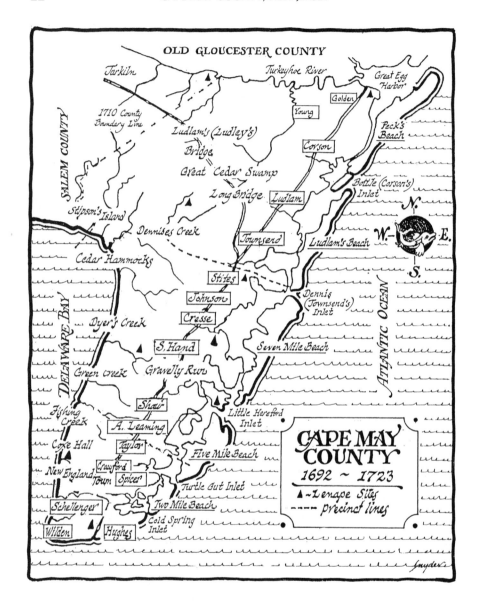

CHAPTER TWO

Whaler Yeoman Ascendancy, 1700–1765

The turmoil that convulsed colonial New Jersey society and politics at the close of the seventeenth century disturbed Cape May County's community of whaler yeomen. George Taylor, Shamgar Hand, and Joseph Shaw, the county representatives to the General Assembly in Burlington in 1700, signed a petition that asked the king of England to assume control over proprietary government. They advocated the establishment of New Jersey as a royal colony.[1]

The surrender of governmental authority to the Crown in 1702 and the uniting of East and West Jersey under one royal governor arose from a number of problems. Land titles held by the West Jersey Society were entangled in utter confusion. Protests against high taxes and quitrents led to mob assaults on local jails in Salem, Burlington, and several East Jersey towns. The militia broke up a meeting in Monmouth County in 1701, and a crowd blocked the path of the justices as they entered the Burlington Court. All the while, Quaker and anti-Quaker factions struggled for power in West Jersey. Factious politics included a bitter pamphlet war and intrigues that reached London, where competing colonial politicians pressed the Board of Trade to grant approbation to their favorite for governor of the province.[2]

The feuding nearly paralyzed government and threatened social order. Cape May County seemed far removed from the strife, but the controversies filtered down to the distant peninsula at the southernmost corner of the colony. Several local justices refused to attend the Cape May County court session of 1700, and when the sheriff rushed to fetch the miscreant officials, he arrived too late. The county justices had already canceled the meeting. Cape May County's whaler yeoman community held a personal stake in the political struggles.

23

One of the more contentious groups included Jeremiah Basse, Joshua Barkstead, and Thomas Hunloke, who had guided the settlement in the 1690s of the whaler yeoman families as a local ruling elite. On the other side, Basse's opponents, Andrew Hamilton, the popular Scottish governor, and the Quaker-dominated assembly also had friends on the Jersey Cape among the Quakers around Great Egg Harbor in the upper part of the county and the Presbyterians along Cold Spring Creek in the lower portion of the peninsula. The ongoing provincial power struggles divided Cape May's loyalties and sympathies.[3]

Politics in East Jersey probably troubled Cape May County's whaler yeomen, as well. They knew about the movement to make Perth Amboy a free port with control over its own customs duties and regulations under the Navigation Act of 1696. The outcome of this controversy promised to affect port and river developments along the Delaware, including the free-port status of Salem, Cohansey, and Burlington. The Jersey Cape had no port, but official records mentioned Cape May in 1697 as the possible station for a royal customs officer. In addition, Cape May County needed protection from pirates and sea marauders. Piracy had increased in the Delaware Bay and along the seaside coast at the turn of the century. According to Cape May County tradition, the notorious pirate Captain Kidd prowled the area and buried a huge treasure cache in 1699 on the bayside beach of Cape May Point.[4]

Cape May County welcomed the transfer of proprietary government to the Crown in 1702. The terms of surrender to Queen Anne favored the evolving whaler yeoman family-controlled community. Voting rights under the new frame of government came from ownership of one hundred acres of land, and thirty-four out of the thirty-five surviving original property owners on the Jersey Cape held at least that many. No one in 1702 owned the thousand acres necessary to hold a seat in the General Assembly of the Province of New Jersey, and Peter Fretwell, a wealthy Burlington Quaker, represented the county until 1707. By that date several Cape May County whaler yeoman families accumulated enough property to qualify for a seat in the General Assembly that met alternately in Burlington and Perth Amboy.

Royal government also encouraged religious toleration. This appealed to Cape May County residents, who by 1702 were divided into three major religious communities. The new government also standardized legal, administrative, and land policies. The latter was most important to the Cape May whaler yeoman leadership. Now they could establish clear title over the lands, a large county land-owner observed, "provided the poor people are not opposed with multitudes of suits to avoid which we in their behalf offer to have one or two Tryals at first on the Indian Purchase on Horse Neck lands with Mr. Chief Justice."[5]

A stable land policy formed the basis for the sociopolitical and economic power for the thirty-five whaler yeoman families who dominated Cape May County for the next two and in most cases three or more generations. During the eighteenth century these families accumulated 70 percent of all improved land, 79 percent of the livestock on the Cape, and 74 percent of the shipping. The thirty-five families held 78 percent of all public offices, which included the posts of county sheriff, clerk, surrogate of wills, assistant land surveyor, road commissioner, overseer of the poor, and justice of the peace. They also had nine out of every ten militia officer posts.[6]

Kinship, intermarriage, and what can be seen as an extended whaler yeoman family system became the essential characteristic of eighteenth-century Cape May County society. Sixty-four percent of Cape May County marriages between 1700 and 1799 remained inside the thirty-five whaler yeoman family network (see Appendix B). The area's sparse population and isolated nature accounted in part for the high rate of intermarriage among a few select families. Intermarriage also became a conscious effort to preserve and promote whaler yeoman domination. Mary Thompson Cresse, a direct descendant of the earliest families, insisted that the first whaling families intermarried to prevent dispersion of wealth and property. They discouraged "outlandish marriage" with anyone outside of the original whaler yeoman clan, Cresse observed. "The reason of intermarriage in the early family," she concluded, "was to avoid that outlandishness."[7]

Intermarriage preserved the homogeneity of the Cape May County community through natural increase of population. A second group of settlers purchased land on the Jersey Cape between 1702 and 1730, but these were the same type of whaler yeomen who had comprised the first group and in fact often were related through marriage to those pioneering families. The second group included the Swain, Bennett, Buck, Church, Downs, Edmunds, Foster, Edwards, Newton, Norton, and Young families. They assimilated quickly into the first group and forged even stronger whaler yeoman community ties. Few additional families entered the county after the initial migration, and Cape May County's population grew more slowly than that of any other New Jersey county during the eighteenth century. Perhaps 350 people lived on the peninsula in 1700. Population increased by another 350 people by 1726, when the first reliable census appeared. The number of people on the Cape May peninsula rose gradually to just over 1,000 by the middle of the century.[8]

The second migration to the county between 1702 and 1730 hardly offset the terrible losses that disease and the abandonment of the area took on the original whaler yeoman families. The domination of thirty-five out of possibly seventy original families can be explained by the early disappearance of some pre-1700 pioneering families. The Jarvis, Short, Dayton, Mason, Whitlock, Carman, and Hoskins families faded from county records after 1700. William Whitlock once owned five hundred acres on the bayside and kept the first official county weights and measures. William Mason served before 1700 as justice, militia captain, and county tax assessor. The Carmans owned the first tidal-powered mill and managed a whaling company and storehouse on the Jersey Cape before 1700. The Carmans sold much of their property by 1710 and apparently started to abandon Cape May County for North Carolina or the Kentucky frontier. Early county sheriff Caesar Hoskins, a Long Island whaler, moved from Cape May County to the Maurice River in what was then Salem County during the first years of the eighteenth century.[9]

Those who remained on the Cape May peninsula confronted the devastating plague of 1714. The influenzalike epidemic killed more than forty people in a four-month period—10 percent of the entire community. It killed most of the Mason family. It removed Arthur Cresse, his son; his wife, Mary; and a daughter. The plague killed Joseph Hewitt, William Shaw, John Stillwell, Nicholas Stillwell, John Reeves, Reuben Swain, Richard Smith, John Foreman, John Matthews, and William Goldin. It also decimated the Hand, Crowell, Holdin, Wells, Hughes, and Garretson families.[10]

The great epidemic of 1714 strained the county's immature institutions. Forty or more funerals and burials taxed the tiny community. Death was an elaborate and expensive affair in early-eighteenth-century Cape May County. It included not only coffin making but also blacking coffins, digging graves, purchasing wine, and often paying for someone "who attended deceased in their sinking." After the burial, the community needed to care for orphaned children or families impoverished by the loss of the head of the household. Officials had to inventory property, administer estates, and redistribute lands. The widow Esther Hewitt explained that the sudden death of her husband, Joseph, in the epidemic left her in charge of a plantation and five young children without resources to settle affairs. She had just given birth, Esther wrote Jeremiah Basse in Burlington, "so that I am incapacitated to travails so far as Burling town for to administer on my husbands Estate."[11]

The county offered no administrative or religious center to organize a response to the epidemic. Whaler yeomen had not built a central courthouse, although possibly in 1707 they had constructed a jail, stocks, and whipping post east of Gravelly Run on the Queen's Road (somewhere along present Route 9 between Burleigh and Mayville in Middle Township). None of the separate religious communities had constructed a meetinghouse, either. The absence of a central place of assembly nearly three decade after the establishment of a settlement on Cape May arose from the first settlement pattern. Whaler yeomen lived along creeks, sounds, and the bay. Unlike Salem, Burlington, or Philadelphia, the rapidly growing colonial city ninety miles upriver, Cape May had no organized town. Only a bayside community known as New England Town, or by early residents simply as Town, held a cluster of buildings. New England Town resembled a town in name only; it contained little more than a string of twelve to twenty log or frame structures built on irregular thirty-acre town lots along the unstable banks overlooking the Delaware Bay. Possibly one of the wooden buildings served as a town hall or meeting house, but Town boasted no central square, village green, or rectilinear street design such as characterized colonial settlements from Boston to Jamestown and Newark to Williamsburg.[12]

Cape May County's founders possessed little of the religious unity that characterized the Newark Calvinists and the Burlington, Salem, or Philadelphia Quakers, who built meetinghouses and churches as soon as they laid out town lines. Religion probably played a small part in the decision of the original settlers to come to the Cape May peninsula. The Townsends, Spicers, and other Quaker families suffered persecution and jailing at one time but had long enjoyed religious toleration when they chose to move to Cape May County in search of whales, land, and economic improvement. Opportunistic early whaler yeoman families turned from the Society of Friends to other congregations depending upon local interests, or married out of Quaker meeting in order to enlarge their landed estates.[13]

Gradually Cape May County families formed churches around their scattered clusters of plantations. Three distinct religious communities emerged. Quaker families of English, Dutch, or Scandinavian origin settled during the 1690s on the northern part of the Cape May peninsula below Great Egg Harbor (present-day Beesley's Point) and down the mainland on the seashore side as far as the middle of the Cape (the current Cape May Court House area). The Townsends, Willets, Garretsons, Badcocks, Baners, Corsons, and Smiths comprised the more active Cape May County members of the earliest Quaker meeting. Timothy Brandreth, Jacob Spicer, Thomas Leaming, and Aaron Leaming also entered the Cape as Quakers. Aaron Leaming had received his education in Salem with Sarah Hall, a leading Quaker teacher. Jacob Spicer was the son of Samuel Spicer, a prosperous Gloucester County Friend.[14]

Thomas Leaming probably suffered some persecution on Cape May as the result of Lord Cornbury's Militia Act of 1704. The first royal governor of New Jersey used this law to weaken Quaker influence by requiring Friends who refused to serve in the militia to pay a fine in goods and property. Leaming surrendered a prize horse to Samuel Matthews, the local militia captain, in 1704 when he failed to train with the militia. Cornbury's militia act had the desired affect on several Cape May County Quakers. Jacob Spicer joined Ezekiel Eldredge, a Presbyterian militia officer, in organizing the local militia for an expedition against the French in Canada. When Captain Eldredge died suddenly in Philadelphia while preparing for the expedition, Major Spicer married his widow within the month. Aaron Leaming also recognized that his fortune lay outside the Society of Friends. He married Lydia Parsons Shaw, a wealthy Baptist, in 1714, shortly after her husband, William, had succumbed to the epidemic. Leaming then allowed the building of a Baptist meeting house on his new property near present-day Burleigh, some four miles below the current town of Cape May Court House. Timothy Brandreth also married out of meeting, joined an anti-Quaker faction in Burlington, and experienced constant difficulties with the Cape May and Egg Harbor Friends.[15]

A group of Quakers in the upper part of the county maintained the unity of the Cape May Meeting. Cape May Quakers joined the Somers, Leeds, Steelmans, Adams, Sculls, and Irelands of what was then Gloucester County in monthly meeting on the northern shore of Great Egg Harbor. They alternated the sites of worship, crossing the bay in a tiny boat to attend meeting. Thomas Chalkley, Jacob Spicer's brother-in-law and an itinerant Quaker preacher, journeyed down from Philadelphia to revive enthusiasm for the Society of Friends. He visited the Cape May Friends in 1706. "They told me, after a meeting we had with them, that they used to spend the Sabbath days in sporting and vanity," Chalkley reported, "until Friends came among them, and now they meet together to worship God and his Son Jesus Christ."[16]

The Cape May Quakers built their own meetinghouse in about 1716, possibly on the Rebecca Garretson property in what was then referred to as Goldin's Point and later as Beesley's Point. The Townsend, Corson, Garretson, and other families provided lumber and labor. In about 1727 the Quaker meetinghouse was moved south to present-day Seaville, where it still stands along U.S. Route 9. Despite a new meetinghouse and vigorous missionary work by Rebecca Garretson and Friend Chalkley, Quakers remained a relatively isolated element in Cape May County's eighteenth century community. They made up less than 5 percent of the total population by 1747. Their interests lay in the uppermost regions of the peninsula. Several held public office under terms of the surrender of 1702 by substituting an affirmation or declaration instead of an oath of allegiance to the Crown. Not until Henry Young, a non-Quaker, entered the upper region in about 1710 and allied himself with the Quaker families did the interests of this remote region become important enough to require a separate political division.[17]

Cape May County's Baptists settled in a line of scattered hundred-acre plantations on the mainland, seaside below the Quakers. Their farms began about two miles above the present town of Cape May Court House and continued as far south as Cold Spring Creek and Turtle Gut Inlet. Early Baptist whaler yeomen included the Taylor, Cresse, Hand, Holdin, Shaw, Stites, and Swain families. Cape May County's Baptists resembled the group of individualistic yeoman farmers that Richard McCormick, a leading New Jersey historian, identified as the backbone of early New Jersey Baptist communities. Unlike other Protestant groups, these small landowners accepted women and African-Americans into full fellowship in the Baptist congregation. Cape May County women led by Lydia Parsons Shaw played a central part in the organization of the Baptist church on the Jersey Cape and in the movement to build a meetinghouse on her husband's plantation.[18]

Apparently a Baptist meetinghouse was completed by 7 July

1719, when the Reverend Nathaniel Jenkins, a Welshman brought into the county by the Cohansey Baptists in 1712, applied to the Cape May County court for a license to hold meetings at a place called Penuel on the west side of the King's Highway. Jenkins guided the Cape May County Baptists until called to Cohansey in 1733. He became a major landowner and political leader, serving variously as royal commissioner on whales and wrecks, county loan officer, tax assessor, surrogate of wills, and colonial assemblyman. Between 1723 and 1733 the latter post brought Jenkins to Burlington and Perth Amboy, where he argued for separation of church and state and for complete religious toleration throughout the colony of New Jersey.[19]

The Presbyterians found a well-educated preacher in the Reverend John Bradner. With a degree from Edinburgh University in Scotland, Bradner apparently ran off to the American colonies in 1712 with the daughter of a rich Huguenot. He made his way to the Jersey Cape from South Carolina, arriving just after the epidemic of 1714 and settling on the old Carman property near Cold Spring along a small stream that today bears the name Bradner's Run. Bradner's congregation included the wealthier and more conservative (in terms of church structure, doctrine, and views toward women and African-Americans) whaler yeoman families residing around New England Town, Fishing Creek, Cold Spring, and Cape Island. Bradner deeded his Cold Spring plantation in 1719 to Humphrey Hughes, Cornelius Schellenger, Ezekiel Eldredge, Jr., William Matthews, and eighteen other whaler yeoman leaders. They became the charter members of the Cold Spring Presbyterian Church. Bradner's deed stipulated that they construct a church building, schoolhouse, and burying yard. When Bradner left the county for Goshen, New York, in 1721, the Cape May Presbyterians had constructed a log meetinghouse with a high pulpit and plain benches near the current site of the Cold Spring Presbyterian Church, commonly called the "old brick church."[20]

John Bradner, Nathaniel Jenkins, and Thomas Chalkley helped to create three distinct and separate religious communities on the Cape May peninsula by 1720. Clusters of whaler yeomen, led by members of the original families, gravitated toward these local assembly places. The religious groupings largely determined the political organization of the county in 1723. At a quarterly session of the county court held at Robert Townsend's house in April 1723, six powerful local leaders voted to have "the county rounded into persinks [precincts] Excepting the Seder [Cedar] swamp." Jacob Spicer, Humphrey Hughes, Robert Townsend, John Hand, Henry Young, and William Smith divided the county into precincts that coincided with religious lines.[21]

The Upper Precinct incorporated the Quaker Meeting area, extending westward from Great Egg Harbor along the "Turkeyhoe" (Tuckahoe) River into the pine wilderness where in 1710 the county line with Salem County had been moved from the Maurice River east to West Creek. The precinct's boundary then extended south along the bayshore from West Creek across East Creek (present-day Eldora) and on to Dennis Creek. The Middle Precinct encompassed the Baptist domain. It began at Thomas Leaming's plantation near Townsend's Inlet and the present town of Clermont, crossed the peninsula to Dennis Creek, ran south down the bay to Fishing Creek, and back across the peninsula to the Turtle Gut Inlet (current Wildwood Crest). The Lower Precinct incorporated the Presbyterian-dominated community from Fishing Creek on the bayside south across the New England Creek, around the point and along Cape Island (Cape May City), and up the seaside to the head of Cold Spring Creek (see map 1).

The formation of precincts in 1723 also was influenced by outside politics. The New Jersey General Assembly passed the first Loan Office Act in 1723 to provide money to yeoman farmers throughout the colony for twelve-year terms at 5 percent interest. The loans were secured on mortgages. The act provided paper money and credit for the cash-starved economy. This act and two succeeding loan laws encouraged whaler yeomen to purchase property and develop business in Cape May County. The law stipulated that each county administer its own share of the loan. For Cape May County to administer the loan more effectively and for the whaler yeomen to protect the interests of their particular part of the county, the county grand jury made up of justices and freeholders (in many ways a forerunner of today's Board of Chosen Freeholders) divided the county into three precincts. The county officials appointed as loan overseers Henry Young for the Upper Precinct, the Reverend Nathaniel Jenkins for the Middle Precinct, and Humphrey Hughes for the Lower Precinct.[22]

The precinct structure reinforced the parochial character of each section already created by geography and accelerated by religious separation. Immediate interest guided each precinct. Lewis T. Stevens, a nineteenth-century county historian, explained that while the Upper Precinct contributed to countywide road maintenance during the early eighteenth century, the Lower Precinct ignored its obligations. Each division became a separate socioeconomic universe. The Upper Precinct looked to its Gloucester County and Atlantic Ocean environment, the Middle Precinct traded with Philadelphia, and the Lower Precinct focused on contacts with Maryland and the Carolinas. Nevertheless the three precincts shared an inherent unity derived from their common tie to whaler yeoman family leadership. The whaler yeoman oligarches joined together four times a year when they assembled with family and kin for Cape May County court day.[23]

Court day had been a gathering time since at least 1692, when the first county justices and freeholders held a court session at Coxe Hall on the bay and in private houses in the lower part of the peninsula. Lord Cornbury continued this practice when he ordered the first court session under the royal surrender of 1702 to convene at Shamgar Hand's plantation at Gravelly Run, located between present-day Mayville and Burleigh, probably on the grounds of what is now the Wildwood Golf Course. Not incidentally, Hand had signed the petition in 1700 requesting royal government. Subsequent quarterly court sessions were held in houses owned by the Eldredge, Hand, Crawford, Shaw, Townsend, and Leaming families. Court day, which sometimes extended to several days, encompassed all community activities. It meant militia training day, particularly when larger colonial affairs required the muster of New Jersey militia to face a French and Native American threat in Canada or along the Pennsylvania frontiers. Court day brought residents together to conduct business, barter and trade, and gossip about developments in their remote corners of the county. Court day might include sporting events such as horse racing and gambling. Apparently the Cape May County court day never evolved into a formal county fair similar to those held in April at Cohansey (now the town of Greenwich in Cumberland County) or in May at Salem.[24]

Whaler yeoman officials heard civil and criminal cases during quarterly court sessions. On court day they established control over local society by enforcing laws such as one that suppressed immorality. Punishment depended on the cost of a case to the public. The grand jury fined Isaac Whilldin five pounds "to save the town or Precinct charge of ye Bastard Childe." The county government required that Randall Hewitt pay thirty pounds for the care of single woman Sarah Hoopes and her baby. In another case, the court ordered Captain Richard Downs, a wealthy Fishing Creek mill owner, to bear all costs for the care of the widow Deborah Russell's child, probably fathered by the already married Downs.[25]

A double standard governed these cases based, it seemed, upon connection of an affair to a whaler yeoman family rather than upon the inferior legal status of colonial Cape May County women. Dinah Fortescue, an indentured white woman, accused a member of the prominent Hughes family in 1705 of getting her with child; she said the family threatened to murder her if she revealed the name of the father. The county grand jury, made up of the Hugheses' kin and fellow whaler yeomen, instead found Fortescue guilty of "scandously calling" one of the Hughes's sons the father. The whaler yeoman jury sentenced Fortescue to receive ten lashes on her bare back. Court records tersely announced the final act: "The said Dina Fortiscue was whiped accordin to Judgment." An identical case involving Mary Holdin, member of a wealthy and prominent whaler yeoman family, ended far differently. When newcomer James Robinson accused Holdin of being "a devilish whore" who lured him into her mother's back bedroom, the court exonerated the woman of any guilt and ordered Robinson punished instead.[26]

Whaler yeoman justices, meeting as a local legislative assembly as well as a judicial body, enforced public order. Remarkably little social unrest occurred in Cape May County's rough frontier seafaring community during the eighteenth century. The absence of a port town or concentration of propertyless residents similar to that in Philadelphia accounted in part for the orderliness of Cape May County society. The separation of different religious groups in their own precincts removed another potential source of conflict. More important, the whaler yeoman families assured stability. Whenever a stranger arrived, whaler yeoman officials examined the visitor's intentions. Constables detained John Crandoll as a suspicious person and released him only when satisfied that he had registered his cattle earmark with the county and established a blacksmith's trade. Strangers who caused trouble received harsher treatment than local residents did for similar crimes. One unlucky visitor, apparently passing through, received fifteen lashes on the bare back for pilfering a piece of ironware.[27]

One aspect of public order defied whaler yeoman control. From the beginning of the county, public drunkenness and the illegal sale of liquor plagued local government. Drunkenness seemed almost endemic on this isolated peninsula. Perhaps people consumed liquor to avoid drinking the water. County residents recognized that putrid water contributed to the epidemics of "Bloody Flux" like those that ravaged similar tidewater communities along the Chesapeake Bay, although Aaron Leaming, Jr., complained that "Idle Stories of waters being unwholsome or dangerous" were "Propagated by physicians to disgrace Creation." Whatever the view, Jacob Spicer, Jr., noted that more rum was sold on the Jersey Cape than any other wet or dry goods. He spotted eighteen hogsheads of rum entering the lower part of the county in one year.[28]

Public drunkenness ravaged Cape May County society. The Presbyterians at Cold Spring removed a preacher in 1726 because of his affinity for strong drink. The Baptists saw one of their ministers break down over liquor. It caused fights between members of the whaler yeoman families. Jacob Spicer, Jr., "merrily Disposed at punch & Beer," became involved in a drunken argument with Elijah Hughes over a fence line. Too much rum probably drove William Shaswood to push his neighbor into his fireplace while the latter lit his pipe. Liquor caused John Stites to attack Aaron Leaming, Jr., with his sword. Lydia Schellenger left her husband because, as Thomas Leaming, Jr., explained, he was a "miserable drunken animal who would have spent everything that he could." A drunken brawl between Joseph Golden and his Native American laborers ended in murder. The Cape May County grand jury indicted Goldin on 4 August 1736 "for striking of Richard Inding in the defense of himself wherewith the said Inding dyed." Meanwhile, Jacob Goldin was denied his inheritance because his family insisted that he was "addicted to the excessive use of spirituous liquors."[29]

Whaler yeoman direction of public works proved more successful than the curbing of public drunkenness or immorality. Building roads, bridges, or causeways took on major significance in a county rendered nearly impassable by deep tidal creeks, tangled underbrush, and treacherous marshes and swamplands. Travel into and out of the peninsula by land appeared impossible during wet seasons. The Burlington Court had ordered a road cut in 1697 from Cape May to the provincial capital, and the following year the Cape May County grand jury instructed Shamgar Hand, John Crawford, and William Golden to form a road commission to build a highway through the Cedar Swamp. The court ordered the commissioners to run a road that started roughly half a mile south of the current town of South Seaville and proceeded northwest over four guts (narrow streams) through the swamp and out of the county near Tarkiln, a region of old cranberry bogs along the county's current northwestern border with Cumberland County. The road passed through a high gravel ridge (now called Mt. Pleasant) and crossed Cedar Swamp Creek, first at a place referred to as Long Bridge and farther north over another bridge known in early records as Ludley's or Ludlam's Bridge.[30]

The Old Cape Road took ten years to complete. County taxpayers together contributed seventy pounds payable in "merchantable Indian corn, wheat, or cattle" toward construction of the road and the bridges. Apparently parts of the road through what is now Belleplain State Forest became impassable soon after the road opened to travel in 1707; in 1716 the New Jersey Assembly passed an act for the construction of a road from the Cedar Swamp Bridge (probably Long Bridge) north to the Tuckahoe River where it would cross at the site of the present-day town of Tuckahoe. This Tuckahoe Road undoubtedly followed the old Native American trail out of the county.[31]

While the county struggled with the old Cape Road, the grand jury instructed road commissioners John Parsons, John Cresse, and Richard Townsend to construct another highway from Golden's fence line near the landing of a ferry that had crossed the Great Egg Harbor since about 1695 and down the coast to "ye olde Road" that went to the bay. This highway, known at various times as the Queen's Road, King's Road, or old Cape Road, passed north to south near the path of present-day Route 9. It followed a course through the fence gates that in 1706 defined the plantations owned by the Corson, Ludlam, Townsend, Hand, Leonard, Johnson, Cresse, Shaw, and Taylor families. Then, this main county road "turned out" at the Cold Spring Path, where it crossed Crawford's Meadow, probably to a windmill located just north of New England Creek near Town Bank. The county ordered yet another road built in 1710; it connected Schellenger's Mill Pond (near the present-day seaside entrance to the Cape May Canal) to New England Town on the bayside. By the end of the first decade of the eighteenth century, the county had completed a basic road network linking lower and upper sections, bayside with seaside, and Cape May County to the rest of West Jersey.[32]

Completion of a system of roads benefited Cape May County's emerging agricultural economy. Soon after road builders dumped their last cartloads of gravel, local farmers drove cattle through the Cedar Swamp to West Jersey markets. County livestock producers found buyers for their cattle, sheep, hogs, and fowl in Cohansey, Salem, Gloucester, Dan Cooper's Ferry (present-day Camden City), and Philadelphia. John Foreman reported that he had received between five and six pounds per head on the Gloucester market for his herd of seven Cape May cattle. The average New Jersey yeoman farmer made sixteen pounds annual income, so the sale of Foreman's small herd for forty pounds suggested the profitability of the cattle business for colonial Cape May County.[33]

The cost of raising livestock on the Jersey Cape remained low. Cattle owners simply let their herds wander on the uninhabited white sandy beaches of a chain of barrier islands that ran the length of the Atlantic coast of the peninsula. Here, they fattened the cattle on grasses, salt hay, and other vegetation found on the Five Mile, Seven Mile, and other beaches. Cape May County cattle raisers needed no fencing. Thoroughfares and channels cut through the coastal salt marshes that separated the barrier islands from the mainland and prevented cattle from leaving the beaches to harm the corn crops on the mainland. At the same time, deep tidal inlets separated one barrier island from another, forcing the herds to remain on their own island. Sheep, cattle, and horses grazed all summer on the beaches. For a time, wolves and panthers endangered the herds, but a bounty of twenty-five shillings "pur Wolfe" and fifteen shillings for the head and ears of a panther eliminated this threat.[34]

The whaler yeomen rounded up their herds in the late autumn and drove them across the channels at low tide, or perhaps loaded them on flatboats. Cape May County cattleowners identified their animals through an elaborate system of earmarks cut into their creatures' ears. The earmark became an important status symbol and form of identification for whaler yeoman families. When a whaler yeoman died, heirs of the estate squabbled over the earmark until the county passed an earmark law in 1734. "The Court & Grand Jury do agree that when any man dieth his Executor or administrator if any hath he shall be allowed to have a right to the ear mark of the deceased for the space of one year," the local law read.[35]

The livestock business dominated Cape May County's early economy. Reputedly the Leaming, Hand, and other Cape families were among the largest sheep and cattle dealers in colonial New Jersey. These Cape May County families also sold some farm products to local markets and probably shipped produce on locally owned vessels to Philadelphia, New York, New England, North Carolina, and possibly to the West Indies. Inventories of the wills of whaler yeomen indicated that their Jersey Cape plantations grew Indian corn, rye, flax, wheat, oats, fruits, and some tobacco. The sandy soil and limited arable land on the Jersey Cape prevented the raising of large crops to rival the marl-rich farmland up the bay in Salem County. Jacob Spicer, Jr., noted that his sixteen-acre plot yielded only sixty-seven bushels of wheat. Aaron Leaming, Jr., imported corn into the county, traveling regularly to neighboring markets to purchase corn from Jeremiah Parvin and other large Salem County planters.[36]

Cape May County whaler yeomen also harvested cedar logs, both cut from the forest and recovered from where they had fallen into the swamps. In 1753 Anthony Ludlam and Lewis Cresse extracted logs from the Cedar Swamp from which they cut 16,500 three-foot-long shingles for export. Jacob Spicer, Jr., employed dozens of swampmen, laborers, and tenant farmers to cut timber and cart it to Dennis Creek, Cedar Swamp, or Goshen landings, where it was loaded on flats and shallops, most likely for the Philadelphia market. The Leamings shipped thousands of board feet of pine and cedar and tens of thousands of cedar shingles to New Castle, Christiana Bridge, and Willing Town, Delaware, and to Delaware Valley lumber merchant John Biddle. Most of the Leamings' lumber came from the vast tract of forestland that lay between the Maurice River and West Creek and had been transferred to Salem County by the boundary revision of 1710. Moreover, the Leamings cut their lumber at their large sawmill on the Maurice River and not in Cape May County where they resided. There were few sawmills on the Jersey Cape in the eighteenth century, and reportedly most of the county's largest trees had been cut down by mid-century. Jacob Spicer, Jr., noted that while the county's oyster crop was valued at £600, and even a woolen mitten industry brought £500 into the county, cedar posts earned county lumbermen only £300 in 1758.[37]

Cape May County whaler yeomen whale-fished throughout much of the eighteenth century to supplement their farming and lumbering enterprises. Upon the sighting of spouts off the ocean coast or bayshore, the whalemen launched tiny boats each February from local beaches. "Went on the Beach awhaling," Aaron Leaming, Jr., wrote in his diary in February 1734. Lewis Cresse left his farming and lumbering to go whale fishing every February during the 1750s. The first whaling families, now primarily yeoman farmers, remained active until the American Revolution in 1776. The Hughes, Swain,

Stites, Hand, and Ludlam families held shares on the barrier island beaches as part of a combined farming-lumbering-whaling business. They launched their own whaleboats from these beaches and leased shares of the beach during whaling season to other whalemen.[38]

Whaling never developed into the dominant Cape May County industry expected by earliest settlers. They whale-fished for two months, Lewis Cresse reported, "and we never saw a whale nor the spout of a whale that we knew of in all the time." Other whalers spotted whales, but their tiny boats, launched through the rough surf, rarely arrived in time to cast irons. During the first sixty years of the eighteenth century, the Cape May County whale harvest probably averaged two whales annually. Aaron Leaming, Jr., wrote in 1772 that the Cape May County whalemen had become nothing more than a band of rabble who plundered wrecks cast upon his Seven Mile Beach, shot waterfowl, and stampeded cattle. The Cape May whalemen, Leaming claimed, had killed only one whale on his beach during the past forty years.[39]

Cape May County developed a few craft industries to supplement the lumber, farming, and whaling businesses. Richard Downs operated a fulling mill for a short time on Fishing Creek but closed it when he sold the property. Encouraged by Benjamin Franklin, who according to tradition visited kin on the Jersey Cape, Jacob Spicer developed a knitted-mitten and -stocking industry that employed a number of Cape May County women and their spinning wheels. The industry flourished briefly during the 1750s and then disappeared. Spicer pursued a wampum trade with Albany, New York, and the many large shell piles left in the county probably came from his industry rather than from an earlier Native American wampum trade. When the strings of beads made from shells lost value as a colonial currency, however, Spicer's wampum industry died out. Spicer talked about developing a salt industry but worried that he could not secure articles of incorporation from the government and probably never started this business.[40]

Cape May County supported no colonial pottery or glassworks during the eighteenth century, although Aaron Leaming, Jr., mentioned that the Hughes family set up an ironworks with Samuel Barnes of Cohansey. The ironworks probably stood in Salem County. Cape May County supported a modest shipbuilding industry during the early eighteenth century. Reportedly, local craftsmen built the sloops *Adventure*, *Dolphin*, and *Necessity* somewhere on the Jersey

Cape between 1705 and 1709. Dennis Lynch, a shipbuilder, held property along Townsend's Inlet before 1710, and possibly constructed these or other small sailing vessels there. There was also a shipyard at Fast Landing (near present-day Petersburg) on the Cedar Swamp Creek in the mid-eighteenth century.[41]

Cape May County's eighteenth-century economy did not support many skilled craftsmen, and therefore whaler yeoman families journeyed to Philadelphia for services. Aaron Leaming, Jr., shopped in Philadelphia, Cohansey, and Salem for iron door hinges and other ironware. Whaler yeomen went to silversmith Philip Syng in Philadelphia if they needed silver buckles repaired. Cape May County planters carried their clocks to Richard Allen on Chestnut Street in Philadelphia. When Jacob Spicer, Jr., and Aaron Leaming, Jr., required a printer for their collection of New Jersey's laws and statutes, they traveled up the bay and across the river to Philadelphia to contract with William Bradford, Printer, for 170 leather-bound copies. Cape May County's whaler yeomen purchased books, newspapers, and pamphlets at Ben Franklin's shop and picked up their mail in Philadelphia (some of it held for months and advertised in the newspaper). They shopped at Jos. Kebby merchants on Market Street for wigs, saddles, sealing wax, or medicines. The Cape May County families purchased nearly everything in the great colonial city, including African-American slaves. "I set out from home to go to Philada. to buy a Negro or two," Aaron Leaming, Jr., noted in his diary.[42]

Slavery had existed in Cape May County since at least 1688, when George Taylor and Joseph Holdin owned five African-American slaves. By the middle of the eighteenth century, Cape May County planters owned more than fifty slaves, mostly African-Americans but possibly some Native Americans. Jacob Spicer, Jr., mentioned a "Red Negroe" in his records, and Abigail Hand suggested that her family held both Indian and "black folk." The original whaler yeoman families owned 91 percent of the slaves on the Jersey Cape in the 1750s. The Leaming, Hand, and Whilldin families owned three or more slaves each. Other families held no more than two each. The smaller farms and diverse economy kept slave owning on a much smaller scale than that of the large East Jersey farms or great southern plantations. Whaler yeomen kept their slaves in the family, willing them to their children and widows. Joshua Shaw left "my Negro wench, Nancy" to his wife. Deborah Hand's "Negro girl Vinah" lived in the main house with her mistress and owned her own "cloaths, bed and bedding."[43]

Many Cape May County whaler yeomen treated their slaves as a part of the family. Jeremiah Eldredge's slave Wanton lived in the master's kitchen near the fireplace. Unfortunately, as Thomas Leaming, Jr., observed, a "wind blew down Jeremiah Eldredg kitchen Chimne and kild his boy Wanton in his bed." Aaron Leaming, Jr., allowed his slaves Tony and Boy to travel alone around the county, carting, logging, and fishing. He gave Tony time off to visit "Penples House warming." Leaming cared for ill slaves as though they were members of the family. "Tony was sick," Leaming explained, "so Boy & myself carted Hay." Regardless of such good treatment and kindness by Cape May slave masters, the county's slaves remained property to be inventoried with the cattle when the master drew up his will. Many remained with the same family, but in other cases the master's death broke up the slave family. The will of Thomas Leaming, Sr., advised that "a negro man and a negro women, whose respective children are disposed of," should be sold. Lewis Cresse recorded the disposable character of the Cape May County African-American in the eighteenth century. "Died Cato a Negro man in Prison with the hurt of the Irons he wore & by cold and long Imprisonment," Cresse observed in 1753.[44]

Farming and landownership remained the county's economic foundation throughout the eighteenth century and determined wealth, social standing, and political power. Yet the peninsula was land poor. Over 70 percent of the acreage lay in swampland, salt marsh, and beach. Not unexpectedly, heated disputes arose over land titles, inheritances, and fence lines that demarcated properties. Aaron Leaming, Jr., viewed with great suspicion the activities of Henry Young and Jacob Spicer, Jr., as they surveyed the Cedar Swamp in the Upper Precinct. "I suppose they are now agoing to run the Line in order to make it come out at the foot of the Cedar Swamp Bridge as Spicer Pretends it ought to do," Leaming wrote, adding that "they have some Sinistere Views."[45]

Land surveyors, such as Henry Young and Jacob Spicer, Jr., and estate administrators became the most powerful officials in the county. The original thirty-five whaler yeoman families controlled these positions, and fought among themselves over influence and property. The surveyor held absolute authority under the law in determining fence lines and the boundaries of property. Not only did he control the division of land, but through access to information and records he could enlarge his own estate. He could do so by assuming guardianship over orphaned children and widows with young children as well as through witnessing wills, drawing up legal documents, and other similar opportunities. Experience Hand petitioned Governor Jonathan Belcher in 1755 to allow Jacob Spicer, Jr., to control all of her extensive lands and tenements because her husband had requested it "verbally on his death bed."[46]

Control of the remaining West Jersey Society lands on the Jersey Cape, mostly swamp and marshlands, caused the most controversy. In 1752 the thirty-five whaler yeoman families formed the majority interest in a General Association to acquire the remaining Society lands, with oystering, hunting, and fishing rights and privileges. The General Association held meetings, probably at the Cold Spring Presbyterian Church, to discuss the purchase. The whaler yeomen failed to agree on a course of action, however, and procrastinated for nearly four years. Jacob Spicer, Jr., reported that the General Association had reached an impasse. "It's morally impossible to Reconcile any kind of partnership to a Multitude, Influenced by different Interests, sentiments, and Principles, which would in Great Measure have impeded, If not totally obstructed the Benefits proposed by the first General Association, had the Publick made the Purchase," Spicer explained.[47]

Spicer took the matter into his own hands in August 1756 when he dined in Perth Amboy with Lewis Johnston, an agent of the West Jersey Society. After some heavy drinking, Johnston apparently told Spicer that if he failed to buy the remaining Society lands at once, Johnston would sell to "another not well disposed" toward Cape May's interests. Spicer insisted that he had to purchase with his own money in order to prevent a "Great Prejudice [that] might Injure both the Publick and me." He concealed his purchase from the General Association, though. Three years later, Jeremiah Hand told Spicer that he had heard rumors about Spicer's purchase and wanted a share in the marshlands. At first, Aaron Leaming, Jr., criticized Hand rather than Spicer. Leaming "told Jere Hand that now hed got a Sherff commission," Thomas Leaming, Jr. recalled; "he thot him self some Lord God or other, but said he was very much mistaken for he was but a damned Indian make the best of him."[48]

Leaming grew suspicious of Spicer's activities. He had probably negotiated unsuccessfully on his own earlier with Lewis Johnston for the West Jersey Society rights on the Cape and had watched uneasily as Jacob Spicer, Jr., and Henry Young seemed to carve out their own claims to the Cedar Swamp. Leaming called for a public meeting in March 1761 to hear Spicer's explanation of affairs. Forty people gathered at the Cold Spring Presbyterian Church on March 23 to learn that indeed Spicer had assumed title to all "waste lands" in Cape May County. He intended to resurvey them and rent out rights for pasturage, logging, and oystering. Apparently the meeting broke up in some confusion, with Leaming threatening to sue Spicer in court. One observer insisted that Leaming never again spoke to Spicer, who had been his longtime legislative partner in the Assembly. Spicer defended himself in a thirty-nine-page statement. He insisted that he planned to share the lands equally with other members of the General Association and to pay them half of all monies received "from the sale of overplus lands."[49]

Spicer controlled this land until his death in 1765. He rented out pasturage, oyster rights, and timber privileges and kept all income. He dominated the county's landless and tenant labor. His economic empire rivaled that of the Leaming family, which over the course of the eighteenth century had through marriage and purchase acquired the largest landed estate on the Jersey Cape. Both families owned ships, mills, and stores. According to historian Thomas Purvis, the Leamings and the Spicers became merchant planters comparable in every way to the Chesapeake Bay tidewater gentry elite. Their great wealth enabled them to join other elite New Jersey planters from other counties and dominate New Jersey legislative politics, financial policies, and elections. The selection of Jacob Spicer, Jr., and Aaron Leaming, Jr., to compile *The Grants, Concessions, and Original Constitutions of the Province of New Jersey* in the 1750s attested to their immense influence over both Cape May County and New Jersey colonial politics and society.[50]

Jacob Spicer, Sr., and his son, and Aaron Leaming, Sr., and his son, held tremendous wealth and power but owed these to their intimate connections, kinship, and intermarriage with Cape May County's original thirty-five whaler yeoman families. Accumulation of wealth and position resulted largely from their connections with the Parsons, Shaw, Foreman, Eldredge, Whilldin, Hughes, and Hand families. "Elijah Hughes says he thinks Uncle Jeremiah L[eaming's] Influence would not have been so great in this County as it was if it had not been for the Family of Eldredges who had always supported him & his Interests," Thomas Leaming, Jr., wrote. The Leamings and the Spicers dared not act without consulting the whaler yeoman leaders. Jacob Spicer, Jr., knew that his one great mistake in defying them by purchasing the Society rights to Cape May County had brought a great "prejudice of my memory when the rubbish of my nature shall sleep in Dust."[51]

Connections with the whaler yeoman community rather than colonial voting patterns and politics defined the social and economic status of Jacob Spicer, Jr., and Aaron Leaming, Jr. They never acted the part of Chesapeake planter aristocrats or lived in the style of Philadelphia's merchant elite. The Spicers and the Leamings toiled daily with their neighbors, kin, and slaves. They dug wells and drainage ditches. They drove their own cartloads of hay, sawed board, and harrowed their fields and those of their whaler yeoman neighbors. They slaughtered their own cattle and hogs. They spent more on themselves than other families in the county, Spicer admitted, and "the populace in general may not live at a proportionate expense with my family." However, the gap in material comfort between the Spicers and the Leamings and the other families narrowed when viewed through the inventories of their personal possessions.[52]

The Spicer and Leaming families lived like their whaler yeoman neighbors in frame houses with wooden barns, sheds, and worm fences, not in grand brick mansions with carriage houses and manicured English gardens. They owned little fine European-crafted furniture, china, or glassware. Like all whaler yeoman families, they filled their houses with woolen and linen wheels, warming pans, pewter and iron kitchenware, and hand mills. They all possessed two-wheeled carts, yokes of oxen, plows, harrows, and husbandry tools. Nearly every whaler yeoman family's inventory of possessions included guns, swords, walking canes, and whale fishing gear. Aaron Leaming, Jr., owned a large library of sixty volumes, but other Cape May County whaler yeomen also possessed Bibles and old books. The Leamings and the Spicers maintained larger vessels for coastal trade, while the other families held shares in these vessels and owned whaleboats and pilot boats, canoes and flatboats. The combined herds of livestock of the Hand, Hughes, and Whilldin families compared favorably to those of the Leaming family and were larger than that owned by the Spicers. The gap in slave owning narrowed, too, when the Leamings lent "our folks" to kin and neighbors at planting, harvest, and barn-raising time.[53]

Cape May County's eighteenth-century society seemed less a county dominated by two colonial tidewater aristocrats than a community run by thirty-five families. By mid-century that whaler yeoman community had started to undergo gradual change that affected future development. A village, possibly with a schoolhouse, had taken shape in the middle part of the Jersey Cape on Shamgar Hand's old plantation between Crooked Creek and Gravelly Run. Residents probably called it Romney Marsh. Despite Cape May County tradition that the village was once also called Middletown, there is no evidence to support this. The Baptists erected a church in the new village by 1741, and that same year the county justices and freeholders consulted in September on the "proper method of erecting and building a Court House and Goal at or near the Midel of the sd County as soon as conveniently" arranged. Instead they repaired the old Baptist meeting house called Penuel on the Aaron Leaming plantation four miles below present-day Court House and built a jail "nere the House of Mr. Leaming." The first session of the quarterly court of common pleas was held at Penuel in May 1745.[54]

County business soon outgrew the old Baptist meetinghouse on the Leaming plantation. Jacob Spicer, Jr., campaigned around the county to build a new courthouse near the property of his son-in-law, Daniel Hand, which was near the center of what is today the county seat, Cape May Court House. Apparently Aaron Leaming, Jr., campaigned just as vigorously to construct a new courthouse on his property. County records indicate that the county justices and freeholders held court sessions in Daniel Hand's house in 1764 while the county constructed a courthouse nearby on an acre of ground purchased from Hand. The county completed a courthouse near the site of the present building and held its first court session there on 21 May 1765.[55]

Now the county had a reference point for eighteenth-century mapmakers and a destination for travelers who braved the old Cape Road or Tuckahoe Road. The increase in "public houses of entertainment," or inns and taverns licensed by the county, during this period suggested that more visitors traveled to the Jersey Cape after the village became a center of county life in the 1740s and county government in 1765. Along the county roads in the 1740s the Reverend Whitefield and other preachers traveled, driven by the fervor of a mid-century religious revival called the Great Awakening. Their visit created considerable controversy and rivalry between Cape May County's Baptists and Presbyterians.[56]

Riders with news of the growing troubles with the French and Native Americans on the Pennsylvania frontier probably passed through the village in the middle of the Jersey Cape as well. Jacob

Spicer, Jr., knew that this meant involvement in a colonial war, "for I hear there has been an Indian killed in this Province & his head exposed to publick view on a pole which I take to be very indiscreet." Spicer, Jeremiah Leaming, Henry Young, Ebenezer Swain, John Mackey, and other Cape May County militia officers began to drill for possible dispatch to the frontier. The General Assembly voted monies to outfit an expedition to fight the French and their Native American allies and sent muskets, powder, and shot to Cape May County's militia. The Assembly ordered Spicer to take charge of the provisioning of New Jersey's force. The Cape May legislator spent months purchasing supplies, during which time he neglected his own farm and store on the Jersey Cape. He complained that the frontier wars had nothing to do with New Jersey and urged the colony to stay out of this "distant Imaginary Danger." Spicer thought that such adventures would be expensive, increase the public debt, raise local taxes, upset trade, and force the British government to interfere in local affairs.[57]

Spicer was right. No sooner had the French and Indian War concluded than the British authorities demanded that the colonies share the burden of their own defense. The Board of Trade dispatched officials to enforce new revenue measures imposed upon the colonists. One of these royal officials settled in Cold Spring. He soon caused a controversy in Cape May County that pulled the region out of its half-century of isolation and plunged it into the events leading to American independence.

CHAPTER THREE

Revolution and the New Nation, 1764–1800

John Hatton's appointment as customs commissioner for the Delaware Bay and River under the British Revenue Act of 1764 brought Cape May County into the larger colonial unrest that led to American independence. Hatton embraced the new revenue measures imposed on the American colonies by the British government after the expensive French and Indian Wars of 1754–1763. He set out to tighten royal authority over the collection of duties along the Delaware River and Bay, ordering an end to the practice of leaving blank port-clearance forms at Cohansey (present-day Greenwich), Salem, or on Cape May, where captains involved in the shuttle trade to Philadelphia and Burlington might fill them out—or ignore them altogether—at their convenience.[1]

John Hatton purchased a small plantation at Cold Spring on the Cape May peninsula to supplement his Raccoon Creek (now Swedesboro) farm in Gloucester County and to watch the activities of Jacob Spicer, Jr., the deputy customs collector. Spicer knew that local pilots and sea captains circumvented the unpopular British navigation laws that regulated colonial trade. He defended the issuance of blank port clearance forms and represented local maritime interests against Hatton. Spicer fought as well in the New Jersey General Assembly for provincial rights. He joined Charles Read and Samuel Smith, Burlington County assembly representatives, as a committee of correspondents in 1764 to send a letter of protest against British taxation practices to Joseph Sherwood, their colonial agent in London. This committee acted as part of a wider colonial protest movement. "The more Active and Expansive part of the Opposition we expect will be upon the other Colonies who are abundantly more Concerned in

Trade," Spicer wrote, "yet it is Necessary so far to Cooperate with them as to Show the Colonies are unanimously of One Mind."[2]

Jacob Spicer, Jr., moved beyond his earlier particularism when he presented regional grievances to the British government. His actions in 1764 suggested that the Cape May County legislator might become a spokesman in New Jersey for the growing Whig sentiment for independence. When Spicer died suddenly at his Cold Spring farm in 1765, however, New Jersey lost a potential revolutionary leader. His death left Aaron Leaming, Jr., as the only Cape May County leader recognized outside of the remote southern county as a political spokesman. Leaming lived until 1780 and saw much of the revolution against Britain unfold, but he never assumed a larger political role in New Jersey's independence movement. Poor health kept him at home much of the time. Moreover, Leaming's keen legal and political mind, which had helped Spicer to compile the New Jersey provincial laws in the 1750s, had become confused during the 1770s by bitter feuds with family and kin over inheritance and property rights. Leaming flogged his brother with a driving gad in an argument over which one held legal title to Nummy Island in Hereford Inlet just south of Seven Mile Beach. He screamed obscenities at relatives and accused leading whaler yeoman families of interbreeding with local Native Americans and with their own African-American slaves. "James Whildin heard A[aron] L[eaming] [Jr.] tell Experience Edmonds that she was a damned black tawny bitch," Thomas Leaming, Jr., observed, "tho his daughter had married her Brother." One whaler yeoman ancestor accused Aaron Leaming, Jr., of having such an obsession with wealth and property that he had lost his mind.[3]

Cape May County thus approached the coming revolution with politically inexperienced representatives who lacked the wider provincial recognition or political power of either Jacob Spicer, Jr., or Aaron Leaming, Jr. With Spicer gone and Leaming preoccupied, John Hatton enforced the navigation laws unchallenged in Cape May County. He seized Jedidiah Mills's Cape May pilot boat in 1770 as it unloaded cargo illegally in the bay from the *Prince of Wales*, just arrived from Liverpool. The rough Cape May County pilots fought back. They assaulted Hatton and recaptured their boat, then charged the official and "Negro Ned, a Molatto slave of said Hattons" with theft. Cape May County justices arrested Hatton and Negro Ned, the latter apparently a large man greatly feared by the pilots. Justices Thomas Leaming, Sr., James Whilldin, and John Leonard threw Ned into the county jail and brought Hatton before the Cape May County court, which indicted him "for willful and corrupt perjury." Finally, Nicholas Stillwell of Upper Precinct posted Hatton's bond and the justices released the royal customs commissioner.[4]

John Hatton protested his treatment in Cape May County to William Franklin, the last colonial governor of New Jersey. Hatton also appealed to the customs commissioners in Perth Amboy and the port of Boston for a redress of his grievances against Cape May County officials. They sided with the local justices and largely ignored the maritime violations that Hatton had revealed in the Delaware Bay. The customs commissioners found that Hatton caused trouble with the colonists wherever he went, and Governor Franklin suspected that Hatton consorted with Philadelphia smugglers. More important, Franklin understood that these local issues threatened to explode into wider revolt against the Crown. In order to preserve British authority, the governor defended New Jersey's colonial interests in the Hatton case.[5]

Governor William Franklin feared the deterioration of Anglo-American relations. Disaffection with Britain appeared each time that the English Parliament passed another measure to tax, regulate, or coerce the American colonies. Colonists dressed as Native Americans responded to a tax on East India tea in December 1773 by dumping a cargo of it into Boston Harbor. Britain closed the port, quartered troops in America, and passed more revenue and enforcement measures. A year later, South Jersey protesters, also dressed as Native Americans, burned a cargo of tea stored a few miles up the Delaware Bay from Cape May County at the port of Cohansey in Cumberland County.

Colonial protests of British imperial policy led to the convening of a Continental Congress in Philadelphia in 1774. Concern for conditions in New England and support for the intercolonial congress reached down to the remote Cape May County community. "I am impatient to hear what news from Boston" and Philadelphia, observed Elijah Hughes, the Cape May County surrogate. Some New Jersey counties organized extralegal political groups. Old Gloucester County formed a Relief Committee to aid Boston's residents, and Essex County assembled a Committee of Observation to defend a Continental Association against trade with Britain. Thomas Leaming, Jr., nephew of Aaron Leaming, Jr., returned from Philadelphia, where he studied law with John Dickinson, to circulate a petition in Cape

May County asking local residents to join the boycott of British trade. "I handed an Association Paper to most of the Inhabitants of Cape May," Leaming wrote, "and had the pleasure to say, that only one Man in that County refused signing it."[6]

Aaron Leaming, Jr., joined the protest against British commercial policy. He urged his neighbors to form a Committee of Observation on Cape May to support the Continental Association. Leaming explained that Britain had no right to tax without granting parliamentary representation. He told the Cape May County justices and freeholders that he opposed the quartering of troops in America and abhorred the treatment of Boston by the British Army as though it was "an Enemy's Town."[7]

The boycott disrupted Delaware River commerce. John Hatton, Jr., the son of the despised customs commissioner, wrote his uncle in England that "the present unnatural contest will soon produce a total stagnation of Trade." Young Hatton expected a complete collapse of order. Instead, local government moved slowly toward a break with Britain. The New Jersey Assembly endorsed the formation of county committees of observation, and most formed such extralegal political associations. Only Bergen and Sussex counties had failed to organize these revolutionary committees when news arrived in April 1775 that Massachusetts minutemen had clashed with British troops along the roads between Boston and the small towns of Lexington and Concord.[8]

Cape May County left no record of a local Committee of Observation during this period, causing one historian to conclude that the county was led by "hard-core royalists." However, county leaders had endorsed Thomas Leaming, Jr.'s, petition, and probably formed such a committee. Cape May County contained few royalists, only inherently cautious and conservative leaders. Elijah Hughes opposed giving anyone a vote on matters concerning the formation of a new government, or a break with Britain, unless he held one hundred acres of land or fifty pounds personal property. Hughes and other whaler yeoman leaders who represented county affairs supported the Whig cause for independence so long as they kept their property. None showed sympathy for Britain. Nearby counties harbored large numbers of Loyalists (or Tories), and their revolutionary governments confiscated Loyalist estates. Cape May County officials seized only John Hatton's small Cold Spring estate for Loyalist activities or sympathies.[9]

Elijah Hughes, elected as Cape May County's first representative to the new state government, moved slowly to support revolution because he had little news about larger developments. He was isolated on the Jersey Cape during the meetings of the Continental Congress in Philadelphia. "The Continental Congress still siting, but nothing respecting their proceedings in particular has traspared," Hughes noted. "God direct them in their delibarations, To such wise, linient and prudent measures, as may become the subject, & at the same time to be a means of preserving unto us, and our posterity our freedom & property, both religeous & civil," he wrote. When finally summoned to Princeton to discuss revolutionary measures, Hughes rode his horse into the deep woods and became lost near the Batsto iron forge on Great Egg Harbor River. He reached the road again only to discover that a recent snowfall had obliterated the only trail through this nearly uninhabited region. Battling sleet, snow, and wilderness, Hughes finally arrived four days later, too late to attend the early meetings.[10]

Cape May County assembled a revolutionary government on 21 September 1775 for "the defense of this and any neighbour colony." Calling together the scattered freeholders took time. Riders had to travel over poor roads to the remote sections of the peninsula to spread news of the meeting. Previous countywide elections had elicited little interest and even less attendance. One emergency meeting to raise money and soldiers during the recent French and Indian Wars had drawn only ten voters. Later, during the height of the revolution, only twelve voters elected Elijah Hughes, Hugh Hathorne, H. Y. Townsend, and Jeremiah Eldredge as the county's representatives. The meeting of September 1775, though, was well attended. Cape May County's white, male voters elected a Committee of Thirty, a type of revolutionary council that in a real sense meant that Cape May County was committed to independence. The freeholders also chose Elijah Hughes and Jesse Hand to represent them in the state legislature. Each township placed ten members on the Committee of Thirty; 60 percent of these came from the original whaler yeoman families. The same families who founded the county and led it through the eighteenth century now guided it into the American Revolution.[11]

Cape May County organized its militia during the meeting of 21 September 1775. The Cape May militia had been a preserve of the whaler yeomen since Jacob Spicer, Sr., Ezekiel Eldredge, and Samuel

Matthews organized the local militia during the first years of the eighteenth century. These same families officered the militia during the periodic frontier crises during mid-century, and now the Revolutionary War officer corps continued this Cape May County tradition. Top posts were held by members of the Hand, Townsend, Leaming, Eldredge, Stillwell, Foster, and Matthews families. John Mackey, who owned a plantation on the Cedar Swamp Creek near the present town of Petersburg and had married into the whaler yeoman elite, became the colonel of a Cape May County militia regiment. These officers recruited fewer than half of the 374 males between the ages of sixteen and fifty who resided in the county on the eve of the revolution. Aaron Leaming, Jr., reported that 151 mustered to arms in 1777.[12]

Early fighting in 1776 and 1777 had little impact on the Cape May County militia force. Operations were carried out in New York City and northern New Jersey. British forces drove General George Washington and his American army out of New York and across the river to New Jersey. Washington frustrated British attempts to march south toward Philadelphia in battles around Princeton and Trenton. The British resolved to strike Philadelphia by a southern route, either up the Delaware River or from the Chesapeake Bay through Maryland. In response, the Continental Congress and local officials fortified the Delaware River with cheveaux-de-frise, iron-spiked logs sunk in the shipping channel to impede the expected British invasion up the bay and river. An incident in Cape May County during the summer of 1776 helped discourage the British from sailing up the Delaware. Two British warships had chased the *Nancy*, an American brigantine loaded with supplies for the revolutionary government in Philadelphia, into Turtle Gut Inlet near present-day Wildwood Crest on the ocean side of the Cape May peninsula. Captain John Barry of the Continental navy held off the British long enough to unload part of the cargo, and then blew up the *Nancy* along with a number of British boarders. The *Nancy* incident, the only Revolutionary War battle to be fought in Cape May County, combined with the cheveaux-de-frise, undoubtedly worried the British navy. A few months after the *Nancy* explosion had killed more than a dozen British seamen, British Admiral Andrew Snape Hamond ordered his squadron to "prevent any vessels going up or down the Cape May channel." At the same time, the British bypassed the Cape May peninsula and sailed for the Chesapeake Bay.[13]

Expecting a British assault on Philadelphia, the Board of War employed James Whilldin, Matthew Whilldin, Abraham Bennett, and David Hand, Jr., on the tip of the Jersey Cape to watch for signs of British fleet movements. These express riders were ordered to carry the news overland whenever sail appeared off the Cape May coast. Meanwhile, Cape May County prepared for war. The Board of War in Philadelphia dispatched gunpowder, a stand of muskets, and probably cannon on traveling carriages to the Jersey Cape. Aaron Leaming, Jr., president of the Cape May County Committee of Safety, ordered armed guards to stand over his herds of cattle and horses. Thomas Leaming, Jr., a member of the First City Troop of Philadelphia, came home to drill the Cape May County militia. During this training, Thomas Godfrey accidentally shot James Parker with a charge of small stone from his musket, used because the local soldiers lacked ammunition. Drs. Frederick Otto and Benjamin Stites amputated Parker's leg in an effort to save his life, but the young militiaman died.[14]

A great British fleet with troop transports left New York in July 1777 and sailed past Cape May County to the Chesapeake in August. The British launched an overland strike from this base through Maryland toward Philadelphia, defeating the Americans along the Brandywine Creek on 11 September. A week later, William Livingston, the governor of New Jersey, called up the militia in southern New Jersey to rendezvous at the Gloucester County court seat of Woodbury a few miles below Cooper's Ferry (present-day city of Camden), where the militiamen would cross the Delaware River to Germantown. The Cape May County militiamen mustered on 19 September as news arrived of heavy American casualties suffered at the battle of Brandywine.[15]

The late summer of 1777 was a particularly bad time to raise troops on the Jersey Cape. The county struggled with another bout of the "bloody flux", which had caused death on the peninsula since the founding of the Cape May community. The "bloody flux" of 1714 had killed 10 percent of the entire population. This time nineteen people died. The call for soldiers also came during the harvest season. Militia farmers worried about how their wives would complete the provisioning for the coming winter. Seth Whilldin, fighting in the vicinity of Mount Holly in Burlington County, reminded his wife on the Jersey Cape that she needed to slaughter the pigs and salt the pork for the winter. Elijah Hughes instructed his wife, Judith Spicer, "to keep the corn clean and mind the fences." The Widow Abigail Smith protested to the Cape May County court about the mustering of her son into the militia. If he left the county, she argued, no one would care for her plantation. Smith's son was released from militia duty. Not surprisingly, Aaron Leaming, Jr., noted in his diary on 19 September 1777, "a considerable number would not go."[16]

About one half of the militia listed on Cape May County muster rolls marched to Woodbury under Col. John Mackey and Lt. Henry Ludlam. They crossed the Delaware River on 22 September with other southern New Jersey militiamen and joined the Pennsylvania militia units before the Battle of Germantown. Aaron Leaming, Jr., learned by letter that the Cape May County men had been under fire at Germantown, but none had received wounds in the fighting as the British routed the Americans and seized Philadelphia. The Cape May County militiamen returned to Woodbury, where they remained on garrison duty. Meanwhile, the British made a concerted effort to reduce New Jersey forts along the Delaware River. They seized Billingsport, near present-day Paulsboro. They attacked Fort Mercer at Red Bank a few miles from Woodbury. British forces breached the lower cheveaux-de-frise and bombarded Fort Mifflin on Mud Island, on the Pennsylvania side, across the river from Fort Mercer. Tiny vessels and fire barges of the Pennsylvania navy fought big British men-of-war, including the sixty-four-gun *Augusta*, on the river. Reportedly the fire and explosion that destroyed the *Augusta* could be heard throughout Cape May County.[17]

Cape May County militiamen remained on the fringe of the great battle for the Delaware River during the Fall of 1777. Henry Ludlam's company skirmished a force of Hessian Jaegers near Cooper's Ferry on 21 October and may have participated in other action around Mantua and Westville creeks in Gloucester County. The Cape May men served in the Woodbury garrison until late November, when Col. John Mackey resigned his commission, and most of the short-term levies returned to the Jersey Cape. Cape May County freeholders wanted to keep them in the county because the British seemed dangerously close to invading the peninsula. During the spring of 1778, British foraging parties scoured South Jersey in search of cattle, hay, and provisions. They engaged Cumberland County militia at Quinton's Bridge and slaughtered some thirty soldiers and civilians sleeping in a great brick farmhouse at Hancock's Bridge in Salem County. It appeared likely that British foraging parties might move farther into Cumberland or remote Cape May counties, where the Americans had reportedly hidden their livestock.[18]

Seventy-four Cape May County freeholders appealed to Governor William Livingston on 10 March 1778 to keep the militia in the county. "Your Petitioners do therefore humbly request that it may please your Excellency to take the premises under consideration, and exempt the Militia of Cape May from performing their Tour of duty abroad" they wrote the governor, "and to point out such methods, as may enable the inhabitants to keep up a regular guard, or any other measure, your Excellency may think most conducive to our safety." In response, Livingston instructed his Privy Council on 19 March not to remove the local militia from Cape May County. When he raised the New Jersey militia to defend Monmouth County in May 1779, Livingston specifically exempted Cape May County as "being too far distant to expect any material service." Instead, the Privy Council voted £570 to support Lt. Amos Cresse's company to stay and guard Cape May County.[19]

The Cape May County petitioners wanted their men to defend the local saltworks from British attack. The war had stimulated a booming salt industry up and down the New Jersey coast. The revolutionary government required salt both for provisions and for the production of gunpowder, and it offered bounties for salt of up to sixteen pence per bushel. Cape May County contained at least five saltworks by early 1777: at Great Egg Harbor, Townsend's Inlet, Turtle Gut Inlet, Cold Spring Inlet, and on the Seven Mile Beach that had been purchased in 1723 by Aaron Leaming, Sr. The Seven Mile Beach saltworks became a lucrative enterprise during the Revolutionary War. Aaron Leaming, Jr., Parsons Leaming, Jesse Hand, and John Holmes, a prosperous Middle Precinct merchant-planter, organized the saltworks in May 1777. They hired Philip Godfrey, a local gristmill owner, and Reeves Isard to set up six iron kettles on the beach to separate salt from seawater. The salt-making business proved so profitable that in July they "concluded to increase our Salt works." Aaron Leaming, Jr., sent John Holmes and Parsons Leaming to the Reading Iron Works in Pennsylvania to purchase ten huge iron kettles, shipping them to the Jersey Cape by wagon teams and ferryboat. The saltworks produced over one hundred bushels per month by late July 1777. Godfrey and Parsons Leaming operated as government contractors and supply masters, providing salt, corn, beef, pork, and horses to the Continental army.[20]

War industry made Cape May County a target for British attack. Already the British had struck the Chestnut Neck community up the coast on the Mullica River. Concern about such attacks had prompted the retention of the local militia on the Jersey Cape during the war. However, the Delaware River, Bay, and southern New Jersey counties ceased to become a part of the fighting after the British evacuated Philadelphia in June 1778. Cape May County functioned during the rest of the war as a base of operations for privateers who plundered British shipping. The peninsula proved an ideal base for these privately owned ships, which were licensed by the government to attack merchantmen legally on the high seas. Inlets, creeks, and bays provided shelter for repair, victualing, and arming of these sea raiders. Skilled sailors and sea captains resided in the county to man the privateers. John Maxwell Nesbitt and Company of Philadelphia considered Salem, Cohansey, and Cape May County as the best recruiting grounds in the entire region for privateers. The Jersey Cape became a supply depot and rendezvous point for Nesbitt's raiders. If a privateer needed shot, powder, and provisions, Nesbitt instructed one captain, "put a letter on shore at Egg Harbour or Cape May, and we can lodge what you want at either of these places."[21]

Privateering became Cape May County's major enterprise during the Revolutionary War. It propelled the bayside communities of Dennis Creek (present-day Dennisville) and Goshen, where the Leaming, Ludlam, Johnson, Smith, and other whaler yeoman families owned sawmills and a shipyard, to a central place in the county's economic life. Thomas Leaming, Jr., Moses Griffing, Jesse Hand, Nicholas Stillwell, and Enoch Stillwell captured thousands of pounds of maritime prizes. Stillwell's privateers, operating primarily from Great Egg Harbor, seized cargoes valued at over £27,000. Nicholas Stillwell sold his prizes at his brother's auction in the Upper Precinct on what is now Beesley's Point. "On Saturday the eleventh instant will be sold at Col. Nicholas Stillwell's in Cape May," read an advertisement of September 1779, "the schooner *Henry* and her cargo consisting of twenty hogsheads of sugar, twenty hogsheads of Molasses, 2,000 lbs. Cotton, and a quantity of Coffee."[22]

Cape May County sea captains and maritime entrepreneurs involved in privateering formed business partnerships with Philadelphia merchant houses, including the Morris, Fisher, Nixon, Wharton, Knox, and Randolph firms. Thomas Leaming, Jr., became the bondsman for the large Philadelphia firm of Andrew Bunner and Company, which helped finance the Continental Congress's war fund. He strengthened his ties during the war with the powerful and wealthy

Fisher family of Philadelphia. "I married the Daughter of Samuel Fisher of this Town," Leaming wrote uncle Jeremiah Leaming in New York, "and have entered into the merchantile Business here."[23]

Cape May County privateers received at least fifty-one letters of marque from the Continental Congress between 1778 and 1782. These licenses for plunder were given to small craft such as Abraham Bennett's tiny, single-gun pilot boat, and to large schooners and brigantines of twenty guns, including the *Mars*, *Hawk*, *Argo*, and *New Comet*. Cape May County men on the militia rolls in 1777 went to sea as privateers in 1778 rather than join the Continental line. Everyone, it seemed, wanted a share in this lucrative privateering business. When Aaron Leaming, Jr., employed Lawrence Powell to cut cedar shingles, he found that Powell "carried them all to Market and sold them, and we hear spent the money and went privateering with Capn. Yelverton Taylor." Abel Lee, a landless entrepreneur in Upper Precinct, trespassed on the Leaming pine forests and cut down two great mast trees to fit out his schooner as a privateer. Leaming planned to sue Powell and Lee after the war, he told Thomas Leaming, Jr.[24]

Cape May County sea captains found privateering profitable but dangerous. Humphrey Hughes and his entire crew disappeared at sea in the privateer *New Comet*, owned by Thomas Leaming, Jr. The British captured Enoch Stillwell, Moses Griffing, Amos Willets, and other Cape May County maritime raiders and imprisoned them in rotting prison ships anchored on the East River in New York. The names of over a dozen Cape May County men appeared on the prison rolls of the notorious death ship *Jersey*. Willets family tradition recorded that Amos Willets died in 1778 on board one of these prison ships. Stillwell and Griffing were more fortunate. The British released them in a prisoner exchange. Reportedly Sally Stillwell Griffing journeyed alone from Cape May County to Sir Henry Clinton's headquarters in New York to win the release of her husband, Moses Griffing.[25]

With their men gone to prison or privateering, Cape May County women defended the county. According to tradition, Rebecca Stillwell Willets fought off a British raiding party in the Upper Precinct by firing a cannon filled with grapeshot at the approaching barge. This story arose, and may have received inspiration from, the Monmouth County legend (developed in the mid-nineteenth century) of Molly Pitcher, about a woman taking over the cannon of her exhausted husband and fighting the British at the Monmouth Court House battle in 1778. Cape May County women also formed a relief society to provide clothing and assistance to men in the Continental army. County leaders included Sarah Leaming Hand, Priscilla Leaming Townsend, Rhoda Mulford Whilldin, and Zabiah Corson Hildreth. The New Jersey Women's Relief Society instructed these wives of Cape May County's representatives in the assembly and council to correspond with similar women in other counties.[26]

American and French forces won a critical victory in 1781 over Lord Cornwallis's army at Yorktown, Virginia. John Grace, a landless resident of Upper Precinct, and possibly Abel Corson of West Creek, participated in the Battle of Yorktown as members of the New Jersey Continental Line. Earlier, Grace had served as a courier for General Washington. After Yorktown, hostilities continued sporadically until 1783, when Great Britain recognized American independence. Both British seizure of ships along Cape May County's coast and American privateering continued until 1782. The last days of the Revolutionary War, though, found few other military activities around the peninsula. Refugee Tories and robbers who reportedly infested other New Jersey pinelands and shorefront regions never bothered Cape May County.[27]

Independence brought economic problems to Cape May County during the Articles of Confederation era (1781–1789), a period of transition government between the Revolution and adoption of the U.S. Constitution. This government lacked a strong central administration. Individual states carried on their own currency, tariff, and western land policies. Some of the newly independent states paid their war debts through the sale of western lands. New Jersey, however, held no public lands; it turned to local taxation to pay for the war. The state legislature assigned each county a percentage of the tax, with Cape May County expected to pay 2 percent of the total.

The county appeared less able to raise this small levy than other New Jersey counties with a larger percent of the tax. Peace had dried up the military market for Cape May County salt, foodstuffs, forage hay, and livestock. The lucrative privateering business had ended. Cape May County, unlike other New Jersey counties, derived little revenue from confiscated Tory estates. At the same time, Jesse Hand, Eli Eldredge, and Nicholas Stillwell, the county committee to assess war damages, made no claims for Cape May County. No British, Tory, or Continental troops had marched through, occupied, or plundered the remote county, as had occurred in nearby Salem and Gloucester counties and as had devastated Monmouth County to the north.[28]

Postwar Cape May County suffered economic hardship. The numbers of debtors and farmers unable to pay their taxes increased during the 1783–1799 period. The Cape May County Board of Justices and Freeholders met in November 1784 to discuss the growing debtor problem. The five freeholders and six justices on the county board voted to enlarge the county jailhouse, recently destroyed by a fire, so that it could accommodate the large number of debtors. They authorized the construction of a large room of stone, brick, and wood, and instructed that, "the said Room . . . be Divided with a stone wall so as the Debtor and Criminal may have their Room."[29]

Sheriff's sales of small farms increased during the period of the Articles of Confederation. James Willets, Jacob Teal, John Mulford, Isaac Hewitt, and other small landowners lost property as a result of the devaluation of the Continental dollar after the war. However, their financial plight benefited the largest whaler yeoman landowners and county leaders. The Hand and Eldredge families purchased most of the land at sheriff's sale, and the Hughes, Godfrey, Stillwell, Corson, Leaming, Ludlam, and Townsend families also recorded large land acquisitions. Henry Young Townsend, wartime army subsistence master, assemblyman, and county sheriff, enlarged his holdings during the 1780s from one hundred to nearly six hundred acres. Townsend also developed a tanyard and built several mills during the decade. Elijah Hughes, a member of the council and delegate to the state's constitutional convention, acquired over fifteen hundred acres of new lands during the Articles of Confederation period. Jesse Hand, the county's wartime legislative representative, enlarged his personal landed estate by five hundred acres and bought shares in a coastal trading vessel. Hand returned from the state convention that ratified the Federal Constitution at Trenton in 1787 with Cape May County's first luxurious four-wheeled carriage.[30]

The old whaler yeoman families increased their numbers of slaves between 1774 and 1784. Cape May County experienced the greatest rise in slave owning in its history during the post–Revolutionary War era. It held the highest percentage of slaves (although not the largest total number) of any of the original West Jersey counties. Other counties responded to the appeals of John Cooper and the Quakers to forbid the importation of slaves into the state and to end slavery, but Cape May County's whaler yeomen accumulated a large group of new slaves. Tax records listed eighteen slaves in the Middle Precinct in 1774 and sixty-three by 1784. Lower Precinct's slave population grew from six to thirty-three during the same period. Possibly Cape May County slave owners, fearing high taxes on property in 1774, failed to list all their slaves. However, whaler yeoman families who owned no slaves prior to the Revolutionary War recorded ownership after the war. Jesse Hand purchased six slaves to work his newly acquired landed estates and timberland. Elijah Hughes owned no slaves before the war but bought three to farm his land while he was away on public business. Jeremiah Eldredge purchased four slaves during the same interval.[31]

Several Cape May County merchant-landowners developed their wartime privateering business into postwar connections with prosperous Philadelphia merchant houses and shipbuilding interests. Moses Griffing opened a firm in Philadelphia on Race between Front and Second streets in 1785 that reportedly included investment in the early China trade. That trade had begun in 1784 when Robert Morris, a prominent Philadelphia merchant who may have been associated with Cape May County families, obtained a half-share in the *Empress of China*. Thomas Leaming, Jr., also participated in the China trade, through his connection to the Fisher family. Leaming prospered in postwar Philadelphia. He purchased extensive city real estate and lived in a magnificent house on South Front Street next to Andrew Bunner, his brother-in-law and wartime business partner.[32]

Philadelphia merchants, particularly those connected with Cape May County privateers during the war and related through marriage to whaler yeoman families, invested in postwar Cape May County lands and businesses. The Benezet, Wood, Ridgeway, Nixon, Morris, and Elmer families owned properties that lay between the Maurice River in Cumberland County and the Cedar Swamp in Cape May County. This region encompassed an area bounded by West Creek, the head of the Tuckahoe River, Cedar Swamp Creek, Dennis Creek, and East and West creeks. Investments included timberlands, sawmills, farmland, shipping, and possibly an early cranberry industry run by the Leaming and Elmer families. Anthony Benezet, a prominent Philadelphia Quaker merchant, bought five thousand acres, extending from the head of the Tuckahoe River south to the East Creek region (present-day Eldora). Daniel Benezet built a mill dam and sawmill on East Creek Pond. The Benezets also constructed a large house between their East Creek properties and Henry Ludlam's inn, which lay on a millpond west of the Dennis Creek settlement (now Dennisville).[33]

The Benezet family built their mill and house along a road that in 1771 had become the first stagecoach route into the county. The stagecoach road followed the course of the present-day East Creek Mill Pond Road and connected Shingle Landing (now Millville) on the Maurice River in Cumberland County with the Hoffman Mill Pond (present-day Hand's Mill Pond) on West Creek. The road continued past Benezet's property and joined with a road that follows the current Route 47 eastward to Henry Ludlam's Mill Pond, past Johnson's Mill Pond, and through the center of Dennis Creek. The stagecoach road turned in a northeasterly direction to Mt. Pleasant, where it connected with the old Cape Road, crossed the Long Bridge over Cedar Swamp Creek, and joined the main seashore road that went down toward Cape Island. This stagecoach road became the major route out of the county.[34]

The new stagecoach road opened Stipson's Island and the West and East Creek regions (now Eldora), heretofore one of the most remote sections of the county, to business and settlement. The region flourished in the immediate postwar period. The Mosslander, Hoffman, Ericsson, Peterson, and other Swedish-American families moved into the region, building sawmills along the West Creek millponds and developing farmland. The community established a West Creek Baptist Church and possibly a schoolhouse along the stagecoach road in 1792. The ancient West Creek Baptist cemetery that stands today on East Creek Pond Road in Cumberland County near the Cumberland-Cape May County border marks the spot of the original church.

The Goff family also contributed during the 1780s and 1790s to the growth of the East and West Creek regions. The Reverend John Goff operated a store on East Creek and four sailing vessels—the sloops *Charming Sally*, *Rebecca*, and *Smith*, and the schooner *Mary Ann*. Local sawmill owners and lumbermen carted loads of boards, cedar post, and rails pulled by teams of oxen to the East and West Creek landings, where the *Rebecca* carried them to Wilmington, Delaware, and to Philadelphia. The *Rebecca* returned from Philadelphia with a cargo of shoe soles, tea, sugar, molasses, powder and shot, and a great variety of cloth to be sold at the Goffs' store. The prosperity of the region extended north toward the Mill Creek branch of the Tuckahoe River, where the Steelman family, which owned large tracts of land north of the Tuckahoe River in Gloucester County, established a sawmill near the present-day location of Steelmantown in Cape May County. A branch of the stagecoach road was opened to the Steelman

Mill Pond in 1794 and continued northeast to Tuckahoe, connecting the West Creek region with the Tuckahoe River community.[35]

Dennis Creek, four miles east of West Creek on the stagecoach road, also experienced spectacular growth in the immediate post–Revolutionary War period. Intermarriage provided the matrix for the development of this community. Thomas Leaming, Jr., who owned a shipyard on the southern bank of the main branch of Dennis Creek, had married into the wealthy Fisher family of Philadelphia. The Ludlam family, founders of the Dennis Creek community, intermarried with the Morris, Whilldin, Hand, Johnson, and Holmes families. Each marriage, particularly that of James Ludlam and Martha Johnson in 1790, brought the Ludlams new landed estates, more saw- and gristmills, and additional cedar swamp timberlands. Intermarriage led to Dennis Creek business partnerships between the Leaming, Smith, Townsend, Cresse, Young, and Goff families as well.[36]

Prosperous newcomers to the Dennis Creek community married into the old whaler yeoman families during the postwar era. John Holmes, a prominent Middle Precinct merchant-landowner, and his brother, Col. Nathaniel Holmes, a Revolutionary War veteran, intermarried with the Ludlam and Hand families. Hannah Holmes, Nathaniel Holmes's daughter, married into the Morris family of Philadelphia. Elizabeth Holmes, executrix of John Holmes's estate, became the first female county official in Cape May history when she served in 1791 as the acting county clerk and county tax collector. Meanwhile Joseph Falkinburg, a shoe merchant, moved to Dennis Creek from Gloucester County and married Abigail Ludlam. Their children further expanded the growing Falkinburg fortune through intermarriage with the Leaming family. James Diverty, a Delaware lumber merchant, moved to Dennis Creek and intermarried with the Hand and Leaming families, thus joining the inner circle of original whaler yeoman families.[37]

The combination of newcomers such as Holmes, Falkinburg, and Diverty with the old whaler yeoman families propelled Dennis Creek to the center of county economic and political power during the closing decade of the eighteenth century. They built saw- and gristmills, stores and houses, connecting them between 1781 and 1800 with new roads, causeways, and bridges during one of the most active periods of road building in the county's history. More than a dozen new or rebuilt roadways connected Dennis Creek to the West Creek region, the Steelman Mill Pond, Tuckahoe, and Littleworth, a community on the Cedar Swamp Creek now known as Petersburg.

Whaler yeoman officials oversaw the construction in 1789 of bridges over the north and south branches of Dennis Creek from the Leaming shipyard to Johnson's Mill Pond. They built a road from David Johnson's sawmill to the old Cape Road leading to the Long Bridge that crossed the Cedar Swamp Creek (near Seaville). Another road connected the Little Mill Dam above Johnson's Mill Pond southward to the Brick Landing on Sluice Creek, a route that long ago disappeared into the salt marsh.[38]

The road building spread to the lower part of the county between 1780 and 1800, suggesting the development of a second center of postwar economic growth. The major activity occurred on Cape Island at the tip of the peninsula. Possibly the new roads in this area reflected the early development of the region that now encompasses Cape May City, West Cape May, and Cape May Point as a seaside summer resort. Apparently the Reverend Samuel Finley, pastor of the Cold Spring Presbyterian Church, saw the possibility of Cape May becoming a resort community as early as 1740. Robert Parsons advertised his plantation for sale in the *Pennsylvania Gazette* in July 1766, as "pleasantly situated, open to the sea, in the lower Precinct of the County of Cape May, within one Mile and a Half of the seashore, where Numbers resort for Health, and bathing in water; and this Place would be very convenient for taking in such People."[39]

Parsons's advertisement suggests that Cape May County was already a seaside resort in 1766, and the road building on Cape Island between 1780 and 1800 supports the conclusion that Cape May County had become an ocean resort before 1800. In June 1783 Silas Swain and George Taylor surveyed a road from the seashore across the Cape Island. Two years later, the county developed a new road between Cold Spring and the current site of Cape May City. This road ran between Ellis Hughes, Sr.'s, inn and Abraham Bennett's public house. The Cape Island road then went to a public house run by Memucan Hughes. The Cape Island road connected at least three licensed public houses, and probably one unlicensed house of entertainment—the Cape May County grand jury indicted Memucan Hughes in 1799 for causing a public nuisance.[40]

The new public roads benefited the Dennis Creek and Cape Island regions, but the entire county bore the expense. Consequently, not everyone favored the postwar road-building boom. Planters opposed roads that cut through their good farmland or divided their property. The residents around Dyer's Creek (Dias Creek), a bayside collection of houses between Green Creek and Goshen Creek, opposed a new road in 1783. At Dyer's Creek Landing, "where now being a number of people collected, and some differences arising about the Propriety of the way the road should be laid," noted Henry Hand and Jonathan Hand, the county road surveyors, "the Road was not continued any further."[41]

The whaler yeoman officials pressed ahead with their roads, bridges, and causeways. They dominated local politics and represented Cape May County in the state assembly and council between 1783 and 1800. Jesse Hand, Jeremiah Eldredge, and Elijah Hughes advocated hard-money policies favored by creditors. They opposed efforts to bail out the Articles of Confederation government with inflationary measures and voted against land bank loan laws that would assist the small landowner or debtor. They formed part of a West Jersey faction in the state legislature that supported the movement for a strong central government under a federal constitution.[42]

Jesse Hand, Matthew Whilldin, and J. Eldredge (either Jacob or Jeremiah) represented Cape May County at the state convention in December 1787 convened to ratify the Constitution of the United States. Cape May County's delegation fit the profile of the New Jersey constitution makers developed by the historian Richard McCormick. Cape May County delegates, like those from other New Jersey counties, had joined the Whig cause early, participated in military and political organizations during the Revolutionary War, and held county office. The Cape May County representatives, like their counterparts from other counties, held modest landed estates, ranging from Whilldin's 150-acre plantation to Hand's larger 1,183-acre farm. They also fit the occupational profile of the majority of the delegates to the New Jersey ratification convention. Whilldin was a farmer, Hand a merchant-landowner with an interest in shipping, and Eldredge a lawyer, merchant, and landowner. All three came from the original thirty-five whaler yeoman families who had founded Cape May County.[43]

Cape May County remained a bastion of federalism throughout the rest of the century. Mahlon Dickerson, New Jersey Jeffersonian Republican leader, thought he found some sympathy in Cape May County for Thomas Jefferson when Jeremiah Hand and one of the Townsends supported the anti-Federalist cause. However, Cape May County never sent a Jeffersonian Republican delegate to the various

Democratic Republican associations and conventions that backed Thomas Jefferson for president against the Federalist candidates. Cape May County became the only New Jersey county without a Jeffersonian Republican political leader and the only county not to send a representative in 1800 to a Jeffersonian rally in Princeton. Federalists in Cape May County removed Jeremiah Hand as county clerk in a disputed election and blocked the appointment of any other Jeffersonian Republican in the county to public office.[44]

Cape May County Federalists endorsed the centralized state and county political structure that emerged in New Jersey at the end of the eighteenth century. The state legislature enacted a measure on 13 February 1798 that replaced the loosely organized county boards of justices and freeholders (established in 1713 and 1714) with more centralized boards of chosen freeholders, forming a structure of county government unique in the United States. "The chosen free-holders in the several townships, precincts, and wards," the free-holder law of 1798 stipulated, "shall be constituted a body politic and corporate in law" as "the board of chosen freeholders of the county." The state legislature passed another act eight days later that incorporated townships, designated their powers, and regulated the town meeting. These two measures established the fundamental framework for Cape May County government, politics, and society in the new nation. The three precincts formed in 1723 now became the Upper, Middle, and Lower townships.[45]

Membership on the first Cape May County Board of Chosen Freeholders between 1798 and 1801 showed the control of county government by the original whaler yeoman families. The members who attended the session for May 1800 were typical of the families who dominated board leadership for the next eighty years. James Ludlam and Cornelius Corson represented Upper Township, Philip Cresse, the director, and Jeremiah Hand sat for the Middle Township, and Robert Parsons and Spicer Leaming held the seats for the Lower Township. These whaler yeoman families controlled all county business. Parsons Leaming served in 1800 as the county clerk and county tax collector. Jonathan Leaming became the Cape May County sheriff, and James Ludlam oversaw the county roads. Israel Stites managed the Public Landing at Dennis Creek, the county's only source of revenue beyond the county tax. In a practice that lasted until the twentieth century, the whaler yeoman families gave themselves county business. They hired Jeremiah Hand to provide cedar weatherboard for county buildings and paid Israel Stites to repair the Dennis Creek Road with a corduroy roadbed of logs cut from his own forestlands. The board of chosen freeholders engaged Jonathan Leaming to put a back door on a county building and paid Jacocks Swain, James Ludlam, David Townsend, Christopher Smith, and Parmenas Corson to repair the bridge over Sluice Creek, the southeastern branch of Dennis Creek.[46]

Cape May County entered the nineteenth century under the leadership of its original thirty-five whaler yeoman families and their kin. They dominated county affairs until development of the railroad and opening of the Atlantic coastal barrier islands to settlement began to expand and change Cape May County society and politics. The new century brought different conditions and challenges to the old whaler yeoman families, however. County slave owners started to manumit their slaves, placing several hundred free but propertyless African-Americans among their former masters. In 1799, the Cape May County grand jury had already indicted local free African-Americans for larceny, assault, and battery.[47]

New social institutions developed during the next decades, including a county almshouse and county farm. Local communities built common schoolhouses and a private academy. Methodism and Catholicism entered the county, and members of these religions built new churches that challenged the older, entrenched Baptist, Presbyterian, and Quaker meetings. Shipbuilding and lumbering along Dennis, Goshen, and Cedar Swamp creeks continued to expand, attracting Irish-American and German-American workers. Throughout the first sixty years of the nineteenth century, Cape Island emerged as one of the great resorts and watering places in America.

ATLANTIC COUNTY

Tuckahoe

Beesley's Point

CUMBERLAND CO.

Steelmantown

Littleworth
Petersburg

UPPER TOWNSHIP

Mt. Pleasant

East Creek Little Mill

West Creek

DENNIS
TWSP.

Seaville

Goshen

DELAWARE BAY

ATLANTIC OCEAN

MIDDLE TOWNSHIP
Almshouse
Dyer's
Creek Court House

Green Creek

Fishing Creek NummyTown

Hildreth

LOWER
TOWNSHIP

Cold Spring

Higbee's
Steamboat
Landing

Cape Island

CAPE MAY
COUNTY
1848

⇒ ✳ Mills
⇒ ● Shipyards

N.

W. — E.

S.

Snyder

CHAPTER FOUR

Cape Island and Dennis Creek, 1801–1849

"SEA SHORE ENTERTAINMENT AT CAPE MAY," the Philadelphia *Aurora and General Advertiser* announced on 1 July 1801. Ellis Hughes, proprietor of a public house on Cape Island (now Cape May City), explained in this newspaper advertisement that he had prepared rooms for summer visitors who wanted to bathe in the sea, dine on oysters and fish, and drink fine liquors. Hughes promised the best care for his guests' horses and carriages. "The situation is beautiful, just on the confluence of Delaware Bay with the Ocean in sight of the Light-house, and affords a view of the shipping which enters and leaves the Delaware" Hughes proclaimed. "Carriages may be driven along the margin of the Ocean for miles; and the wheels will scarcely make any impression upon the sand, the slope of the shore is so regular that persons may wade out a great distance." Hughes concluded, "It is the most delightful spot the citizens can retire to in the hot season."[1]

Transportation overland by stagecoach to Cape Island had improved between 1783 and 1800. A weekly coach ran from Cooper's Ferry (now the city of Camden) with stops in Woodbury, Glasshouse (now Glassboro), Lehman Mill (near present-day Millville), and Port Elizabeth. The stagecoach road entered the county near Hoffman's old millpond on the West Creek. The stage ran through the northern side of Dennis Creek (present-day Dennisville) to the old Cape Road at Mt. Pleasant, through Seaville, and down the seashore route to Cold Spring and Cape Island. Possibly some stagecoaches took a poorly developed road down the bayside across Wills Creek (the current site of Bidwell's ditch below Goshen) and passed through the communities of Dyers (Dias) Creek, Green Creek, and Fishing Creek before they entered Cold Spring. "A stage starts from Cooper's Ferry on Thursday in every week, and arrives at Cape Island on Friday," Ellis Hughes explained. Travel by boat down the Delaware River from Philadelphia followed no regular schedule to Cape Island in 1801. Hughes assured travelers, however, that "those who choose water conveyance can find vessels almost any time."[2]

Cape Island had entertained summer visitors since the middle of the eighteenth century, giving credence to Cape May County's claim to be America's earliest seaside resort community. The *Philadelphia Gazette* had mentioned the Lower Precinct in 1766 as a place where visitors resorted for health and bathing. Ellis Hughes's advertisement in 1801 marked the start of a new era for Cape May County as a summer resort for the emerging nineteenth-century gentry. Not until his public advice in the Philadelphia press had the tiny beachfront community of Delaware River pilots and mariners at the southernmost tip of the Cape May peninsula promoted itself directly as an American seashore resort.[3]

Cape Island became an essential part of Cape May County social and economic development during the next fifty years. Thousands of summer visitors from New Jersey, Pennsylvania, Maryland, Virginia, and New York flooded the Jersey Cape between 1 July and 1 September each summer season. A regular steamboat service between Philadelphia, Delaware, and Cape Island developed during the 1820s. The steamboats landed passengers on the bayside, probably near the current site of the wrecked concrete ship just off Cape May Point. Previous sailing packets to Cape Island reportedly sailed around the peninsula, entered Cold Spring Inlet, and unloaded passengers at Schellenger's Landing. Entrepreneurs invested in Cape Island lands and built large, rambling wooden hotels along the beachfront. Construction of these barnlike hotels could not keep pace with the demand for summer accommodations. "I have never seen the Island so full," John Watson, a Philadelphia writer, reported in 1822. "All the gentry of Delaware and Philadelphia" had arrived, Watson continued, and they "set to dancing" and some to "an excess of drink."[4]

Isaac Mickle, a young Camden lawyer and newspaperman, found Cape Island even more vibrant in 1843. "Visitors are still pouring down" Mickle wrote, "and to night I and four others slept in the reading room." They frolicked in the surf, where men and women entered the water at separate times of the day, gathered seashells on the beach, and took carriage rides along the strand. Mickle and his friends played quoits, billiards, and tenpins. Mickle discovered that the following summer was even busier. "We arrived at the Island about four o'clock, and found it so crowded that [Jonas] Miller could do no better for us than give us a room to sleep in out in the country two miles," Mickle noted in his diary. Cape Island, it seemed, rivaled Newport, Rhode Island, and Saratoga, New York, as the premier American watering spot.[5]

A less spectacular community developed on both banks of Dennis Creek at the same time that Cape Island was becoming a leading resort town. Nathaniel Holmes, Joseph Falkinburg, James Diverty, J. Fisher Leaming, and Jonathan Leaming, among others, built stores, churches, schools, and large frame (and one brick) residences. They constructed shipyards and landings at Dennis Creek. They were part of an emerging nineteenth century business gentry that on the Cape May peninsula included the old whaler yeoman families and a number of post–Revolutionary War newcomers. "Whaler yeoman" no longer described the socioeconomic status of the leading families of Cape May County during the early nineteenth century. Instead, a new, largely well-educated, and gentrified occupational group that was involved in diverse economic activity and business enterprise emerged as the county's leaders.

In 1803 Dennis Creek's business leaders began to build the massive Dennis Creek Crossway, which connected the north bank of the community to the southern part (now called South Dennis). Previous causeways, banks, and creek crossings had washed away each year with Dennis Creek's tidal flow, which cut off this vital passage between the northern and southern parts of the Cape May peninsula. Maintaining a permanent wagon and stagecoach road across the treacherous tidal creek became an essential step in the development of the two Dennis Creek communities on either side of the waterway. The crossway assured that the main route from Cumberland County down the bayside to Cold Spring and Cape Island would pass over the Dennis Creek rather than take the more northerly route through Mt. Pleasant to the old Cape Road. Joseph Hughes, a Lower Township freeholder, recognized the importance of the Dennis Creek corridor to his hotel-keeping kin on Cape Island when he voted in 1803 to employ county funds to improve the Dennis Creek road, causeway, and bridge.[6]

Dennis Creek became the hub of political-economic life in the county during the first half of the nineteenth century. Commerce, travel, and business from remote West and East Creek, the Tuckahoe River area, Cedar Swamp, and seaside communities along the shore road passed through Dennis Creek. The bayside community overshadowed the Middle Township courthouse town that lay along the shore road. The first U.S. post office in Cape May County opened in 1802 at Dennis Creek. The county seat received a post office in 1803 and became the post office address of Cape May Court House. A few months later in 1804, Cape Island opened its own post office in Ellis Hughes's hotel.[7]

Shipping and shipbuilding provided the economic base for Dennis Creek's prosperity. J. Fisher Leaming shipped thousands of dollars of cordwood during the 1820s to Philadelphia from Dennis Creek. He employed six coastal sloops and schooners to carry this cargo from the Dennis Creek Landing. James Diverty began constructing ships on the Dennis Creek in 1821. "It is agreed between James Diverty & Enoch T. Godfrey," James Smith's memorandum book noted, that "the said Enoch agreed to cutt all the timber in the woods, and Build and Complet, Launch a vessels in workmanlike manner all at his owen Expense." Jeremiah Leaming established a shipyard across the creek from Diverty's yard on the south bank of Dennis Creek, probably in the old Thomas Leaming, Jr., shipyard. Leaming built at least ten coastal sailing vessels on the Dennis Creek during the 1830s.[8]

Dennis Creek continued to grow in importance. The New Jersey State Assembly created Dennis Township out of the southern half of Upper Township in November 1826. This new township included the Dennis Creek community, the East and West Creek regions, the southern portion of the Cedar Swamp, and the seashore region between Townsend's Inlet and Ludlam's Bay. Dennis Township formally organized its local government in March 1827 and sent Jacob G. Smith and Samuel Bishop as its first representatives to the board of freeholders, which now became an eight-member board. Dennis Township's leaders began to demand recognition of Dennis Creek as the site for the county seat to replace Cape May Court House.[9]

Only Cape Island shared Dennis Creek's importance to Cape May County's early-nineteenth-century development. These communities formed an intersecting political-economic axis. Richard S. Ludlam's experiences show the linkage between Cape Island and Dennis Creek. Ludlam established a general store in Dennis Creek, where his family had founded the original settlements on either side of the creek in the 1720s. Ludlam began to vacation on Cape Island in about 1812; there he discovered that the rambling wooden hotels and small pilots' houses used to board summer guests were filled to capacity. He invested in Cape Island property and in 1832 constructed the Mansion House, a three-story structure famous as the first hotel on Cape Island with plaster walls. From his dual political-economic base on Dennis Creek and Cape Island, Ludlam became a leading political figure and represented Cape May County in the New Jersey legislature, where during the 1847–1848 session he gained incorporation of Cape Island as a separate borough government.[10]

The joint development of Cape Island and Dennis Creek in the early nineteenth century led to prosperity for the tiny Delaware bayshore communities that lay along the road between the two largest county settlements. The smaller bayshore communities formed an arc of settlement along the road that wandered down the bayside toward the tip of the peninsula. It passed through the tiny clusters of houses called Goshen, Dyer's Creek, Green Creek, and Fishing Creek. Narrow dirt roads across the peninsula linked each to the courthouse village in the middle of the cape, pulling the loyalties of these tiny bayshore communities between the old county seat and the newer, aggressive commercial town of Dennis Creek.

Goshen, just south of Dennis Creek, had a history older than that of its bigger neighbor to the north. The Leaming, Crowell, and Johnson families had established hay and cattle plantations at what they called the Cedar Hammocks by the beginning of the eighteenth century. Aaron Leaming, Sr., probably built a house in Goshen about 1703 when he moved from Salem, where the Widow Hall had tutored him in law and the Quaker faith. Goshen Creek provided sheltered anchorage for the coastal schooners that by 1805 loaded lumber, cordwood, and farm products from landings owned by Mathew Tomlin, Benajah Tomlin, Jesse Hand, and Jonathan Leaming. Goshen established a schoolhouse about 1804 and a post office in 1818. The Philadelphia to Cape Island mail stagecoach stopped at Goshen in 1843. A large tavern and inn stood at the crossroad between the main bayshore road and a corduroy road that led to the Goshen Creek and landings. Goshen seemed important enough that by 1848 it was considered as one of three potential sites for the county seat of justice.[11]

Immediately to the south of Goshen lay Dyer's Creek (later called Dias Creek), a collection of houses, a schoolhouse, and a wind-powered sawmill located on an unruly, meandering tidal creek that flooded nearby meadows and fields. Residents of Dyer's Creek met in 1814 at the house of Daniel Cresse to form the Dyer's Creek [Meadow] Banking Company, one of a number of corporations formed under the New Jersey statute of 1778 that authorized owners of meadows and swampland to form themselves into corporate bodies to bank and drain their wetlands. The Dyer's Creek Company organized "to lay out bank, dam, sluices, floodgates, and other works necessary for securing the said meadows from the overflow of the tide."[12]

Joseph Falkinburg, Thomas Beesley, and Abijiah Smith oversaw the Dyer's Creek project, which cut a twelve-foot-wide, three-foot-deep sluiceway to drain the surrounding meadows between Joseph Hildreth's Landing and Pierce's Point. Reclaiming swamps and meadows encouraged the growth of this community, which by 1830 boasted a wind-powered saw- and gristmill owned by Jesse Springer, a general store where the stagecoach stopped, a school built in 1811 on Joseph Hildreth's land, and a Baptist church. A post office was established in 1824 with Stillwell Hildreth as the postmaster. In 1831 Dyer's Creek became the site of what was most likely the first religious camp meeting in county history.[13]

Moving down the bayside from Dyer's Creek, the rough road crossed Green Creek, which contained a cluster of houses. This brought the traveler to Fishing Creek, one of the oldest communities on the Jersey Cape. Several plantations had existed there as early as the 1690s. Fishing Creek's importance increased in 1806 when the Fishing Creek [Meadow] Banking Company authorized the banking and draining of nearby meadows. Parsons Leaming, Shamgar Hewitt, Parsons Edmunds, and Judith Hand, the area's most prominent residents, comprised the company's major stockholders and managers. Christopher Ludlam, Isaac Smith, and Abijiah Smith, county road commissioners, assisted the private company in draining meadows and banking lowlands. The county contracted with Aaron Woolson in 1817 to build a new wooden bridge over Fishing Creek. Jesse Springer's windmill, which employed a unique reciprocating device with two vertical saws, provided the cedar planks for the county bridge. Fishing Creek established a post office in 1818 and became a stop of the mail stagecoach route by 1843.[14]

As the communities between Dennis Creek and Cape Island began to prosper and grow, the Anglo-American War of 1812 threatened to destroy their progress. The bayshore and Cape Island beachfront were vulnerable to attack by the powerful British fleet prowling the American coast. The causes for this war seemed far removed from Cape May County's interests. The United States and Britain went to war largely over the impressment of American sailors into the Royal Navy and British policies toward Native Americans along the western frontier that impeded westward expansion and settlement. Joseph Falkinburg and Robert M. Holmes, Cape May County's representatives in Trenton, joined their Federalist colleagues from New England, New York, and New Jersey in opposition to the war. British maritime and frontier policies had not hurt Cape May County's coastal trade or economic development, but war meant that the Delaware Bay and coast would become a target as it had during the Revolutionary War for British warships or foraging parties. In fact, British naval forces during the next two years constantly threatened Cape May County. British landing parties foraged for cattle and fresh water on the peninsula, seized several Cape May County residents, including two women, and burned local saltworks and fishing vessels.[15]

War with Britain, over the opposition of Falkinburg, Holmes, and other Federalists, forced Americans to raise the militia, mobilize a national army, and build a navy. Cape May County participated reluctantly in the preparations. One month after the Democratic Republican "War Hawks" in Congress had voted for war in July 1812, the Cape May County Board of Freeholders resolved to place the two cannons left over from the Revolution under cover in sheds at Court House and Cold Spring. First they had to mount them on carriages. Robert Holmes, the county treasurer who opposed the war, refused to disburse funds either to mount the guns or to place them in gunsheds. The county government voted in March 1813 to raise $300 for Thomas Hughes to purchase amputating instruments, gunpowder, and "100 weight of large buckshot." The county instructed Colonel John Dickinson—a Revolutionary War veteran, county physician, and tax collector—to distribute the supplies to the Cape May County militia. Several months later, the Board of Chosen Freeholders diverted $150 slated for further development of the Dennis Creek Causeway to purchase six hundred weight of cannon balls, two kegs of gunpowder, and canvas and flannel for making cartridges.[16]

When the British fleet appeared off the Delaware Bay and began a tight blockade in 1813, Cape May County residents took measures for coastal defense. William Douglass, a Dyer's Creek farmer and ship carpenter, reportedly devised huge logs painted to resemble cannons and mounted them on the Cedar Hammocks (Goshen Creek) to discourage British invasion. In another episode of wartime Cape May County tradition, Abigail Hughes protected her Cape Island community from British bombardment by standing in front of her husband's cannon, thus preventing a fight certain to lead to the destruction of wooden hotels and pilots' houses along the shore of the seaside resort town. Cape May County farmers defended their interests by hiding cattle and sheep, according to tradition, in the swamp and woods along the south branch of Fishing Creek. They probably dug a deep channel from the bay to Lake Lily near Cape May Point so that salt water would foul this freshwater pond and discourage the British from landing to replenish the water kegs on their warships.[17]

Defense of the Delaware bayshore began in the summer of 1814. Governor William Pennington of New Jersey ordered the militia units in southern New Jersey to man posts at Billingsport, Port Elizabeth, and on the Cape May peninsula. At least six different companies, mostly from Cumberland, Salem, and Gloucester counties under the command of Brigadier General Ebenezer Elmer, saw duty in Cape May County. Cape May County's own forces included Captain George Norton's Company of the Cape May Independent Infantry Regiment and the Fishing Creek Independent Artillery Company. Once again the families of the original whaler yeomen dominated the local military organization. The Cape May Independent Regiment contained eight Corsons, three Ludlams, and three Hughes. The artillery company was slightly more elitist. The wealthiest young men from Dennis Creek and Cape Island composed the bulk of the unit.[18]

Militiamen manned an alarm post on Dennis Creek, supposedly at the site of an old fort said to stand near Jake's Landing (also called Mosquito Point) sometime before the Revolutionary War. Militiamen camped near the beach on Cape Island, on the banks of Cape May Point, and along the bay to watch for British sails. They complained about late payrolls, suffered from alcoholism, and at least one died from disease on Cape Island during the War of 1812. Joshua Townsend was appointed adjutant to improve supply and payroll conditions. "The men he represented to be in a state of mutiny, 37 deserted last weeks & the remainder threaten to follow," Lucius Elmer, a Cumberland County officer, noted in his diary. The militia in Cape May County encountered the British in 1813 and 1814. Reportedly the local force fought under Joshua Townsend and Furman Leaming against British landing parties at Town Bank, killing more than a dozen invaders, and repulsed other British landing parties at Edmunds' Landing on Fishing Creek and on Pierce's Point between Fishing Creek and Dyer's Creek.[19]

Cape May County prospered during the War of 1812 despite the constant British menace. The foreboding of Joseph Falkinburg and other local Federalists that the war meant economic disaster to the Jersey Cape proved to be without foundation. The British failed to interrupt local cordwood or agricultural trade. By contrast, the terrible killing frost during the summer of 1816 did more than any British foraging party to damage Cape May County's crops. The war accelerated the development of southern New Jersey's iron industry, including the establishment of the Etna Furnace in 1816 just across the Tuckahoe River from Cape May County. Cape May County lumbermen supplied wood for the furnace, which stimulated the settlement of the region around present-day Belleplain and Steelmantown in the northwestern corner of the county.[20]

The Etna Furnace forged ironware for Cape May County shipbuilders, particularly yards on the Tuckahoe River and at the Stephen Young shipbuilding yard on the Cedar Swamp Creek near the present town of Petersburg in Upper Township. Young enhanced his family fortunes during the war by developing a saltworks on Peck's Beach (now Ocean City) that continued in operation for several years after the war. Young joined Thomas Beesley, Peter Corson, and the Van Gilder family in 1815 to organize the Cedar Swamp Meadow [Banking] Company, which, like its bayshore counterparts, reclaimed farmland and salt hay meadows by draining wetlands and banking tidal streams and creeks. During the war, the area from Littleworth (present-day Petersburg) to the town of Tuckahoe evolved into an important economic region, although it was overshadowed by the Dennis Creek community to the south. Stephen Young became the wealthiest resident in the Upper Township, and one of the ten most prosperous men in Cape May County.[21]

For Cape May County and for the United States the end of the war with Britain in 1815 ushered in a period of nationalism, prosperity, and expansion called by some the Era of Good Feeling. The deep financial and social problems that would soon emerge were not apparent as patriotic celebrations swept over the nation. This postwar patriotism manifested itself in the growing popularity of the Independence Day celebration each Fourth of July. Cape May County celebrated the Fourth of July with an intensity and pageantry that brilliant Camden lawyer and diarist Isaac Mickle found in no other New Jersey community. Young Zerulia Stillwell Edmunds attended one July Fourth celebration at Cold Spring Church that included a full day of patriotic orations by county leaders, picnics, and the constant firing of guns.[22]

The end of the war brought a complex period of change to the United States. Removal of frontier problems with the British opened a new era of westward exploration, land speculation, and migration to Ohio, Indiana, Illinois, and beyond. The war stimulated internal developments that included canals, turnpikes, and the railroad. Old political factions eroded during the war, blurring the lines between Federalist and Democratic-Republicans, and leading to the emergence of new political coalitions around Henry Clay and the Whigs and Andrew Jackson's Democrats. The war also unleashed speculation in land and manufactures, and revealed the lack of a central banking and financial system. This led to the creation of a badly managed Second Bank of the United States in Philadelphia in 1817 and a terrible financial panic in 1819. Rural and emerging urban industrializing communities experienced problems with debtors, paupers, and labor unrest. All the while, the slavery question plagued the nation, leading to uncomfortable compromises over the admission of the new states to the Union and the abolition of slavery in the United States.

Each aspect of this turbulent era of American history shaped the character of Cape May County's society and institutions between 1815 and 1848. The opening of the trans-Appalachian frontier after the war attracted thousands of settlers, including several hundred from the Jersey Cape. As many as one hundred county families joined this westward migration during the first part of the nineteenth century. Maurice Beesley, a Dennis Township physician and amateur historian, noted in 1857 that between sixty and seventy Cape May County families had migrated west since 1830. The migration actually started before the war. Esther Leaming and Eli Foster ventured to Lebanon, Ohio, about 1806. David and Jeremiah Van Gilder left the Cedar Swamp and forests of Upper Township for Hamilton County, Ohio, between 1809 and 1811. Jonathan Hildreth, Dorcas Mills, and their three children left Cape May County during the War of 1812 and according to family tradition walked overland from Philadelphia to Pittsburgh, where they flatboated down the Ohio River. The land was higher, drier and healthier than "ever she was at the Cape,"

Thomas and Phebe Leaming Yates wrote from Ohio. "We are perfectly satisfied in the Exchange we have made," the Yates continued, "and would not come back to the Cape to Live if we Might have all we Left given to us & our Expenses back."[23]

Not everyone shared the Yates's enthusiasm for the West. Pulling up roots from Cape May County entailed certain risks. Lewis Ludlam wrote his family in Dennis Creek that his dry goods and commission business had encountered a serious setback. "We met with a heavy loss last summer of abt. 3200 Dolls. which arose from our taking notes of an unchartered bank in Indiana territory in the West Country which we could not dispose of at any rate," Ludlam complained in 1816. Despite such difficulties, the West continued to attract Cape May County residents in several waves that drained the county and accounted in part for the very slow rate of population increase from 4,000 to 6,000 between 1820 and 1850. During the financial panic that plagued the county and nation in 1837, members of the Nickelson, Corson, Tomlin, and Hand families joined a wagon train that assembled at West Creek and headed for Sangamon County, Illinois. The Sangamon County census for 1850 showed twenty different Cape May County families residing there.[24]

The movement west arose partly from limited landowning and business opportunities on the Cape May peninsula during the early years of the nineteenth century. Though a number of older families and a few new entrepreneurs such as Holmes and Falkinburg prospered, the county saw a constant increase in the number of debtors, paupers, and propertyless former slaves. John Price, a blacksmith and merchant, noted that an expanding number of his accounts stood uncollected because his customers remained confined in the county jail for their failure to pay debts. "Take notice that the Judges of the County of Cape May Common Pleas," one customer wrote to Price, "have apptd Sat., the 14th day of December next at one o'clock in the afternoon at the Court House of said County to hear me and my creditors on what can be alleged for or not against my liberation from confinement for debt from the jail of said County."[25]

The Cape May County Board of Freeholders complained that the jail had run out of beds and voted to expand the prison with an upper floor for debtors and the lower rooms for criminals. A number of American communities met the problem of poverty and debtors during the early nineteenth century by developing more formal institutions to replace the church, family, and voluntary poor relief measures.

Nantucket, Massachusetts, a community much like Cape May, turned to the almshouse movement to solve some of its problems with paupers and debtors. Cape May County, too, employed the almshouse as a central institution with which to provide welfare to local residents. Cape May County constructed a new almshouse in 1821 and an addition in 1833 on the old Johnson farm two miles north of the Court House village, on the grounds of the current Crest Haven complex. The Board of Freeholders named Robert Holmes, the county tax collector, Spicer Hughes, and James Townsend as trustees of the county almshouse. The county appointed John S. Ludlam as the poorhouse steward, with instructions to keep the institution "free from disorder." The freeholders mandated that "if any are disorderly and obstanately perverse [the steward] is authorized immediately to confine them, and feed them bread and water for any time—not exceeding twenty four hours at a time."[26]

Establishment of almshouse rules and policy during the first months of operation revealed how Cape May County's gentry leadership hoped to maintain social order and provide care for the poor. Freeholders Abijiah Smith, Richard Thompson, Jeremiah Leaming, Ezekiel Stevens, and Joshua Townsend resolved on 20 February 1821 that all the poor in the county must be lodged at county expense in the new almshouse. Stephen Young, Parmenas Corson, Lewis Corson, and Recompense Badcock collected bedding, farm implements, food, and a woolen wheel from the old township overseers of the poor and delivered them to the county almshouse in Middle Township. Robert Holmes brought to the almshouse barrels of potatoes, corn, beans, salt, molasses, and fifteen hundred clams taken from nearby waters. Isaac Swain and James Corson donated six pairs of shoes for indigent children at the almshouse. County almshouse trustees established an account at one of their general stores, expending $31.79 of county monies for calico and cotton cloth, sewing supplies, coffee, crackers, tea, tobacco, soap, and a broom. They also purchased cattle, hogs, sheep, and fowl for the almshouse, hoping to make it a self-sufficient farm.[27]

Thus supplied, the county welcomed the first paupers in the spring of 1821. These represented the complex texture of Cape May County's early-nineteenth-century society. Nathan Baner and James Townsend, Upper Township overseers of the poor, delivered "a parcel of paupers of said Township whose names are as follows—Elizabeth Ludlam, commonly call'd Crazy Betts—Jeremiah Johnson an idiot and Martha Johnson a female child of Letitia Townsend's perhaps three years old." Two days later, Lower Township deposited Ezra Eldrege, Judith Flowers, Dinah Turner, and her child Eliza Pierson "whose name [the county steward] alter'd as being spurious and call'd her Imprudence Bull." Flowers soon left in search of work, but then returned in the fall with her sickly husband, who died at the county poorhouse. Meanwhile, the Middle Township brought to the almshouse a pregnant woman, who gave birth to a baby daughter and then left with the infant. Abraham Woolson entered the county almshouse in early January 1822, only to be evicted by the trustees, "believing his bodily powers too good to remain here a charge to the publick."[28]

The county admitted African-Americans to the almshouse in 1821, after James Townsend and Ezekiel Stevens consulted lawyers about their legal responsibility to care for aged, infirm, or indigent former slaves. The almshouse accepted Dinah Turner in 1821 and Sylvia Jackson, "a dark and sick woman," in January 1822. Jacob Brown soon arrived at the county almshouse and offered to take care of Jackson if the steward paid him twenty-five cents a week. The almshouse became the residence in 1823 of Emeline and Dan Humphreys, "two Cullered children." A few years later, Dennis Township officials brought Richard Jackson to the poorhouse with both his feet so badly frozen that Joseph Fifield, the county physician, amputated them. Incredibly, Jackson left the almshouse in 1835 to earn his own living. The number of African-Americans in the county almshouse increased steadily, until by 1850 they made up 45 percent of the permanent residents, though less than 5 percent of the total county population.[29]

The large percentage of African-Americans under county care arose because the manumission of slaves cast free blacks too old or too young to work into the community without shelter, property, or family. County gentry business leaders searched for ways to absorb the freed slaves. The Baptist meetinghouse in Cape May Court House cared for elderly former slaves, including Rumy, once owned by Baptist leader Nathaniel Holmes. Holmes bound out seven-year-old Benjamin Turner, who was "chargeable upon the county," to Stephen Young until Turner reached the age of twenty-one. In another case, Jesse Hand established a collection for the maintenance of Jonah Collins, a seventy-five-year-old "masterless slave." Collins appeared later on the almshouse rolls along with Susan Taylor, a blind eighty-one-year-old former slave, and James Green, manumitted in 1812 by Abigail Townsend.[30]

Cape May County began to record manumissions in 1802 (see Appendix C). The county followed the gradualist approach to manumission set by the New Jersey legislature, which passed a law in 1786 prohibiting the further importation of slaves into the state. At the same time, the New Jersey government authorized the voluntary manumission of "any Negro or Mulatto Slave" after the master had recorded the act in a document signed by two township overseers of the poor and by two county justices of the peace. Eighteen years later, the legislature provided that children born of slave parents after 1804 should be freed when the female reached the age of twenty-one and the male the age of twenty-five.[31]

New Jersey abolished slavery, at last, in 1846. By then Cape May County slaveowners had manumitted all their slaves with the exception of Dorothy Jackson, an eighty-one-year-old slave still owned by Amariah Corson of Upper Township in 1860. Some slave owners seemed reluctant to part with their slaves. Jacob Cresse, a prosperous farmer and lumber merchant, gave his wife Ruhama in 1816 "all my blackpeople, namely Prudence, Bethany, Marshal, Alphus, [and] Angeline Seagraves." Jonathan Leaming died without freeing his slaves, and they became entangled in the disposal of the estate. In such cases, the slaves might become county charges and end up in the almshouse.[32]

Freed slaves and possibly runaway slaves from other areas settled in pockets of remote Cape May County woodlands before the middle of the century. One of the first black communities developed above Cold Spring in present-day Erma, where the Shunpike crosses Tabernacle Road in Lower Township. Thomas Hughes sold property in Lower Township to Derick Turner, Griffin Cox, John Armour, Peter Murkens, and Manuel Davis, "colored men," in June 1831, to erect a meetinghouse and burying ground. In 1847 Hughes transferred land on the former John Hand farm to Edward Turner, Robert Cox, Jr., William Cox, Griffin Cox, and Peter Umphries, Jr., to build a Methodist church and burying ground. This was probably the start of the Union Bethel settlement, and perhaps the place where Jarena Lee, the first known female preacher in the African American Methodist Episcopal Church attended meeting.[33]

Another African-American settlement, possibly an offshoot of the first, built the Mt. Zion chapel below Union Bethel in Cold Spring. This settlement moved farther south on the present-day Shunpike to be closer to hotel jobs on Cape Island. Today, the Mt. Zion cemetery, nearly invisible along the Shunpike below Batt Lane, in thick weeds, underbrush, and ivy, marks the spot of the second Mt. Zion settlement and meetinghouse. These freedmen and women, mostly kin of the earliest slaves in Cape May County, formed clusters of families and a community that through intermarriage resembled, in some respects, the whaler yeoman family and community. Original African-American families in the county included Armour, Turner, Taylor, Coachman, Cox, Humphreys, Harmon, Lively, Moore, Seagraves, Collins, and Squirrel. The Turner, Trusty, and Batt (or Batteast) families, some free-born mariners, moved to the county and intermarried with the original slave families.[34]

Most manumitted slaves became farm laborers or domestic helpers for prosperous white families. Twenty-six out of the thirty heads of African-American households in Lower Township in 1850 listed their occupation as that of common laborer. Four said they were mariners. Lower Township African-Americans between the ages of fourteen and nineteen lived and worked in the houses, general stores, or hotels of the leading business gentry families. Joseph Squirrel worked at George Stratton's hotel, and Lemuel Harmon waited on guests at W. B. Miller's establishment. John Obekiah labored in George Bennett's general store, while Anthony Trusty worked for Israel Townsend, one of the wealthiest men on Cape Island. Ann Trusty, Susan Armour, and Julia Jackson lived as domestic servants in the households respectively of Humphrey Hughes, Elijah Bennett, and Dr. Samuel S. Marcy.[35]

Three African-American families owned taxable estates in Lower Township by 1850. Edward Turner farmed a small plot of land and drove a team and wagon. Turner's family intermarried with the Cox, Armour, Trusty, and Taylor families, establishing wide kinship ties throughout the county. According to tradition, Turner employed his wagon, remote woodland farm in the Union Bethel community, and family ties to operate an Underground Railroad station in Cape May County that shuttled fugitive slaves to Snow Hill (Lawnside), Haddonfield, or other stations farther north. Turner may have assisted Harriet Tubman, a leading Underground Railroad conductor, who worked in a Cape Island hotel about 1850.[36]

Another community of freed and fugitive African-Americans developed before 1850 between Goshen and Townsend's Inlet in Middle Township. Sarah Hand sold land to Abel Cox and Samuel Robertson on the Eldredge plantation along the seaside road in 1819 "for [a] burial ground for the People of Colour." John West, possibly a runaway slave from South Carolina but more likely a free black preacher from Tennessee, came to Goshen about 1823 and worked for Jedediah Tomlin. West and George Taylor, a mariner, formed a church in the 1830s. West eventually purchased a building from a white congregation and in about 1853 moved it to the site of the current John Wesley Methodist Church and Mt. Olive Cemetery near the old Swainton railroad station. Apparently Lovina Armour-Coachman owned a small house and an acre of land nearby. The Widow Coachman worked in the Hand and Garrison households in Goshen and ran a cake-and-ale stand at the shipyard on the Goshen Creek. The Seagraves, Wrights, and Armours formed a cluster of houses between the African-American church and the seashore road, later known as Siggtown.[37]

Freed Cape May County slaves often remained with their former slave-owning families. Prudence Seagraves, once a Holmes family slave, lived in Robert Holmes's household as a domestic servant after manumission. Jonah Armour joined Reuben Holmes and Jinkins Holmes as Nathaniel Holmes's employees. The trio plowed the turnip patch, harrowed corn, and split wood for the Dennis Creek business leader. They "hauled out dung on [the] shop field" and loaded cordwood on coastal vessels at Holmes's Landing on Dennis Creek. Armour carted dirt and gravel to fill the Dennis Creek Crossway and lumber for the bridge over Green Creek. These latter jobs were part of an extensive road-, bridge-, and creek-banking enterprise undertaken by Armour's boss, Nathaniel Holmes, the most influential and powerful Dennis Creek merchant, freeholder, and road builder in early-nineteenth-century Cape May County.[38]

Stephen Young, Nathaniel Holmes, and his brother-in-law Richard Thompson continued Cape May County's internal improvements, which had been started before the War of 1812. The New Jersey legislature had passed an act in 1816 that authorized the banking of certain meadows and swamps in Cumberland and Cape May counties. In response, nearly every Cape May County tidal-creek community organized a meadow-banking company. Holmes, Thompson, and Young associated with Joseph Falkinburg, Jeremiah Leaming, Downs Edmunds, John Williams, Thomas Beesley, and Israel Leaming to form a public-private combination to develop county public works. These county leaders owned extensive properties along the tidal creeks, held major shares in the meadow-banking companies, and dominated the seats on the Cape May County Board of Freeholders. They formed a nineteenth-century business gentry elite tied together, like their eighteenth-century whaler yeoman ancestors and kin, by intermarriage and political-economic associations.

A corporation called the South Branch of the Dennis Creek Meadow Company organized in 1815 and led the postwar internal improvement movement in Cape May County. Joseph Falkinburg, the county's Federalist representative, secured legislation for this corporation from the Democratic-Republican state legislature in Trenton, which had adopted a policy of public improvements advanced by Albert Gallatin, the Democratic-Republican U.S. secretary of the treasury. Falkinburg sat on the board of directors of the South Branch company with Nathaniel Holmes, Henry Ludlam, James Diverty, Jeremiah Leaming, and Elizabeth Ludlam. Inclusion of the latter on the board of managers, and the presence of female directors on the Cedar Swamp and Fishing Creek Meadow Banking companies, suggest that women from the inner circle of families who had directed county affairs from the beginning held voting power and influence on this early-nineteenth-century Cape May County internal improvement program.[39]

Similar meadow-banking companies were organized to reclaim meadowland along New England, Coxe Hall, Dyer's, and Fishing creeks. The same business gentry leaders oversaw these projects. They directed the road and bridge improvements that supported the creek-banking projects. They maintained the public works between Dennis Creek and the Cape Island. They built new bridges over West, Cedar Swamp, Green, Fishing, and Cape Island creeks. They erected milestone markers in 1826 along the county's dirt and gravel wagon paths and resolved to "affix directors at the forks of such publick roads." They met with the Cumberland County bridge commissioners to construct a bridge over West Creek. The Cape May County leaders cooperated with John Estell, Benjamin Weatherby, Philip Emmel, and Jesse Bowen, Gloucester County freeholders in 1830 and 1831, to build a drawbridge over the Tuckahoe River. Stephen Young and John Williams, Cape May County's representatives, advised that they should design "the draw of said Bridge to work on the Pivot after the plan of the Bridge on the Delaware and Chesapeake Canal."[40]

Cape May County's business gentry made progress in the reclamation of swampland and tidal marshes and the development of a network of roads and bridges. An English physician who visited the county in 1833 marveled at the unusually fine roads, elaborate dikes, and carefully sluiced meadows. He found the worm fences of cedar rails that divided these meadows rather ugly, however. "Ugly" also described the Cape May County courthouse in 1833, with its decaying white wooden siding and faded red ocher trim. The county had erected new brick buildings to house the county clerk, surrogate, and jail in 1825 but had not repaired the courthouse beyond an occasional new coat of paint. The board of freeholders appointed Samuel Springer, the designer of wind-powered sawmills, and Jeremiah Hand and Samuel Matthews, carpenters, to draft a plan in May 1833 for a new courthouse building.[41]

The decision to construct a new courthouse in 1833 led to a lengthy and at times bitter debate over the location of Cape May County's seat of justice and government. This controversy delayed action on the construction of a new courthouse for nearly fifteen years. The issue was complex. The county almshouse and care for the poor absorbed 30 percent of the annual county budget of three thousand dollars. Road and bridge projects, needed to keep the county open for travel, took up the rest. Conservative county taxpayers hesitated to support additional expense for a new government building. The courthouse question also involved larger historical and geographic factors of a county divided into four distinctive townships that were separated by tidal creeks, religion, and local interests. The location of the original courthouse in the middle of the peninsula along the seashore road had been subject to heated debate in the mid-eighteenth century. Followers of Jacob Spicer, Jr., and Aaron Leaming, Jr., had hotly contested the location of county government. Though situated in the middle of the peninsula, the Cape May Court House village remained isolated from active county life around the Dennis Creek, Cape Island, and Tuckahoe River communities.[42]

When Dennis Creek broke away from Upper Township, the two new freeholders from Dennis Township formed a faction with those on the board who shared the same interests as Dennis Creek. Together, they dominated county business. Eighty percent of public works authorized by the board of freeholders between 1815 and 1848 directly benefited Dennis Creek. The first resolution, on 14 June 1827, following introduction of the Dennis Township freeholders, authorized Nathaniel Holmes to expand the Dennis Creek causeway with huge "heart of pine" pilings filled with gravel carted for the county by "Holmes' boys." The board of freeholders voted to construct a new bridge over the Dennis Creek, contracting with James Diverty, a wealthy Dennis Creek lumber merchant and shipbuilder, to construct bridge abutments. These Dennis Creek business gentry allied in 1830 and 1831 with Stephen Young to grant a number of public works around Young's store, lumberyard, and shipyard at Lower Bridge, where the current Tuckahoe Road between Marmora and Middletown crosses the Cedar Swamp Creek in Upper Township. The board also contracted with Young to repair the public roads and bridges in his neighborhood.[43]

At first, the Dennis Creek coalition developed good relations with the Lower Township business gentry, who were intent upon developing their own Cape Island resort community. In 1832 the board of freeholders authorized the construction of an expensive stone bridge at Aaron Schellenger's crossing over Cape Island Creek. This provided a direct route to the "large houses" kept by Richard S. Ludlam and Samuel Richardson. So long as visitors to Cape Island continued to use the stagecoach route that passed through Dennis Creek on their way down the peninsula to the resort, Dennis Creek's interests coincided with that of Cape Island. When Wilmon Whilldin, Aaron Bennett, Joseph Higbee, and other Lower Township pilots and entrepreneurs developed regular steamboat service and built steamboat landings at Higbee's Beach and Cape May Point, travelers bypassed Dennis Creek. Mutual interest eroded, and Dennis Creek's enthusiasm for Cape Island projects cooled.[44]

Cooperation between Cape Island and Dennis Creek ended between 1844 and 1845. After twice agreeing to build a large bridge over Cape Island Creek, representatives of Dennis, Upper, and Middle townships rescinded their original resolution. Stephen Young, director of the board of freeholders, decided on 14 May 1845 that he wanted bridges over Dennis Creek and Cedar Swamp Creek instead, and shelved the Cape Island project. Ten days later, in a meeting held without Lower Township representatives, the freeholders resolved to build a new Dennis Creek bridge. The six northern freeholders voted on 27 May 1845 "that a new Bridge over Dennis Creek be constructed upon the old foundations of sufficient width for a carriage and walkway, and to be properly *enclosed and roofed over*" (emphasis added). Stephen Young headed the commission to oversee the construction of this covered bridge.[45]

The Dennis Creek coalition appeased the Lower Township in a May 1845 meeting at the house of Jonas Miller, the leading Cape

Island hotel and land owner. County administrators promised to build a bridge in the Lower Township and appointed Spicer Hughes, Abraham Reeves, and Thomas Hewitt to draw a plan for the structure. The freeholders warned, however, that the county could only bear half the cost of the project and that Lower Township would have to raise the rest. No such restriction appeared in the contracting of the Cedar Swamp or Dennis Creek works. Then, on 7 December 1847, the board of chosen freeholders abruptly rejected the Lower Township bridge commissioner's report.[46]

Cape Island development became hostage between 1847 and 1848 to the politics of building the county courthouse. Lower Township might secure its badly needed bridge to Cape Island if it supported Nathaniel Holmes and his Dennis and Upper township allies in their movement to relocate the seat of county government from Cape May Court House to Dennis Creek (or, as it was called after 1848, Dennisville). Similar fights over the location of county seats had divided other New Jersey counties. Voter fraud and political corruption marked the election in 1807 between Newark and Elizabeth for the courthouse site of Essex County. The Salem County election to select a county seat in 1823 ripped the northern and southern sections apart and shattered Federalist and Democratic-Republican factions. The Cape May County election promised a similar schism as John Wiley, a Court House physician, determined to battle the Dennis Creek forces.[47]

Dr. John Wiley distributed a handbill "To the Independent Voters of Cape May" that listed the reasons for retaining the county seat at its original location. He noted that in the current location, Daniel Hand, his wife's great-grandfather, had given the county "perfect title so long as the County chooses to occupy it with either a Court House or Jail." Wiley explained that the courthouse village was accessible to Cape Island and other sections. He suggested that Nathaniel Holmes had a personal stake in the Dennis Creek site because all materials for new construction would come through "N. Holmes's landing." Wiley's most effective argument with the always frugal county voters centered on the cost of moving the entire county government to Dennis Creek. "Now, shall we voluntarily assume an additional debt of $20,000, and increase our taxes threefold, which are sufficiently heavy already, for the sole purpose of destroying one place and increasing the importance of another?" Wiley inquired. "Let us leave Cape May Court House and Dennis Creek villages to take care of themselves, while we take care of the county, and look to her interests rather than to individuals; and this can best be done by keeping out of debts and exercising economy."[48]

John Wiley's appeal saved the Court House location as the county seat. In an election held on 25 April 1848, an incredible 1,003 out of 1,005 registered county voters cast ballots that gave Cape May Court House an 89 vote edge over Dennis Creek. Forty-four votes went to Goshen as an alternative site. By contrast, only 129 county voters had cast ballots in 1844 in an election over whether to accept the new state constitution. The politics of the Cape Island bridge backfired on Dennis Creek in 1848 as Jonas Miller, in whose house the board of freeholders made promises that it later broke, led an overwhelming Lower Township vote in favor of the Cape May Court House site. As expected, Stephen Young delivered the Upper Township vote for Dennis Creek. Jonathan Hand, the county clerk, invalidated only 4 votes, all in the Lower Township, and certified on 29 April 1848 that Cape May Court House had been retained as the county seat.[49]

The aftermath of the Cape May County courthouse battle resulted in surprisingly little recrimination. No discussion of voting fraud or corruption attended the results. Nathaniel Holmes and Stephen Young united with Israel Townsend of Lower Township and Samuel F. Ware of Cape Island on the board of freeholders to authorize, fund, and construct an attractive new county courthouse on its original location. Ware, Holmes, Young, and Richard Thompson served as the building committee. They dispatched Samuel Ware, a Cape Island carpenter, and James L. Smith, a West Creek surveyor and large landowner, to study the architecture of the courthouses in neighboring counties. The board of freeholders accepted their design for a two-story courthouse with floors of Carolina heart pine, sills of white oak, and joists and rafters made of hemlock. Completed at the cost of $6,284.33, the new courthouse opened for its first meeting of the Cape May County Board of Chosen Freeholders on 7 May 1850.[50]

County leaders united behind the courthouse project. Developments in the Lower Township defused possible animosities toward the rest of the county in the wake of the recent political battle. Cape Island secured separate borough government in 1848 and incorporated in 1851 as the City of Cape Island (it would become Cape May City in 1869). Joseph Ware and William Cassedy, representatives on the board of freeholders from the City of Cape Island, joined Abraham

Reeves and Israel Townsend of Lower Township in 1851 to form their own little four-member coalition on the board. The four-member Upper and Dennis township group no longer dominated the lower region of the county when the board met to conduct county business in the new courthouse. Meetings of the board of freeholders immediately reflected the new power shift. James L. Smith, Dennis Township freeholder, and Matthew Marcy, a wealthy Middle Township merchant and the brother of Samuel Marcy, the leading Cape Island physician, joined the new coalition in 1851 to advance the interests of the Cape Island Turnpike Company. The board voted on 10 June 1851 to allow the company "to alter and enlarge a wing of the Cape Island Bridge."[51]

The political energies and interests of Cape Island, so long frustrated by the Dennis Creek politicians, found outlet in the organization of Cape May County's first urban government. The Borough of Cape Island leadership met at Cape Island School on 2 May 1848 and organized the new borough. They appointed James L. Kennedy, Richard L. Ludlam, and Joseph Leach as a Common Council "to draft the laws and ordinances for the better government of the Borough of Cape Island." They passed ordinances to "suppress riotous conduct," prohibit the explosion of fireworks, and prevent swimming without "suitable bathing apparrel." Another ordinance restricted the parking of carriages so that they blocked the street. The three-member council appointed Thomas B. Hughes as the high constable for the borough and Jediah Bellangee as a special constable to enforce these laws.[52]

Cape Island had grown into a dynamic but undisciplined community that county leaders, intent upon developing Dennis Creek, had neglected for years. Cape Island's somewhat unregulated expansion stemmed from the seasonal nature of the population. During the summer months, Cape Island teemed with thousands of visitors. For the rest of the year, it remained a quiet coastal village of Delaware Bay pilots and local fishermen. During the summer season Henry Clay, William H. Harrison, and other Whig politicians mixed on the island with their bitterest Jacksonian Democrat opponents. Isaac Mickle noted in 1844 that every political conversation at the resort ended up in a heated debate. Southern slave-owning guests stayed in hotels attended by recently freed African-Americans. "We have had a great battle in one hotel between the black servants and the white gentlemen, which has caused some bloody heads," observed Frederika Bremer, a Swedish visitor. Southern gamblers and big players from the region, including James A. Bayard of Delaware, gambled at the Blue Pig, a notorious Cape Island gambling den. All the while, hundreds of young men and women ate, drank, danced the "hop," set off firecrackers, and romped until early hours of the morning. For a time, the Benevolent Society of Forkers operated as a type of vigilante group to restore order, but apparently these Forkers deteriorated into drunken revelers and mischief makers, as well. It was a boisterous, highly volatile summer resort community that required better regulation by Cape May County leaders.[53]

Cape Island had become a vibrant resort business community by 1850. Ten of the nineteen wealthiest men in the county owned businesses in the borough. These included Jonas Miller, George Stratton, Israel Leaming, and Jeremiah Mecray, hoteliers, and John Rutherford and John Dougherty, store owners. The success of both Cape Island and Dennis Creek during the first half of the nineteenth century drew Cape May County into larger regional and national developments. The board of freeholders petitioned the federal government in 1849 to build breakwaters and improve navigation on Delaware Bay. Meantime, more outside investors and entrepreneurs engaged in Cape Island hotel business and in Dennis Creek shipbuilding. During the next decade, New York and northern New Jersey financiers established Cape May County's first banks. Most important, Pennsylvania and New Jersey railroad men planned to extend into the county a rail line that promised to change Cape May County's society and economy dramatically.[54]

CHAPTER FIVE

The Railroad and the Civil War, 1850–1878

Southern New Jersey presented an untapped market for the railroad entrepreneur of the 1850s. Despite a burgeoning glass industry and the rise of manufacturing centers at Bridgeton and Millville in Cumberland County, no rail line yet connected the region to the rest of New Jersey. This was partly because the Camden and Amboy Railroad-Delaware and Raritan Canal monopoly discouraged railroad development. New Jersey legislators would not charter any line without the approval of the joint transportation companies, which in 1832 had been granted exclusive right-of-way through the state. Finally, the West Jersey Railroad Company secured a charter to build a line from Woodbury to Glassboro in Gloucester County and to Millville in Cumberland County. This proposed route bypassed Bridgeton and stopped short of Cape May County. "It has become a serious matter with us," Charles Elmer, a Bridgeton banker and later president of the Cape May and Millville Railroad, wrote Richard C. Holmes, a Cape May County businessman, "as I have no doubt but that if the West Jersey road is continued to Glassboro and a road is made from Millville to Glassboro, that our prospect of a road is cut off, for a long time to come."[1]

Atlantic County, formed out of Gloucester County in 1837, became the first southern New Jersey coastal area to develop a railroad. Jonathan Pitney, an Absecon physician, and Enoch Doughty, an Atlantic County merchant, convinced South Jersey glass barons and Philadelphia investors to undertake a railroad project that would connect Camden City with the Atlantic coast near Absecon Island. Dr. Pitney lobbied in Trenton and secured a charter in 1852 for the Camden and Atlantic Railroad. Pitney, Doughty, and Samuel Richards, a glass manufacturer, also organized the Camden and Atlantic Land Company to sell building lots on Absecon Island. The rail line to the seashore opened in 1854, and the new community that formed on Absecon Island incorporated in 1855 as Atlantic City. After a period of gradual growth, this new shore resort became the region's major watering place for Philadelphia and New Jersey visitors. Atlantic City eventually eclipsed the older, genteel resort City of Cape Island to the south.[2]

Entrepreneurs turned their attention to Cape May County during the 1850s, but with less spectacular success than that obtained in Atlantic County. New York and Jersey City investors incorporated five banks in Cape May County between 1851 and 1853. These included the American Exchange Bank, Atlantic Bank, and Second City Bank of Cape Island, all incorporated in 1851, the Farmers (later Traders) Bank in 1852, and the Bank of Cape May County in 1853. Cape May County investors held interests in two of these financial institutions. Dr. John Wiley and Franklin Hand, a prosperous Court House farmer and real estate developer, owned the majority of shares in the Atlantic Bank. William F. Garrison, a Goshen Creek shipbuilder, and Richard S. Ludlam, a Cape Island hotel owner, held the largest shares in the Bank of Cape May County. None of these banks lasted beyond 1855.[3]

Cape May County merchants and farmers continued to transact business as they had for over three decades with the conservative Cumberland Bank, incorporated at Bridgeton in 1816. Reportedly, the Cumberland Bank never missed payment on its annual dividend to stockholders, a practice made possible by cautious loan and deposit policies. Cape May County business gentry maintained close ties to the Cumberland Bank and to Bridgeton's legal and financial community, particularly the Elmer and Nixon families. James L. Smith, West Creek landowner and Cape May County freeholder, was a director of the Cumberland Bank. The Cape May County Board of Chosen Freeholders retained the Nixon and Elmer law firms in Bridgeton when they needed legal services. Jeremiah Nixon of Cumberland County owned East and West Creek timberlands and a shipbuilding concern on Dennis Creek. The Elmer and Leaming families had been business associates in cranberry bogs and timberlands since 1759. Consequently, Bridgeton remained Cape May County's banking and legal center until after the Civil War, and early efforts to establish independently chartered state banks in the county failed.[4]

Restrained by the conservative banking practices of the Cumberland Bank, Cape May County entrepreneurs invested in a more traditional enterprise, the turnpike company. Richard Holmes and other county business gentry formed a local turnpike syndicate. They incorporated the Cape May Turnpike Company in 1854 to build a toll road from Court House to Cape Island (roughly along the path of present-day Route 9). Progress was slow as county subscribers hesitated to purchase shares in the turnpike company. Wilmon Whilldin, owner of a Cape Island steamboat, apologized to his friend Richard Holmes for not buying any of the turnpike stock. Whilldin explained that the economic panic of 1857 made it impossible to turn securities into cash and he needed all his assets to build another steamboat for the Cape Island-Philadelphia passenger and freight line. A steamboat, not a turnpike, Whilldin suggested, promised to bring the county out of the depression that had settled over local business. "If we are satisfied nothing can be done here, that Cape May is blighted and mildewed," Whilldin wrote, "we had better pitch our wigwam in California, New Mexico, Oregon, or Texas, for there will be those improvements directly be."[5]

Local landowners held out for higher prices for their land along the proposed Cape May Turnpike route. Richard Holmes and Henry Swain, county loan commissioner and a turnpike director respectively, failed to obtain a right-of-way across Elijah Hand's pasture and in front of Samuel Hoffman's place. These farmers refused to sell. John Tomlin of Goshen also opposed the turnpike monopoly, which would force farmers to pay tolls when they delivered their produce to the Cape Island hotels and dining rooms during the summer season. Tomlin determined to build a toll-free road (the Shunpike) parallel to and just west of the Cape May Turnpike.[6]

The turnpike company pushed ahead. Downs Edmunds, Jr., a company director, purchased a tollhouse in 1857 from the Cape Island Turnpike Company, which operated a road between the bayshore steamboat landing and the City of Cape Island. Edmunds installed the tollhouse near Cold Spring. Apparently the turnpike company erected another tollhouse nearer Court House and hired Martha Gentry as "keeper of tollgate." Inhabitants along the route carted gravel, stone, and plank for the new turnpike. Finally, John Wiley, who had organized the successful forces that kept the county seat at Court House, took charge of buying land for the company and persuaded Elijah Hand and Samuel Hoffman to sell. The popular county physician also convinced Jeremiah Cresse to part with his timberlands in the path of the turnpike. "I now have every reason to hope that the two sections or ends of the turnpike will be joined together in less than three weeks making a continuous road from Cape Island to Cape May Court House," Wiley announced in April 1858.[7]

The Cape May Turnpike Company never showed a large profit. The collection of tolls and stock subscriptions could not offset the cost of repairs to the roadbed, which was constantly being washed away. Probably John Tomlin's Shunpike, a rough wagon track through the woods nearby, allowed travelers and loads of farm produce to reach Cape Island without paying tolls. Waters B. Miller, a large investor, dropped out of the turnpike syndicate. Miller preferred to invest in a railroad enterprise. He knew that a committee of southern New Jersey state legislators (including Joshua Swain, Jr., of Cape May County) had hired William G. Cook, engineer for the Camden and Amboy Railroad, to conduct a line survey through the Cape May peninsula.[8]

Cook proposed three possible railroad routes in 1852 from the Camden City waterfront to Cape May County's resort community at the tip of the peninsula. He drew a straight course through Millville, another that swung west to connect Bridgeton, and a third that lay farther west through Salem. Cook favored the last route because it linked the entire Gloucester, Salem, Cumberland, and Cape May counties economic region. The cost of bridging the creeks for this railroad line was too expensive for investors, however, and the engineer recommended the second course. "The establishment of a railroad on this route," Cook advised, "would open to the market a new and valuable agricultural country, abounding in cedar swamps, and timber of various kinds."[9]

No railroad would enter Cape May County for eleven years after William G. Cook's engineering report of 1852. The chartering and construction of a railroad line became entangled in New Jersey and regional politics and in a contest between competing groups of entrepreneurs and businessmen. After the New Jersey General Assembly had granted the joint companies exclusive rights to railroad development in 1832, any project for completing a line into Cape May County required the support or approval of this monopoly. It had taken Dr. Jonathan Pitney of Absecon two years of negotiation before he had obtained a charter for the Camden and Atlantic Railroad.

Similar "sidewalk persuasion," Charles Elmer explained, was necessary to convince the legislators in Trenton to charter a railroad for Cumberland and Cape May counties. One local businessman thought their chances of securing a charter were good. "I suppose the northern part of the State will be willing to allow us the same privileges for improvement as they have had," he wrote Richard Holmes.[10]

Holmes remained cautious toward railroad investment. He showed little interest in pushing a line that would compete with his struggling turnpike company. The Cape May County businessman found economic conditions too unstable for new enterprise. Recently, the Townsend family of Dennis Creek and Port Elizabeth (Cumberland County) had suffered severe financial losses in a glassworks, and had been forced to sell much of their Cape May County cedar swamplands in 1851 for far less than their value to Daniel Estell, an Atlantic County speculator. Holmes suffered his own disappointment when the U.S. government refused to buy his patented "Self-Righting Surf and Lifeboat," which he had developed at considerable personal expense. A business associate warned Holmes to move slowly on future investments such as a Cape May County railroad line. "I received a letter from Doct. [Maurice] Beesley that you [Richard] Thompson & myself had been talking about getting up a petition to the Legislature authorizing the companies to subscribe," he advised Holmes, and "I wrote him that I thought it would be bad policy."[11]

Debate over a Cape May County rail line dragged on for a decade. Competing syndicates squabbled over different routes. The Cape May and Atlantic Company, an arm of the Camden and Atlantic Railroad group that had built the Atlantic City line, proposed constructing a track from Absecon to Egg Harbor and across the Tuckahoe River into Cape May County. Such a line assured that travel and trade would pass through and benefit Atlantic County and Atlantic City. At the same time, a group of speculators led by E. L. B. Wales, Upper Township's wealthiest resident, formed the West Jersey Central Company and suggested a route through Port Elizabeth to Cape May County. This company never raised operating capital. Delays in building a railroad down the peninsula to the Cape Island resort hurt the local economy. "I wish it would be built, if it is not, Cape Island must go down as a watering place, to a certainty," worried William Baird, Richard Holmes's brother-in-law, "and now that the shore birds are exterminated [by overhunting] along your coast, I should not like that to happen on account of the unfavorable influence it would exert on the value of land in Cape May County."[12]

The *Ocean Wave*, Cape May County's first newspaper, established between 1854 and 1855, kept the railroad issue alive. "We have heard little said for some time past about the railroad question," wrote Joseph S. Leach, the editor, in 1857, and "we hope that the citizens of our county have not given up the idea." Leach appealed to county residents to subscribe to a newly organized Glassboro and Millville Railroad Company led by Samuel Whitney and Thomas Whitney, Glassboro glass barons, and Richard D. Wood, a Philadelphia and Millville manufacturing tycoon. These were "men of wealth, influence, enterprise and perseverance," Leach insisted. The Wood family already held deep roots and major economic interests in the South Jersey iron industry, and Richard Wood had recently invested in a glassworks and cotton mill at Millville just a few miles from the Cape May County border. Wood and the Whitneys received a state charter for a railroad in 1859, and in twelve months had laid track, purchased rolling stock, and obtained a locomotive engine from a Philadelphia works.[13]

The directors of the Glassboro and Millville Railroad combined with a group of Cape May County investors in March 1860 to construct a railroad from Millville in Cumberland County "to any point on or near Cape Island." The syndicate planned to begin work when it had raised $175,000. This new railroad group contained the type of aggressive mid-nineteenth-century business entrepreneur who had built the Camden and Atlantic Railroad ten years earlier. Dr. Maurice Beesley of Dennis Township served much the same role for the Cape May County project as that performed by Dr. Jonathan Pitney for the Atlantic County enterprise. Beesley had developed extensive ties throughout New Jersey during the 1840s as a member of the state general assembly and council (state senate), organizer of the New Jersey Historical Society, and one of the founders of the New Jersey State Asylum for the Insane. Beesley employed these statewide connections to advance Cape May County's railroad interests. The Cape May County railroad syndicate also included Jeremiah S. Nixon, a Dennis Creek shipbuilder, Israel Leaming, Cape Island hotelier, Joseph Ware, mayor of the City of Cape Island, Samuel Ashmead, an Upper Township merchant, and Dr. Coleman F. Leaming of Court House.[14]

The Leaming family pressed hard for the railroad because they owned property through which the proposed line would pass. The route of what would soon become the Cape May and Millville Railroad entered the county near the spot where the old Cape Road crossed into Cumberland County just south of the current boundaryline between Upper and Dennis townships. It proceeded easterly through cedar timber and swamplands to the high gravel ridge known as Mt. Pleasant, and began a great arc as it extended south toward Cape Island. The Leamings, like their whaler yeoman ancestors, speculated in the land along the railroad line, and Coleman Leaming became a leading county railroad promoter. Charles B. Dungan, a Philadelphia traction entrepreneur, also joined the Cape May and Millville Railroad syndicate and provided vital support for the Cape May County enterprise from the Philadelphia financial community.[15]

Formation of a Cape May and Millville Railroad syndicate in 1860 promised to bring the long-delayed railroad to Cape May County. Still, final connections were not completed for another three years. Outside forces that buffeted the county were in part responsible for this further delay. Cape May County was a border region, lying precariously between feuding sections of the country and subject to pressure during the late 1850s from both unionists of the industrial North and secessionist from the southern slave states. A South Carolina secessionist state flag flying defiantly in front of one Cape Island hotel symbolized the fragile geographic and socioeconomic character of New Jersey's southernmost county. Joseph Leach, the local newspaper editor, hoped that a break between North and South might be avoided, because it would hurt Cape Island resort business. He observed that the secessionist rumbling in the wake of Abraham Lincoln's presidential election in 1860 was "more smoke than fire."[16]

Joseph Leach understood that Cape May County held sympathies for both the North and the South. Southerners made up a large portion of the summer population on Cape Island. Slave owning had been a central aspect of Cape May County life and economy until recent years, and some Cape May County business gentry opposed the abolition of slavery in the South. "I am confident that slavery is a curse [and] its effects are like the blight of the mildew," Henry Swain proclaimed, "but I believe that turning loose of four millions of Negroes upon the country would be a much greater evil than this." The Upper Township "Union" committee declared that antislavery agitation was the "deadly poison" that had caused the present crisis between the sections. The Upper Township unionists announced that they would never tolerate abolitionist sentiment in their schools, houses, or meeting halls. They opposed meddling in the "domestic institutions of our Southern brethren," and wanted to restore relations with the slave-owning South "at any cost." A similar "Grand Union Meeting" on Cape Island "condemned all Fanaticism" such as that displayed by John Brown, an abolitionist, in his violent raid on the federal arsenal at Harper's Ferry.[17]

Cape May County's desire to stay out of the problems between North and South reflected the county's geographic location and historic character. Cape May County remained an isolated cluster of villages far from the main Philadelphia-New York corridor in 1860. "If you were not so far on one side of the great route," a Washington friend wrote Richard Holmes in 1860, "I could often see you as I travel a great deal in the litigated cases which seem destined to form the greater part of my business, and am frequently in Philada."[18]

Holmes admitted that travel on and off the Jersey Cape was difficult. A two-day round trip to Philadelphia required some combination of private conveyance, ferryboat, stagecoach, and catching an occasional sloop out of Dennis Creek Landing. The steamboat service from Philadelphia to Cape Island remained unreliable. Wharves on the bayside fell into disrepair and had to be rebuilt for each approaching summer season. After decades of good roads and bridges, the county's transportation network had disintegrated during the 1850s. The Cape Island bridge, probably at Schellengers Landing, "had been nearly all swept away" by 1854. Christopher Ludlam raised his millpond so that it flooded the main stagecoach road between the village on Dennis Creek (Dennisville) and West Creek (Eldora).[19]

A telegraph line had connected the City of Cape Island with Kaighn's Point in Camden City since the early 1850s, but service was erratic, and it closed down completely on the eve of the Civil War. Cape Island leaders appealed to Charles Olden, the governor of New Jersey, to reopen the telegraph line in 1861 so that Cape May County might receive war news from Philadelphia. Joseph Leach complained that he was so isolated from events that he knew nothing about a huge forest fire that had burned through Dennis Township a few miles up the peninsula. "We frequently receive no intelligence of such occurences in our own County," the Cape Island journalist observed in 1857, "until we learn them from our Philadelphia Exchanges."[20]

Isolated from the outside world, Cape May County society in 1860 had not changed much since early settlement. Like their ancestors, the county's 7,130 residents (an increase of only 697 people from the 1850 census) came from English, Welsh, Scottish, or Irish stock. Eight out of ten countians on the eve of the American Civil War had been born in New Jersey, mostly in Cape May, Cumberland, Salem, and Gloucester counties. Almost 10 percent of those born outside the county had migrated to the peninsula from nearby Pennsylvania or Delaware. A few families entered the county from New England and, like the early settlers, intermarried with the older families. The most prominent of these pre–Civil War newcomers included the Wales and Marcy families from Connecticut. Less than 2 percent of Cape May County's population in 1860 had been born outside the United States, and of these 70 percent came from Ireland.[21]

This homogeneous Cape May County community pursued farming and maritime livelihoods on the eve of the Civil War, as had the original whaler yeomen. Seven out of ten countians labored on the farm and in maritime-related occupations, many combining agriculture, livestock raising, and fishing. Cape May County's agrarian communities continued to raise small herds of cattle, flocks of sheep, and horses and oxen, although the county no longer recorded these in the cattle earmark book. Cape May County farmers still grew their potatoes, corn, and peas, and their yield per acre and value of the crop stood at the bottom of the list of New Jersey's counties. Cape May County continued to harvest rye, wheat, oats, and salt hay cut on meadows drained by the banking companies. These grain crops ranked among the poorest in New Jersey's twenty-one counties. Maurice Beesley saw some changes, though. He noted in 1857 that Cape May County had become, for the first time in its history, nearly self-sufficient in agriculture.[22]

Cape May County remained in 1860 a county that could be described best as clusters of houses rather than a community of towns. Each cluster had its own shop for a blacksmith, wheelwright, and shoemaker. Most had a grist and sawmill, including a steam-powered mill on Goshen Creek. There were wind-powered mills along the shore road in Seaville, the Springer's windmill on Dyer's Creek (now Dias Creek), the Cummings's on Green Creek, and Daniel Cresse's windmill in Cold Spring. The Pilgrim, Steelman, Van Gilder, Marshall, Creamer, and Hoff families operated water-powered mills along Upper Township's millstreams and ponds. Clinton Ludlam cut wood at his sawmill in South Dennisville.[23]

A few manufacturing enterprises developed on the Jersey Cape before the Civil War to supplement the local farming, fishing, and lumbering occupations. Randal Marshall, a Cumberland County glass manufacturer from Port Elizabeth, bought land in Cape May and Cumberland counties at the head of the Tuckahoe River in 1811 and established a glassworks on the Mill Creek branch by 1814. When the Cumberland-Cape May line was redrawn in 1841, Marshall's glass manufactory, general store, houses for glassworkers, and the town of Marshallville, which grew up around them, lay partly in Cape May County. Marshallville also contained at least one small shipyard before the Civil War, providing periodic employment for skilled craftsmen. The Godfrey family operated another shipyard just east of Marshallville on the Tuckahoe River. Further south, Jeremiah Nixon built vessels on Dennis Creek, William F. Garrison constructed schooners on Goshen Creek, and Joshua Swain's boatyard on Townsend's Inlet repaired and built boats. Swain's yard was the site in 1811 for the invention of a new type of patented centerboard for small, fast-sailing craft.[24]

County life in 1860 revolved around the country store, which probably differed little from the one that Jacob Spicer had operated in Cold Spring during the 1750s. The country store was the center of the mid-nineteenth-century Cape May County community, serving as stagecoach stop and post office. Country stores, often barnlike wooden structures with large porches, stood at important crossroads, where the north-south routes connected with the roads that led from bayshore to seashore. Their importance can be seen in the number of mid-nineteenth-century communities that took the name of the local store owner, including Bennett (now Erma), Hildreth (present-day Rio Grande), Williamsburg (now Tuckahoe), and Petersburg (formerly Littleworth but renamed after local store owner and postmaster Peter Corson).

Country store proprietors dealt in everything from groceries to manure and shoes to "seegars" (cigars). Joseph Schellenger's store at Schellenger's Landing advertised grain, ground feed, dry goods, hardware, groceries, boots, shoes, and stone coal "at Philadelphia prices." The country store proprietors usually owned farms and held shares in coastal schooners. They speculated in real estate and timberland. Often, the country store owner ran a horse stable, blacksmith shop, and wheelwright's shed to repair and sell wagons, carriages, and farm equipment. Country store proprietors formed a prosperous business gentry sector in mid-nineteenth-century Cape May County. Samuel

Ashmead, owner of a country store in Upper Township, was a county cultural leader as well, contributing studies on plant life and marine algae in 1856 for George H. Cook's *Geology of Cape May*. The Edmunds, Swain, Hildreth, Bennett, Rutherford, Hand, and Schellenger families comprised a lower-county merchant gentry community. The Ashmead, Gandy, Corson, Van Gilder, Holmes, Shoemaker, and Steelman families ran country stores in the upper portions of the county. Members of these families served on the county board of freeholders and held other local political offices.[25]

The country store spawned an economic subgroup of female merchants in Cape May County before the Civil War. The wives and daughters of country store owners opened millinery shops, sometimes as part of the main store, but many managed their own hat, sewing, and clothing stores. Martha Gandy, Angelina Corson, and Melison Corson operated two stores in the Seaville area. Caroline Hand and Jane Hildreth ran millineries at Court House. Sallie Woolson opened a shop at Fishing Creek, and Lydia Foster managed a country store in Dennisville. Most made their own business trips to Philadelphia to purchase merchandise. Mary C. Price, a Cold Spring milliner, announced that she had "just returned from Philadelphia and calls the attention of the Ladies and friends in general to her new and fashionable assortment of Millinery Goods."[26]

The meetinghouse or church rivaled the country store as the most important local institution on the Jersey Cape before the Civil War. The Cape May County community church organization served a vital social, cultural, and moral role. It sponsored Harvest Home festivals, fairs, and picnic excursions to the wild oceanfront barrier islands along the Atlantic coast of the Cape May peninsula. Churches held quilting sessions, music education and Bible study classes, and public meetings of all kinds. Sunday school played a significant part in the education of Cape May County children. Residents traveled miles every Sabbath morning and again in the evening to worship in their local church building or to attend a church-related social event. During the late 1830s, Elizabeth Woolson walked three miles from Fishing Creek to Tabernacle Church to attend the Reverend Parsons Townsend's bible study class. Recompence Hand and Nancy Schenk Hand trudged on foot over muddy lanes and crossed swollen creeks, pushing their youngest children in a wheelbarrow each Sunday as they went from Cape Island to Cold Spring to attend Presbyterian service in the Brick Church.[27]

The spread of Methodism through Cape May County led to the construction of eleven church buildings before the Civil War, more than twice the number of Baptist meetinghouses. Cape May County Presbyterians had only two churches, including the Cold Spring brick building constructed in 1823. The Catholics erected a small wooden church on Cape Island in 1848. Methodism dominated the county. Circuit riders introduced John Wesley's Methodist doctrine to the Goff family in West Creek during the 1770s, and apparently the Goffs brought Methodism to Dennis Creek by the turn of the century. James Ludlam and others incorporated the Methodist Episcopal Meeting House of Dennis Creek in July 1802. Cape Island and Fishing Creek held Methodist prayer meetings by 1810, and the Methodists incorporated the Tabernacle Church in 1823 near present-day Erma in Lower Township. Three years later, Charlotte Weatherby, Charlotte Swain, Judith Ludlam, and Rebecca Douglass formed a prayer group that led to establishment in 1829 of the Ebenezer Methodist Church at Court House. Other Methodist Episcopal churches were organized in rapid succession, including churches in Tuckahoe (1829), Petersburg (1831), Beesley's Point (1836), Goshen (1839), Cape Island (1843), Green Creek (1850), and Seaville (1856). African-American Methodist Episcopal leaders organized the Mt. Zion Methodist Church near Cold Spring in 1848, and another east of Goshen (present-day Swainton) sometime between 1832 and 1852.[28]

The common school joined the country store and church as basic institutions in the nineteenth-century Cape May County community. Before the New Jersey common school law of 1829, county schools operated through private subscription. Community members incorporated and built twenty-seven small school buildings (probably one-room structures), paid tuition for their children, hired teachers, and cut cordwood for the iron stoves that kept the schoolroom warm during winter months. Three-member township school committees administered education at the local level between 1829 and the passage of a New Jersey District School Law in 1851. Under the district law, Maurice Beesley, Jonathan F. Leaming, Moses Williamson, and other community educators replaced the township committees as district superintendents. This reform had little impact on the county educational system before the Civil War. The two thousand students continued to walk long distances to their widely dispersed community schools, where they sat all day on hard benches in one room that contained the first through the eighth grades. Most early-nineteenth-century school buildings undoubtedly resembled the tiny Friendship School, built in 1831, and restored by the Historical Preservation Society of Upper Township in 1983 along U.S. Route 9 in Palermo.[29]

The schooling of Reuben Willets was typical of Cape May County education during the mid-nineteenth century. Willets walked two miles to his schoolhouse but attended irregularly during harvest and planting times. He learned to read and write, and "ciphered some" under "Lack," a strict old schoolmaster whose beard reeked of tobacco juice. Such schoolmasters enforced order with a hickory rod and, in one case, poured ice water on the students to maintain quiet in the classroom. Willets differed from most Cape May County common school students, though. He went on to Burnell's Academy in Port Elizabeth (Cumberland County) and to the Jefferson Medical College in Philadelphia. Roughly 10 percent of Cape May County's students attended higher schools in other counties. Cape May County had no higher academy (high school) until the late 1830s or early 1840s, when the Reverend Moses Williamson opened the Cold Spring Academy, just south of the Presbyterian Brick Church and parsonage. Only the sons and daughters of more prominent and wealthy county families attended Williamson's academy.[30]

Cape May County's clusters of houses, stores, churches, and little schoolhouses extended along both sides of the bayshore and seashore roads up and down the peninsula. They differed slightly in layout from the original settlement pattern. The cluster was more concentrated in Dennisville, but there still was no town square, village green, or regular street plat. Cape Island, incorporated as a borough in 1848 and as a city in 1851, stood out as the single area of socioeconomic change. This small resort city held the only sizable percentage of foreign-born residents (Irish-American and German-American) in the county. Over 6 percent of the city's population had been born outside the United States, compared to 1.5 percent in the rest of the county. The City of Cape Island had a higher percentage of African-Americans in 1860 than the rest of the county, over 8 percent compared to 3.83 percent. The people in the city of Cape Island held a more complex set of occupations than the farming and fishing livelihoods pursued by those in the rest of the county. The community at the southernmost tip of the peninsula housed tinsmiths, horticulturists, plasterers, carpenters, hack drivers, and fishing-boat captains. The city had gamblers, drug store operators, and journalists who worked for the county's only newspaper. Fifteen tailors resided on Cape Island in 1860, compared to one at Cape May Court House and two in Dennisville.[31]

The City of Cape Island experienced remarkable growth during the 1850s as the rest of the county struggled through a cycle of economic depression. John West, a British immigrant, and a syndicate of Philadelphia and southern New Jersey investors incorporated the Mount Vernon Hotel Company in February 1852 and built one of the largest hotels in the world along the southwestern beachfront of the city. The partly completed Mount Vernon accommodated nearly three thousand guests by 1854 in rooms served by hot- and cold-water faucets and gaslights. Ayers Tompkins, a wealthy Philadelphian, built the United States Hotel, and Lilburn Harwood, a veteran Cape Island hotel manager, constructed the Columbia House, importing the first professional architect to design interior space in any Cape Island hotel. Jonas Miller turned the management of Congress Hall over to Waters B. Miller, his son, and subdivided his Cape Island properties into cottage sites for Baltimore, Philadelphia, and New Jersey gentry vacationers. Before a devastating fire completely destroyed the Mount Vernon Hotel in 1856, the City of Cape Island contained twenty-four hotels that entertained several U.S. presidents, senators, and other prominent personages.[32]

Cape Island assumed some characteristics of a modern mid-nineteenth-century American city with a gasworks, gas street lighting, and a telegraph. Between July and September regular steamboat service tied the resort town to New York City and Philadelphia. Visitors embarked on a bayside steamboat landing near the current site of the concrete shipwreck off Cape May Point. Passengers stopped first at Sarah Little's Ice Cream Saloon, which served confections made at the People's Manufactory in Cape Island City, or went across the way for liquor and cigars at John C. Little's Oscar House. Summer resort guests then took wagons and carriages, driven by Cape May County farmers and African-American teamsters, along a shell-covered Cape Island Turnpike (now Sunset Boulevard) to the hotels in the city two and a half miles to the east.[33]

The City of Cape Island introduced the first county newspaper between 1854 and 1855 under the editorship of Joseph Smallidge Leach, a schoolteacher who had moved to the peninsula from Massachusetts in 1840. Leach called the original editions of his newspaper the *Cape May County Ocean Wave*, in an effort to make it more than a Cape Island edition. He sought news from the New York City and Philadelphia telegraphs and canvassed the upper regions of the county for information. Leach hired Samuel Magonagle, a veteran Philadelphia newspaperman, as writer and reporter. Leach became the county's voice for modern organizational developments such as the railroad and industrial and agricultural associations. He joined Dr. John Wiley, who had organized the Cape May County Medical Society, in the establishment of the Cape May County Republican party organization to promote Abraham Lincoln's presidential candidacy. "In all departments of society and business, concert of thought and action are necessary to improvement and prosperity," Leach wrote. "In religion, morals, politics or business," he continued, "there must be organization, in order to concert action."[34]

The organizational principles espoused by Joseph Leach and Dr. John Wiley would become a central aspect of industrial, corporate society after the Civil War. Leach had the opportunity to advance modern organizational society in Cape May County before the war: he controlled the one county newspaper; he was a leading county educator; he had helped to organize the Baptist congregation on Cape Island. Leach claimed both Mayflower and Revolutionary War ancestries, prerequisites for success in Cape May County's mid-nineteenth-century society. His organizational energies focused increasingly on national union, though, as the disintegrating conditions between North and South led in 1861 to civil war. He devoted his efforts to organizing military preparedness in the county rather than on larger social and economic reorganization. He urged an apparently reluctant Cape May County Board of Freeholders to provide money to train local volunteers. "Why should Cape May have stood in the rear," Leach asked the county government in early 1861, "when it is known that her homes are more exposed and are more liable to receive invasion than any others on the seaboard from Maine to New Jersey?"[35]

Pressed by Leach and aware of growing threats to the region from Confederate forces moving north toward Washington only one hundred miles away, Cape May County began to espouse the Union cause and support Lincoln's national government. Representatives from every township formed committees of vigilance in April 1861. The Cape Island Home Guard enrolled seventy volunteers and commenced twice-a-day drills on the hotel grounds. Joshua Townsend organized a group of volunteers in Seaville. Townships competed to stage the most elaborate patriotic ceremony. Cape Island women and Home Guard trekked by carriage to Cold Spring for a great flag raising at the schoolhouse. Reuben Foster, the area's oldest resident, raised the flag as the Reverend Moses Williamson, Joseph Leach, and Abraham Reeves, a popular former freeholder, made patriotic speeches. Not to be outdone, Dennis Township held a unionist rally at the South Dennisville schoolhouse. After rousing talks by the Reverend Jesse H. Diverty and William Ashmead, the school principal, a crowd assembled in the school yard to raise the American flag. This exercise showed their "purest" patriotism, one Dennis Creek resident wrote, and "I am happy to say, that not a single traitor can be found in Dennis Township, notwithstanding reports [that] have been circulated to the contrary."[36]

The Civil War came home to Cape May County in July 1861 when news arrived that Sgt. Richard T. Tindall, the son of Cape Island schoolteacher and Baptist minister Napoleon Tindall, had died of typhoid fever while guarding the approaches to the national capital. Tindall's death was the first of 32 suffered by Cape May County men during the next four years of war. Over 360 Cape May County volunteers fought during the Civil War. Four died on the battlefield. John Mecray and Townsend Ireland were killed in the battle for Williamsburg, Virginia, in May 1862. Albert Edmunds died during the Battle of Fredericksburg in December 1862, and Richard Townsend at the Battle of Gettysburg in July 1863. Seven other Cape May County soldiers succumbed to wounds received during these three battles. Twenty-one countians died of typhoid, measles, and other diseases contracted during the Civil War in army camps and hospitals.[37]

Cape May County volunteers fought in some of the bloodiest battles of the Civil War. J. Granville Leach, son of the *Ocean Wave* editor, led his unit against Confederate entrenchments at Fredericksburg. Andrew J. Tomlin of Goshen won a U.S. Medal of Honor for leading a company of marines in the attack on Fort Fisher. Dr. John Wiley ministered to the wounded on both sides in the middle of the Gettysburg battlefield. Henry W. Sawyer, a Cape Island carpenter and first county resident to volunteer for the New Jersey Cavalry, fell captive to Confederate forces in 1863. The Rebels imprisoned Sawyer at the notorious Libby Prison in Richmond and sentenced him to death for the earlier Union execution of two Confederate cavalry officers. Sawyer's plight momentarily unified New Jersey, which was badly divided between peace Democrats and Republican unionists.

Finally, Lincoln's threat to shoot two prominent southern captives, including Robert E. Lee's son, saved Sawyer from execution.[38]

New Jersey called upon Cape May County to help fill War Department troop quotas. The townships met their quotas of volunteers. The board of freeholders facilitated recruitment in June 1862 by authorizing a bounty. "My bounty from the County is $300," Daniel Wheaton wrote. "We get $65 now Cash," Wheaton continued, and "I am going to have 30 dollars brought to me and the rest I will leave for Father to collect at Coleman F. Leaming's, Cape May Co." Most Cape May County nine-month levies joined the Twenty-fifth Regiment, New Jersey Volunteers. Early recruiting was a wild affair in the county, with drums banging and guns firing. Mary Thompson Cresse claimed that her father was thrown from his horse onto a picket fence at Court House when Mat Hand suddenly struck a drum next to his mount. They found the horse two miles away, impaled on John Spaulding's fence in Mayville, a tiny community southeast of Court House.[39]

Gradually the drain on county manpower, combined with the knowledge that the Civil War had become a series of bloody battles of attrition, discouraged Cape May County men from volunteering for military service. "Why, one more draft of this kind will have to fall on dead men," Joseph Leach wrote, "as after that number is made up, we shall not have over 10 men left subject to military duty." The Enrollment Board in Millville rejected 80 percent of the Cape May County men in the military draft of July 1864 for physical disability, age, or commutation (paid deferment). Another sixteen Cape May County men bought substitutes to fight for them. In addition, the local Enrollment Board "rejected Gideon Holmes because he was dead." Dennis Township initiated a poll tax on every white male citizen of draft age who had not enlisted. The township committee resolved "that any man who can furnish satisfactory proof to the assessor of said township that he has furnished a substitute or paid commutation money on the last call, shall be exempt from the aforesaid poll tax of $10." Partly to meet its draft quota, Cape May County enlisted African-American residents during the summer of 1864. Charles S. Boze, Isaac Pepper, David M. Trusty, Henry Turner, Israel Cox, and others joined the Twenty-fifth Regiment, U.S. Colored Volunteers.[40]

The war made a tragic impact on Cape May County's home front. Amelia Hand of Cape May Court House recorded poignantly in her private diary on 18 December 1862 that this day "will be remembered by some of us at Cape May with sorrow." She had learned that during the last charge at the battle of Fredericksburg "among those that fell, was my dear friend & to-be husband, Edward L. Townsend." A few months later, Richard Townsend of Dennisville received a letter sent by Richard Thompson from Gettysburg with news about his son. "He was shot through the heart & died instantly," Thompson wrote, and "is buried in a garden lot at the apex of the line of battle upon which he fought with the grave properly marked."[41]

The Civil War also had an economic impact on the Jersey Cape. It raised the price of everything, Amelia Hand explained. Wool, which cost twenty-five cents a pound before the fighting, cost $1.50 per pound by 1863. The price of cotton had risen from seven cents to $1.00 a pound, coffee from twelve and one-half cents to forty-five cents, and tea from forty cents to $1.50 a pound. At the same time, the county tax for 1862 reached an unprecedented sum of $5,000 to pay interest on war bonds and bounties for volunteers. County businesses suffered as well. Before the war, Cape Island had filled with southern guests who spent nearly $50,000 a season in the Cape May County resort. Profits during the war fell to $10,000 for the summer season. One summer visitor found the largest hotel closed and others in disrepair. He walked streets and sidewalks covered with hot blowing sand and observed that the unpainted picket fences had crumbled in the blazing sun. "The lawn and big patches of open ground are filled with rank grass, weeds, and clovers—safe harbors for mosquitos, as one may easily find out who attempts to walk across one," the visitor wrote.[42]

Steamboats and schooners employed to carry summer visitors to the Jersey Cape resort, or to ship cordwood and cedar rails to Philadelphia, had been taken by the U.S. government for troop transports and blockading vessels. Albert H. Ludlam, a Dennisville mariner, told Richard Leaming that his large schooner had been damaged off Port Royal by Confederate gunboats and was now a worm-eaten and rotten hulk. Without ships to carry lumber to market, cordwood and cedar rails lay on the Dennis Creek landing. "The rails is in bad a condition when the tide is full," wrote Ephraim Sayre, Leaming's foreman at the landing, and "the water is two feet deep and all the bottoms wet and muddy."[43]

During what seemed to be these darkest days of the Civil War, an event occurred in the summer of 1863 that transformed life on the Cape May peninsula. Amelia Hand recorded the day: "We at last have a Rail Road from Cape Island to Philadelphia & August 26th the cars made a trip for the first time, the route was performed in three & a half hours, quite an improvement over our old way of going to Philadelphia which took the most part of one day," she wrote. Hand continued, "[We] have two trains per day & that brings us as near to a large city as one need wish to be." Amelia Hand took her first train ride to Philadelphia in October 1863 to visit her uncle, Alexander Whilldin. In subsequent trips the Court House woman attended concerts at the Academy of Music and visited the Central Fair to benefit the Sanitary Commission, where in June 1864 she saw President Abraham Lincoln as he visited the New Jersey horticultural exhibit. A few months later, Franklin Hand, Amelia Hand's brother, also traveled by train from Court House to see Lincoln in Philadelphia. This time, however, it was to view the president's body as it lay in state at Independence Square.[44]

News of Lincoln's assassination in April 1865 hit Cape May County particularly hard. It had been one of the few New Jersey counties to unite behind Lincoln and a moderate Union Republican political organization, and one of the only areas in the state without Democratic party opposition to Lincoln's conduct of the war. Cape May County women draped churches in mourning. Great audiences assembled on Cape Island and at Court House to show their sorrow for the fallen wartime leader. A general state of sadness set in throughout the county, Mary Thompson Cresse recalled, dampening the celebration that accompanied the end of the war. Dr. Jonathan Leaming, a popular Cape May County legislator, tried to revive the people's spirits by holding a great "Jubilee" at Court House. "He went personally over the whole county, arousing people into new life," Mary Cresse explained.[45]

Arrival of the railroad in the county in 1863 and the end of Civil War eventually introduced that new life promised by Jonathan Leaming. First, however, Cape May County had to pass through a postwar period known on the national level as the Era of Reconstruction, 1865–1877. Radical Republicans in the U.S. Congress struggled with Andrew Johnson, the new president, for control over postwar policy to reconstruct the defeated South. A Tennessee Democrat selected in 1864 to balance Lincoln's presidential ticket, Johnson followed what he believed had been Lincoln's plan to let secessionist states back into the Union with an oath of allegiance and little federal intervention to ensure the constitutional rights of the freedmen. The

Radical Republicans advocated a harsher reconstruction policy that divided the South into military districts, protected the civil and voting rights of the freed African-Americans, and advanced economic and educational opportunities under a federally funded Freedman's Bureau. The bitter struggle over Reconstruction between the executive and legislative branches led to Johnson's impeachment.

Reconstruction politics reverberated all the way to Cape May County. The Cape May County Republican party supported Congressional Reconstruction. The county's Union Republican Convention passed a resolution introduced by Wilmon W. Ware of Cape Island on 27 October 1866 that condemned President Andrew Johnson for "harmonizing with traitors." Cape May County Republicans organized in preparation for upcoming elections into five-member committees for each township. Cape May County physicians, in the tradition of Dr. John Wiley, founder of the county's Republican party, dominated political organization. Drs. Alexander Young, Maurice Beesley, James Kennedy, Jonathan Leaming, Coleman F. Leaming, and Wiley headed their respective local Republican party organizations.[46]

The excitement surrounding the presidential election campaign of 1868 demonstrated the dynamic role that national politics played in Cape May County during Reconstruction. "A month before the election the excitement was intense," Amelia Hand observed, "every night the Grant & Colfax Club of C.M.C.H. [Cape May Court House] was out going to different neighborhoods in two & four horse wagons to stir up the people with their band of music, several very pretty transparencies & their torches." F. Sidney Townsend of Seaville attended a huge political rally with "both Republicans & Demmy's" on 26 October 1868 and four days later watched the largest political "Grand Mass Meeting at Court House" ever held in Cape May County. Republican party candidates—U. S. Grant for president and Thomas Beesley for the state assembly—swept to victory in the county, although New Jersey overall went to the Democrats in the 1868 election.[47]

The Cape May County Democratic party organization challenged the entrenched local Republican party during Reconstruction. Christopher S. Magrath, the abrasive owner of the *Ocean Wave*, became local party leader and spokesman. Magrath attacked the Republican-dominated Cape May County board of freeholders, claiming that it "plundered the county." Magrath was upset that the Board of Freeholders had appointed William Seigman, editor of the *Star of the Cape*, the county's second newspaper, organized in 1868, as the new clerk of the board. Magrath had coveted the job, and he launched into a vituperative newspaper campaign against the board of freeholders when they selected Seigman. On his part, Seigman defended the county governors and the Republican party. He condemned Magrath as a "miserable creature" for his "mean and contemptible attack on the Board of Freeholders of Cape May County." The bitter newspaper controversy finally led to a movement to curb the traditional practice of distributing county work to members of the board of freeholders. The county board resolved in September of 1874 that for "members to furnish their own labor, teams and material is improper and should be abolished in the future."[48]

The uncharacteristic intensity and prominence of politics in Cape May County during the immediate post–Civil War era reflected the changing nature of the community. The railroad opened the peninsula to outside influences. Shortly after the first train had passed through the county, a visitor observed how the railroad had altered the local population. "The new people are those who have made money, either directly or indirectly, through this war," he explained. "The gun contractor, the harnessmaker, the clothing contractor, the groceryman, the officers and their wives, and also the borer, the second man, the middle man," the visitor continued, "all combine to make up the class now flourishing at Cape May."[49]

The Cape May and Millville Railroad spawned new communities along the station stops. The first stop, at Belle Plain (later Belleplain), actually lay just across the county line in Cumberland County until boundary revision in 1891 placed the town in Cape May County. Jeremiah F. van Rensselaer, the railroad's general superintendent, named the station in honor of Annabelle W. Townsend, daughter of William S. Townsend, a prominent Dennis Township landowner, lumber merchant, and railroad stockholder. Belle Plain served the extreme western region of Cape May County as a rail terminal for the shipment of lumber and farm products. Daniel Goff traveled north from West Creek to hold Methodist services in the new station town in 1863. Belle Plain remained a tiny cluster of houses with a brickyard and lumberyard until the late nineteenth century, when dozens of Italian-American families began to settle and farm the region.[50]

Just to the east of Belle Plain, in Cape May County, Jeremiah van Rensselaer and William S. Townsend laid out streets and buildings lots in 1863 on either side of the tracks and the station stop that they called Woodbine, after the wildflowers that grew in the region. They advertised Woodbine as the ideal location to settle, "lying between Tuckahoe on the North-east and Dennisville on the South-west" with "soil, sandy loam, very fertile, with abundance of excellent water." Woodbine attracted few buyers. By 1872 only the Champion and Holmes families had built structures in Woodbine. Nathaniel Holmes operated a dry goods, grocery, and lumber business next to the railroad tracks. Not until establishment of a Jewish-American agricultural and industrial community at Woodbine in 1891 would this wilderness railroad stop grow into a large town.[51]

Mt. Pleasant was the next stop on the Cape May and Millville Railroad in 1863. The origins and naming of this site are obscure. As the highest spot in the Great Cedar Swamp, it had served as part of the old Cape Road since the early eighteenth century, and probably as the site of a tavern or inn and several houses. Perhaps the inn was called Mt. Pleasant. More likely, the name came from the original whaler yeomen in the region who had migrated from the Monmouth tract in East Jersey, where one of their communities had been called Mt. Pleasant. Likewise, a cluster of houses directly northeast of Mt. Pleasant in the Cedar Swamp was known originally as Littleworth (now Petersburg), a name probably brought by the whaler yeomen from Long Island, where there was a community with the same name.

The railroad at Mt. Pleasant began to curve into a great arc on its way down the peninsula toward Cape Island. Just before the rail line emerged from the curve it passed near a cluster of old settlements—including Gracetown, Cressetown, and Cedar Grove—and stopped at a train station designated in 1863 as South Seaville. Already a crossroads community, where the old Cape Road intersected roads to Dennisville, Seaville, Beesley's Point, and Petersburg, South Seaville became one of the most important stops on the railroad. The railroad stimulated remarkable growth, including the establishment in about 1863 of the Seaville Methodist camp meeting grounds, a fairground, and racetrack. Oystermen and clammers from Townsend's Inlet shipped their harvest to Philadelphia from the South Seaville station. The Van Gilder Cannery on Magnolia Lake in Ocean View brought tomatoes for shipment by rail to market. The community expanded so rapidly that South Seaville residents agitated to move the county government to their railroad town, and according to tradition so angered the residents of Court House that they took away the fairgrounds and racetrack by establishing a county racetrack and fairgrounds on the seashore road just above Court House.[52]

The settlements along the Cape May and Millville Railroad developed during the period of greatest growth in population in Cape May County's history. More newcomers entered the Jersey Cape between 1865 and 1870 than during any previous decade. By contrast with the preceding five-year period, when the county increased by only 123 people and Middle and Lower townships actually experienced a decline in population, Cape May County grew by 1,090 residents between 1865 and 1870. African-Americans, including freed slaves from Maryland and Virginia, made up the largest single group of immigrants to enter the lower half of the county during this postwar period. German-Americans settled in the county as well; most of them were born in the German states of Bavaria, Hanover, Württemburg, and Saxony. Some migrated first to Pennsylvania, moved to Atlantic County, and then relocated in Cape May County. German-American families became farmers, cabinetmakers, bakers, and innkeepers in Court House, Cold Spring, and the City of Cape Island. The Caramille Mirabella family immigrated from Naples, Italy, and probably became the first Italian-American family to settle on the peninsula, operating a small inn on Cape Island before 1870.[53]

The promise of jobs on the Jersey Cape attracted these newcomers. Entrepreneurs expected a postwar resort business and real estate boom in Cape May County. A syndicate of speculators formed the Burlington, Atlantic, Cape May and Philadelphia Glass Manufacturing Company on 1 July 1865 to exploit the predicted postwar economic opportunities on the peninsula. The company planned to manufacture glassware and boots; operate hotels, boardinghouses, and sawmills; and build ships on the Jersey Cape. John Dougherty, a Lower Township merchant, was the only local stockholder in this highly speculative enterprise. Similar schemes abounded in the immediate post–Civil War era. A West Creek speculator, the *Star of the Cape* reported, "contemplates erecting a factory to utilize the mosquito the coming season by converting them into an article of food; and also that same party intends manufacturing genuine imported Japanese wash basins from the shell of the king crab."[54]

Land development offered safer investment. Waters B. Miller, the wealthiest man in Cape May County at the end of the Civil War, and Return B. Swain, a Cape Island surveyor and real estate developer, laid out streets along the Cape May and Millville Railroad from Court House to the southeast as far as Mayville. Miller and Swain advertised a "Great Sale of Truck Farms and Town Lots" in 1865, assuring prospective buyers that "the atmosphere is dry, sufficiently near the ocean for the benefit of the sea air, and is free from the dampness and mildew of clothing, which occurs at Atlantic City and Cape Island." Miller organized the Cape May Provision Company to can fruits and vegetables, and a clam- and fish-canning factory at the Shellbed Landing on Jenkins Sound, both to provide employment for new property owners.[55]

Shipbuilding provided the largest employment in Cape May County during the immediate post–Civil War era. Federal government demands for ships during the war had stimulated local construction, and Cape May County yards launched sixteen vessels between 1861 and 1865. The shipbuilding boom continued during the Reconstruction Era. Local yards launched thirty vessels between 1866 and 1870, nearly as many as those built during the entire first half of the nineteenth century. Cape May County shipbuilders constructed another fifty-one vessels between 1870 and 1879, making the 1870s the most productive decade in the county's shipbuilding history. The Garrison and Harker shipyard on Goshen Creek, Richard S. Leaming and Jesse H. Diverty yards on Dennis Creek, and Jonas Steelman shipyard at Tuckahoe produced the largest ships. Sixty percent of the vessels built on the Jersey Cape during the 1870s were three-masted schooners of 200 to 300 tons. The *Mair and Cranmer*, launched sideways into Goshen Creek at high tide from the Garrison and Harker yard in 1871, was typical of the larger schooners built on the Jersey Cape during this era. A three-masted schooner with a raised poop deck, the *Mair and Cranmer*, displaced 230 tons and was 115 feet long. She was owned by thirty-two shareholders and carried coal to New England, returning with cargoes of ice during the winter months and carrying pinewood, fish, and coal between North Carolina and Philadelphia during the summer.[56]

Dennis Creek shipyards constructed several schooners well over 400 tons during the 1870s. In March 1877 the Richard S. Leaming yard launched the *William E. Lee*, an 800-ton oceangoing schooner built by George S. Wentzel, master shipbuilder. The hull was towed to Philadelphia, were it was fitted out with sails and rigging. Tuckahoe builders steadily increased the size of their vessels until in 1874 Lewis Williams, Upper Township freeholder, called for the county to widen the Tuckahoe drawbridge because "vessels being built at the ship yards on Tuckahoe River at Tuckahoe are of such size as to make it difficult for their egress through the draw of the Tuckahoe Bridge without inflicting injury."[57]

Other Cape May County industries experienced a postwar expansion. Thomas Beesley's cancerine in Goshen ground bayside king (or horseshoe) crabs into fertilizer, doubling production during the war. The crab-grinding business increased in value from $2,000 in 1865 to $12,500 by 1870. Vincent Miller opened another cancerine in Dennis Township. The shingle-mining business expanded as well. Dennisville "shingle getters" dammed up Robbins Swamp along Dennis Creek to gain access to the huge buried cedar logs. This business attracted Civil War veteran Charles Pitman Robart, who after starting an unsuccessful postwar grain business turned to shingle mining. Skilled shingle getters extracted cedar logs from the swamps with long poles known as progues, split the cut sections with a tool called the froe, and sliced and shaved them into shingles. Robart routinely shaved 500 shingles in one day and contracted with Philadelphia to deliver 25,000 shingles for the roof of Independence Hall. The cedar shingle business became an integral part of Cape May County's postwar commerce. Coleman F. Leaming delivered 20,000 cedar shingles to Camden City in one shipment in 1865.[58]

Cape Island City's recovery as a summer resort contributed to the postwar business revival in Cape May County. Vacationers began returning to the resort during the closing days of the Civil War. Hotel owners refurbished their dilapidated buildings and, as one noted, "in two years the influx of visitors will compel the building of new hotels." A New York newspaperman who stayed on Cape Island in 1865 predicted that, with the railroad connections to northern New Jersey and New York City, more New Yorkers would come to the southern New Jersey shore resort for summer bathing. Some Cape May County businessmen expected the southerners to return to Cape Island as well.[59]

Philadelphia and South Jersey investors connected with the West Jersey Railroad, which took over operation of the Cape May and Millville Railroad line in 1868, developed the City of Cape Island, incorporated as Cape May City in 1869. John C. Bullitt, a Philadelphia corporate lawyer and railroad counsel, and William J. Sewell, Civil War veteran and director of the West Jersey Railroad, filled in the marshland east of the city and built the Stockton Hotel in 1868. Sewell purchased Poverty Beach (site of the U.S. Coast Guard station, today) and opened a horse trolley line in 1868 across the beach to Cold Spring Inlet, where he built the Fish House restaurant on Sewell's Point. Bullitt, Sewell, and Joseph Q. Williams, a Cape Island carpenter and later mayor, controlled city government through a state-legislated commission. The commission allowed the West Jersey Railroad syndicate to secure a traction monopoly on Cape Island for the Cape May City Passenger Railway Company.[60]

Cape Island maintained twenty-two hotels in 1866, including an African-American establishment on Lafayette Street. Jacob F. Cake, a veteran Washington hotelier, arrived to manage the Columbia House and then became the proprietor of Congress Hall. Henry Sawyer, the Civil War hero who had barely escaped execution in Libby Prison, took over the Ocean House in 1867 and then in 1875 opened the Chalfonte Hotel. William Sewell, Richard D. Wood, John Wanamaker, E. C. Knight, and other wealthy Philadelphia and southern New Jersey industrialists and merchants purchased land and cottages in and around the City of Cape Island in the years after the Civil War. They organized a yacht club in 1871, and encouraged President U. S. Grant to take up permanent summer residence at the Cape May County resort. Grant visited Cape Island in 1874, but decided instead to spend his vacations at Long Branch on the northern New Jersey seashore.[61]

The introduction of baseball to the City of Cape Island during the summer of 1865 symbolized the postwar recovery and expectations of the beach resort community. Founded in 1845 by Alexander Joy Cartwright, the modern game of baseball had received a boost during the Civil War as New Jersey and New York soldiers spread the game to both sides during lulls in the fighting. It had become "a national amusement," Samuel Magonagle, editor of the *Ocean Wave*, explained in July 1865. It seemed appropriate that the national game should arrive on Cape Island as it reemerged from the war as a national watering place and vacation resort. Cape May County's first recorded baseball game was played on the lawn of Congress Hall between a team of Philadelphia and Camden players staying at Congress Hall and nine gentlemen vacationing in Columbia House. "The tour of the victorious Athletics of Philadelphia," Magonagle boasted, "witnessed no better batting and fielding than that displayed yesterday."[62]

Baseball spread throughout Cape May County during the follow-ing summer of 1866, until Samuel Magonagle reported that county youth "have baseball on the brain pretty bad." Cape Island leaders expected baseball to boost summer business in the resort, and they organized the Cape Island Base Ball Club. Cape May County business gentry in the mold of Alexander Cartwright and the New York City gentlemen who first played the game in 1845 at Hoboken, New Jersey, organized the Cape Island club. James Mecray, a local physician, served as baseball club president. Other officers included Walter A. Barrows, an attorney, William F. Cassidy, a local builder and businessman, and Christopher Magrath, a Cape Island newspaper owner. The club successfully promoted baseball as a leading summer attraction for the City of Cape Island.[63]

Cape Island entrepreneurs promoted horse racing to revive resort business at the close of the Civil War. In 1866, Joseph Heis, a hotel and stable owner, selected a racetrack site between Town Bank and Cox Hall Creek along what was then called Diamond Beach (not to be confused with present-day Diamond Beach farther south toward Cape May Point). Diamond Beach had been named for the small shiny stones that washed up on the bayshore beaches and were taken to Cape Island for polishing and cutting so that they resembled tiny diamonds. Diamond Beach had attracted summer visitors since the 1840s and contained a hotel and several cottages. The Diamond Beach Park and Hotel Association purchased this property in 1867 and constructed a mile-oval racetrack and a clubhouse. John West and Aaron Miller, owners of the United States Hotel in the City of Cape Island, managed the track and clubhouse when the first sulky races were held during the late summer of 1867. Charles A. Rubicam purchased the property the next year and planned to further expand the race track. Rubicam lost all his cash in a Cape Island hotel fire in 1869, however, and abandoned the racetrack project.[64]

Cape May County society experienced an increase in disorder and violence during the Reconstruction Era. The first death from the Cape May and Millville Railroad symbolized the quickening pace of postwar life on the peninsula. Edmund S. Smith fell between two railroad gravel cars at the South Seaville station in November 1865 and was crushed. Vandalism also plagued the county. The destruction of property in 1867 prompted the board of freeholders to offer a fifty-dollar reward for the apprehension and conviction of anyone found guilty of "defacing Bridges, mile posts, finger boards," and other county property.[65]

Arson caused the most damage to postwar Cape May County property. Arsonists became so bold that William L. Cummings, a Lower Township freeholder, introduced a resolution to hire Pinkerton detectives "to ferret out the offenders." Alexander Corson of Upper Township blocked the use of county monies to fight arson, insisting that it was only a problem in Lower Township. The worst cases of arson centered in Cape May City, which had three suspicious fires between 1869 and 1878. The fire of 1869 devastated one of the oldest sections, along Jackson and Ocean streets. Another fire, which gutted Benezet and Brothers store on Jackson Street in 1876, was the "work of an incendiary," the *Star of the Cape* reported. The most destructive fire in Cape May County history burned thirty-five acres of Cape May City on 9 November 1878. This wind-driven conflagration destroyed nine large hotels, including the historic Atlantic Hotel, Congress Hall, Columbia House, Centre House, and the Ocean House, where the fire apparently had started. Fire apparatus shipped by rail from Camden City and Millville arrived too late to save any of these hotels.[66]

The fire of 1878 coincided with and probably contributed to the steady economic decline of Cape May City as a major resort during the 1870s. The *Star of the Cape* reported that many "idle men" roamed the city, unable to find employment. In response, W. B. Miller, a former mayor and large hotel owner, called a citizen's meeting to discuss the resort's decline, particularly in comparison to the continued prosperity of Atlantic City. The citizen's meeting blamed local government for levying high taxes and refusing to grant liquor licenses to hoteliers such as W. B. Miller. The citizen's group also faulted the West Jersey Railroad for not granting free passes, similar to those given out by the Atlantic City Railroad, to Cape May County businessmen or low excursion rates for summer visitors. Wilmon W. Ware, a city councilman, argued that the resort's economic problems lay in the continuing national financial depression caused in 1873 by the collapse of the Credit Mobilier company and other overspeculation. "The depression in business had arisen not alone from local causes," Ware explained, "but from a depression in business and general 'hard times' [that] prevails all over the country."[67]

Dr. Palmer Way of South Seaville agreed that larger national financial policies had created the economic crisis in Cape May County during the 1870s. Way organized a Greenback Club in 1878 as part of the nationwide Greenback Labor party movement of workers and farmers. Way and Captains Thomas Townsend and Thompson Van Gilder represented Cape May County Greenbackers at a state convention held in Vineland, Cumberland County, to press for government issuance of treasury notes to pay the national debt, equal taxation of all property, a graduated income tax, and the abolition of national banks. Opposition to the Greenback movement in Cape May County was led by William Seigman, editor of the *Star of the Cape*, who attacked the Greenbackers for their inflationary and destructive economic schemes.[68]

Economic depression added to unrest and violence that plagued the entire post–Civil War society in the Delaware Valley. Eight murders occurred in the city of Philadelphia in April 1866 alone. A crime spree in nearby Milton, Delaware, led to the reinstitution of the public pillory and floggings in 1873. Cape May County recorded at least three murders between 1871 and 1875, including that of Jonathan Hoffman of Lower Township. In May 1873 an assassin shot at Dr. Alexander Young, the director of the Cape May County Board of Freeholders, as he traveled home to Goshen after a meeting at Court House. The pistol ball passed through the curtains of his carriage, narrowly missing Young. The stunned board of freeholders offered a five-hundred-dollar reward for the capture of Young's attacker.[69]

Criminals filled Cape May County's tiny jailhouse, located next to the courthouse building. Five prisoners broke out of the jail in April 1871 by burrowing into the dirt floor and under the decrepit wall. The board of freeholders fired the "underkeepers" of the county jail, and in June 1871 ordered the installation of an iron jailhouse floor. Overburdened county officials met with representatives of other South Jersey counties in late 1873 to discuss the need for a regional house of correction.[70]

Cape May County's gentry leaders formed new organizations to restore order to their rapidly changing postwar community. They turned—as did many post–Civil War American communities—to educational institutions such as the high school as an instrument with which to rebuild community stability by replacing the old apprentice work-school system with high school and vocational training. Jesse H. Diverty and twenty-four other county gentry leaders incorporated the Cape May Academical Institute for this purpose in April 1865. This probably opened as the Mayville Academic Institute in 1868. County leaders somewhat reluctantly endorsed Dr. Maurice Beesley, a noted scholar and physician, as the first county superintendent of public schools appointed by the New Jersey Board of Public Instruction. The opposition to Beesley's appointment that appeared from five of the eight members of the board of freeholders arose from traditional county suspicion of outside interference in local affairs and from the fear that the new system placed an additional tax burden on the economically depressed county. The board of freeholders eventually endorsed Beesley as the county school superintendent, and he worked to bring unity and order to the sometime chaotic county school system. "Scholars will not have knives or sticks or any other unnecessary or dangerous articles about," declared the new school rules.[71]

Temperance organization became another county response to post–Civil War disorder. Antiliquor temperance had been part of a reform movement that included abolitionism and had swept the Northeast before the Civil War. Cape May County had embraced temperance while rejecting abolitionism. Jesse H. Diverty of Dennisville and James L. Smith of West Creek were elected during the late 1840s and 1850s from the county to the New Jersey legislature on the temperance issue. After the war, Diverty, Socrates Townsend, Dr. Jonathan Leaming, and Samuel Magonagle organized the Cape May County Temperance Association. The association held meetings in 1866 at the Methodist Episcopal churches in Dennisville and Court House. County temperance leaders pledged to assist the Reverend Simon Lake of Atlantic County and the Grand Division of the Sons of Temperance in their crusade throughout New Jersey to ban the sale of liquor.[72]

Temperance organization contributed to the founding in 1875 of Sea Grove (now Cape May Point), Cape May County's third-oldest resort community after Cape Island and Beesley's Point. Alexander Whilldin, a Philadelphia cotton merchant and Presbyterian leader, transferred 266 acres of Stite's Beach on Cape May Point that he had inherited through marriage to the Sea Grove Association for five dollars in 1875. The association included religious leaders, businessmen, and real estate speculators such as Philadelphia merchant storeowner John Wanamaker, William Sewell, Thomas Beesley, Downs Edmunds, and Franklin Hand, Whilldin's brother-in-law. The Sea Grove Association drew up rules for the "systematic and businesslike conduct of affairs" that included a complete ban on all liquor and amusements. Whilldin organized the Union Hall Association to build hotels and houses, and the Sea Grove Association hired James C. Sidney, a Philadelphia architect, to design an octagonal pavilion at the center of the planned community with streets radiating out from the pavilion. William Sewell chartered a special excursion train for Presbyterians to inspect the Sea Grove site and incorporated the Cape May City Passenger Railway to connect the resort to the West Jersey Railroad depot in Cape May City.[73]

The temperance connection also became a central aspect of early interest in the development of the Cape May County barrier islands. Toward the close of the 1870s, Simon Lake and other prominent southern New Jersey and Philadelphia temperance leaders and clergymen began to consider Peck's Beach, the county's northernmost barrier island, as a potential site for a great oceanfront temperance resort city. They examined ancient land titles and began to survey the vast white beach as the first steps in what became a new era for Cape May County—the development between 1879 and 1899 of the Atlantic Ocean barrier islands.

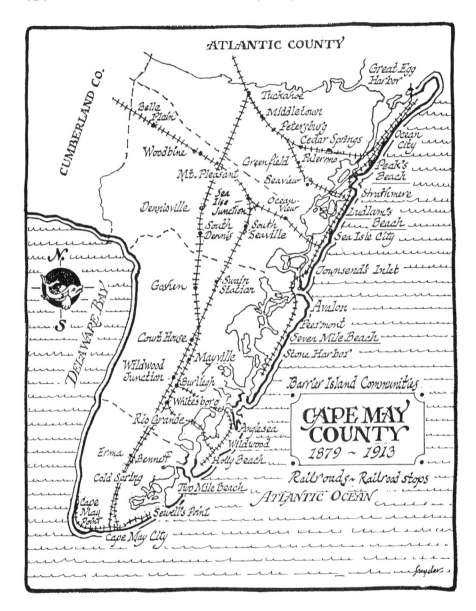

ATLANTIC COUNTY

CUMBERLAND CO.

Great Egg Harbor

Tuckahoe
Belle Plain
Middletown
Petersburg
Cedar Springs
Woodbine
Palermo
Greenfield
Mt. Pleasant
Seaview
Dennisville
Sea Isle Junction
Ocean View
South Dennis
South Seaville

Ocean City
Peak's Beach
Strathmere
Ludlam's Beach
Sea Isle City

N.
S

DELAWARE BAY

Goshen
Swain Station

Court House

Townsend's Inlet

Avalon
Peer'mont
Seven Mile Beach
Stone Harbor

Wildwood Junction
Mayville
Burleigh
Whitesbor'o
Rio Grande

Barrier Island Communities

CAPE MAY COUNTY
1879 ~ 1913

Erma
Bennett
Cold Spring
Anglesea
Wildwood
Holly Beach
Two Mile Beach

Railroads ~ Railroad stops

Cape May Point
Sewell's Point

ATLANTIC OCEAN

Cape May City

Snyder

1. Seventeenth-century whaler yeomen recorded their property in the Cape May County Cattle Earmark Book. Photographs of brands from the Cape May County Clerk's Archives.

2. The Cold Spring Presbyterian Church, known as the Old Brick Church, built in 1823 and a center of nineteenth-century Lower Township life. Photograph from the Cape May County Historical Museum.

3. Ishmael Armour and wife. Armour had been a Cape May County African-American slave and was manumitted by his master in 1826. Photograph from the Cape May County Historical Museum.

4. The old jailhouse, sheriff's office, county office building, and courthouse built in Cape May Court House in 1850 and still standing, shown here c. 1900. The original courthouse was erected in 1765 when the town became the center of county government. Photograph from the Cape May County Historical Museum.

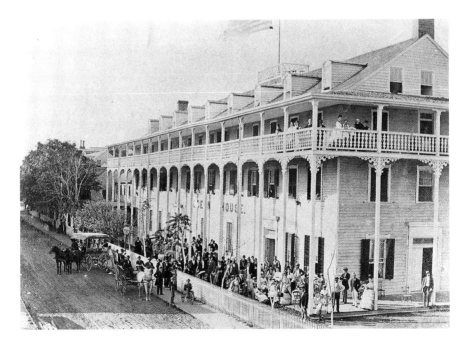

5. The Ocean House hotel in Cape May City, origin of the fire that burned down most of the resort in 1878. Photograph from the Cape May Historical Museum.

6. The Gatzmer House in Dennisville, built by Mackey Williams in 1871, served as the shipbuilding town's major hotel in the 1870s and 1880s. Photograph from the Cape May Historical Museum.

7. A rare photograph of a nineteenth-century Cape May County windmill along the shore road in Ocean View. Photograph from the Cape May Historical Museum.

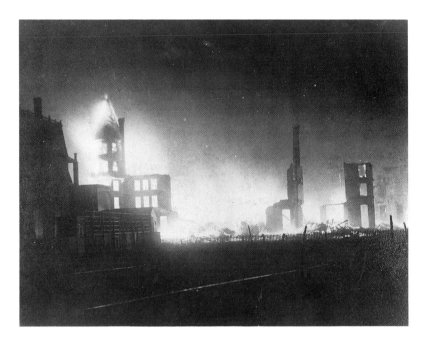

8. Cape May City never entirely recovered from the fire of 1878 that burned the entire downtown beachfront hotel district between Congress and Gurney streets. Photograph from the Cape May Historical Museum.

9. The main Shore Road (Route 9) looking south toward Calvary Baptist Church, c. 1880. Photograph from the Cape May Historical Museum.

10. The great oak tree at Green Creek on the Bayshore Road, where Woodrow Wilson reportedly gave a campaign speech. Photograph from the Cape May Historical Museum.

11. The Goshen Road from Cape May Court House, probably near the spot where an assassin shot at Freeholder Director Dr. Alexander Young in 1873. Photograph from the Cape May Historical Museum.

12. Large schooner under construction on the Goshen Creek sometime between 1870 and 1890. Photograph from the Cape May Historical Museum.

13. A three-masted oceangoing schooner would be launched sideways into the creek (either Dennis or Goshen). Photograph from the Cape May Historical Museum.

14. The Cape May City iron pier and broadwalk built in 1885. Photograph from the Cape May Historical Museum.

15. The Rio Grande sugar factory was built in 1881. By 1889, when this picture was taken, the building was used as a cannery. Photograph from the Cape May Historical Museum.

16. The Anglesea (North Wildwood) Life Saving Station. Photograph from the Cape May Historical Museum.

17. North Wildwood's cottages and electric railway were typical of turn-of-the-century barrier island settlements. Photographs from the Cape May Historical Museum.

18. The interior of the Brotherhood Synagogue in Woodbine, constructed in 1894. Photograph from the Cape May Historical Museum.

19. Woodbine's factory workers, Russian visitor Korolenko reported in 1894, lived in frame houses along sandy streets of this "Jewish city." Photograph from the Cape May Historical Museum.

20. The Cape May Hotel (now the Christian Admiral), built along the Cape May City beachfront by Peter Shields in 1908 and used during both world wars as a military facility. Photograph from the Cape May Historical Museum.

21. Wildwood's railroad station for the West Jersey and Seashore Line, c. 1910. Photograph from the collection of the Wildwood Historical Society.

22. Katharine Baker of Wildwood, an educational reformer, suffragette, Progressive Era essayist, and decorated World War I Red Cross nurse. Photograph from the collection of the Wildwood Historical Society.

23. U.S. Navy Section Base Nine, Cape May City, seen at the end of World War I. Photograph from the Cape May Historical Museum.

24. A violent storm and flood tide in 1920 destroyed Cape May City's waterfront, boardwalk, and street railroad. The old Convention Hall, built in 1917, can be seen on the left. Photograph from the Cape May Historical Museum.

25. The all-male lifeguards of the Ocean City Beach Patrol during the 1920s. Photograph from the Cape May Historical Museum.

26. The automobile brought large resort crowds to Ocean City during the 1920s. Photograph from the Cape May Historical Museum.

27. Plans to use the concrete ship *Atlantus* as part of a dock for a proposed Cape May-Lewes ferry fell apart, leaving the wreck aground just off Sunset Boulevard at Cape May Point. Photograph from the Cape May Historical Museum.

28. Dr. Margaret Mace of North Wildwood operated the only general hospital in Cape May County until the Burdette Tomlin Hospital opened in 1950. Photograph from the collection of the Wildwood Historical Society.

29. The first female mayor in Cape May County History, Doris W. Bradway of Wildwood, appealed to women, African-Americans, and Italian-American voters during the 1930s. Photograph from the collection of the Wildwood Historical Society.

30. The huge dirigible hangar, built in 1919 and demolished in 1941, at the Naval Air Station Cape May in the 1930s. Photograph from the collection of H. Gerald Mc-Donald.

CHAPTER SIX

Settlement of the Barrier Islands, 1879–1900

Two centuries after the first settlement of the mainland portion of the Cape May peninsula (what early residents called the upland), the five barrier islands along the Atlantic seaboard side remained uninhabited. These islands included Peck's Beach (now Ocean City), Ludlam's Beach (now Strathmere and Sea Isle City), Seven Mile Beach (now Avalon and Stone Harbor), Five Mile Beach (the Wildwoods), and Two Mile Beach (Wildwood Crest). A series of twisting saltwater channels and thoroughfares, small sounds, and mile-wide marshes isolated the barrier islands from the upland, and deep tidal inlets separated the islands from each other. Passage to these beach islands, even at low tide, required a boat, and the wide muddy salt marshes prevented the construction of roads or causeways to the islands (see map 3).

Early Cape May County settlers used the barrier islands to forage cattle, horses, and sheep. They rented shares of the beaches for timbering, oystering, and whale fishing. Aaron Leaming, Sr., who purchased Seven Mile Beach in 1723, made annual trips to the Two Mile, Five Mile, and Seven Mile beaches (the latter sometimes called Leaming's Beach) to bring his cattle to pasture on the beach grasses in the spring and to take them offshore (to the mainland) in the winter. Seven Mile Beach remained in the possession of the Leaming family until it was sold to the Tathams, who constructed a farmhouse and barn on the island in the 1850s. A farmhouse also existed on Peck's Beach before the 1870s, built about 1859 by Parker Miller, a marine salvage and insurance company agent. These were the only houses on the barrier islands.[1]

Lifesaving stations stood on Cape May County's coastal beaches before the 1870s. The U.S. government established the Life Saving Service in 1848 and assigned stations to Cape May County's barrier islands, where almost every year ships foundered and wrecked off the Jersey Cape's treacherous Atlantic coastal waters. Early stations stood on Peck's Beach and near Townsend and Hereford inlets. John Stites, Platt Brower, John Ludlam, and other county residents manned these Life Saving Service wooden buildings with their observation towers and sheds to house surfboats. In 1855, the U.S. Life Saving Service erected additional stations on Corson's Inlet, and near Tatham's farm on Seven Mile Beach, Turtle Gut Inlet, and Cold Spring Inlet. The latter was probably located on Poverty Beach below the Two Mile Beach and near the site of the present-day U.S. Coast Guard training station. In addition to lifesaving stations, the U.S. Lighthouse Board built the Hereford Inlet Light between 1873 and 1874, and according to the board's annual report for 1875, "John March, the [first] keeper of this station, was drowned by the capsizing of his boat, on returning from the mainland to his station." Freeling Hewitt replaced the ill-fated keeper in September 1874.[2]

The occasional farmhouse and lifesaving station on Cape May County's barrier islands had not disturbed the pristine white beaches and sand dunes, which teemed with wildlife and were covered with grass and shrubs. Fields of flowers and patches of thick forest and undergrowth flourished along the high spots on these long, narrow islands. They were the "chosen spot[s] of nature," observed Mary Townsend Rush, an early barrier island resident. Lewis T. Stevens, who visited the barrier islands from his home in Cape May City, likened the islands to great vineyards. "Gigantic grape vines here flourish," Stevens wrote in 1897, with "one monster nearly a yard in circumference ten feet from the ground, spreading away over the branches of the oaks a distance of two hundred feet." The holly bushes in the middle of Five Mile Beach were so beautiful that the earliest settlers there named it Holly Beach, and called the neighboring beachfront community Wildwood, after the exotic twisted trees that had been shaped by the constant ocean winds that crossed the island.[3]

The images of natural beauty and purity accompanied development of Cape May County's barrier islands. "Hardly any form of disease originates [there]," Mary Rush explained, "while upon many diseases acquired elsewhere, simple residence and the use of salt waters in the bathing season, together with hot sand baths, are more beneficial than ordinary medical treatments." The barrier islands were pictured by developers and visitors as a rural frontier to the expanding Philadelphia and Camden City urban industrial centers. Settlement of the islands was part of a movement to escape the polluted industrial city by going to the healthful beaches of southern New Jersey. Charles Funnell found in his study of Atlantic City that this motivation lay behind promotion of that oceanfront resort during the late nineteenth century. Promoters of Cape May County seaside resorts likewise stressed the rural nature and healthful purity of the barrier islands by contrast with the ugliness of nearby factory cities. There were "no furnaces poisoning the air with smoke and gas," wrote Mary Townsend Rush; there were no "manufactories with ceaseless hum of machinery suggesting toil and weariness."[4]

The desire to escape urban industrial society (where they all lived or worked) was one factor that drove the group of Methodist ministers, temperance reformers, and real estate developers who founded Ocean City on Peck's Beach in 1879. William B. Wood, William H. Burrell, Simon Lake, Sr., Simon W. Lake, and Ezra B. Lake met in Philadelphia in October 1879 and organized the New Brighton Association, a land improvement company and camp meeting association. The association added James E. Lake and S. Wesley Lake and incorporated a month later as the Ocean City Association. The syndicate instructed William Lake to survey the island and search the titles to Peck's Beach.[5]

The Ocean City Association employed modern business methods to develop their planned religious resort on Peck's Beach. The association involved Dr. Gilbert E. Palen in the Ocean City enterprise. A mining and chemical industry entrepreneur, Palen had founded several frontier towns in northeastern Pennsylvania and had run once as the Prohibition party candidate for mayor of Philadelphia. Palen threw his political-economic power behind the development of Ocean City and became one of the religious resort's first summer residents in 1880. William Lake, in the meantime, searched every title and surveyed every corner of the island. The Ocean City Association needed complete and clear title to Peck's Beach so that it could restrict property ownership to those who pledged to uphold the community's strict regulations against liquor and immorality. Violation of the rules could lead to the loss of property. "The reservations and restrictions embodied in our deeds of conveyance," Lake explained, "I am sure, are salutary in their nature and should be strictly enforced."[6]

Parker Miller, the original island resident, caused some trouble for the Ocean City Association. He claimed a one-sixteenth part of Peck's Beach under a deed obtained in 1867 from Jesse Somers. Miller incorporated a land and turnpike company in 1881 and planned to develop his own part of the beach without any of the religious restrictions imposed by the Ocean City Association. Parker's actions led to an extended legal dispute with the Methodist developers. Eventually, the Ocean City Association gained control over Peck's Beach and served as the governing body until 1884, when residents voted for incorporation as a borough. Ocean City borough sent William Lake as its first representative to the Cape May County Board of Freeholders. The Methodist association passed and enforced a set of ordinances against Sunday travel and bathing. "So far as the Sabbath is concerned we place no impediment in the way of those who came with the purpose of uniting with us in the worship of God," wrote William B. Wood, president of the Ocean City Association in 1883, "but we cannot allow mere pleasure or business transportation to and from Ocean City on the Lord's Day."[7]

The Ocean City Association selected lot owners carefully, choosing what one barrier islander called the "better class of enterprising people." These fell into three categories of original residents, who established the fundamental character of the Ocean City community. The first group of residents came with Simon Lake from Atlantic County. Original Atlantic County settlers included Hiram Steelman and Rush Cox, grocers; S. B. Sampson, a house builder; and R. C. Robinson, a printer who edited the barrier island's first newspaper. A second group of original Ocean City residents moved from Philadelphia, including Ira S. Champion, an ice cream parlor operator; R. Howard Thorn, a hardware store owner; and Dr. J. S. Waggoner, a drugstore owner. A third group relocated in Ocean City from nearby Upper and Dennis townships, often retaining their mainland (offshore) properties as well. The first local people to settle on Peck's Beach were Nicholas Corson, a Seaville carpenter; and Richard B. Stites, a lumber dealer.[8]

Ocean City's early leaders were driven by a combination of religious utopianism and practical business spirit. "We present to the capitalist a wide field for enterprise, to the artisan work," Mary Rush explained. Ocean City Association members cleared land, laid out sidewalks, graded streets, and built cottages and hotels. The work of founding Ocean City was interrupted briefly by a tragic accident. In 1880, Simon Lake died from a severe axe wound received as he cleared brush for a Methodist pavilion. Other members of the association continued to construct their religious resort, ironically bringing to the seashore frontier region the very urbanization from which they had sought escape. The Ocean City Association built steamboat wharves, sewer lines, and plants for electric light and heat. They constructed a foundry and factory, managed by the Lakes, to manufacture iron shade rollers and other hardware. Ezra B. Lake, James E. Lake, S. Wesley Lake, and Gilbert Palen organized the Ocean City Electric Railroad Company, creating the type of traction monopoly that epitomized late-nineteenth-century big-city politics and society.[9]

The Methodists were not the only entrepreneurs interested in the Cape May County barrier islands in 1879. Charles Kline Landis, arguably the greatest real estate entrepreneur and townbuilder in the history of southern New Jersey, turned his attention to the development of Ludlam's Beach in the late 1870s. He had helped to establish the town of Hammonton in 1857 as the fruit-growing center of Atlantic County and in 1861 had founded Vineland in Cumberland County. Landis carefully planned the city of Vineland. He designed wide tree-lined boulevards, sold large building lots to Italian American and other enterprising settlers, and attracted railroads and industries to the city. The restless and creative Landis was not satisfied with these projects; and he searched for a new city to build. "Doing nothing in Vineland and having debts with plenty of assets which are available," Landis wrote in 1878, "I must do something—what shall I do?"[10]

Charles K. Landis pursued a variety of business schemes. He interested speculators in the construction of a narrow-gauge railroad through Cape May County in order to break the West Jersey Railroad Company's monopoly. Landis held rallies for the narrow-gauge line in Dennisville and Cape May City but was unable to raise the necessary capital for a Cape May-Philadelphia Short Line Railroad. Landis tried to join William Sewell and John C. Stevens, West Jersey Railroad bosses, in the development of Sewell's Point and Poverty Beach between Cold Spring Inlet and the city of Cape May. The railroad men rebuffed Landis. "They have offered me no share of the enterprise," Landis observed, concluding that the entire affair was "a mean piece of business."[11]

Landis settled at last upon development of what he called his "sanitary and art city by the sea" on Ludlam's Beach in Cape May

County. "Have been thinking closely about the Island all day," Landis observed in early 1880. He prepared sketches for the proposed city, complete with a design for a protected harbor and a thousand-foot wooden pier and pavilion. Landis envisaged a seaside city with an elaborate canal and drainage system and public baths and fountains somewhat like Venice, Italy. He wanted to build Italian-style piazzas and public buildings decorated with Renaissance artwork, sculpture, and statuary. Landis designed a grand hotel with reading rooms and wide verandas. He dreamed about creating "arcades of stores" and convinced the University of Pennsylvania to consider his city for a marine science laboratory and research center.[12]

Charles Landis meticulously organized Sea Isle City. He purchased titles to Ludlam's Beach in 1879. "This is a stupendous job," Landis explained, and "I have now over 150 signatures." The founder of Vineland dispatched John L. Burk, his chief clerk, to Ohio and Illinois to buy interests in the island from heirs of the Ludlam and Edwards families, who had migrated earlier to the Midwest from Cape May County. Landis attached wealthy investors to his Sea Isle City project, including Philip P. Baker, a Vineland merchant and Cumberland County legislator; Jonathan Cone of Bristol, Pennsylvania, owner of the *Republic*, a steamboat that plied between Cape May Point and Philadelphia; and John Wright, heir to the immense Cooper family fortune in Camden County. Landis associated with Thomas E. Ludlam, prominent Dennis Township businessman and a descendant of one of the original family owners of Ludlam's Beach.[13]

Charles Landis built the political alliances necessary to obtain public support for development of his barrier island. He consulted with Cape May and Cumberland county representatives—including James H. Nixon, Jesse D. Ludlam, and Waters B. Miller—about passage of legislation for a right-of-way across the salt marsh from the upland to Ludlam's Beach. The local legislators introduced such a law for Landis. "This bill enables me to build a wagon road to the Island," he explained, "and it opens up all the islands on the coast to the main land." Landis also revealed his plans for Sea Isle City to General William Sewell, New Jersey's Republican party boss and Pennsylvania and West Jersey Railroad director. "He may steal my ideas and then deceive me," Landis worried. Without Sewell's support, Landis could not obtain a railroad spur to Ludlam's Beach. The railroad "may be my sole dependence for the Island," Landis wrote, and he decided to "strike a deal" with Sewell. The deal led to establishment of a railroad branch line from just north of the South Seaville station (known as Sea Isle Junction) across the marshes to Ludlam's Beach in 1882.[14]

The railroad connection assured Sea Isle City's growth. Charles Landis, John Burk, and Philip P. Baker incorporated the Sea Isle City Improvement Company to sell land and build houses, hotels, docks, seawalls, and piers. Landis offered one million dollars in capital stock and took investors on tours of the beach, serving them picnic lunches of "Cape May salts" (oysters from the nearby bays). He directed installation of gas, waterworks, and electric lighting. An excursion house and ten frame cottages were completed in November 1882. That year residents voted for incorporation as a borough, and Jesse Ludlam of Dennis Township moved that Thomas E. Ludlam and William L. Petersen be admitted to seats on the county board of freeholders. "It would seem," the *Cape May Wave* observed, "as if Sea Isle City is taking the wind out of the sail of Ocean City."[15]

Difficulties accompanied the founding of Sea Isle City. A brush fence used as a seawall failed to protect choice beachfront properties from the incessant pounding of surf, and Landis discovered that the ocean eroded the most valuable part of his island. The railroad track to Sea Isle City constantly washed away. Landis complained that the West Jersey Railroad dumped gravel on the salt marsh, expecting it to secure the track. "It is not being done right," Landis wrote, "it is not staked and pinned down and is weighted too much with gravel, but the mud bank they are making may defend it." The mud bank did not hold back the flood tide caused by a violent storm in September 1882 that swept away entire sections of the track as well as the railroad bridge across Ludlam's Thoroughfare, a deep channel that connected Ludlam's Bay to Townsend's Inlet. Landis hired a crew of twenty Italian-American railroad workers to repair this vital lifeline to the mainland.[16]

Charles Landis encountered trouble with John Burk, his trusted business agent and shareholder in the Sea Isle City corporation. Apparently Burk had some deeds signed over to him rather than to Landis and allegedly swindled Matilda Landis, Charles Landis's sister, out of shares of Sea Isle City. Landis dismissed Burk, charging him with forgery and fraud. The disenchantment with Burk arose less from alleged theft of properties than from Burk's development of a competing barrier island community on Five Mile Beach to the south. A few weeks before Landis fired him, Burk formed the Holly Beach Improvement Company with Dr. Aaron Andrew of Vineland (whose interest in the beach was stimulated by the need to find a healthful spot for his ailing wife), John L. Davis of Chicago, and other investors. The company purchased tracts of land on Five Mile Beach from the Bennett, Schellenger, Cresse, and Hildreth families.[17]

Development of Five Mile Beach began slowly. "There was [sic] houses along the beachfront, few streets graded and covered with hay and sidewalks was [sic] boardwalks elevated on piling," recalled Cecil T. Ober, a general contractor who lived on the island in 1883. John Burk hired William H. Bright of Philadelphia to run his real estate office in Holly Beach, and Bright soon opened his own realty and insurance business, becoming the island's political and economic leader. Burk and Bright made Holly Beach into a vibrant resort community. Holly Beach became a borough in April 1885, with John Measy as the first representative to the board of freeholders. Measy made an immediate impact on the unwieldy county governing body, which had reached sixteen members by 1885. He introduced a resolution in June 1885 that sought to reduce the county tax for all the new barrier island communities. Though defeated by a coalition of mainlanders, the Measy resolution suggested that the barrier island settlements had become part of an increasingly complex and less stable Cape May County society and polity.[18]

Carpenters and workmen who had completed reconstruction of Cape May City after the fire of 1878 moved to Holly Beach to construct roominghouses, hotels, and cottages. Some of these were elaborate houses with large fireplaces, towers, porches, and gingerbread trim. One cottage boasted an observatory on the roof. Most were painted dark red with red slate shingled roofs. Mainland farmers carried on business with the new settlement. Horace Richardson brought his farm produce from Rio Grande by boat. Jeanette DuBois Meech moved to the seashore community from Vineland and opened a country store and established the *Holly Beach Herald* in 1885, the community's first newspaper. The railroad entered Holly Beach in 1885, with Charles Mace directing the laying of tracks down the Five Mile Beach from the tiny fishing village of Anglesea (now North Wildwood) located on the northern tip of the island.[19]

The settlement of Anglesea (North Wildwood) predated Holly Beach by at least two years. Located on Hereford Inlet near the best offshore fishing banks in Cape May County waters, Anglesea contained a collection of fishing shacks and harbored a small fleet of fishing boats before 1880. Development of Anglesea as a resort community started in 1879 when Humphrey Cresse sold his title to Anglesea to the Five Mile Beach Improvement Company headed by Frederick E. Swope, a Philadelphia real estate and railroad entrepreneur. Swope incorporated the Anglesea Land Company in 1882 and began selling lots and constructing cottages.[20]

Swope built the Anglesea Railroad across Grassy Sound from the West Jersey Railroad junction at Burleigh, a settlement formerly named Gravelly Run but renamed in 1883 in honor of John J. Burleigh of Camden City, the chief operator of the West Jersey line. The tracks were extended from Anglesea to Holly Beach in 1885. The West Jersey Railroad absorbed the Anglesea line in 1888. Anglesea contained a hotel, several dozen cottages, and a tiny boardwalk by 1884. It attracted permanent residents, including Joshua Shivers of nearby Mayville on the mainland, a fishing boat captain. Dr. William A. Tompkins, a retired U.S. army surgeon, came to the island for his health and stayed to serve as Anglesea's first postmaster and mayor. Anglesea was incorporated as a borough in 1885 and sent Hewlett Brower as its representative to the Cape May County Board of Freeholders.[21]

Philip P. Baker, one of Charles Landis's partners in the Sea Isle City project, and Latimer Baker bought ninety acres between Anglesea and Holly Beach in 1885 to develop yet another resort community. Joined by their brother, J. Thompson Baker, the trio incorporated the Wildwood Beach Improvement Company. The Baker brothers first named their beachfront enterprise Florida City, but renamed it Wildwood after the wild, wind-twisted trees found on their beach. Over the next decade, when Wildwood incorporated as a borough in 1895, the Bakers created a major resort community. Thomas R. Brooks, editor of the *Star of the Cape*, visited Wildwood in 1890 and found a dance pavilion, photograph gallery, hotels, and "beautiful cottages which have sprung up all over town." That summer, U.S. President Benjamin Harrison visited Wildwood as a guest of the Bakers. The following year, Brooks returned to Wildwood and visited the new pier, railroad station, boardwalk, excursion house, and swanboats on Magnolia Lake. The newspaperman praised Philip and Latimer Baker as the type of businessmen needed in Cape May County. "They are both very enterprising," Brooks wrote, "and are pushing along Wildwood in a very successful and thorough manner."[22]

Seven Mile Beach between Ludlam's Beach and Five Mile Beach remained the only undeveloped barrier island by 1885. The salt marshes were wider and the channels and thoroughfares more treacherous between this beach and the mainland than for any other barrier island, discouraging travel and delaying development. The early rail link came over Townsend's Inlet from Ludlam's Beach, not across the salt marsh. Joseph L. Wells of Germantown, Pennsylvania, and a syndicate of investors took a chance on development of the beach in 1887, purchasing three thousand acres from the Tatham family. Wells incorporated the Seven Mile Beach Company and offered lots. According to tradition, the company's secretary named the new development after the mythical Arthurian city of Avalon. Two other syndicates of Philadelphia and Camden land speculators followed, forming the Avalon Beach Improvement Company in 1888 and the Avalon Beach Hotel Company in 1889. Wells's company sold a tract of land just south of the original tract in 1894 to the Peermont Land Company, incorporated by Daniel G. Evans of Philadelphia and a group of Camden, Avalon, and Philadelphia investors. An Atlantic City investment company took over the Peermont Land Company in 1902, and for a time the resort community was called Peermont-Avalon.[23]

Joseph Wells's development company constructed a dozen cottages and the Hotel Avalon. The company attracted guests to the hotel by advertising the delights of its "braided wire torsion spring mattresses." Carpenters, laborers, and merchants moved to Avalon from Cape May City, where jobs had become scarce. Enos Williams, Cape May City's most prominent builder, arrived in Avalon in February 1888 with five carpenters and thirty laborers to construct a hotel. Avalon experienced growing pains from the beginning. Four attempts to bridge Townsend's Inlet from Ludlam's Beach for the railroad resulted in washouts until 1891, when the Phoenix Iron Company (builders of the Iron Pier in Cape May City) erected an iron bridge for the West Jersey Railroad. Now, "Avalon will boom," the *Wave* predicted. Avalon incorporated as a borough the following year. The new bridge across Townsend's Inlet also opened the lower end of the beach to a group of Philadelphia speculators, who purchased a four-mile stretch of beach, laid out streets, and built cottages in what would become the resort community of Stone Harbor.[24]

Barrier island communities assumed population and settlement patterns that differed from those of the older Cape May County mainland communities. Living space was so limited on the narrow strips of land that building had to be organized tightly along central streets and around standard-sized square building lots. Summer residents demanded both the solitude and quiet of the rural seashore frontier and the services that they had come to expect from their industrial, urban centers of Philadelphia or Camden City, including gas, electricity, railroads, and trolleys. The new barrier island boroughs introduced these modern utilities and urban improvements before many of the mainland communities. All the barrier island resorts, including the quasi-utopian experiments on Ocean City and Sea Isle City, were founded as business ventures by investment companies formed to sell shares and develop property. The first permanent residents of the islands reflected the business origins and formed an inner core of builders, real estate dealers, shopkeepers, and hotel and boardinghouse proprietors.

The barrier island resorts contained a greater percentage of foreign-born residents than the mainland communities where the foreign-born populations comprised less than one percent of the total population of Upper, Middle, Dennis, and Lower townships. By comparison, 15.4 percent of the barrier islands' combined population in 1895 was foreign-born. Twenty-three percent of Anglesea's population and 22 percent of Holly Beach's permanent residents came from Scandinavian countries, mostly Sweden, and became menhaden fishermen, employing this coastal fish in a fish oil and meal industry. Scandinavian-American families who settled Cape May County's barrier islands in the late nineteenth century included the Axelsons, Andersons, Carlsons, Colbergs, Johansons, and Berglunds. The first barrier island census of 1895 also listed thirteen permanent Italian-American residents in Sea Isle City, probably recruited by Charles Landis.[25]

African-Americans settled on the barrier islands during the early years of development. John Burk sold a lot on Holly Beach to John Vance, a Cape May City African-American property owner, in August of 1885. Other early African-American barrier island resident families included Barker, Moultrie, and Johnson. African-Americans made up 8 percent of Holly Beach's year-round residents by 1895. Joseph Vance and other members of the Mt. Pisgah African Methodist Episcopal Church of Cape May City organized a small chapel in Holly Beach in 1891 for some thirty members.[26]

As the barrier island resorts took shape, a new community formed on the mainland at Woodbine, the wilderness stop on the West Jersey Railroad three miles north of Dennisville. Over six hundred Jewish immigrants from eastern Europe moved to Woodbine during the last decade of the nineteenth century. The founding in

1891 of the "Russian Jewish colony" made Cape May County an integral part of the mass immigration movement to America. Driven out of eastern Europe by a combination of severe social and economic conditions and anti-Semitic pogroms, hundreds of thousands of Russian, Polish, Rumanian, Austro-Hungarian, and German Jews emigrated to the United States during the late 19th century. American industrialists actively recruited these immigrants in order to provide labor for their factories, mines, and businesses. Many of these eastern Europeans entered New York, Philadelphia, and other urban centers, becoming trapped in festering tenement districts. Urban reformers and organizations such as the Baron de Hirsch Foundation, established by Baron Maurice de Hirsch, a wealthy Jewish industrialist and banker, sought to ameliorate urban problems by resettling Jewish-American immigrants in rural communities, including a number in southern New Jersey.[27]

Woodbine became the most ambitious—and in the short run most successful—Jewish-American agricultural and industrial colony in the United States. It presented the same quasi-utopian vision that drove the Lakes in Ocean City and Charles K. Landis in Sea Isle City as they sought to provide an escape from industrial machines and urban decay by establishing planned, healthful communities in rural Cape May County. Woodbine, one promoter said, was filled with "luscious woodbine" and other sweet, fragrant flowers. Landis provided a blueprint to Woodbine's planners for the wide boulevards and building lots that he had used successfully earlier to lay out Vineland in Cumberland County. The original Woodbine town plan had been prepared by Jeremiah van Rensselaer and William S. Townsend for the Cape May and Millville Railroad, but the final design adopted by the Jewish-American leaders of the colony followed the plan that Landis gave in March 1891 to Mayer Sulzberger, a leading trustee of the Baron de Hirsch Fund and the Jewish Colonization Association, which financed the Woodbine settlement.[28]

The Baron de Hirsch Foundation bought the Woodbine tract (except for the Nathaniel Holmes property near the railroad station) in July 1891 and hired Hirsh L. Sabsovich to superintend the development of a Jewish colony in the northwestern corner of Cape May County. Educated at Odessa University and a member of a secret agrarian reform faction, Sabsovich fled Russia and came to the United States, where he taught for a time at the Fort Collins Agricultural College in Colorado before coming to Woodbine. Sabsovich combined an idealism that helped him build a reformist agricultural school with an authoritarianism that caused some of the Jewish farmers to revolt against his iron-fisted leadership and leave the colony. Sabsovich's methods guided the growth of the wilderness settlement. "Woodbine is a city, but a peculiar city," Vladimir Korolenko, a Russian Jewish writer, observed in 1893. Korolenko saw thirty houses, sandy streets, a factory, two schools, a post office, and a hotel in Woodbine. "This is the city of the future, an American embryo of a Jewish city; around it there are sixty-six farms," Korolenko wrote.[29]

Continual financial support from the de Hirsch Fund subsidized Woodbine. The money helped Sabsovich overcome a series of economic setbacks. It sustained Woodbine against Dennis Township, which placed obstacles in the path of the foreign community's growth by refusing to use tax monies to improve roads or public schools. The de Hirsch Fund continued to bring immigrants to Woodbine. Most had large families, such as the Abraham Marcus and Samuel Marcus families with their sixteen children. The large families worked in the clothing factories or on the farms. Though a number of relatively poor Russian and Polish Jews came to Woodbine among the earliest settlers, the original Woodbine community presented a far more complex set of peoples, including Jewish families of German and Austro-Hungarian origin and several Italian families. The first residents were farmers, laborers, merchants, craftsmen, shopkeepers, mechanics, teachers, and professionals such as Achiles Joffe, a physician. Nacham Diamond became a leading county merchant and built a cranberry factory in Marshallville. Michael Bayard founded a machine shop. Joseph Kotinsky and Jacob Goodale Lipman, among Woodbine's earliest settlers, graduated from the de Hirsch Agricultural and Industrial School, founded by Hirsh L. Sabsovich, and went on to Rutgers College. Lipman later directed the New Jersey Agricultural Experiment Station between 1911 and 1939.[30]

Woodbine attracted industry during its first decade. The de Hirsch Fund established a coat factory to provide employment for the first residents. Louis Zech, Louis V. Freund, and a syndicate of New York City textile manufacturers incorporated the Woodbine Manufacturing Company in 1894 to establish a men's and boy's clothing factory. Other small shops and factories for clothing, hats, baskets, and machine tools followed.[31]

The late-nineteenth century American political-economic environment stimulated industrial development in Woodbine and contributed to modest industrial growth throughout Cape May County between 1879 and 1899. It was an era of laissez-faire capitalism with few regulations or restraints on the accumulation of wealth and expansion of big business, and it encouraged industrial growth even in the more rural communities such as those on the Jersey Cape. The Lake brothers built a factory and iron forge in Ocean City in 1885 to manufacture steering gears, stove lid lifters, and iron spring shade rollers. Simon Lake III, later inventor of a modern American submarine, managed the Ocean City factory with a firm hand that crushed labor unrest or strikes. The Reverend Isaac W. Dawson founded a canning factory in West Creek on the old Mosslander Mill Pond around 1890, and the Springer brothers of Philadelphia and Gloucester City incorporated a West Creek Paper company in 1893 to manufacture paper pulp and products. West Creek's industrial growth required the renaming of the community. Apparently shippers and business correspondents confused the Cape May County address with that of West Creek in Ocean County. Dawson held a contest to rename West Creek, and in 1892 he chose the name Eldora. Eventually, Eldora included the communities of West Creek, Stipson's Island, and East Creek. Dawson's company became the Eldora Canning Company, and Springer's Manufacturing Company was renamed the Eldora Paper Company in 1894.[32]

Local industrial development contributed to the formation in 1884 of the borough of West Cape May, just across Cape Island Creek from Cape May City. George H. Reeves moved back to his family's homestead along the Cape Island Turnpike (now Sunset Boulevard) because of poor health in 1879 and established a branch of the Hastings goldbeating company of Philadelphia. Two years later, Reeves moved the business to West Cape May. Reeves employed eight to ten beaters to pound one-inch strips of gold into gossamer-thin sheets, and fifty local women to cut the sheets into tiny squares to be used as gold leaf in the decorative arts, for edging Bible pages, and in printing. The new industry, combined with the development of lots and streets by real estate speculators, led to the creation of the borough. John W. Reeves became the borough's first representative on the board of freeholders in 1884, and George H. Reeves served as mayor of West Cape May during the 1890s.[33]

Another Cape May County industry was founded in Rio Grande (the former community of Hildreth) during the 1880s. Charles M. Hilgert and other Philadelphia businessmen incorporated the Rio Grande Sugar Company in 1881 for the "manufacture and sale of sugar, made from beets, sorghum, amber or other sugar cane." The company purchased twenty tracts of land in Lower and Middle townships that comprised nearly two thousand acres to grow sugar beets and cane. The New Jersey legislature passed a bounty to be paid on every ton of sugar manufactured. For a time the sugar plantation and large mechanized sugar factory in Rio Grande prospered. The company employed 140 wagons and teams in 1883 to cut and haul sorghum from Lemuel Miller's farm in Green Creek to the Rio Grande factory. "This industry may have a great future," Charles Landis observed, "and it was scarcely expected in South Jersey." Unfortunately cost far outweighed profit. Hilgert went bankrupt. The Rio Grande sugar factory had several owners (and probably two different buildings on either side of the railroad tracks), and several agricultural experiments were undertaken to raise new, more productive strains of sorghum. In the end, the sugar industry failed in Cape May County. The Rio Grande sugar factory became a cannery in 1889, and later a slaughterhouse.[34]

The shipbuilding industry continued to be Cape May County's leading enterprise during the 1880s. Cape May County yards launched forty-six vessels of over 200 tons between 1880 and 1890, fourteen in Dennisville and thirteen on Goshen Creek. The Richard S. Leaming shipyard on Dennis Creek launched a double-decked schooner of nearly 900 tons in 1882. The shipbuilding industry peaked in 1891 with the launching on Dennis Creek for a group of Baltimore and South Jersey owners of the *Samuel B. Marts*, an 800-ton, three-masted schooner. Launching day celebrations brought visitors from all over southern New Jersey. They alighted from the railroad train at the Woodbine station and traveled to the "picturesque village of Dennisville" in Lloyd's horse-drawn bus. Young ladies in spring bonnets traveled by carriage from every small village in the county to attend the launching party. Ship captains and master builders from Mauricetown, Leesburg, Port Norris, and other shipbuilding and port towns up the Delaware Bay congregated to watch George Wentzell and Frank Wentzell, Dennisville's master shipbuilders, launch their big schooner. Most visitors attended a launching banquet held on the veranda of the Gatzmer House, Dennisville's hotel, built by Mackey Williams of Tuckahoe in 1871.[35]

An ominous portent for Cape May County's shipbuilding industry occurred during the launching of the *Samuel B. Marts*. Thomas Brooks, editor of the *Star of the Cape*, observed that when the large vessel slid into the water it struck a wharf on the opposite bank of the narrow Dennis Creek, "crushing it down at the edge and obstructing the boat so much as to prevent her sliding squarely into the water and causing her to rest on her bilge from which position it will be necessary to relieve her by considerable hard work." Launching of big ships into the silt-filled Dennis Creek had become too dangerous. Richard S. Leaming and other shipbuilders began to leave the county for better locations. Moreover, the need for coastal schooners declined. The railroad now served as the main transportation in and out of Cape May County and as the main connection to the urban centers. Production of ships fell steadily during the 1890s to less than half the number produced the previous decade, and by the end of the century county shipyards constructed no large vessel. Shipbuilding, like whaling and cedar mining before, disappeared from the county, ending a way of life that had sustained portions of the community for over a century.[36]

The decline of the shipbuilding industry coincided with and contributed to growing economic problems on the Jersey Cape during the 1890s. Despite a post–Civil War boom that lasted through the 1880s, the county's economic base of shipbuilding, farming, and resort development was fragile and particularly sensitive to fluctuations in the larger national economy. As early as 1891 Charles Landis had predicted a financial depression because of the overexpansion of the barrier island resorts. "Sea Isle is full of Bears, Growlers and speculators, who expected to have money fall in their laps without work," Landis wrote. He prepared to unload his remaining oceanfront building lots for as little as fifty dollars each. Aaron Hand, the county tax assessor, noted that Avalon was also in deep financial trouble. "The Seven Mile Beach Company set out with a flourish of trumpets and were going to pay dividend on stock the first year," Hand explained, but "several years have passed and stock can find no purchasers." Holly Beach failed to pay its taxes, and the county prepared to bring suit against the tiny seaside borough for delinquent payment.[37]

The economic cycles of the 1880s and 1890s most affected Cape May City, the county's oldest resort. The city never recovered completely from the fire of 1878. Instead of rebuilding with the bold new Victorian architectural styles that marked Atlantic City and other urban centers, Cape May City returned to the simple rural style that had been popular on Cape Island before the Civil War. Most hotels, villas, and cottages constructed after the fire reflected the traditional design, with verandas, flat roofs, and little ornamental trim. Only the New Columbia's soaring towers and brick and stone surfaces departed from the dominant conservative designs. Victor Denizot's Lafayette House and George Hildreth's Carroll Villa, built in 1882, resembled the plain L-shaped hotels built in the 1840s. Stephen D. Button, an elderly architect, and Enos Williams, a conservative local builder, designed old-fashioned cottages for E. C. Knight, Thomas Whitney, and others intent upon preserving Cape May City as a quiet, gentrified resort village.[38]

Several innovative entrepreneurs sought to revive and modernize the Cape May City resort during the 1880s. Jonathan Cone, owner of the *Republic*, the sidewheel steamer that carried passengers and freight between Philadelphia and the bayside steamboat landing near Cape May Point, promoted railroad, trolley, and real estate business around Cape Island. Cone developed the Delaware Bay and Cape May Railroad in 1879 with a new covered station at the steamboat landing and a modern double-ended locomotive. He improved the narrow-gauge track that carried thousands of passengers during the summer season from the steamboat landing, along Lincoln Avenue in Cape May Point, past the Cape May lighthouse, along the beach to the Sea Breeze Excursion House and the Grant Street depot for the West Jersey Railroad. Cone incorporated the Cape May and Sewell's Point Railroad Company in 1880 to operate a horse trolley from the Sea Breeze along the beach as far as Madison Avenue in the eastern corner of Cape May City. A steam locomotive then resumed the trip along Poverty Beach to the Inlet House and yacht pier at Sewell's Point. Cone also joined William Sewell and other West Jersey Railroad directors to organize the East Cape May Beach Company in February 1883 to develop streets and building lots east of Madison Avenue.[39]

Theodore M. Reger, a Philadelphia land speculator, concentrated on the development of the beaches and meadows just to the west of Cape May City. Reger, Thomas H. Williamson, and Albert B. Little of Cape May City incorporated the Neptune Land Company in 1882 to develop the old Mark Devine tract, the site of the former Mount Vernon Hotel. This tract extended from the Sea Breeze House westward to the lighthouse and from the beachfront to the Cape Island Turnpike. The Neptune Land Company issued $300,000 in capital stock to finance the banking of the salt meadows, reclamation of land, and construction of seawalls, wharves, roads, hotels, and cottages. Reger hired Nathan Culver to design and build a huge wooden and

tin-sided elephant in the meadows near the beach, along the Delaware Bay and Cape May Railroad tracks. Named the Light of Asia (and
Old Jumbo by residents), the fifty-eight-foot-high elephant was completed between 1884 and 1885. Reger organized the Mount Vernon
Land Company in 1887 to accelerate the slow development of the
property, and used the Light of Asia as a real estate office. Sales
remained slow, but the oceanfront development incorporated in
1894 as South Cape May; it lasted as a separate borough until 1945,
when most of the cottages had been washed away by the tides.[40]

Theodore Reger and James Henry Edmunds, one of Reger's partners in the Mount Vernon Land Company, organized the West Cape
May Improvement Company in May 1884 to develop lots and streets
in this newly incorporated borough. Edmunds became a major political and economic figure in West Cape May and in Cape May City,
where he served as mayor between 1885 and 1892 and 1895 and
1896. He purchased the *Cape May Wave* in 1886 and made the
county's oldest newspaper the voice of the local Democratic party
organization. Edmunds directed urban development in Cape May
City. He held stock in and sat on the boards of directors of every
major local traction, railroad, water, gas, electric, and telephone company. He once attempted to sell the city's waterworks to his own
syndicate of investors, but Republicans on the city council blocked
the scheme. Edmunds's main project to advance the resort community on the lower end of the Jersey Cape was the development
between 1887 and 1888 of the Cape May Driving Park, an oval horse-
(and probably bicycle-) racing track located in an area bounded by
present-day Columbia Avenue, Fourth Avenue, Sunset Boulevard, and
Stevens Street in West Cape May.[41]

James Edmunds advertised the inaugural meeting of the Cape
May Driving Park Association in late July 1888 as "the most important
ever held in the State." He assured fans that a splendid grandstand
could accommodate three thousand people and that soon the railroad would run a spur from Cape May City to the driving park.
Probably three thousand saw one hundred thoroughbreds compete
in four races that first day, but attendance quickly declined. Without a
rail link to West Cape May, the driving park attracted few fans. The
conservative Cape May City community opposed the gambling, drinking, and no doubt the Democratic party politics that surrounded the
racetrack. F. Sidney Townsend, a city councilman and Republican
party stalwart, reported with obvious satisfaction that fewer than

three hundred people saw the last race of what he termed the "dull season" of 1888.[42]

Far more sports fans went to the Cape May Athletic Park to watch a baseball game between the Cuban Giants, one of the best African-American clubs, and the "Cape May boys." Baseball proved the bright spot in Cape May City's summer season during the 1880s. U.S. President Benjamin Harrison, members of his cabinet, and local dignitaries attended baseball games in Cape May City. William Sewell, John Edgar Reyburn, a U.S. congressman from Pennsylvania and onetime mayor of Philadelphia, and other wealthy patrons financed the star athletes from Princeton College and the University of Pennsylvania who played for the Cape May Athletic Club baseball team. This amateur Cape May County ball club dominated a league comprised of teams from Staten Island, New York, Riverton, New Jersey, and Chester, Germantown, Pottstown, and Danville, Pennsylvania.[43]

Despite its growth during the 1880s, Cape May City remained a conservative community of gentry cottage owners, summer visitors, and year-round residents. Almost no outside investors spent money in the resort during the decade. Land development companies found few buyers for lots in either East Cape May or the Mount Vernon tract. Old Jumbo, the Mount Vernon Land Company's elephant, fell into disrepair, was moved to Cape May Point, and was eventually dismantled for its tin sides. The Cape May Driving Park Association went bankrupt, and the race track and grandstand closed. Cottagers resisted the introduction of electric trolleys until 1892. Cape May City fell further behind Atlantic City as southern New Jersey's leading seashore resort, and as one observer commented, no longer deserved its title as queen of the seaside resorts.[44]

The boss politics that choked many New Jersey cities during the late nineteenth century appeared in Cape May City. James H. Edmunds accused William Sewell, state Republican party boss, and Robert Hand, the local party chief, of buying the votes of Cape May City's "degraded colored citizens." The Republican party struck back through the *Star of the Cape*, accusing Edmunds and the local Democratic party of wide-scale corruption. The atmosphere of boss politics (and racism) permeated every municipal election in Cape May City and generated bitterness, explained F. Sidney Townsend, because of "the fact that 'White Man' is so uncertain and that 'Nigger' is never to be depended on that it is mere conjecture who will win."[45]

Cape May Point, the former Sea Grove Presbyterian retreat,

suffered more serious problems than Cape May City. Incorporated as
a borough in 1878, Cape May Point struggled to pay its county taxes
and confronted constant bankruptcy. Alexander Whilldin and other
original investors lost over $1.7 million in resort development. In
order to revive the fortune of Cape May Point, William Sewell, John
Wanamaker, and other wealthy Republican party friends and financial
backers of Benjamin Harrison, tried to interest the president in spending his summers at the resort. Earlier Monmouth County promoters
had successfully exploited President U.S. Grant's summer residency
in Long Branch to enrich that northern New Jersey oceanside resort,
and perhaps the Cape May Point entrepreneurs could do the same
thing with Harrison. Wanamaker, Sewell, and the others donated a
large cottage on Cape May Point to the Harrisons, hoping that the
president and his family would use it as the summer White House.
Harrison rarely visited the cottage, however. "The place is two and a
half miles from Cape May City," the *Star of the Cape* explained, "and
why General Sewell ever permitted his chum Harrison to go over
there is a mystery."[46]

A terrible financial panic hit the United States in 1893, ushering
in one of the worst depressions in American history. The Depression
of 1893 upset an already troubled Cape May County economy. Businesses went bankrupt. Camden City banks foreclosed on the Cape
May and Sewell's Point Railroad in 1893 and sold it at sheriff's sale.
An ambitious project begun in 1890 to build Highland City on-the-
Bay, six miles north of Cape May City in the Fishing Creek area,
stopped development. Upper Township business suffered as the price
of cordwood fell. Clothing factories closed in Woodbine, and the
Hotel Woodbine received no business. "I have an empty house for the
last two months and have had no success with the Newburg-
Rosenberg factory," Morris Bernheim, the hotel proprietor, wrote in
early 1894. Bernheim insisted that unless his hotel secured a liquor
license from county officials it would be forced to close, like most
other "Temperance Hotels" in Cape May County. Labor violence accompanied the economic troubles. Railroad workers employed by
the Reading-Seashore line to lay a new line from Winslow Junction in
Camden County through Tuckahoe to Sea Isle Junction fought with
crews employed by the older Pennsylvania and West Jersey Railroad.
The bloodiest confrontation occurred when the newcomers tried to
cross the old tracks below Woodbine Station.[47]

The depression hit Cape May City hard. Even during good times, the resort suffered from off-season unemployment, and for years the overseer of the poor had distributed winter relief among African-Americans employed by Cape May City hotels during the summer season. The *Cape May Daily Wave* declared in December 1894 that the city stood on the brink of complete bankruptcy and that local residents desperately needed a soup kitchen. Freeholder Alfred L. Haynes distributed beef among the city's poor during the winter. City employees went on half-pay. Dr. Emlen Physick, a wealthy Cape May City estate owner and man-about-town, donated a piece of land for a clothing factory to provide work for the city's idle labor force during the off-season, but the developer lost his money when a local bank failed.[48]

Cape May City's newspapers searched for a cause of the financial crisis. Thomas Brooks blamed "the evils of ignorant alien-born citizenship" for the hard times. James Edmunds felt that the depression had been caused by the Populists, a disparate group of farmers, labor organizers, free silverites, and single taxers who in 1892 had formed a third political party to press for more regulation of the railroads and businesses. "The Populist mouth," Edmunds wrote, "can create a panic in short order." The Populists won some sympathy in Cape May County among farmers hurt by high railroad shipping and bank interest rates. Cape May County Populists nominated Israel Swain Townsend of Seaville and Thomas Van Gilder of Ocean View to run for the state senate and the general assembly in the election of 1894. Neither seriously challenged the regular party candidates, but they demonstrated the growing disaffection with the existing political response to industrial problems and depression.[49]

The fear of Populists and foreign immigrants expressed by Cape May County's leading journalists in 1894 was partly a reaction to the changing conditions that transformed America from a rural, agrarian country into an urban, industrial nation. The tensions and adjustments that accompanied this transformation reached down into New Jersey's southernmost county, affecting the character of Cape May County's traditional society. Industrial technology had opened the long isolated peninsula to outside influences and to new population, particularly in Woodbine and along the barrier islands. Two railroads crossed the county by 1894, and the bicycle brought remote sections closer together and increased weekend travel into the Jersey Cape from nearby counties. Court House cyclists routinely made the fifty-five-minute trip to Cape May City to attend baseball games during the

1890s, and hundreds of wheelmen made the six- to eight-hour journey down the pikes of southern New Jersey into Cape May County each weekend during the summer beach season. The installation of a quarter-mile oval bicycle-racing track at the Cape May County fairgrounds above Court House in 1895 attested to the popularity of the wheel for travel in late-nineteenth-century Cape May County.[50]

Edmund Bennett Leaming, whose ancestors were among the original thirty-five whaler yeoman families, called all the newcomers "carpet-baggers" and insisted that no one with less than fifty years permanent residence on the peninsula could be considered "a Cape Mayman." Alfred Cooper, one of Leaming's carpetbaggers, who had entered the county in 1880 to establish the *Cape May County Gazette*, disagreed that distinctions between outsiders and old county families existed any longer. "The present generation neither knows nor cares whether their neighbors are to the Manor Born," Cooper wrote, "or who their forebears were." Nevertheless, traditional family connections continued to play a central role in county politics and society. The *Wave* explained in 1897 that intermarriage still dominated Cape May City politics as it had for two centuries. "President of Council Walter S. Leaming is a brother-in-law of City Solicitor J. Spicer Leaming, who in turn is a brother-in-law to Councilmen F. Sidney Townsend and Edward F. Townsend," the newspaper revealed.[51]

Cape May County's traditional community, dominated by the older families, resisted change and reacted against the new conditions brought about by industrialization. Some county residents joined the Prohibition party, which opposed the granting of liquor licenses to resort hotels and inns. Prohibition was an issue around which Cape May County voters showed opposition to outside ("foreign") influences. Local Prohibition party candidates polled 5 percent of the vote in the county and came close to holding the balance in some towns between the Democratic party and Republican party candidates. Cape May County members of the Women's Christian Temperance Union (WCTU) put up booths at polling places to serve coffee and to preach against proliquor licensing candidates. Prohibition divided barrier island communities. "Wildwood is a temperance town, but just across the line Holly Beach provided all the wet goods which are required," the *Cape May Daily Star* reported. The main controversy arose in Cape May City, where a liquor license meant the economic survival of many hotels and saloons. Lewis T. Stevens, a city councilman, led the forces against Mayor James H. Edmunds and his proliquor Democratic party organization. Stevens accused Edmunds of squeezing liquor dealers for money and using political influence among the saloonkeepers of the city to win votes in return for the coveted liquor license.[52]

Cape May County's traditional society also resisted more participation by women in county affairs during the late nineteenth century. There had been a quiet increase in the role of women when Dr. Anna Hand became the first female physician in Cape May County, establishing a medical practice in Cape May City in 1892. The WCTU also became politically active under the leadership of Alice Canfield of Ocean City, but in 1894 the county temperance group split badly over the question of women's suffrage. No county woman secured election to a local school board under the New Jersey law of 1887, which permitted women to vote for and hold office on school boards. Only twelve women, four of them African-Americans, voted in the Cape May City school board election of 1888 for Jennie Champion Hughes, a veteran public schoolteacher and Methodist Sunday school leader. "Thus it was contended that Mrs. [Memucan] Hughes was entirely competent," F. Sidney Townsend admitted, "yet it was developed that at the present time women are not desired to act in the capacity of school directors."[53]

Minor events seemed more intense or perhaps exaggerated in the tiny Cape May County community, which remained largely apart from modern urban and industrial developments. A woman running for the school board caused far more interest than it might in larger communities. So too did a battle between groups of immigrant railroad workers near Woodbine, or the hanging in effigy of a Tuckahoe minister in 1894, which created countywide excitement. Each incident revealed tensions in late-nineteenth-century Cape May County society, and this environment provided the setting for the only public execution to take place on the Jersey Cape. Sarah Pierce, a Swainton African-American, was found murdered in April 1894 inside a Goshen barn. Richard Pierce, Jr., her husband, was charged with the slaying, found guilty by a Cape May County jury, and hanged by the county sheriff in the yard behind the county jail at Court House, all in less than three months. Alfred Cooper, foreman of the coroner's jury, reported that the sheriff removed Pierce's body to the courthouse building, where two University of Pennsylvania physicians severed the head and removed it for study in Philadelphia.[54]

Social tensions and economic problems continued in Cape May County until the middle of the 1890s. Signs of national recovery from the depression appeared by late 1896 or early 1897 with the discovery of gold in the Klondike and improvement of agricultural prices. "The Alaska gold discovery and the passage of the tariff bill should assist in setting the wheels of business into active motion," observed the *Cape May Star* in July 1897. There was recovery throughout Cape May County. Stores in Cape May Court House received electricity. Gangs of Western Union Telegraph Company linemen strung wires between Cape May City and Philadelphia to accommodate "the large volume of business." The Delaware and Atlantic Telephone Exchange opened an office on Washington Street in Cape May City, instituting in 1897 the first long-distance telephone service in the county. A syndicate led by John J. Burleigh, Camden County traction and railroad entrepreneur, consolidated the five separate street railway and narrow gauge railroad companies under the Delaware Bay and Cape May Railroad Company and provided efficient electric trolley service from the bay to Sewell's Point and to Schellenger's Landing. The railroad combination helped stimulate a "new boom" in financially troubled Cape May Point.[55]

Holly Beach, long delinquent in payment of its county tax, was the first community in 1897 to pay its taxes. The upper part of the county recovered as well. The cranberry industry showed a profit for growers around the Tuckahoe bogs. Cape May County cranberry shippers sent twenty-four carloads from the Tuckahoe railroad station on the South Jersey Railroad and twenty thousand crates of berries from the Belle Plain station on the West Jersey Railroad line in December 1897. That same month, the Tuckahoe Building and Loan Association began lending money for the first time since the onset of the depression in 1893.[56]

The war with Spain in 1898 did not interrupt the economic recovery. One Cape May County newspaper editor predicted that the Spanish-American War would bring additional prosperity to the peninsula. "The war may cause a booming season," the *Star* observed, "for undoubtedly there will be from time to time unusual and warlike things to see." A crowd of beach bathers had spotted steamers going around Cape May Point and up the Delaware Bay to the League Island Navy Yard in Philadelphia for outfitting as auxiliary naval cruisers. The Cape May City council voted $150 to train Captain Miller's Independent Rifles, a volunteer group that drilled in the local armory.

The detention of a stranger with a foreign accent suspected of being a Spanish spy caused momentary excitement, and rumors circulated that Spanish cruisers planned to raid the Jersey Cape. U.S. Senator William Sewell assured his Cape May County summer neighbors that the U.S. Navy would protect them. In the end, cloudy, cold weather during 1898 wreaked more havoc on Cape May County resort business than did the fear of Spanish raiders.[57]

The nationalistic spirit and economic confidence that swept the United States after the defeat of Spain filled Cape May County during the closing days of the nineteenth century. Earlier antiforeign sentiment transformed into a confidence that America offered opportunity to absorb these newcomers and make them part of the prosperity. Woodbine became Cape May County's model for this Americanization. "It is indeed a splendid place for foreign boys," Thomas Brooks enthused, "they learn the English language, [and] Americanize in every way." The county showed a renewed enthusiasm for business enterprise. Harry O. Douglass, Joseph Douglass, Jr., and Dr. Julius Way, the county coroner, incorporated a glassmaking company to erect a great works just below Cape May Court House along the railroad tracks. Luther Ingersoll, Robert E. Hand, Joseph P. MacKissic, and other Lower Township businessmen organized the Citizen's Local Telephone Company in 1899 to provide telephone service between Cold Spring and Woodbine.[58]

Entrepreneurs planned to expand both the barrier island and Cape May City resorts. In the latter, a new group of businessmen that the local newspapers called progressives led the end-of-the-century boom. These business progressives included Thomas W. Millet, Luther C. Ogden, William Porter, and John Halpin, who in March 1897 incorporated the Board of Trade of the City of Cape May to plan and organize more efficiently the expected progress of the new century.[59]

CHAPTER SEVEN

Progress and World War,
1901–1919

Americans entered the new century confident that it would bring continued progress and prosperity. The crowds that welcomed the new year on 1 January 1901 in the Delaware Valley exuded that optimism. "In Philadelphia the new year and century were greeted enthusiastically," the Cape May *Wave* announced, "and for nearly five hours the streets were black with a surging mass of sight-seers." Revelers in Camden, Merchantville, and other South Jersey towns gathered to view the fireworks across the river. "The statue of William Penn stood out against the black background in a blaze of glory," the *Wave* observed. Cape May County's celebrations were smaller but equally enthusiastic. Residents danced along Cape May City's streets, blowing tin horns and whistles. Hundreds attended the masquerade ball at the Auditorium on Washington Street to hear Bellangy's orchestra. It was the largest New Year's Eve celebration in the old resort's history, the *Star of the Cape* noted.[1]

There was a more serious side to Cape May County's celebration. Solemn New Year's Eve church services suggested to some "the birth of the epoch which promises to eclipse all previous centuries in religious expansion and the uplifting of fallen humanity to a higher sphere of life." The new century also forecast the birth of a new era for the resort community in Cape May City. "Never before in the history of this old resort," the *Star* enthused, "has the pulse of business men and citizen alike beat so quickly with expectancy as at present." After years of depression and decline, Cape May City appeared to be on the way back to major resort status. The Queen Anne's Railroad now connected Baltimore with Lewes, Delaware, and a ferry service linked Lewes to Cape May City. Cape May City businessmen planned to construct a thousand-foot iron pier to accommodate the Lewes-Cape May ferryboats. The Queen Anne connection promised to revive that old southern business that had earned antebellum Cape Island the title as queen of the seaside resorts.[2]

The Cape May City council launched an advertising campaign contracting with Lewis T. Stevens to provide stories about the resort to over four hundred newspapers nationwide. Marcus A. Scull, a local real estate developer and printer, introduced the *Cape May Herald* in February 1901 to promote the resort's growth and development as the city's third major newspaper. Not to be outdone, James Henry Edmunds announced that he would make his *Wave* the voice for "the progressive future of Cape May." Noting the political success of Progressive Republicans such as Mark Fagan in Jersey City, Edmunds switched to the Republican party and began to attack the coal and ice trust owned by Cape May City's mayor, Thomas Millet.[3]

Cape May City bustled with activity in 1901 in what the local newspaper called the "New Cape May" movement. Neither the news of President William McKinley's assassination nor the raids on Cape May City businesses led by the Law and Order League dampened the spirit. The Law and Order League, organized by South Jersey clergymen and prohibitionists, convinced county officials to seize slot machines and liquor from Rose Halpin's Congress Hall, Victor Denizot's iron pier amusements and opera house, and other popular city establishments, but the proprietors paid their twenty-five-dollar fines and returned to business. The Cape May Golf Club on Washington street boomed with women's golf tournaments and mixed foursomes that "are now the Fad." Citizens held mass meetings in the Auditorium to promote electric lighting rather than gaslight to illuminate their city. Lewis Stevens led a movement to clean up the sewage and waste that clogged Cape Island Creek. The construction of a $35,000 brick, two-story city high school in 1901 symbolized the dynamic "New Cape May" movement.[4]

Only the lack of a modern electric street railway system seemed to stand in the way of continued expansion of this resort city of more than two thousand year-round residents at the southern tip of the Jersey Cape. A narrow-gauge railroad line connected the steamboat landing at Cape May Point with the city, and another ran between the city and Sewell's Point to the east. However, no trolley lines ran north and south, and after abandonment of a horse trolley in the late 1880s, no trolley linked the city to Schellenger's Landing. James E. Taylor, former city tax receiver, and Lemuel Miller, a former state senator, purchased the local railroad and trolley companies in early 1901 and combined them into the Cape May, Delaware Bay and Sewell's Point Railroad Company, forming a railroad and traction monopoly in the city and a holding company for the Philadelphia and Reading Railroad.

The Cape May, Delaware Bay, and Sewell's Point Railroad Company became a powerful political machine, similar to those early-twentieth-century traction monopolies that dominated many larger urban centers. It influenced the city council and secured rights of way along main city streets over the opposition of residents. When the city council hesitated to grant a right of way, the company took matters into its own hands. The company laid tracks on 3 May 1902 from the railroad depot on Washington Street next to Lemuel Miller's Arlington House hotel down Ocean Avenue to the beach. Five hundred workers arrived suddenly on the Reading Railroad on Saturday afternoon and started to grade streets, lay tracks, and prepare poles for overhead wires. They labored straight through the night into Sunday morning. A citizens group led by Cape May City clergymen protested the activity to Mayor Thomas Millet. Millet told them that he could not issue a restraining order until Monday morning. By then, the tracks were finished, a trolley car run over the line, and the work force returned to Philadelphia.[5]

While the Cape May, Delaware Bay and Sewell's Point Railroad established a monopoly, rumors surfaced that a syndicate led by wealthy Pittsburgh and New York steel tycoons intended to develop the eastern part of Cape May City, Poverty Beach, Sewell's Point, and Two Mile Beach across Cold Spring Inlet. This largely undeveloped beach and marshland had long attracted speculators. For a time, General William Sewell and the West Jersey and Pennsylvania Railroad people had dreamed of building a seaside resort there. Charles K. Landis had shown interest in the project. Dr. Emlen Physick had purchased much of the marshland as part of his vast Lower Township speculations in real estate. Nothing had been developed in East Cape May by 1901, however. Late that year, the *Cape May Wave* and the *Cape May Herald* circulated rumors that an unknown syndicate had bought the property. The *Herald* insisted that Henry Clay Frick, Pittsburgh steel magnate, and Charles W. Morse, who had just founded the New York Shipbuilding Corporation along the banks of the Delaware River in Camden, headed the syndicate. In fact, a group led by William Flinn, a Pittsburgh steel company owner and former state senator, and

Peter Shields, a Pittsburgh real estate entrepreneur, had purchased some four thousand acres in East Cape May.[6]

Peter Shields guided the East Cape May enterprise. He attended Cape May City council meetings and secured the promise of city bulkheads, boardwalks, sewerage pipes, and waterworks. Shields purchased the local electric light plant. He hired architects and builders for what was to be the most modern hotel in the world. Shields introduced investors from Mellon Bank, Standard Oil Company, and Carnegie Steel to the East Cape May project. He brought potential investors from New York, Philadelphia, and Baltimore to Cape May City in a specially leased private palace car over the new Delaware River railroad bridge at Delair, Camden County, through Winslow Junction, and down the peninsula. Shields publicized the East Cape May project as another Newport, Rhode Island, which would have the same stately homes, yacht clubs, golf courses, and entertainments as the posh New England resort.[7]

Constructing a deep harbor between Sewell's Point and Schellenger's Landing became the central feature of Shields's East Cape May enterprise. Work started on dredging a new harbor and building jetties on either side of Cold Spring Inlet for the harbor entrance in October 1903, when the huge dredge *Pittsburgh* arrived from Baltimore. The fill was used to build up the marshlands east of the city. Shields secured the cooperation of state and federal governments. The New Jersey riparian commission granted his private real estate company permission to fill in all the blind creeks and waterways, and State Senator Robert E. Hand of Lower Township introduced legislation for an inland waterway commission to develop a protected boat channel between the mainland and barrier islands that extended from Cold Spring Inlet north to Barnegat Bay in Atlantic County. War Department engineers surveyed Cold Spring Inlet and the proposed Cape May harbor site in 1906 as part of the projected inland waterway favored by both the Theodore Roosevelt and the New Jersey Governor George F. Fort administrations. Congress voted funds in 1907 to deepen the inlet and build jetties to protect the channel. The U.S. Army Corps of Engineers began building the jetties in 1908.[8]

Despite governmental support for the East Cape May development, the project ran into trouble. Workmen struck the hotel construction job in 1906. Racial tensions, probably tied to the strike, plagued work on roads and buildings. A trolley carrying African-American workers from Schellenger's Landing to East Cape May was sabotaged by a spiked board, and only an emergency maneuver by the conductor prevented a disastrous derailment. Then, in November 1906, the *Pittsburgh* sank suddenly into thirty feet of water, bringing harbor dredging to a standstill. The Hotel Cape May (now the Christian Admiral Hotel), a magnificent million-dollar steel-and-brick structure, opened two years behind schedule in April 1908.[9]

During the opening ceremony Governor George F. Fort presented the Hotel Cape May Cup to the winner of an automobile race from Philadelphia to the hotel.The automobile race was the featured event in the hotel dedication, attesting to the importance that Cape May County resort leaders placed on automobile travel and good roads to the development of resort business. In 1905, State Assemblyman Lewis Cresse of Ocean City, and Mayor Thomas Millet of Cape May City had organized the Cape May Automobile Club "to conduct automobile tournaments and speed contests on the Cape May Beach and to promote the interests of good roads." The club sponsored races on the strand in front of the partially completed hotel during the summer of 1905. Twenty thousand people watched in August of that year as racing machines driven by Louis Chevrolet, Walter Christie, A. L. Campbell, Henry Ford, and other racers tore along the beach between the Life Saving Station off Madison Avenue and Sewell's Point.[10]

Henry Ford came in last in the races and sold his touring car to Dan Focer, a local railroad engineer, in order to pay his bill at the Stockton Hotel. Focer later established the first automobile agency in the city. Despite his setback, Ford considered Cape May County as the location to construct an automobile factory and test track. In October 1908 he purchased the old George Hildreth mill and farm property in Lower Township just north of the new Cape May harbor. Ford bought the property for $40,000 from Emlen Physick, who had paid $2,000 for it five years before. Rumors circulated that Ford planned to erect an automobile and marine engine plant on the northern shore of the harbor. These reports increased in 1911 when Ford bought another tract adjacent to the first on the "northeast end of the Bridge over Cape Island Creek at Schellenger's Landing."[11]

The entrepreneurial activities that agitated Cape May City during the first years of the new century extended to the African-American community. In March 1901 Joseph G. Vance, a prosperous storeowner, William L. Selvy, an hotel porter, and James W. Fishburn, pastor of the Cape May City African Methodist Episcopal Church, organized the Colored American Equitable Industrial Association. This organization sought to establish institutions for the care and welfare of African-Americans and to purchase land for a town. The desire to build an African-American town somewhere in Cape May County derived, at least partly, from a growing pattern of discrimination in Cape May City. R. J. Cresswell, city councilman, refused to allow any blacks on a city-sponsored trip to Wilmington in June 1901 to watch the launching of the *City of Cape May*, a ferryboat. A few months later, the city administration excluded African-American students from the new city high school. The "apartments for the colored annex," the county superintendent of schools explained, had not been completed. Black students had to attend the dilapidated Franklin Street school until the construction of the segregated wing of the Cape May City High School.[12]

The *Cape May Herald* campaigned during 1901 to remove African-American residents from Cape May City. Marcus Scull, the newspaper's editor, who owned property along an African-American section of Lafayette Street, printed lurid accounts of Cape May City's "colored population" who allegedly loitered about Lafayette Street drinking heavily and insulting white vacationers as they passed by in their fine carriages. The *Herald* insisted that Cape May City could never return to the glories of pre–Civil War days until the community rid itself of its African-American population. Scull published a letter on the front page of his newspaper from a reader who wanted to make Lafayette Street "an attractive avenue for settlement by white families" and "free from mixture with the colored population which now chiefly occupy the avenue for some distance north of Franklin Street, with gas works and all things else objectionable removed farther back toward the creek or to another locality."[13]

Perhaps such racism prompted Joseph Vance and the others to organize the Colored American Equitable Industrial Association the same month that the *Herald* campaigned for the removal of African-Americans from the city. The Reverend James W. Fishburn, a South Carolina clergyman who moved to Cape May City circa 1900, led the movement to build an African-American town. However, Fishburn represented not Cape May City's black community but a syndicate of wealthy southern investors. This real estate group included Paul Laurence Dunbar, the preeminent turn-of-the-century African-American poet and novelist, Harriet Aletha Gibbs of Washington, D.C., Wiley H. Bates of Annapolis, Maryland, and Samuel Vick of North Carolina. The syndicate's largest investor was George Henry White, a former North Carolina educator and state legislator, prominent Washington, D.C., lawyer, and the last post-Reconstruction Era African-American to hold a seat in the U.S. House of Representatives (1896–1901). White probably employed the Reverend Mr. Fishburn to purchase seventeen hundred acres in Cape May County for the syndicate from Robert E. Hand in August 1901. Fishburn paid $14,000 for a tract of land in Middle Township eight miles north of Cape May City. Ironically, the land on which the African-American investors hoped to build their agricultural and industrial town had once been the property of Aaron Leaming, Jr., and Thomas Leaming, Jr., the largest slave owners in Cape May County history.[14]

Only George White actually developed the Cape May County property. It was doubtful whether Paul Dunbar and his wife, Alice Ruth Dunbar, major shareholders in Cape May County real estate, intended to settle in Middle Township. Plagued by poor health and marital problems, Dunbar moved instead to his hometown of Dayton, Ohio, where he died in 1906. White settled in Philadelphia in 1905, founded the George H. White Realty and Development Company, established a bank, and assumed charge of town building in Cape May County. The new African-American community's post office was first named White, after the town's founder, and later renamed Whitesboro. White's plan for developing an industrial and agricultural community probably received inspiration from Booker T. Washington, founder of Tuskegee Institute and leading exponent of African-American agricultural and industrial communities. White's law office represented Washington, and the two leaders may have associated together in business.[15]

Booker T. Washington visited Cape May County and attended a ceremony where George White, Joseph Vance, and other African-American leaders discussed the founding of Whitesboro. Possibly Washington visited Woodbine as well when the Jewish community became a separate borough in 1903. There was a close similarity between the Woodbine street and lot plans with wide boulevards and the plan adopted for the town of Whitesboro. An editorial in the *Star*, owned by Robert E. Hand, who sold the land for Whitesboro to Fishburn and may have helped to lay out the town, noted as early as 1902 that there was a connection between Woodbine and Whitesboro. "It will be an agricultural colony on the same plan as the Jewish colony of Woodbine," Hand's newspaper explained.[16]

George White sold shares in Cape May County's planned "Negro town" to African-Americans from North Carolina and Virginia, not to blacks already in Cape May County as proposed by the original trustees of the Colored American Equitable Industrial Society. Henry W. Spaulding, a North Carolina carpenter related through marriage to White, became White's manager, developing streets and constructing houses. Early lot owners included Henry S. Beaman, a North Carolina merchant who established Whitesboro's first country store, and North Carolina farmers General Scott Askew and Earnest A. Cherry (possibly the Noah Cherry who is buried in a plot near the Garden State Parkway). White's real estate company sold an additional fifty-four building lots in Whitesboro, mostly to North Carolinians, and a lot to the Middle Township Board of Education to build a schoolhouse in 1909. Maggie Beaman, John and Levi Stanford, and members of the Macedonian Baptist Church of Cape May City organized a church in Whitesboro and built a meetinghouse by 1904. Four years later, General Askew, Lena M. Askew, the Reverend Ezra Pearsall, and Maggie Pearsall incorporated the Mt. Olive Baptist Church, probably holding services in Court House. A local newspaper praised the development around Whitesboro. This "new settlement for the Colored Race," the *Cape May Wave* explained, showed that the "spirit of Progressivism is not confined entirely to the Caucasian race."[17]

Other new communities developed in Cape May County during the first decade of the twentieth century. Philip P. Baker purchased a tract of land south of Holly Beach in 1905 and developed Wildwood Crest, which incorporated as a borough in 1910. In another transaction, the Avalon Development Company sold the southern portion of Seven Mile Beach, known as Stone's Harbor, to the South Jersey Realty Company for $90,000 in September 1907. First surveyed in 1825 by Ephraim Hildreth, this 3,674-acre tract included "accretions to said hereby conveyed hereditaments and premises formed by the gradual receding of the Atlantic Ocean." This term of the property transfer revealed the unstable and potentially litigious nature of real estate along the barrier islands. The tides could wash away or deposit new beachfront at any time. The South Jersey Realty Company immediately distributed property to Howard S. Risley and David Risley, the company's president and secretary, and to their brother, Reese P. Risley. The Risley brothers created the resort community of Stone Harbor and secured its incorporation as a borough in 1914. The Risleys built hotels, developed sidewalks and streets, constructed cottages, dredged harbors and basins, built a yacht club and street railway, and connected the community to the mainland via Stone Harbor Boulevard. They sponsored automobile races and, in 1912, the first airmail flight on the New Jersey coast from Stone Harbor's beach to Ocean City.[18]

Stone Harbor was the last incorporated town built on the barrier islands, and in many ways exemplified the larger settlement pattern and development of the earlier barrier island communities. The Risleys, like the Lake family and the Baker brothers, organized real estate development corporations, sold shares in the enterprise, and attracted cottagers, hotel proprietors, shopkeepers, and restaurateurs to their oceanfront resort. Like Charles K. Landis, the Risleys used Italian-American laborers and road workers to level sand dunes and grade streets. Some of those employed by the South Jersey Real Estate Company settled permanently on the island. The Risleys, like the Bakers and John Burk on Holly Beach, brought African-American hotel workers, cooks, and teamsters to the island. The Risleys also hired Scandinavian and German carpenters, builders, and fishermen. Thus, the first hundred residents of Stone Harbor assumed the population characteristics that appeared in other barrier island resorts, forming communities that differed substantially from the mainland, where eight out of ten residents had been born in New Jersey or Pennsylvania.[19]

The Risley brothers recognized, like Landis and other barrier island pioneers, that their community's survival depended upon establishing a connection to the mainland. Stone Harbor's isolation had long discouraged development, and the Risleys determined to construct a roadway and bridge from Stone Harbor directly to the mainland near Court House. They also drafted a plan for a cross county canal from Stone Harbor to Dias Creek through the center of Court House. The proposed five-mile canal would be one hundred feet wide and ten feet deep and crossed by two railroad and two automobile drawbridges. Only the Stone Harbor roadway was built, and in 1911 Howard S. Risley, president of the South Jersey Realty Company, traveled to Trenton and asked Governor Woodrow Wilson to visit Cape May County and dedicate the Stone Harbor Ocean Parkway.[20]

Woodrow Wilson welcomed the opportunity to return to New Jersey's most remote county. He had campaigned for governor briefly at Court House and Wildwood in 1910, where he found the forces of the Democratic party and progressivism in disarray. Wilson discovered a county dominated by a Republican party political machine headed by Robert "Bob" Hand and by Hand's *Star and Wave*, a Republican newspaper combination formed in 1907 when the *Star of the Cape* company purchased the *Wave*, the county's oldest newspaper. The *Star and Wave* had attacked Wilson unmercifully during the campaign, portraying the Princeton University president as a haughty intellectual out of touch with the people. Cape May County rejected Wilson, when the rest of the state swept him into office. Thus, Wilson agreed for a number of political and personal reasons to return in July 1911 and dedicate the opening of this major automobile route to the barrier islands.[21]

The Stone Harbor visit generated the political reaction that Wilson had expected. A few months later, J. Thompson Baker, Oliver Blackwell, George N. Smith, and Charles A. Norton, Wildwood and Holly Beach Democratic party organizers, invited the governor back to the county. They chartered a special train from Kaighn's Point, Camden, and arranged a motor cavalcade along the bayshore to Rio Grande, a tour of Cape May City, and a motorboat ride from Cape May harbor up the Middle Thoroughfare to Wildwood. During this trip around the county, Woodrow Wilson stopped at Norbury's Landing on the bayside, where he met the Dias Creek Fishermen's Association, angry over a new state law that outlawed net fishing. Wilson told the fishermen that he had signed the law because their state senator, "Bob" Hand, had insisted that county residents favored passage. Wilson promised the Cape May County net fishermen that he would revise the law. The governor next visited the boardwalk in Wildwood as a guest of the Bakers. He rode along the boardwalk in the famous rolling chair and dined at the Holly Beach Yacht Club, where he called for consolidation of the towns on Five Mile Beach. In fact, a few months later, on 1 January 1912, the boroughs of Holly Beach and Wildwood consolidated into the city of Wildwood, although North Wildwood, incorporated in 1906, and Wildwood Crest, formed in 1910, opted to remain separate borough governments.[22]

Woodrow Wilson returned to the county a fifth time in October 1912, as he ran for president of the United States. His visits had strengthened the Democratic party in Cape May County, as had his appointment of Curtis T. Baker of Wildwood to the Cape May County court of common pleas instead of Matthew Jefferson of Dennis Township. Wilson's political alliance lay on the barrier islands, particularly in Wildwood, where he campaigned successfully for J. Thompson

Baker, who in 1912 became the first Cape May County resident since Thomas H. Hughes (a Whig representative, 1829–1833) to win a seat in the U.S. House of Representatives. Wilson knew that he had built a political organization in Cape May County. "I have come to feel very much at home in Cape May County," he told an enthusiastic Court House crowd. "It is delightful to find this old county, which has been so systematically neglected, so systematically forgotten by the other parts of the state," Wilson continued, "now coming into the running and saying, 'we, too, are part of the new force, of the new age, and we are going to take part in a rejuvenation of American institutions which will be worthy of the great founders of this ancient county.' "[23]

Woodrow Wilson had stirred the county's political forces but doubted that he had instilled the proper spirit of progressive reformism among the conservative residents. "You had a much more vital part with contracts for roads in Cape May County, than you have had with the people of the United States," he confided to one group of Cape May County voters. In this observation, Wilson displayed an intimate understanding of county politics. Road and bridge politics had absorbed local government ever since the 1690s, when Shamgar Hand, John Townsend, and Rem Garretson had been appointed road commissioners to construct a road out of the county. Road politics remained at the center of local government throughout the next two hundred years and became more dominant still during the first decade of the twentieth century as the automobile introduced an entirely new era to Cape May County seashore resorts. Motor cars brought weekend vacationers into the county by the thousands, and high-speed automobiles raced about the county's dirt wagon paths and over the narrow bridges that spanned creeks and thoroughfares. Automobiles hurtled through unguarded railroad crossings and over causeways covered with loosely packed gravel. Automobiles competed with horse and wagon for the narrow lanes. Such confrontations ended tragically for Isaac Pepper, a Cape May City African-American wagon driver. An automobile frightened his team, throwing Pepper against a fence and killing him instantly in July of 1904, probably the first automobile-related death in Cape May County.[24]

The Cape May County Board of Chosen Freeholders undertook a massive road- and bridge-building program during the first fifteen years of the twentieth century, improving nearly one hundred miles of county roadways for automobile travel. Road and bridge building became a most lucrative business for local contractors and gravel pit owners. From the beginning, suggestions of graft and corruption accompanied the large-scale public works contracting. Freeholders Henry S. Rutherford and Samuel E. Ewing voted in 1901 against granting a road contract to Robert E. Hand, county Republican party boss, because his $45,000 bid for the Rio Grande-Holly Beach Road was not the lowest bid. When Hand blocked Ewing's reelection to the board, the former freeholder asked the New Jersey Supreme Court to investigate Hand's contract. The court dismissed the case. The following year, the Board of Chosen Freeholders suspended N. C. Price, county engineer, when he complained that the poor quality of gravel used by the county risked injury to travelers. In 1903 Stillwell H. Townsend, county engineer, again attacked Robert E. Hand, this time for not using top-quality material on the Holly Beach Road. Hand insisted that Townsend's motives in criticizing his road work were strictly political.[25]

Cape May County's road building came under increased scrutiny by New Jersey state government, which during the first decade of the twentieth century developed a state highway system. In early 1907, E. C. Hutchinson, the New Jersey commissioner of public roads, warned Anthony B. Smith, director of the Cape May County Board of Chosen Freeholders, to exercise more caution in his road expansion program. "I do not approve of the county's purchasing the gravel for new roads," Hutchinson wrote Smith, "and I am absolutely opposed to any allowance for over hauls." Smith ignored the warning and rushed ahead with new county roads, including the Tuckahoe-Ocean City, Dennisville-Marshallville, and Dennisville-Sea Isle City roads. Smith pushed work on the latter route in "anticipation of receiving the State's share of said road." The Cape May County Board of Chosen Freeholders also condemned and tore down the old wooden covered bridge over Dennis Creek in 1907, and contracted to build a steel bridge over this important county route.[26]

Alfred Cooper, who made the *Cape May County Gazette* into an organ for good government and municipal reform, suggested that problems over roads stemmed from inefficiency in the administration of county business. He argued that the twelve-member board of freeholders (already reorganized between 1896 and 1897 by reducing membership from sixteen to twelve members) was still too large to conduct business and was subject to too many individual interests. Cooper called for replacement of the large board with a three-member commission, an idea that echoed the movement toward a commission form of government led by Woodrow Wilson and other New Jersey progressives who sought to streamline and democratize government through popularly elected commissions. "The time has come," Cooper wrote in 1911, "when something more in keeping with progressive government should be adopted."[27]

The concept of a commission, which progressive reformers argued was less susceptible to manipulation by boss politics than other forms of local government, received support in Cape May County from the boards of trade, chambers of commerce, Commercial League of Cape May Court House, and the Young Men's Progressive League of Ocean City. The latter was formed in December 1911 to "aid and assist in the pure and honest administration of public affairs." Lewis T. Stevens, while the county representative to the state assembly in Trenton, supported a form of commission government where the three candidates in a municipal election who received the largest vote regardless of party would become commissioners. Stevens later edited a collection of documents about New Jersey commission government.[28]

Not everyone favored municipal reform. Nelson Z. Graves, the largest property owner in Lower Township and Cape May City and the proprietor of the Cape May Casino, Hotel Cape May, and Cape May Farmstead, took out a front-page newspaper advertisement in the *Star and Wave* one week before a Cape May City election, announcing that he opposed a proposed change in city government. In response, city voters overwhelmingly defeated the commission form of government in September 1911. The *Star and Wave* opposed any type of progressive municipal reform. "The initiative, referendum and recall are named in the bill merely to catch the gullible," the city newspaper explained, "and would be of no value from the people's standpoint." Cape May City voters resisted the commission concept until 1915, when they elected the first Cape May City Commission, consisting of William L. Stevens, Joseph H. Hanes, and William S. Shaw.[29]

Opposition to political reform appeared in Cape May County's response to women's suffrage during this era of progressivism. "The greatest majority of women in the state do not want to vote," announced the *Cape May County Times* in 1915. William A. Haffert, the editor, led local opposition to women's suffrage, urging women to stay home and not disrupt the harmonious, prosperous Cape May County society. Haffert rejoiced when New Jersey and Cape May County voters defeated a suffrage amendment in October 1915, announcing in bold headlines: "SUFFRAGETTES ARE BADLY BEATEN." Haffert failed to note that while 44.5 percent of the county's voters (all male) supported women's suffrage, Woodbine voters endorsed the reform by a two-to-one margin and the barrier islands divided evenly over the question. Woodbine, after some indecision, seemed to identify with the communities on the barrier islands rather than with the older mainland townships or Cape May City. Woodbine and the barrier islands shared similar characteristics. They were all late-nineteenth-century creations by outsiders. They held far larger foreign-born populations than any of the older sections of the county; and their social and political alliances more nearly reflected national political forces. Woodbine and Wildwood became centers of Democratic party politics in a county controlled by the Republican party.[30]

Leadership of the women's suffrage movement in the county centered in the barrier islands and in Woodbine. Mary V. (Mrs. Reese P.) Risley of Stone Harbor, Priscilla F. (Mrs. William H.) Bright of Wildwood, and Margaret Elizabeth (Mrs. J. Thompson) Baker and her daughters Frances, Katharine, and Mary led the barrier island suffragettes. Frances Baker and William H. Bright toured the county together, speaking for women's rights at Payne's Store in South Seaville, Way's Store in Ocean View, and other traditional mainland gathering places. Woodbine suffragettes held the largest rallies; in 1914 they turned away from the borough hall hundreds who came to hear Anna Lowenberg and Dille Hasting, Philadelphia suffragette leaders.[31]

The women's suffrage issue reflected a growing division over social and political change between mainlanders and the newcomers in Woodbine and on the barrier islands. The differences appeared in the growth rate and characteristics of the population in the respective regions of the county. Cape May County population increased between 1900 and 1910 from 13,201 to 19,745, a 49.6 percent increase. While the mainland averaged under 10 percent growth, the barrier island population increased by over 200 percent during the decade. From their former uninhabited status, the oceanfront beaches by 1910 held nearly 30 percent of the entire county population. The contrast was even starker in the percentage of foreign-born residents in each section. Woodbine and the barrier islands contained over 80 percent of the county foreign-born population.[32]

The differences between the older and newer communities were reflected in political leadership. Older families dominated the mainland and represented their sections on the board of freeholders, where they tangled for influence and money with the newcomers from the barrier islands. Descendants of the original whaler yeoman pioneers still held power on the mainland. These families included the Hands, Ludlams, Townsends, Corsons, Smiths, Gandys, and Cresses. Three Cresses ran for county office in 1901. Alfred M. Cresse of Green Creek, the county's leading harness racetrack driver, became the Republican party candidate for sheriff. Lewis M. Cresse ran for the state assembly, and Clinton S. Cresse for county sheriff on the Prohibition party ticket. There was a "superabundance of Cresses," the *Wave* noted, adding that, "if the Democrats can find a Cresse for their candidate for sheriff it will be easy to tell what the next sheriff's name will be."[33]

Newcomers to the county such as J. Thompson Baker and William H. Bright emerged as county leaders on the barrier islands. Bright became locked in a countywide political power struggle with mainlander Robert Hand. At the same time, the Bakers fought political battles against the Hands and Cresses. Stillwell Townsend of Court House assailed the selection of Charles E. Clouting of Sea Isle City, J. Thompson Baker of Wildwood, and Reuben Edwards of Ocean City to the Cape May County Sinking Fund Commission. Townsend claimed that the barrier islands now controlled county finances.[34]

Not surprisingly, the barrier islands produced Cape May County's female leadership during the progressive era, 1901–1917. Dr. Margaret Mace, the daughter of Charles Mace, one of the founders of Anglesea (North Wildwood), graduated from the Woman's Medical College of Pennsylvania in 1905 and opened a medical practice on the northern part of Five Mile Beach the following year. She cared for wealthy summer cottagers, but, as one visitor recalled, also went "into the homes of the poor and sick and helpless suffering ones and fed and ministered to them, treating them without compensation." Mace crusaded for a county public health service and a county hospital. She served as a police surgeon and cared for the injured in every major accident or disaster in the county for two decades. She delivered hundreds of babies. Margaret Mace joined J. Thompson Baker and several Five Mile Beach businessmen in the incorporation of the Samaritan Hospital of Cape May County in 1911. This organization intended to construct the first county hospital. Instead, Mace purchased the Frederick Sutton mansion in Wildwood in 1915 and founded the Mace Emergency Hospital. The twenty-five-bed hospital served as the county's major hospital, dispensing all types of medical services until the establishment of the Burdette Tomlin Hospital at Court House in 1950.[35]

Wildwood was the home of Katharine Baker, who except for her premature death as a Red Cross nurse in World War I might have become a national leader for women's rights. Baker attended Bucknell and Goucher colleges and passed the Pennsylvania bar exam. She taught school in Wildwood, introduced the Montessori method to the county board of education, and in 1912 became the first elected female member of the county board of education. Katharine Baker wrote between 1911 and 1914 for the nation's leading progressive reform magazines, publishing essays in *McClure's*, *Forum*, *Atlantic*, *Collier's*, *Hampton*, and *Harper's Weekley*. In a series of short stories that were based upon her own experiences and observations of life on Cape May County's barrier islands, Baker criticized the subservient status of women in the United States. "American women are petted, helpless dolls," she wrote in the *Atlantic* magazine in 1913. Baker demonstrated through her stories and essays that women could be strong, independent leaders in business and politics, equal to men.[36]

Clearly two different worlds had emerged in Cape May County during the first decade of the twentieth century: the mainland and the Woodbine-barrier island community. Within these there existed a number of lesser divisions—between the upper and lower parts of the peninsula, and between Ocean City and Wildwood—thus adding to the complexity of Cape May County society. The division underscored the fragile nature of the county's resort economy. After a decade of vigorous growth and prosperity between 1900 and 1910, Cape May County experienced a decade of decline between 1910 and 1920, when population actually decreased for the first time in county history. Every section suffered. The East Cape May project collapsed in bankruptcies and sheriff's sales. Trouble had appeared in 1909 when Peter Shields quit as president of the Cape May Real Estate Company. The following year, Frederick W. Feldner of Baltimore, the new president, and Fritz Mergenthaler, the major stockholder in the real estate company, were killed when their speeding Locomobile automobile crashed into the Pennsylvania Railroad express train at the Cold Spring crossing. Nelson Z. Graves, a wealthy Philadelphia and Camden paint and varnish manufacturer and longtime Cape May City cottager, took over the East Cape May enterprise. He temporarily revived East Cape May, making the Hotel Cape May a major convention center, improving trolley lines, and in 1913 building a "fun factory" (amusement park) on Sewell's Point. In the end, Graves went bankrupt.[37]

Other Jersey Cape communities also suffered. Whitesboro failed to attract businesses or large numbers of new settlers after 1909. The town became a dumping place for barrier island refuse, and boxcars with rotting seafood stood on the sidings at Wildwood Junction, just below Whitesboro. Court House was devastated by a fire in 1905 that destroyed most of the business section. On Seven Mile Beach, the Princeton, Avalon's only hotel licensed to serve liquor, burned to the ground. The Peermont and Avalon fire companies could not fight the blaze because the town's fireplugs were broken. Ocean City's problems were more complex. The *Cape May County Times* summarized that resort's dilemma. "High taxes, increasing County debt, shark frights, scares, infantile paralysis, and what not," the *Times* explained, "have been ascribed as the cause for little or no activity in the building line in our County resorts the past year or so." The most important sign of the county's troubles appeared in Woodbine: the Baron de Hirsch Foundation decided to move the agricultural and . industrial school to New York State in early 1917.[38]

The sudden loss one after another in remarkable succession of prominent Cape May County figures between 1913 and 1917 added to the gloom. Curtis T. Baker, an immensely popular young county judge, collapsed and died in August 1913. The following summer Ocean City mayor and former assemblyman Lewis M. Cresse, apparently despondent over financial problems and poor health, took his own life in an Ocean City garage. The next year Thomas W. Millet, one of Cape May City's most popular mayors, died suddenly. Then Emlen Physick passed away unexpectedly in 1916. Though an eccentric and often self-serving real estate speculator, Physick had long promoted Cape May City's progress and prosperity and had become something of a gadfly for good government and municipal reform. The following year, Robert E. Hand, one of the most dominant Cape May County political figures, died.[39]

Some county businessmen thought that advertisement and public relations might pull Cape May County out of the doldrums, revive business, and bring the crowds back to the resort. Cape May County had received too much bad publicity, explained William Porter, Cape May City drugstore owner and political reformer. "There is a feeling abroad," Porter wrote, "that Cape May is so corrupt, so absolutely in the grip of 'boodlers' and 'grafters,' that her condition is hopeless." James E. Whitesell, Wildwood city clerk, hired the Philadelphia advertising firm of H. R. Whitcraft to produce an attractive brochure that promoted the benefits of the oceanfront resorts on the Jersey Cape. "Senator Baker and I called on the Pennsylvania Railroad this afternoon and showed them the booklet," Whitesell wrote, "and they at once asked for 2,000 to distribute in their various passenger agents." The Wildwood city clerk intended to circulate thousands more. "The Reading R. R. no doubt can make good use of at least 1,500," Whitesell explained in 1914.[40]

Philip P. Baker, mayor of Wildwood Crest, hoped to use parades, carnivals, and events such as baby parades and the Old Home Week Celebration to boost business. Thomas Brady of Amusement Enterprises in New York promised to provide Baker with all the necessary equipment for Old Home Week, and to "use our best efforts to book and arrange for the appearances of side shows, platform shows, merry-go-round, ferris wheel and other riding devices besides numerous concessions." Charles A. Norton, one of the original founders of the Board of Trade of Holly Beach City, offered to produce a moving picture in 1917 to advertise Wildwood.[41]

Judge James M. E. Hildreth, Luther Ogden, president of the Cape May City Board of Trade, and other city leaders suggested that cleaning up Cape May County's mosquito problem might better revive the summer shore business. The salt marsh mosquito had plagued Cape May County since earliest settlement. Ephraim Sloan, a Court House farmer, claimed that clouds of mosquitoes often darkened the sky and that one swarm had killed entire herds of cattle around Dennisville. F. Sidney Townsend noted in his diary that mosquitoes and green-head flies destroyed nearly every summer season between 1880 and 1890. Finally, in 1901, John M. Rogers, owner of the Marine Villa in Cape May City, agitated for the organization of a mosquito extermination commission in the county. A few years later Peter Shields pressed the New Jersey legislature to pass a mosquito control law. The legislature appropriated funds for mosquito extermination and in 1912 passed a statewide county mosquito commission law, authorizing each county to form an organization to combat the hated mosquito. Cape May County organized such a commission in 1915, and the following year a number of residents petitioned the freeholders to appropriate $10,000 to drain and ditch lowlands and to spread oil on breeding ponds. "There seems to be a demand by the taxpayers of the county, particularly from the Seaside Resorts for an appropriation to be used for the extermination of mosquitos in the county," observed Henry S. Rutherford, the director of the board of freeholders, in 1916.[42]

It would be the great European war that erupted in August 1914 that revived Cape May County business. The giant Bethlehem Steel Company of Pennsylvania brought war industry to the Jersey Cape when it established several ordnance-proving grounds on the peninsula. The decision to locate testing grounds in Cape May County came from Eugene G. Grace, president of Bethlehem Steel. Grace knew the county. He had grown up in Goshen on the old bayshore road, where his parents operated a country store, and he had attended the Goshen public schools before going on to Lehigh University. Grace directed the purchase in 1915 of a tract along the Delaware bayshore now known as Higbee's Beach. The company purchased another tract north of Coxhall Creek and leased land near Grace's old homestead along the bay from Goshen south to Pierce's Point. Adella Reed, a resident of Dias Creek, also recalled that Bethlehem Steel built several buildings and a tiny railroad on Reed's Beach to bring test guns down to the bayside. The munitions company tested artillery shells probably manufactured at the Bethlehem Loading Company plant (Belcoville) in Atlantic County and contracted for by the French, Russian, and British armies.[43]

Bethlehem Steel was not finished with its Cape May County acquisitions. A few months after the United States became involved in World War I in April 1917, the company bought additional land from Rolla and Mary Garretson, heirs to the Theophilus Corson estate in Upper Township. This testing ground for naval ordnance extended from the Tuckahoe River south across the Tuckahoe-Marmora Road and then north to Willets Thoroughfare. The company fenced off the land, posted armed guards, built ammunition storage sheds, and secured permission from the county board of freeholders to use a railroad spur to Petersburg. The *Cape May County Times* reported that by May 1917 seven carloads of ammunition lay on the Tuckahoe siding waiting for shipment to Petersburg. Several residents complained about the noise of the incessant gunfire from the proving grounds, but county administrators ignored the complaints. Recognizing that Bethlehem Steel meant a revival of prosperity, Freeholders Joseph MacKissic of Lower Township and Uriah Gandy of Upper Township introduced a resolution to the board to "commend the said Bethlehem Steel Company and its manager for the orderly manner in which its business had been conducted in the County of Cape May."[44]

While Bethlehem Steel developed its proving grounds, the federal government considered Cape May City harbor as the site for a naval training station and airfield. Rumors of U.S. Navy interest in the area surfaced during the summer of 1913 when a Cape May County delegation reportedly met with Franklin D. Roosevelt, then assistant secretary of the navy. "It is an open secret," the *Star and Wave* reported, "that the government military and naval authorities are considering making of the harbor a naval base and of ultimately fortifying it." Rumors became stronger that the local Life Saving Force would be stationed in a new naval base in Cape May City when in January 1915 Congress created the U.S. Coast Guard by consolidating the old Life Saving Service and the Revenue (Marine) Cutter Service and by providing that in wartime the Coast Guard would become a part of the U.S. Navy.[45]

Naval reservists from Fourth Naval District Headquarters in Philadelphia frequented Cape May City harbor in their submarine chasers and tenders during the summer of 1916. The *Absecon*, a government dredge, started to dig out the harbor channel to permit access by submarine boats. At the same time, a Curtiss flying boat landed near the Corinthian Yacht Club on Cape May harbor's western shore, demonstrating the feasibility of the area for a naval air station. Naval reservists joined local residents and summer cottagers for a July Fourth celebration in 1916 that included dances, fireworks, and a grand parade through Cape May City featuring floats by Little's Bath House, the Grand Army of the Republic, Women's Christian Temperance Union, and the Bethlehem Steel Company, the latter float a huge pyramid of hollow artillery shells. That month, the navy announced that it would establish a training station in Cape May. "The preparedness units will make a very valuable asset to the attractions of the resort," the *Star and Wave* enthused, "and will present a very imposing appearance at any gala day on the waterfront."[46]

After years of uneasy neutrality, the Woodrow Wilson administration asked Congress for a declaration of war against Germany on 2 April 1917, in response to German announcement that it would launch unrestricted submarine warfare against all shipping. The following day, Governor Walter Edge of New Jersey appointed Joseph G. Champion, the mayor of Ocean City, to the State Preparedness Commission. Champion organized his city for war. "Ocean City has several organizations of Ladies who are no doubt anxious to do something to display their patriotism and in order that all may work together in harmony with the general preparedness scheme," the mayor announced, "I am taking the liberty to appoint one lady from each organization to form a Central Committee for the purpose of bringing all organizations together in this great work." Champion also told the Cape May County Board of Freeholders that "in view of the impending crisis in international affairs and the possibility of spies or enemies attempting to destroy property" the county should appropriate money for defense of the bridges and beaches. A few days later Joseph MacKissic of Lower Township introduced a resolution to the board to raise $500 for the maintenance of a "Home Guard" to subdue disorder in Cape May County.[47]

A patriotic fervor swept through the county unlike anything that had occurred since the Civil War. Mayor William L. Stevens organized a patriotic demonstration in Cape May City and opened a recruiting station in City Hall. Stevens called upon Cape May County men to enlist and "strike down the ruthless and lawless assailant of the Imperial Government of Germany upon our ships and cargoes." In Court House, the high school graduated seniors early so that they could volunteer for military service. Wildwood held a huge rally in Hunt's Theater where former U.S. Congressman J. Thompson Baker implored the crowd to do their duty for the nation. Already Baker's daughters, Katharine and Frances, had volunteered for the ambulance service and had left for France. Meanwhile a large crowd gathered at the Music Pavilion on the boardwalk in Ocean City to say farewell to their National Guard Company as it prepared to leave for the Sea Girt camp in Monmouth County.[48]

Contractors from the Cramp Construction Company of Philadelphia descended upon the Ford property in Lower Township north of Schellenger's Landing in June 1917 and began building thirty wooden barracks as part of the $1.5 million Wissahickon Naval Training Station. Across the harbor in East Cape May and on Sewell's Point, navy enlisted personnel built machine shops, repaired docks, erected steel hangars for flying boats and a dirigible, and drove pilings for submarine and destroyer slips in what became the Cape May Section Base (No. 9), U.S. Navy. The U.S. Navy commandeered the Corinthian Yacht clubhouse for a communications center, and the county granted permission for the navy to dig sewer lines and a water main and build a railroad track across Schellenger's Landing Road.[49]

The *Camden Post-Telegram* predicted that all the activity would bring unprecedented prosperity to Cape May County. "Cape May is experiencing something like a revival of its aforetime prosperity," the Camden newspaper observed, "now that Uncle Sam is making it a center of activity in connection with the war." Woodbine clothing factories boomed with war work. Sol Needlemen, a Cape May City businessman, opened a factory in his city. Cape May City bustled with excitement. Sailors filled the resort town with a steady round of parties, sporting events, and dances. Naval officers took over most of the summer cottages. Residents found the summer season of 1918 "the gayest" in the resort's history. Hotel Cape May became a military hospital where George W. Childs Drexel, a wealthy Philadelphian, sponsored parties for wounded patients. Cape May City opened a new convention hall in 1917 to provide further facilities for wartime amusements. Even the fire (termed suspicious by naval investigators) that on 4 July 1918 destroyed part of the old amusement pavilion and skating rink on Sewell's Point used by the Cape May Section Base failed to dampen the enthusiasm that accompanied wartime duty on the Jersey Cape.[50]

The First World War did cause difficulties for Cape May County, however. Shortages in lumber, coal, and railroad rolling stock meant delays in the development of barrier island resorts. The Strauss Bascule Bridge Company explained that it could not provide steel to complete the Sea Isle City bridge. "It is, owing to the war in Europe," the company told the board of freeholders, "impossible to get such steel castings under a period of ten months." The federal government's refusal to allow railroad shipments of material for the Strathmere Bridge hindered development of a new community organized by the Whale Beach Realty Company in 1913 on the northern tip of Ludlam's Island a few miles above Sea Isle City. Strathmere remained the only barrier island community under a mainland township government. At the same time, the government restricted the use of gondola cars to bring gravel into the county from Millville to construct county roads. Most troublesome, the railroad stopped the daily excursion train to the shore. Reese P. Risley, a Cape May Chamber of Commerce member, cabled New Jersey Senator Joseph Frelinghuysen for help and dispatched Sea Isle City Mayor Richard W. Cronecker to Washington to press for resumption of the excursion line. The Cape May County businessmen argued that the shore resort trade was an essential war service. "We folks at the shore resorts who derive our livelihood from tourists consider pleasure as much a business as any other line of endeavor," explained Carlton H. Brick, Cape May County Chamber of Commerce president.[51]

Coal shortages coincided in January 1918 with the coldest winter on the Jersey Cape since 1880. Temperatures fell to minus seven degrees at night and rose no higher than four degrees above zero during the days. Basins, bays, and creeks froze over, killing ducks and shorebirds. A bitter northeast wind drove snow across the frozen peninsula. Without coal, the Vulcan Electric Light plant near Court House could not produce electricity. Stone Harbor and Avalon went dark. Wildwood closed its schools, and the Cape May County court canceled sessions. Mainlanders burned wood in their stoves and sold cordwood at a greatly inflated price of ten dollars per cord to their freezing barrier island neighbors.[52]

The war intruded upon the lives of county residents as had no other event in the peninsula's history. Canvassers for the Liberty Loan drives, Cape May County YMCA war work fund, and the county Red Cross organization scoured the countryside, pressing residents to contribute money. Alfred Cooper, a leading county Red Cross and YMCA organizer, admitted that at times teams of solicitors used any method, including threats and intimidation, to secure funds. Cooper's organizations consolidated in 1918 under the United War Work Campaign with Mary Baker's Cape May County YWCA, Jacob Feldman's Jewish Welfare Board, and other county wartime fund-raising groups to increase efforts to collect contributions from local citizens. At the same time, residents were afraid to travel about the county. Greatly agitated by the suspicious fires at the Cape May Section Base and by news of explosions and supposed sabotage at New Jersey and Philadelphia munitions factories, Coast Guardsman fired at suspicious characters along the county's beachfront and seized fishermen in bay waters. Coast Guard patrols shot and killed a man on the Ocean City beach in September 1918.[53]

News of the deaths of county men in the war added to the solemn Cape May County wartime conditions. Six hundred Cape May residents served in World War I, and at least nine were listed by the "Soldier's Record" service as dying in the war. Mr. and Mrs. Joseph Douglass of Court House lost two sons, Charles G. and Herbert S. Douglass, from disease contracted on a troopship carrying New Jersey soldiers from Hoboken to France. Abram N. Morgan of Ocean View died in action in the Argonne forest in 1918. Disease killed

David Horenstein of Woodbine and Lawrence R. Henry and Nicola Impaglizzo of Ocean City. George E. Lloyd and Bryon Pennington Croker, both of Wildwood, died in battle. The American Legion post in Wildwood was named after Croker, who died in the Meuse-Argonne battle in 1918. The county appeared particularly moved by news that Thurston Elmer Wood, a former Court House resident and great-grandson of Dr. John Wiley, had died while commanding a battery against German positions near Vierzy, France. After the war, Wood's remains were brought from France to Court House for a memorial service before burial in a navy cemetery in Annapolis. The county American Legion post at Cape May Court House adopted Wood's name.[54]

Returning troops brought disease from the war zones back to Camp Dix and other New Jersey military camps. They spread Spanish influenza into every New Jersey town. Hundreds of people died in the larger cities of Newark and Camden. The disease raged through Cape May County, schools were closed and the county court session canceled. Woodbine recorded the most cases, but the influenza epidemic hit Cape May Court House, Tuckahoe, Ocean City, and Wildwood as well. Only three physicians—Joseph Joffe in Woodbine, Eugene Way in Dennisville, and Julius Way at Court House—were available to care for the ill in the entire upper half of the county.[55]

There were not enough doctors or nurses in Frances Baker's hospital in France either, and Katharine Baker was anxious to leave Wildwood, where she had recently returned from the battlefront to recuperate from exhaustion and disease, to assist her sister. The hospitals were overcrowded with too few nurses to care for "my wounded boys," she wrote a friend in January 1919. "They sleep in beds built up like layer cakes, three deep," Baker explained. She added, "It is very unsanitary, but on reflection the authorities decided it was more sanitary than the streets." Katharine Baker never returned to France. She was seriously ill and went to a hospital at Saranac Lake, New York, where she died a few months later. Devastated by his daughter's death, J. Thompson Baker, one of the most successful barrier island political figures and pioneer settlers, collapsed a few weeks later.[56]

CHAPTER EIGHT

Prohibition, Depression, and the New Deal, 1920–1938

For Cape May County, the First World War closed an era of change that had started with the opening of the barrier islands to settlement. Between 1879 and 1919 the Jersey Cape community had been transformed from a collection of quiet mainland agricultural villages with one resort town at the tip of the peninsula into a region with eight dynamic oceanfront resorts and a mainland industrial town. A more diverse and complex Cape May County society had emerged. Eastern Europeans had settled the Jewish borough of Woodbine, where they had established an agricultural and industrial school and factories. Italian, Scandinavian, Irish, and German immigrants formed nearly one-quarter of the population of the barrier island resort towns. The Cape May *Star and Wave* called these newcomers "irresponsible alien born," suggesting that they threatened the county's traditional social order and stability. Just as undesirable from the perspective of the county's oldest newspaper were the outside speculators who had accompanied the newcomers to the peninsula and had exploited the Jersey Cape, taking business away from the older residents. They were "parasites," the *Star and Wave* continued. "The syndicates which purchased the larger tracts," explained Albert Hand, "permitted the land to lie idle for years and blocked instead of promoted resort progress."[1]

Years of progressive agitation and reform had affected the remote Cape May County community. Woodrow Wilson swept through the peninsula between 1910 and 1912, bringing the progressive movement into the county, stimulating the commission form of government, and mobilizing a new coalition of barrier island politicians around the Baker family of Wildwood. Wilson encouraged local Democrats to challenge the old mainland Republican party machine and advanced the movement for women's suffrage and other social change. Then in 1917 Wilson led the United States into the First World War. On the Cape May peninsula, local Red Cross, YMCA, and other war relief agencies mobilized the county for the war crusade. At first, the war promised jobs and renewed prosperity. But war contractors such as the Bethlehem Steel Company descended upon Cape May County, tested ammunition, and departed as abruptly as they had come. Bethlehem Steel left a legacy of dangerous live shells buried in the sand. One exploded on Pierce's Beach in 1920, killing a vacationing fisherman and maiming Bentley Hoffman, a county resident. At the same time, U.S. government facilities around Cape May harbor deprived the county of thousands of dollars in tax ratables, and after the war, the city sued the federal government for damages and won a $31,000 settlement.[2]

Cape May County voters had shown their displeasure with Wilsonian politics and the accompanying changes in 1916 when they had rejected the former New Jersey governor in the presidential election. Four years later, Cape May County warmly endorsed Warren G. Harding, the Republican U.S. senator from Ohio, for president. "Harding is a splendid type of clean American manhood," the *Star and Wave* insisted, "a notable example to every American-born boy of the opportunities the country offers them all." Cape May County particularly welcomed what Harding called the return to "normalcy." The Republican party candidate promised to prevent American entanglement in the League of Nations, Woodrow Wilson's postwar international peace-keeping organization. Harding promised to save the nation from foreign influences such as those believed to have been unleashed by the Bolshevik Revolution of 1917 in Russia. When Harding won, Cape May County's leading newspaper announced, "We are delivered from Wilsonism."[3]

More important for the resort county, Harding's election meant "firm business-like constructive administration." Harding's successors, Calvin Coolidge and Herbert Hoover, continued this businesslike government, and received overwhelming support from traditionally Republican Cape May County. Coolidge's election results in 1924, the first broadcast into the county over a radio set, surpassed in popular votes all previous Republican victories. Four years later, Hoover won by an even larger margin, 12,190 to 3,737, over Democratic candidate

Al Smith. Smith, the Irish Catholic governor of New York, received a majority only in Woodbine, where the ethnic composition and economic character of the voters most closely reflected the emerging Democratic urban, liberal, and labor coalition that became a base for Franklin D. Roosevelt's political organization in 1932.[4]

Most Cape May County political leaders during the 1920s embodied a corporatist political-economic philosophy of business-government cooperation and organization advanced at the national level by Herbert Hoover. Cape May County Assemblyman Charles C. Read, an Ocean City hardware merchant, advanced these corporatist ideals. "The keynote of his campaign," the *Star and Wave* explained in 1924, "is business-like government, with fewer laws, and better enforcement of those we have." T. Millet Hand, the clerk of the Cape May County Board of Chosen Freeholders, explained in 1928 to the Chamber of Commerce that Cape May County government had become a business corporation, not a political body, and that the freeholders served as the board of directors of this hundred-million-dollar corporation. Similarly, Cape May County's state senator, William H. Bright, a Wildwood real estate entrepreneur and banker, chaired a joint legislative committee in Trenton in 1925 that reorganized New Jersey state government along "modern business lines."[5]

Business-government leadership throughout South Jersey provided the larger regional setting for Cape May County's economic development during the 1920s. Camden City bankers extended favorable credit terms to those who invested in Cape May County real estate and resort business. The Greater Camden Movement of business expansion led to development of new ferry slips at the Reading terminal in Camden for seashore travelers in 1924 and the surfacing of the White Horse Pike with concrete from Camden to the seashore. A spur was built from the pike to Tuckahoe; by 1926 it furnished a "motor trail to the year-round playground" of Cape May County. The Camden Bridge (now the Ben Franklin Bridge) opened for automobile traffic in 1926, accelerating the flow of visitors to New Jersey's southern seashore resorts. Cape May County surfaced the seashore road and parts of the bayside road with concrete by 1920 to keep pace with increased motor vehicle traffic. Robert S. Miller, the director of the board of freeholders, ordered the prosecution of anyone running over these new concrete roadways with iron-wheeled tractors, still the major piece of farm equipment for Cape May County farmers during the twenties.[6]

Air transportation came to Cape May County during the 1920s. It was the decade when Charles Lindbergh flew alone across the Atlantic Ocean, aviation entrepreneur Nicholas Ludington opened a transcontinental air service at Central Airport in Camden County, and Secretary of Commerce Herbert Hoover supported the development of American commercial aviation around the nation. Cape May County leaders joined the movement to develop aviation and air travel. Mayor Gustavus W. Bergner of Avalon announced that his barrier island resort would build the first airfield in the county, and Mayor Joseph G. Champion of Ocean City quietly secured a tract of land for an airport and brought in airport developer Erwin L. Schwatt of Atlantic City to plan the Ocean City airport. The first airport in the county was established by Harry F. Greaves, editor of the *Star and Wave*, Paul A. Volcker, Cape May city manager, and William R. Sheppard, the mayor of Cape May City. This airport syndicate leased one hundred acres from the U.S. Navy Department on the old naval air station used during the First World War to train pilots. It had become nothing more than a weed-filled patch of beachfront sand that extended from Sewell's Point to Yale Avenue, the easternmost street of Cape May City. The Cape May Airport Association headed by Greaves raised funds from county businessmen to grade the rough field, pull out shrubs, build a small terminal, and erect a fence to separate the airport from Section Base Nine, then and now a U.S. Coast Guard station. The county board of freeholders voted in July 1929 to contribute $300 from its special advertising fund to construct what the freeholders considered the county airport. The airfield opened for private flights in July 1929 and operated until 1934, when the Navy Department revoked its lease.[7]

Potential investors showed an interest in the giant dirigible hanger located at the center of Section Base Nine. This 700-foot long, 100-foot high structure had been completed at the close of the First World War to house ZR-2, a huge airship under construction in Britain. Lt. Charles G. Little, U.S. Navy Reserve Force, left the Cape May naval base to take command of the new airship and bring it back to the county for coastal patrol duty. While in England, Little married Joy Bright, daughter of William H. Bright of Wildwood. A female yeoman at the Cape May naval base during the war, where she had met Little, Joy Bright (Hancock-Ofstie) later became the highest-ranking female officer in the United States Navy. Unfortunately, ZR-2 crashed on a test flight before reaching Cape May County, killing Lieutenant Little.[8]

The dirigible hangar stood empty for several years. Goodyear Rubber Company, Consolidated Air Lines, and other business expressed interest in renting it. The Aero Corporation of America considered the Cape May section base facility in 1926 as part of a proposed coastal dirigible passenger service with mooring masts in Camden, Atlantic, and Cape May Cities. For a time, Anton Heinan, designer of the ill-fated dirigible *Shenandoah*, built baby blimps in the hangar on the Jersey Cape and tested one in flights over the county. The Navy Department housed four small airships in the hangar on the former naval air station, but high winds tore the largest airship from its mooring in November 1931 and ripped it open on the county airport's barbed wire fence, undoubtedly discouraging further navy use of the hangar. In 1941 the U.S. Navy pulled down the dirigible hangar during renovation of the base.[9]

The transportation revolution in South Jersey during the 1920s revived interest in a ferry line across the Delaware Bay connecting Cape May County to Lewes, Delaware. Earlier efforts to develop this line had ended in failure. The Queen Anne ferry service had folded in 1904, partly over the company's inability to develop a safe landing facility on the Cape May side. During the 1920s, William H. Bright, Cape May County state senator, introduced ferry legislation as part of the state highway appropriation bill of 1921, and Lewis T. Stevens, a former state assemblyman from the county, lobbied in Trenton for passage of the ferry bill. In 1926, Jesse Rosenfeld of Baltimore, president of the National Navigation Company, developed the idea of using concrete ships to form a Y-shaped ferry dock at Cape May Point near the old steamboat landing. Rosenfeld purchased the *Atlantus*, one of four concrete freighters built during the world war by the Liberty Shipbuilding Corporation of Georgia. The 250-foot concrete hulk was raised from the mud in Virginia's James River in June 1926 and towed from Norfolk to Cape May County.[10]

As reports of a new Cape May-Lewes ferry line circulated through the county, the board of freeholders straightened and paved the old shellbed toll road between Cape May Point and the city, rededicating the road as Sunset Boulevard in August 1926. Real estate speculators purchased land along either side of Sunset Boulevard from the West Cape May town line to the bay and south to the beachfront cluster of houses called South Cape May. The Marks Construction Company of Philadelphia brought in steam-powered shovels, dump trucks, and teams of horse drawn wagons to grade streets and lots for a new community called Cape May Gardens. In the process of excavation on the old Reeves farm, the developers uncovered Native American burial mounds, disinterred three skeletons, and discovered numerous artifacts, probably revealing the original site of a permanent Lenape settlement on the Cape May peninsula.[11]

Jesse Rosenfeld's project ran into trouble. The *Atlantus* slipped its mooring in a high wind and plowed bow first into the sand. Floated free, the hulk dragged its anchor and became fouled in the discharge pipe of the Cape May City sewer. The huge concrete mass could not be stirred further from its resting place, and indeed sixty-five years later it still lies just offshore at the end of the Sunset Boulevard. Rosenfeld failed to obtain support from either the New Jersey or the Delaware state legislatures, and his company fell apart. "Those who had subscribed and paid for their stock in good faith," Albert Hand's *Star and Wave* writers recalled, "felt that they had been misled by excess enthusiasm on the part of the promoters."[12]

Another attempt to establish the Cape May-Lewes ferry was made by New Jersey Governor Morgan F. Larson. Larson signed a bill that authorized the state highway commission to construct a ferry dock and access highway in Cape May County if a properly bonded private operator could be found to run a ferry franchise. An Ocean City syndicate incorporated to operate the ferry, but lacked financial backers. Then, a group of Delaware, Philadelphia, and Cape May County investors formed the New Jersey and Delaware Transportation Company to sell shares, purchase ferryboats, and secure a company to run the ferry. Harry F. Greaves, fresh from his success in establishing an airport, headed the ferry company. Directors from Cape May County included Ralph T. Stevens, owner of the Cape May Sand Company located near the site of the proposed ferry terminus, George A. Redding, mayor of North Wildwood, and George L. Markland, a wealthy Philadelphia machinery manufacturer and the mayor of Stone Harbor. Once again, political and financial obstacles, combined with the difficulty in locating a protected spot for a ferry landing along the Cape May County bayshore, delayed development of a Cape May-Lewes ferry.[13]

Despite setbacks in ferry and airport development, the Camden Bridge and the construction of modern concrete roads ushered in a boom era for Cape May County real estate developers and a decade of rapid population growth. Between 1920 and 1930, Cape May County's population increased by over 51 percent, from 19,460 to

29,486, nearly twice New Jersey's statewide growth rate during the same decade. Liberal credit terms from Camden County and Cape May County banks and the general speculative frenzy in real estate characterized on the national level by the Florida real estate boom fueled Cape May County's own land-buying explosion. The *Cape May County Gazette* claimed that Ocean City's expansion compared to the Florida real estate boom of the 1920s. "Many real estate men assert that activities at the up-county resort are greater than at the best known resorts of Florida," the newspaper noted in 1925. The Cape May County Clerk's Office received more business in 1925 than in any prior year, and the inability of the overcrowded office to handle all the work convinced the county board of freeholders to build an addition to the county jail and a new courthouse with offices for the county clerk, surrogate, freeholders, and judges. The new buildings opened in July 1927.[14]

Cape May City expanded during the 1920s with the construction of dozens of new cottages that used the materials taken from the demolished Wissahickon Barracks. Joseph P. Cox remodeled the Palace Theater and built a new amusement pier in 1922 near the old Iron Pier that had been erected between 1884 and 1885 at the foot of Decatur Street. Adam Suelke, an electrical engineer, built the Liberty Theater in 1923. Leonard H. Davis, president of the Cape May Progressive League, remodeled the Lafayette Hotel. Julius Denizot constructed the American Stores building, and Jeremiah E. Mecray built the Focer-Mecray Block on Washington Street to house a city post office, lodge rooms, public meeting hall, and the Ford-Lincoln automobile showroom. The Merchants National Bank was completed in 1924, and under the leadership of Judge Henry H. Eldredge, John W. Mecray, and Everett Jerrell it became a prime lender for the development of Cape May City during the 1920s.[15]

The real estate boom spread north from Cape May City to the African American community at Whitesboro. "Lots at Wildwood Junction Heights are being sold rapidly by the George H. White Land and Improvement Co.," the *Cape May County Gazette* observed in early 1923, "the buyers being mostly colored and hailing from all parts of the country." East of Wildwood Junction, Robert J. Kay, a Wildwood real estate and insurance agent and state assemblyman, developed Five Mile Beach properties with State Senator William H. Bright. To finance the real estate business Bright assembled a banking network that included the First National Bank of Cape May Court House, the

Marine National Bank of Wildwood, and the Holly Beach Building Association. Bright's daughter Eloise Bright, educated at Mount Holyoke College and the University of Pennsylvania, ran her father's business on Five Mile Beach during the boomtime of the 1920s. Down the beach and across the Turtle Gut Inlet, which had been filled in 1922, developers built Wildwood Gables on the southern boundary of Wildwood Crest. In Sea Isle City, Herman Diamond and Caroline Cronecker, widow of one of Ludlam Beach's earliest hoteliers, built brick buildings and bungalows. William McLaughlin, developer of the Ventnor section of Atlantic City, purchased a large tract on the northern border of Ocean City in 1923 and began laying out Ocean Gardens and a million-dollar hotel.[16]

The real estate boom extended to the bayside, where the Philadelphia Development Corporation surveyed the Beach Estates community on the old Price Farm opposite Town Bank (later North Cape May). Joseph Millman of Philadelphia and a group of county investors incorporated the North Wildwood Villas Company to develop the bayshore south of Norbury's Landing Road in Green Creek (now Villas). The Miami Beach Builders Corporation of Philadelphia surveyed the bayshore from the Bate Farm below Fishing Creek and subdivided the property for the Miami Beach development.[17]

Joseph P. MacKissic, one of Lower Township's most successful real estate developers, was ready to plunge further into this real estate boom. As a member of the board of freeholders since 1911, MacKissic had joined E. Riley Mixner, a Goshen contractor, and other developers to lay out new roads through his properties as rapidly as the county board appropriated road money. MacKissic celebrated another reelection to the board of freeholders in November 1920 with a great pig roast at his Mayville farmstead. The real estate speculator and county freeholder welcomed over 150 county political and business allies and friends who had helped with his reelection, this time by a dangerously close margin of victory. Conversation at the party turned to the main purpose of those gathered at the MacKissic farm. "Everyone was loud in their praise of the county Board of Freeholders for the excellent macadam roads now completed in the county," one guest observed.[18]

Joseph MacKissic was reelected in 1920 to a Cape May County Board of Chosen Freeholders that was dominated by political cronies and fellow real estate speculators and building contractors such as John Fox and John R. Groves of Ocean City and Otto Koeneke of

Wildwood. Joseph Camp, known as the "King Crab King of New Jersey" for his factory on Pierce's Point, which ground bay horseshoe (king) crabs into fertilizer, represented Middle Township. Augustus Hilton, owner of the Consolidated Fisheries and the putative "Pound Net King," was a representative from the Five Mile Beach community. Hope W. Gandy represented Upper Township. He was known as the mayor of Tuckahoe, although Tuckahoe had no official mayor. Gandy joined MacKissic in working for road projects in Lower Township and Wildwood Crest in return for MacKissic's support for Gandy's road projects in Upper Township. Henry Rutherford, an elderly Cape May City undertaker, directed the board in 1920. Over the years, Rutherford had opposed MacKissic's more expensive road projects, often voting against appropriations. But in the end Rutherford had accepted the ever-increasing road and bridge budget.[19]

Joseph P. MacKissic, Hope W. Gandy, Joseph Camp, and the board of freeholders had directed the greatest road and bridge expansion program in the county's history between 1910 and 1920. Local real estate and resort business depended to a great extent upon the development of this transportation network. The prosperity of many county residents lay in securing county road building contracts, particularly projects for filling in Turtle Gut Inlet and construction of the road from Wildwood Crest to the Two Mile Beach. There were signs in 1920, however, that the board of freeholders might not be able to resume its traditional method of granting contracts, conducting business, and spending money. Rumors circulated that a Wildwood citizen's group (mostly members of the Democratic party) sought to eliminate what had become a fourteen-member board of freeholders (comprised entirely of local Republican party leaders) and replace it with a three-member county commission by informing the county prosecutor about evidence of gross mishandling of county monies and contracts.[20]

There had been earlier rumblings of wrongdoing on the part of county government. Allegations had surfaced briefly in 1911 that Hope W. Gandy had misused county funds to build a private road in front of the Marshallville general store. Two years later, rumors circulated that Ocean City's two freeholders had hired the Burns Detective Agency to put a "detectaphone" on the telephone used by the Cape May and Atlantic County freeholders to discuss the construction of a bridge between Somers Point and Beesley's Point that would effectively bypass and isolate Ocean City. A few years later, Charles C.

Black, a state supreme court justice, had reviewed E. Riley Mixner's contracts with the county for the Avalon and Stone Harbor roads. Justice Black also had examined a charge that Charles H. Clouting, a Sea Isle City freeholder and lumber merchant, had contracted with his own company to build a county bridge to his city.[21]

Little evidence of criminal conduct and only one indictment, quickly quashed, had arisen from these investigations. Seemingly, traditional road politics remained immune from serious probes. Then, in December 1920, Justice Charles C. Black acted upon a petition presented by thirty-seven Wildwood voters for an investigation of the Cape May County Board of Chosen Freeholders. Black appointed William J. Kraft, a Camden County prosecutor, and Edward P. Bacon of Jersey City to investigate the charges against the county. Kraft and Bacon examined county records and interviewed former and present county officials and private contractors. They uncovered evidence of widespread malfeasance, bribery, conspiracy to defraud the county, and bid rigging. In response, Justice Black called the Cape May County grand jury to hear the case of the *State of New Jersey* v. *Board of Chosen Freeholders*.[22]

The grand jury that convened in Cape May Court House in April 1921 was representative of the county's changing population and politics, with membership divided evenly between mainlanders and barrier islanders and between the upper and lower sections of the county. Everett Jerrell, a Cape May City banker, served as the foreman of the jury. Two Corsons, a Townsend, a Swain, and a Garrison represented the oldest families on the jury. The Cape May County grand jury of April 1921 also reflected passage of the women's suffrage amendment, ratified in August 1920. The jury contained the first women to sit on a county grand jury, Jennie Thompson of Wildwood and Nellie C. Towner of Ocean City.[23]

This representative grand jury returned a sweeping series of indictments against Cape May County's government. The grand jury brought in thirty-nine bills of indictment against Joseph P. MacKissic and Hope W. Gandy and forty-five indictments against the board of freeholders, several county officials, and private contractors. "In many instances public office has been bartered and sold, payments being made to members of the Board," the grand jury found. "Open and flagrant violation of the law has been willfully and corruptly permitted," the jury charged, "and extravagant programs of public improvements has been laid out and county money expended without due regard as to the necessity for the public improvements and the ability of the County to finance the same."[24]

The largest crowd since the Pierce murder trial of 1894 assembled at the county courthouse in June 1921 to hear Henry S. Rutherford and James F. Eustace, a retired Sea Isle City engineer and freeholder, change their pleas from not guilty to guilty without intent to commit a crime. Eustace and Rutherford agreed to resign from the board of freeholders, turn state's evidence, and testify against the others. Judge Henry H. Eldredge, a leader of the county Democratic party, fined Rutherford and Eustace five hundred dollars each for their part in the alleged conspiracy to defraud the county. At the close of this sensational court session, N. A. Cohen, a Wildwood physician, told the court that his patient John W. Young, one of the indicted freeholders, had collapsed. Young was "not always mentally clear [enough] for him to appear at this time," Cohen wrote Justice Charles Black.[25]

Judge Henry Eldredge fined Joseph MacKissic and Leaming M. Rice, county engineer, and sentenced both to prison terms of from one to three years. Joseph Camp defended MacKissic and the other freeholders. He insisted that they never intended to break the law. He blamed the county engineer. "Rice drew the contracts and put one over on us!" Camp claimed. Eventually attorneys for both parties worked out a plea bargain whereby all entered pleas of guilty without intent, paid ten thousand dollars in fines, and thus avoided possible jail sentences. The court lifted the prison terms for Rice and MacKissic. "By the acceptance of pleas," explained Judge Henry Eldredge, "the state has broken up the system; removed the defendants from office; discharged itself of the necessity of additional trials, collected in fines a large portion of the expenses of the investigation, and saved the county thousands of dollars of expense."[26]

The trial and conviction of the Cape May County Board of Freeholders led to the elimination of the large board, a primary goal of the barrier island petitioners. The grand jury recommended the creation of a small board of commissioners and centralization of all county offices and records in Cape May Court House. The grand jury advised the reorganization of the contracting system and the deposit of money in banks that paid interest to the county. The jury concluded as well that county government needed to coordinate business better with the smaller municipalities.

County voters adopted a three-member board of freeholders,

and the board organized on 5 January 1923 into three divisions, each headed by a freeholder. Robert J. Kay of Wildwood directed the division of public affairs, Joseph G. Champion of Ocean City oversaw finances, and Charles E. Foster, a South Seaville undertaker, headed the division of public buildings in the first elected small board. Kay drafted a set of rules for honest and efficient management of county business. A month later, Ralph T. Stevens, state assemblyman from Cape May County, responded to criticism that the barrier island free-holders controlled the board and introduced legislation to add two members from the rural mainland districts. The five-member board, Stevens hoped, "would do away with any possibility of factional fights between one resort and the other, or from the countryside." A five-member board made up of Champion, Foster, Robert S. Miller, Luther C. Ogden, and H. Foster Goslin was adopted and first met on 2 January 1925, introducing the format of the present-day board of freeholders.[27]

The Cape May County freeholder scandal coincided with a de-cade of wide-scale corruption around the country, including that of the Warren G. Harding administration. The 1920s were years of change and contrast between older values and modern technological society that caused deep tensions and conflict. The dramatic changes helped bring about a decline in morality and helped to explain the widespread corruption. Passage of the Eighteenth Amendment, which prohibited the manufacture, sale, and transportation of alcoholic beverages, cre-ated an environment that led some to regard the era as the Roaring Twenties. Prohibition nurtured an entire subculture of gangsters, speakeasies, and rumrunners. Cape May County became a center of this Prohibition culture because of its many hidden harbors and water-ways for bootleggers and its seaside resort towns filled with speakeas-ies. The county became a focal point during the 1920s for the struggle between those who sought to enforce Prohibition and those who violated the anti-liquor ordinances.[28]

Throughout the 1920s, eight seventy-five-foot Coast Guard pa-trol craft stationed at the wartime Cape May Naval Air Station and Section Base, now designated as a Coast Guard station, battled against rumrunners who raced up the Delaware Bay or along the barrier islands in powerful motorboats. Rumrunners unloaded Scotch whis-key from freighters beyond the three-mile limit off the Jersey Cape and smuggled it to the Consolidated Fisheries warehouse in North Wildwood, where the liquor was repacked in barrels of fish for shipment to Atlantic City and other local markets. Reportedly, the son of the Consolidated Fisheries owner ran one of the largest "rum rings" on the Atlantic coast. At the same time, Max ("Boo Boo") Hoff, reputed Philadelphia bootleg kingpin, purchased several thousand acres in Upper Township along the Thoroughfare separating the mainland from Ocean City, where he allegedly ran a bootlegging operation. Rumrunners found refuge all over the county—in Ottens Harbor, Schellenger's Landing, Hereford Inlet, Higbees Beach on the bayside, and at Jake's Landing on Dennis Creek.[29]

Cape May County also produced illegal moonshine. Prohibition officers located dozens of stills in the upper parts of the county, particularly in the northwestern corner around Belleplain, Woodbine, and the small community of Martintown. State police and county law enforcement officers raided a chicken coop in Belleplain, a sparsely settled community, where they found 350 gallons of moonshine. Another huge still was found a few months later in Ocean View, a community in Middle Township where the shore road and route to Sea Isle City met. This "poison hooch," the *Star and Wave* reported, was sold by "grocery stores, fruit stores and other places kept by foreigners, and Americans with no principles."[30]

Prohibition accelerated violence around the county. Bathers along the seashore reported seeing gun battles between Coast Guard patrols and rumrunners. A "rain of gunfire" pelted Ocean City as gangsters in powerful Stutz motorcars fought city police in their pursuing cars. A gunman in Wildwood shot and wounded Oakford M. Cobb, the community's popular chief of police. Violent crime came to the sleepy town of Tuckahoe in Upper Township in 1925 when three bank robbers shot and beat to death Edwin L. Tomlin, president of the Tuckahoe National Bank, and blackjacked Edward L. Rice, the bank cashier, and his wife.[31]

One angry county newspaperman suggested that the Ku Klux Klan (KKK) be used to fight the criminals and Prohibition violators. "We do not advocate violence," Harry Greaves noted, "but it would do some of these birds good if the Ku Klux Klan happened to make a visit here, and make them skiddoo, never to return." The KKK presented a strange blend of Protestant Christian morality, racial purity, hatred, and terror, and won support throughout South Jersey in the 1920s as a vehicle to restore traditional racial, religious, and social values and to repel what they saw as foreign threats. The KKK burned crosses on African-American, Jewish, and Catholic properties and held rallies and parades, including a march down Broadway in Camden City in 1927. U.S. Senator Walter Edge of Atlantic City came to Court House in 1923 and warned against the Klan, but local membership swelled nonetheless. The *Star and Wave* reported hundreds of mainland farmers in the KKK, and large crowds attended Klan rallies in Wildwood. "One of the meetings was held in the old Atlantic Pier on the boardwalk," the *Cape May County Gazette* reported in April 1924, "and the other took place March 26 in the high school." That July, the Klan burned a cross in Wildwood, and when an Anglesea fisherman rushed to knock it down, Klansmen beat him. The KKK burned another cross on the Columbia Avenue ballpark in Cape May City near an African-American neighborhood. African-Americans throughout the county, particularly in Sigtown near Swainton, the *Star and Wave* reported, were terrified by the prospect of a visit by the white-hooded Klansman.[32]

Other organizations, far different in character and methods from the KKK, searched during the 1920s for ways to restore fundamental social values and to strengthen traditional society. One of these organizations formed in 1927 as the Cape May County Historical and Genealogical Society to study the origins and traditions of the county's first settlers. Inspiration for the formation of a society came partly from the Reverend Paul Sturtevant Howe, rector of the Church of the Advent in Cape May City. Howe had recently discovered the direct genealogical connection between Cape May County's first families and the Pilgrims who had come to America in 1620 on the *Mayflower*. Further impetus for a Cape May County historical organization came from Edward M. Post and his close friend H. Clifford Campion, Jr., of Swarthmore, Pennsylvania, a wealthy electric supplies manufacturer and summer resident on the Jersey Cape. Post and Campion collected genealogical information about the families who had migrated to Cape May County from Long Island during the late seventeenth and early eighteenth centuries, data that eventually became part of the collection of the county historical and genealogical society.[33]

Many of those who founded the Cape May County Historical and Genealogical Society in 1927 came from the Townsend, Ludlam, Leaming, Hand, Gandy, Smith, and other original whaler yeoman families. Lewis Townsend Stevens, author of a comprehensive county history in 1897, served as the organization's first president, and Mabel Clay of Beesley's Point, whose roots went back to the earliest colonial families, became the society's first vice president. Clay, regent of the Cape May Patriots Chapter of the Daughters of the American Revolution (DAR), sponsored the society and became a driving force behind the organization's philosophy of genealogical research into those county families with ancestors who had served in the Revolutionary War. Far more than a genealogist, Clay became an important political force in the county during the 1920s as a Republican party committeewoman and the leader of the county council of Republican women. Clay represented "all the sentiments of womankind in her devotions to the cause of clean government and law enforcement," the *Star and Wave* declared.[34]

Clay employed the resources of the county historical and genealogical society to counteract threats to clean government and law and order that she found in the alien ideas and foreign influences of "communistic literature." Clay joined Lila M. Gandy, DAR librarian and one of the historical society's original members, in selecting what they considered proper books for county schoolchildren and residents to learn about their county's historical heritage and traditional values. Gandy and Clay chose three basic books: Lewis T. Stevens's *History of Cape May County*, the Reverend Paul S. Howe's *Mayflower Pilgrim Descendants in Cape May County*, and John E. Stillwell's *Historical and Genealogical Miscellany*.[35]

T. Millet Hand, the Cape May County prosecutor, launched his own campaign to curb foreign influences and restore traditional values. The youngest prosecutor in county history, Hand crusaded against corruption and vice. He dispatched Wardell Higbee of Ocean City and Charles W. Unfreed of Wildwood, county detectives, on dozens of raids against speakeasies, gambling dens, and illicit stills, reportedly run by foreign-born residents. At Ottens Harbor in North Wildwood, Hand's raiders "confiscated enough liquors, beers and wines together with home brew apparatus to fill a five-ton truck," the *Star and Wave* noted with approval.[36]

County Prosecutor Hand investigated Ocean City government in 1929 after a citizens group accused Mayor Joseph G. Champion of protecting gambling and liquor interests in his resort town. Reportedly, a detective hired by Hiram S. Mowrer, Clayton Haines Brick, and other Ocean City bankers and businessmen found twenty-seven locations in this traditionally dry town where alcohol was sold and consumed. The citizen's group demanded Champion's immediate recall. This attack by his former political and business allies stunned Champion. "It is inconceivable that the master minds back of this movement could have been actuated by sincere motives," Champion wrote in March 1929, "otherwise they could have hesitated to broadcast to the world news that cannot help but reflect discredit to the fair name of the cleanest and best governed Resort City in the county."[37]

The attack on Mayor Joseph G. Champion arose from a complex set of issues that reflected the dynamics of county politics and society in the late 1920s. T. Millet Hand of Cape May City represented traditional mainland and lower-county society anxious to unseat this upper-county barrier island boss from the board of freeholders and to undercut his growing countywide influence. Champion seemed to embody barrier island politics, with its foreign-born newcomers and other influences that threatened older values. Ocean City contained the second-largest concentration of Italian-American, Irish-American, and African-American residents in the entire county. Mayor Champion's political organization represented, at least to the mainland and lower county politicians, these groups. Moreover, Champion allied himself with other barrier island bosses such as Gustavus Bergner, the Philadelphia brewery owner who became the mayor of Avalon in 1925. Bergner contracted with Champion's construction company to build the Avalon amusement pier and convention hall.[38]

Joseph G. Champion weathered the investigation and recall but lost his seat on the board of freeholders in 1931 to Charles B. Powell, an Ocean City Democrat. Less fortunate was Hiram S. Mowrer, plagued by financial difficulties and worn out by the fight against Champion, who walked to an Ocean City jetty and jumped to his death. Banking problems at the First National Bank of Ocean City contributed to Mowrer's death. The stock market crash of October 1929 and the ensuing economic depression hit the resort banks particularly hard, forcing the temporary closing and reorganization of Mowrer's Ocean City bank and other barrier island financial institutions. This economic collapse caught Cape May County bankers completely by surprise. Just three months before the stock market crash, Edward Arnett, president of the First National Bank of Sea Isle City and a director in Mowrer's Ocean City bank, predicted the "greatest banking season in county history."[39]

Edward Arnett had reasons for such optimism in early 1929. County agriculture showed a steady increase in profits in poultry, blueberries, and cranberries. Roland B. Mason of Belleplain expanded his basket factory to produce more fruit containers. Similarly, the cranberry crop of late 1928 had been the best in county history, earning $100,000 for Thomas J. Durell, Manton Godfrey, and other Upper Township growers. The moving picture business expanded with the introduction in June 1929 of the first "talkies" to the William C. Hunt Theater chain in Cape May City, Court House, and Wildwood. At the same time, new housing starts at Brighton Shores on Corson's Inlet and Wildwood Villas and Miami Beach on the bayside promised a building surge in early 1929. Harry Headley, the county treasurer since 1921, announced on 28 December 1928 that "today will practically wind up our financial transactions for 1928 which will show the largest surplus for any one year in the history of Cape May County." Bolstered by this news, the board of freeholders embarked on new public works programs for 1929 that included the funding of a Shade Tree Commission to landscape and beautify the county.[40]

The stock market crash upset such optimism and revealed underlying weaknesses in the credit buying system, wild land speculations, and failure of the Federal Reserve to control lending and inflation. The *Cape May County Times* predicted in November 1929 that Cape May County business was facing a very tough winter. New construction ceased along the seashore by early 1930, and Ocean City and Wildwood recorded an unprecedented number of unemployed among the year-round residents. The jobless in Sea Isle City mobbed the city commissioners, demanding work. "We are willing to go out now and do for 40 cents an hour work for which we would get 75 cents an hour later in the year," the spokesman for the unemployed told the Sea Isle City commissioners. Earl M. Waddington, director of revenue and finance, promised to cut salaries of city workers so that others might be hired, but warned that "the city cannot purposely create unnecessary work in order to relieve unemployment, or the city will go broke." Sea Isle City defaulted on the payment of its county taxes in 1931. Other tax-delinquent resorts included Stone Harbor, North Wildwood, and West Wildwood, the latter a borough formed in April 1920 out of the real estate developed by Warren D. Hann, a railroad and land developer.[41]

As the Depression deepened, county leaders expressed confidence in President Herbert Hoover's program of rugged individualism and voluntary business cooperation. Harry F. Greaves claimed that Cape May County could pull out of the Depression through hard work and business-government cooperation, and without federal government interference. Luther C. Ogden, director of the board of freeholders in 1931, blamed high taxes and overexpansion of public improvements for the county's economic hardships and promised to cut back on all spending to solve the problems. In response, the board reduced the appropriations for highway maintenance from $85,000 to $20,000 and laid off twenty-five highway workers. "There is only one cure for unemployment," county leaders insisted, "industrial development that will put men to work without taxing them for the privilege." To this end, a group of Middle Township businessmen and bankers raised money in 1931 to build a factory on the east side of South Main Street in Court House to attract Harry A. Norris's Colonial Knitting Company to manufacture hosiery.[42]

Unemployment continued to rise. Alfred Cooper, organizer of county relief during the First World War, became the director of emergency relief for Cape May County in 1931 under the state emergency relief bureau. Cooper served as a volunteer without salary, as did members of his advisory council, which included Dorothy Rice, the county health nurse, Rev. William Ewen of Court House M. E. Church, and Arlington B. Corson, municipal director for Dennis Township. Cooper selected volunteer relief managers for each municipality, including Dr. Harold H. Hornstine, the county coroner, for Wildwood, and Irving Fitch, the county surrogate, for Sea Isle City. Volunteer relief work meant doling out flour and sugar provided by the Red Cross and convincing local businessmen and contractors to hire the unemployed. Cooper encouraged private business to raise relief money. William Hunt's moving picture theaters held welfare unemployment fund-raisers, and Mary Gregory Ogden, president of the Women's Community Club of Cape May, held the Cape May Capers, a charity ball.[43]

Despite such voluntary relief, the Depression grew steadily worse in Cape May County. Banks restricted withdrawals, unemployment climbed to eighteen hundred, and towns failed to pay their taxes. Once-prosperous Avalon foreclosed on the beachfront properties owned by the Avalon Development Company in order to collect $200,000 in back taxes. For some, these foreclosures brought new opportunities. The Paramount Company of Newark bought up tax-delinquent titles throughout the county and "cleaned up handsomely," wrote land entrepreneur Erwin L. Schwatt, and "delinquent owners redeemed their real estate, after foreclosure, for a song." Most suffered, though. Thomas J. Durell, county superintendent of schools, admitted that teachers would not receive paychecks for the year 1931. The goldbeating factory in West Cape May laid off fifty-five employees. A beleaguered county government argued over whether to adopt a central welfare board as proposed by the state or continue the traditional local methods of relief.[44]

A threat to traditional relief measures appeared when elements of a group of disgruntled veterans known as the Bonus Army marched toward Tuckahoe in search of land. They were stragglers from the seventeen thousand marchers from all over the United States who had camped in Washington in May 1932 to ask Congress for their promised bonus pay from World War I. A frightened President Herbert Hoover had ordered General Douglas MacArthur to drive the bonus marchers from their encampment along the Potomac River. Using more force than the president had authorized, General MacArthur drove the Bonus Army from Washington and burned their camp. He had saved the country from a Communist insurrection, MacArthur claimed. Harry Souders of Cape May Court House, a veteran who had gone to Washington with the marchers, echoed General MacArthur when he told the *Cape May County Gazette* that Communists and other troublemakers had taken over the Bonus Army. With these supposed dangerous troublemakers about to reach Tuckahoe, Alfred Cooper warned Upper Township officials to keep them away. "Every thoughtful man must realize that the gathering of several hundred indigent men or families in any section of this county for even one week's stay," Cooper explained, "would be little short of a calamity at this time, when all our municipalities are put to their wits' end to provide food for their own unemployed citizens."[45]

The Bonus March incident and the continuing Depression did not shake the county's faith in Herbert Hoover. When Franklin D. Roosevelt swept the Democrats into office in an election landslide around the nation in 1932, Cape May County voters gave President Hoover a three thousand vote majority over Roosevelt, the candidate who offered a New Deal for the nation. Only Woodbine gave Roosevelt a large margin. Local Republicans won as well. William C. Hunt of Wildwood Crest, operator of a chain of motion picture theaters in the county, defeated Evans G. Slaughter, a Wildwood banker and the county Democratic party leader, for the state assembly. Republicans Robert S. Miller and Henry Y. Clouting, an Upper Township farmer, were reelected to a board of freeholders that had been laying off county workers and cutting public services for the past year.[46]

The election of 1932 showed Cape May County's mistrust of FDR as much as it reflected support for Herbert Hoover and the local Republican party candidates. Alfred Cooper voiced a common fear on the Jersey Cape that Roosevelt meant more and bigger government and more controls and regulations. Cooper claimed that his local relief program had faltered only after the Roosevelt government "entered the picture with its socialism and communistic theories [and] the whole system changed—laziness became a virtue." There were other reasons for Roosevelt's poor showing in the county. William A. Haffert insisted that Doris W. Bradway, a Wildwood city commissioner, damaged the county Democrats by temporarily bolting the Republican party and campaigning for Roosevelt. Bradway went "raging up and down the county," Haffert wrote, "hurling wild charges, names and accusations at the Republican administration of the county." Cape May County Republicans brought out their own female politician, Frances Baker, daughter of the late Democratic party leader J. Thompson Baker. Baker defended county Republicans against Bradway's tirades and against the "male politicians who hid behind her skirts."[47]

Doris Bradway's incredible rise to political prominence in Cape May County during the 1930s reflected both the increased role of women in politics and the volatile nature of New Deal–era county politics where for one of the few times the local Democratic party became a serious challenger to Republican party domination. Doris and Edwin T. Bradway arrived in Wildwood in 1920 and established with Noble Bright (son of W. H. Bright) a tin-roofing and sheet metal-business. The Bradways became active in the tumultuous world of Five Mile Beach politics, supporting William H. Bright, the Holly Beach realtor who had served as county sheriff between 1905 and 1908 and as state senator for three consecutive terms between 1918 and 1927. Doris Bradway, an abrasive and emotional debater, worked tirelessly for Bright and once made a "tearful plea" for retention of Bright's son as the assistant director of health for Wildwood. Bradway's own public career began suddenly in 1932 when Bright, then mayor of Wildwood, appointed her to fill the city commission seat left vacant by Commissioner Kenneth K. Kirby's death in an automobile accident. A few months later Bright died suddenly, and Bradway became the mayor of Wildwood.[48]

At first, Doris Bradway won the support of many groups that had remained outside Cape May County politics. Bradway included

African-Americans in her Bradway Republican Club of Wildwood. An African-American clergyman called Bradway the "Joan of Arc of Cape May County" and expected her to mobilize black voters as had no other politician in the county's history. At the same time, Bradway appealed to Italian-Americans, telling one gathering at Court House that she would see that the county hired Italian-Americans. She protested against the county's refusal to give work to the Versaggi Brothers Construction Company of Wildwood, although this Italian-American firm had turned in the lowest bid. Bradway seemed to represent county women. Bradway, Josephine Bright, and Grace McGonigle organized the Bradway Republican Club of Wildwood in 1934 as a political and civic organization exclusively for women. Over two hundred cheering women watched Bradway take her oath of office as mayor, and several hundred women rose in unison and applauded wildly as Bradway entered the old courthouse building in 1933 to address the board of freeholders during a tax protest meeting.[49]

Doris Bradway's appeal to female and ethnic voters made her a potential ally of FDR and the Democratic party, and in 1932 she worked for Democratic candidates in the county. Bradway never left the Republican Party, however. Entanglement in the sometimes tawdry world of barrier island politics, combined with Bradway's own abrasive style, destroyed her promising political career. Every newspaper in the county turned against her as Bradway lashed out indiscriminately against New Dealers and the county's most respected Republican party leaders, T. Millet Hand, Judge Palmer Way, and William C. Hunt. Bradway's feud with the latter became personal. Mayor Bradway attacked Hunt and closed down his Wildwood theaters and amusements on Sundays. Hunt sued Bradway for fifty thousand dollars. "Wildwood is doomed," Hunt warned, "if we are to have a continuation of such government.[50]

Bradway continued to make powerful enemies who brought indictments against the female mayor for alleged corruption. She lost a bitter recall election in 1930. "So heated was the contest," the *Star and Wave* reported, "that Mayor Bradway informed all city police and firemen to protect city government from the hands of a mob which, it was reported, threatened to seize city hall." Sadly, by 1939, the once-rising leader of Cape May County women lost an election for justice of the peace 153–73 to Grace McGonigle, an original founder of the Bradway Republican Club of Wildwood.

Bradway placed sixth among eight candidates in the city council election of 1944.[51]

Doris Bradway publicized the role of women in county politics and undoubtedly contributed to the increase in the number of female officials in Cape May County during the New Deal decade. Four women held county posts. Louisa R. Carlson of Ocean City became the assistant county treasurer, and Phoebe Grace of Dennisville the deputy surrogate of the county. Annabelle Spaulding of Whitesboro served as the assistant county nurse. Sarah A. Thomas held the post of Cape May County librarian. A tiny, dynamic woman, Thomas embraced nearly every worthy cause from the late 1920s through the 1930s, helping to organize the Stone Harbor heron sanctuary, the Cape May County Art League, and the movement to save the old courthouse building from destruction when the new county courthouse opened in 1927. Women also controlled several boards of education during the decade. Sara R. Way and Lillie Bradshaw headed the North Wildwood board and battled during the Depression to prevent the total collapse of the public school system. "To make the matter even worse," Sara Way told the people of North Wildwood in 1938, "we have received no state school money since 1933."[52]

Female political organization expanded in Cape May County during the 1930s. Women dominated the leadership of the Colored Regular Republican Organization Circle, incorporated in December 1933 in Wildwood. Women organized the Cape May County Democratic party for FDR, including the Roosevelt Democratic Club of Wildwood and the New Deal Democratic Club of Ocean City. Patience Ludlam helped to mobilize the Democratic party behind her husband, Jesse Diverty Ludlam, a Court House banker and realtor, as he ran for the state legislature. She formed a Roosevelt Club as well. The Roosevelt organizations never became popular, though. Cape May County expressed little confidence in Franklin D. Roosevelt, and formed an uneasy relationship between 1933 and 1938 with his massive New Deal program, which brought money and jobs into the county but also extensive federal government intervention and controls.[53]

After Roosevelt's election in 1932, Cape May County leaders had sought their own solutions to relief and recovery without turning to the new administration in Washington for help. The local chamber of commerce studied plans in December 1932 to promote Cape May County as the poultry and small-farm mecca of New Jersey in order to attract outside private business investment. H. Foster Goslin, a Wildwood lumber dealer and Wharton business school graduate, and Elmer Jackson Pearl, vice president of the New Jersey Taxpayer's Association, tried to get the county to solve its own budgetary and financial problems without federal assistance. Gustavus W. Bergner, mayor of Avalon and the head of a local bridge corporation, applied for funds to build bridges along the barrier islands for a coastal highway from the Reconstruction Finance Corporation, a public-private partnership set up by President Hoover to strengthen private enterprise.[54]

Local efforts at relief and recovery were not enough. It became obvious by the end of 1932 that Cape May County required outside help to deal with the Depression. County deposits had been frozen in the Wildwood Title and Trust Company, and other local banks had suspended business. The entire county school system went bankrupt and paid teachers in promissory notes called scrip. The board of freeholders decided in a split vote (3–2) to issue scrip for the payment of taxes and transaction of business with the county clerk, surrogate, sheriff, and almshouse. Several municipalities refused to accept county scrip in payment of taxes, and the board of freeholders authorized Robert K. Bell, county solicitor, to take legal action against them. A near-riot rocked the county courthouse in January 1933 during hearings over the county budget. Doris Bradway and Elmer Jackson Pearl led a crowd of five hundred county residents in shouting down the freeholders as they tried to explain the budget. "Insults, boos, jeers, and outbursts of vulgarity all aimed at the freeholders were frequent," William Haffert reported.[55]

Social conditions deteriorated. The county announced that it no longer had relief money. Thomas J. Durell reported that schoolchildren came to class hungry because they had no food at home. Thefts of food and pilfering from coal bins spread. "The reason for the unusual activity of the thieves at this time is that so many are unemployed," the *Star and Wave* noted, "and some have turned to this type of theft in order to live without applying for aid." The *Cape May County Times* and the Chamber of Commerce printed free advertisements for people who offered to do any type of work in exchange for food and clothing. These listings revealed the growing despair. "Nurse practical, Ocean City, husband will do common laboring, needs clothes for four children and self," read one listing. "Engineer, Cape May, will do work of any kind and can do most anything," another explained, "will accept food, seeds for planting garden or live chickens."[56]

FDR's administration and programs for relief began to make an impact on the county in early March 1933, when the president declared a bank holiday. Then, federal examiners visited county banks. The First National Bank of Ocean City, First National Bank of Sea Isle City, and Tuckahoe National Bank went into receivership, and the troubled Ocean City National Bank was placed under a conservator, George S. Groff. Meanwhile, Congress legalized 3.2 beer preparatory to the repeal of the Eighteenth Amendment. Surprisingly, 72 percent of Cape May County voters, including those in traditionally dry Ocean City, supported the repeal of Prohibition. Petitions from local church groups convinced the Middle and Upper township committees to ban Sunday sales of beer, however.[57]

Local officials turned to New Deal programs to help Cape May County battle depression. The board of freeholders resolved in July 1933 "to obtain State or Federal aid (or both) to relieve erosion and tide conditions on the Delaware Bay Shore within the boundary lines of Middle Township." Edwin C. Mann, a Strathmere resident, asked his old friend Harold Ickes, Roosevelt's secretary of the interior, to grant federal monies to the barrier islands to stop beach erosion. The Cape May County Chamber of Commerce petitioned Frances Perkins, U.S. secretary of labor, to locate one of the reforestation and reclamation camps in the county provided for under the Reforestation Relief Act of 1933 that created the Civilian Conservation Corps (CCC).[58]

Sixty Cape May County residents, nearly half of them African-Americans from Wildwood and Middle Township, enrolled in the forestry service and went to Camp Dix in Burlington County for training in May 1933. Five months later, the government established a CCC camp in Woodbine and another at the Tuckahoe-Petersburg crossroads on the former Bethlehem Steel Company proving grounds. A third CCC camp was built in 1935 at Dias Creek on the bayshore to fight mosquitoes. The development of the CCC camps caused considerable controversy. Upper Township residents feared that the government planned to encamp hundreds of African-Americans from New York City and northern New Jersey at the Tuckahoe barracks. A citizens group rushed to Ocean City to see Charles C. Read, state assemblyman, and to protest against "such a large number of colored men being sent here." Upper Township women sent a letter of protest against the CCC camp to U.S. Congressman Isaac Bacharach. Nevertheless, two hundred African-American workers lived in the CCC camp and developed the Tuckahoe Hunting and Fishing Grounds in the thirties. Workers at the Woodbine CCC camp stayed in the old Bayard machine shop and used the facilities of the Jewish community center and gymnasium. These CCC laborers traveled five miles west to the Belleplain State Forest, a huge tract of land acquired as a recreation site by the state at the behest of Roland B. Mason, powerful county Democratic party leader and Belleplain basket factory owner. The CCC workers in the state forest developed roads and campsites and created scenic Lake Nummy out of an old cranberry bog.[59]

Cape May County endorsed the controversial National Recovery Administration (NRA) created by the National Industrial Recovery Act of June 1933, and later declared unconstitutional by the U.S. Supreme Court. The NRA established a wage, hour, and price scale designed to stimulate fair employment and selling practices. Those who subscribed to the NRA code received a blue eagle insignia; customers were encouraged to patronize businesses that displayed this symbol. Alfred Cooper claimed that his *Cape May County Gazette* was the first local business to earn the blue eagle, signifying that the newspaper had instituted a thirty-five-hour work week with the same wages paid for a fifty-hour week. Close behind, the *Cape May County Times* displayed the blue eagle on its masthead and promoted countywide compliance with the NRA code. The Bradstone Rubber company of Woodbine and Colonial Knitting Mills at Court House cut hours and increased wages, securing immediate NRA endorsement. Other businesses followed, led by the Goslin and Baker lumber companies of Wildwood. The barbershops owned by Dominick Trombetta and John Battendieri and Clyde Spalding's meat market at Court House joined the NRA and displayed the blue eagle in their shop windows.[60]

NRA organizers sought to enroll every resident in the system. Harry Greaves claimed that 80 percent of the people in his district had signed an NRA pledge to buy only under the blue eagle. Irma White, wife of the county agricultural agent, Henry H. White, organized NRA canvassing districts and dispatched Roxana S. Gandy of Dennisville, Rosalie Howe of Ocean City, and other county women "house to house" in order to reach every purchaser. "Woman's greatest weapon against the forces of depression," Irma White said, "is her buying power."[61]

NRA wage and hour schedules, combined with increased labor union activities, contributed during the summer of 1933 to a series of strikes in Woodbine's clothing, hat, and rubber products factories. The Bradstone Rubber Company strike led to incidents of violence, and T. Millet Hand warned that state forces might be required to preserve law and order. The county prosecutor offered to assist Mayor Nathaniel Rosenfeld of Woodbine to maintain the peace. Rosenfeld, the youngest mayor in New Jersey, told Hand that Woodbine Borough could handle its own problems without interference from the county prosecutor. Rosenfeld arbitrated the labor dispute and settled the strike, although Woodbine's factories continued to suffer from periodic labor and financial troubles, and the Woodbine Borough Clothing Company, the largest factory, declared insolvency in 1938.[62]

New Deal assistance for Woodbine, the only Cape May County community to vote for Al Smith in 1928 and to consistently support Franklin D. Roosevelt, partly offset economic problems caused by labor strife and factory closings. Woodbine Borough acquired a CCC camp in October 1933 and received a constant flow of New Deal money from the Public Works Administration (PWA) and Works Progress Administration (WPA). The PWA and WPA helped to rebuild Woodbine's roads, sidewalks, curbing, and drainage system. New Deal grants renovated playgrounds and buildings at the Woodbine Colony for Feeble-Minded Males, a state agency built on the grounds of the de Hirsch agricultural school, and in the borough itself. During the Depression decade, Woodbine became the shopping and entertainment center for Dennis and Upper townships. Crowds filled the Colonial Theater of Woodbine, advertised as "the Theater of perfect sound," and the Palace roller-skating rink operated by the Levenson brothers. Woodbine also became the center of the county's poultry industry. The Cape May Egg Producers Association organized in Woodbine in 1931 and the Woodbine Cooperative Poultry Association erected a huge store and warehouse on DeHirsch Avenue in 1938.[63]

New Deal monies refurbished public works throughout Cape May County from Woodbine to the tip of the peninsula at Cape May Point, where the WPA developed Lake Drive. The New Deal left permanent monuments, including Lake Nummy in the Belleplain State Forest, the Tuckahoe Fish and Game Preserve in Upper Township, and Cape May County Park just above Court House in Middle Township on the old almshouse grounds. The CCC barracks in Dias Creek became the headquarters later for the Cape May County Mosquito Control Commission. New Deal assistance helped Middle Township Mayor Edmund Burke rebuild the Court House Sewerage

System. WPA grants rebuilt Dennis Township's roads and repaired a bridge over Cedar Swamp Creek near Petersburg. The most ambitious PWA program granted $744,545 and loaned another $910,000 to Cape May County to build bridges between the barrier islands as part of the Ocean Drive.[64]

Despite the New Deal programs, throughout the 1930s Cape May County never completely shook the affects of the Depression. There were still two thousand unemployed in the county by 1937. Seemingly the lingering Depression made the county more susceptible to bizarre situations. When a huge, unexplained hole appeared in the woods between South Dennis and Clermont in 1938, local residents claimed that it had been caused by a half-human, half-animal creature said to have roamed through the New Jersey Pine Barrens since the eighteenth century. "Is the 'Jersey Devil' abroad in Cape May County?" the *Gazette* wondered. In another bizarre incident, a large lion escaped from the Wall of Death arcade on the Wildwood boardwalk, killed auction attendant Thomas Saito, and dragged him under the boardwalk. More mundane but equally unusual, a mysterious fever carried by ticks invaded the county in July 1936, killing Charles Cossaboon, the popular Avalon fire chief.[65]

A series of sensational accidents also plagued the county during the 1930s. The dirigible *Akron* plunged into the sea off the Jersey Cape in 1933, and Cape May County fishermen located the wreckage. The search for survivors was directed from the Coast Guard base in Cape May City. Pieces of the *Akron* continued to wash up on county beaches for weeks thereafter. News reached Cape May County that the giant German zeppelin *Hindenburg*, which had passed over Wildwood and Strathmere and had flown along the barrier island beaches earlier, had burst into flames at Lakehurst in Ocean County. Coast guardsmen from Cape May City were rushed north to guard the wreckage. Probably the first airplane crash in the county occurred in 1936 when a spray plane used to dust Thomas Durell's crops in Belleplain plunged into a cranberry bog. Mostly, automobile crashes shook the county. Unable to take long vacations because of the Depression, thousands of motorists raced down to the Jersey Cape for weekends. Traffic deaths hit a county record twenty-two in 1936, and more than one hundred people died in automobile crashes in Cape May County during the decade. A double tragedy occurred on a December evening in 1938, when Flora Devaul of Ocean View and Eleanor Van Gilder of Seaville, two elderly lifelong residents from old county families, were struck and killed instantly by a speeding auto-mobile as they walked along Shore Road to a prayer meeting at the Seaville M. E. Church.[66]

This tumultuous era came to a close for Cape May County largely as it had begun, with a political scandal surrounding the elec-tion of William C. Hunt to the state senate. Hunt epitomized the successful resort businessman. He had introduced the moving pic-ture theater to Cape May City in 1906 and had incorporated the United Theaters Company of Holly Beach City in 1910 to show mo-tion pictures, vaudeville, and dramatic performances and to manufac-ture films. Over the next twenty-five years Hunt built an amusement empire that included seven theaters in Avalon, Wildwood, Court House, and Cape May City, amusement piers in Cape May City and Wildwood, and the Starlight Ballroom in Wildwood. Hunt's enter-prises included banks, a Wildwood newspaper, and the Wildwood Golf Club. Hunt promoted countywide projects including a cross-county canal and Lewes–Cape May ferry, and won election to the state assembly in 1933. Three years later, Hunt defeated Charles C. Read of Ocean City, the immensely popular Cape May County state senator, in the Republican party primary. Read won most of the county's municipalities, but a large vote in Wildwood secured the victory for Hunt. In an even closer vote, Hunt defeated Jesse D. Ludlam of Court House, the county's Democratic party leader, for the state senate seat. Once again, a huge majority in Wildwood meant the difference.[67]

For one of the few times in county history, a local election held major statewide and national implications. Ten Democrats and ten Republicans deadlocked the New Jersey state senate, and the Cape May County vote determined party control over that body. Moreover, Jesse D. Ludlam and Patience Ludlam had been organizers for FDR, and Ludlam's defeat symbolized the president's political weakness in the county. The Democrats demanded a recount, citing massive vot-ing fraud as the reason for William C. Hunt's margin of victory. Stirling W. Cole, county clerk, impounded ballot boxes, and French B. Love-land of Ocean City, county prosecutor and Democratic party leader, launched an investigation of the election. Agents from the Federal Bureau of Investigation assisted Loveland in his probe of the alleged election fraud.[68]

Judge Wilfred H. Jayne started hearings on the election at the county courthouse in December 1936. Testimony revealed that hundreds of voters had been rushed from Philadelphia to vote in Wild-wood. One Philadelphia "waitress" testified that she had voted seven different times for Hunt in the primary and five times in the November election against Ludlam. She claimed that she never realized it was illegal to vote more than once. Others testified that dozens of "floaters" operated from Mae Wolf's Cafe in North Wildwood, coming and going to receive new voter registration cards for each vote that they cast. A laborer at the Tuckahoe CCC camp admitted that bus-loads of African-Americans had been sent down to Wildwood and paid two dollars apiece to vote for Hunt.[69]

After the hearings, Judge Wilfred Jayne refused to certify the election, and William C. Hunt stepped down from his seat in the New Jersey State Senate in April 1937. By then, county residents had started to redirect some of their attention to the collapsing world order in Asia and Europe. Cape May County's residents saw signs already that distant overseas events might affect the Jersey Cape. Rumors circulated that the U.S. Navy planned to train aircraft carrier pilots at Section Base Nine in Cape May City and to build a new, larger naval air station somewhere else in the county. Similarly, U.S. Army engineers showed renewed interest in digging a canal across the Cape May peninsula as part of an intracoastal defense system. In the months ahead, as world unrest led to another world war, increased national defense activity and war would fundamentally alter the nature of Cape May County's landscape and population.

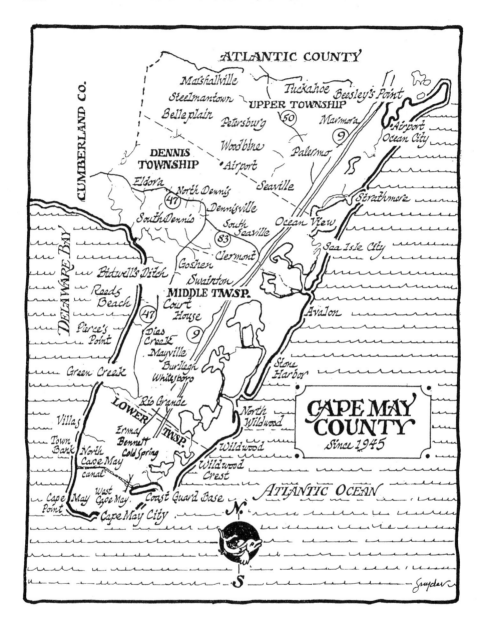

CHAPTER NINE

A Wartime and Postwar Resort Community, 1939–1961

Cape May County tried to ignore the world war that broke out in Europe in September 1939. Woodbine's leaders worried about the Nazi persecution of Jews, but most county residents expressed isolationist sentiments. "The people of Cape May County, with the people of the rest of the nation, want no part of a European war," the *Cape May County Gazette* observed, adding that "any man in official life who hopes to continue to serve his constituents and his nation will tread carefully lest he be a party to a move which might embroil this country in the fighting overseas." Lt. Richard L. Burke, commandant of the Cape May Coast Guard base, assured residents that the facility was not on a wartime status, although he had increased patrols in the Delaware Bay to enforce neutrality laws and customs rules.[1]

Cape May County wanted to enjoy the returning prosperity in 1939. Some residents found jobs at the New York Shipbuilding Company in Camden City or across the river in Wilmington, Delaware, and Chester, Pennsylvania, where government contracts for naval construction had created a shipbuilding boom. The Holtz Boat Works and Basin Company of Atlantic City relocated in Ocean City, where it joined the Ocean City Engine and Yacht Company and the Moyer shipbuilding firm in the manufacture of boats for the U.S. government. New Deal agencies continued to provide jobs. Over seven hundred county workers labored on Works Progress Administration (WPA) projects in 1939 and 1940; these included the cutting of fire lanes, road building, and construction of a Woodbine municipal airport located on two hundred acres just east of Woodbine and the

221

Pennsylvania-Reading Seashore Railroad tracks. Leaming M. Rice, borough engineer, developed the airport and employed one hundred local workers. The Public Works Administration (PWA) program to construct the Ocean Drive gave jobs to dozens of county contractors and hundreds of laborers, who completed this oceanfront network of roads and bridges between the barrier islands in June 1940. Construction of the South Dennis overpass, which opened to traffic in June 1941, also provided local employment. The bypass took the main road (now Route 83) from Dennisville to Clermont over the tracks, eliminating one of the most dangerous railroad crossings in the county.[2]

There were signs throughout Cape May County of economic recovery in the months before American entry into the Second World War in December 1941. County farmers led by Henry H. White, county agricultural agent, produced a record lima bean crop in 1940. Contracts with Seabrook Farms, which employed a new quick freezing process in their Cumberland County packing plants above Bridgeton, stimulated the expansion of the Cape May County agricultural industry. The Cape May County fishing business also prospered in 1940, producing 25 million pounds of fish worth $3 million. George A. Reddings's Cold Spring Fish and Supply Company, the largest plant in the county, packed 13 million pounds of fish in 1941 alone. Business recovery was reflected in bank deposits around the county, which increased by $500,000 each season between 1938 and 1941. The Cape May County resort in 1941, the local press announced, "witnessed its best season since the Depression." The returning prosperity improved county finances. Most back taxes from the Depression era were collected by 1940, and the county received a top bond rating from Philadelphia brokers. The county steadily reduced its debt, and in 1940 cut local taxes. "Money bags bulge as county faces 1941," the *Cape May County Times* observed, and the *Cape May Star and Wave* reported that "one feels the underlying current of progress."[3]

Cape May County obtained unprecedented political influence in Trenton in January 1941. John E. Boswell of Ocean City became speaker of the New Jersey State Assembly and I. Grant Scott of Cape May City was elected president of the state senate. At the same time, Thomas J. Durell of Belleplain, a Princeton University graduate and former county superintendent of schools, became assistant state commissioner of education. With such representation, the often-neglected county expected more attention, money, and influence than at any time in its history. Scott introduced measures to improve the Inland Waterway by dredging Sunset Lake in Wildwood Crest and Beach Thoroughfare near Ocean City to enlarge the county's tourist, boating, and fishing facilities. The county representatives pressed for development of a four-lane "super-road" (later the Garden State Parkway) through the county, connecting Beesley's Point with Cape May City. Cape May County's legislators promoted the cutting of a cross-county canal from the Cape May harbor to the Delaware bayshore and advocated the development of a county airport.[4]

Despite its focus on local developments, Cape May County was not isolated from the preparedness program pursued by the Roosevelt administration in 1940 and 1941. Bayshore residents could see the destroyers going down the Delaware Bay as part of the Destroyers-for-Bases deal that gave overage warships, mothballed in the wet basin of the Philadelphia Navy Yard, to the British in exchange for leases on key British bases in the Western Hemisphere. Rumors persisted that the Navy Department planned to reopen the old airfield between Cape May City and Sewell's Point. "The field at Cape May will be utilized this Summer by the squadrons of the aircraft carriers U.S.S. *Yorktown* and *Enterprise*," declared Rear Admiral A. B. Cook, chief of the Bureau of Aeronautics. A board of naval officers visited the old Cape May Section Base and naval air station and recommended that in the event of a national emergency the field should be expanded. Meantime, the U.S. Marine Corps used the small arms firing range on Sewell's Point for officer training. After the fall of France to the Nazis in June 1940 and the Roosevelt administration's declaration of a national emergency, the Coast Guard turned the Section Base over to the navy in August. The navy recommissioned the Naval Air Station, Cape May, in September 1940.[5]

Cape May County learned more about the possibility of American intervention in World War II when James H. R. Cromwell, former U.S. ambassador to Canada, dedicated the Ocean Drive in June 1940. "If Hitler wins we will live in a different world," Cromwell told the huge crowd gathered at the bridge over Middle Thoroughfare in Lower Township. "We must help the Allies win the war," Cromwell concluded. The announcement of the first peacetime draft in American history in September 1940 brought the world conflict closer to the county as draft board headquarters were opened at the Music Pavilion in Ocean City and in the old courthouse building at Cape May Court House. The county registered 2,705 men for the draft.

There was a growing concern for security around the Cape May peninsula during the winter of 1940. Informants claimed that Wildwood fishermen had supplied a German submarine just off the Cape May County coast with food and fuel. An investigation disclosed no such activity, but rumors continued that Cape May County barrier island residents with families in Italy and Germany had helped Nazi U-Boats.[6]

German submarine activity in the Atlantic Ocean, combined with the fall of Greece and Yugoslavia to Axis forces, led Roosevelt to declare a state of unlimited national emergency in May 1941. This meant the call to active duty of reserve officers. Major Clarence W. Way of Sea Isle City, a veteran medical officer who had served in France during the First World War, was placed on active duty. Edward L. Rice, Jr., the tax collector in Avalon, reported for duty at the Philadelphia Naval Yard. Many county towns organized defense councils. Dennis Township planned to convert trucks to ambulances and turn schools into emergency hospitals. An army coastal artillery unit arrived at Cape May Point in July 1941 and pitched tents near the old lighthouse. All the while, WPA workers rebuilt the Cape May Section Base, U.S. Navy. They constructed nineteen buildings, nine new jetties, seaplane slips, and underground fuel storage tanks. They reroofed and painted the dirigible hangar, then tore it down in October 1941 to make space for other construction. The Cape May County Board of Freeholders authorized the installation in August 1941 of underground telephone cables to the Naval Air Station, Cape May, "in the interest of national defense."[7]

Japan's surprise airstrike against Pearl Harbor brought the United States into World War II on 7 December 1941 and accelerated military activities on the Jersey Cape. Volunteers from the Aircraft Warning Service manned aircraft observation posts in Mayville, Erma, Swainton, Petersburg, and Woodbine. Lookouts maintained a twenty-four-hour watch on top of the Music Pier in Ocean City. These aircraft spotters were Cape May County's first line of defense, claimed Henry Roeser, Jr., the director of finance for Ocean City. "Let a single air raid be made anywhere along the New Jersey coast; let a single enemy submarine be discovered anywhere along this coast," Roeser told the Cape May County League of Municipalities, "and the seaside resorts may just as well blow up all their bridges and close up shop for all the summer season they will have."[8]

Precautions against air attacks that might destroy the beachfront resorts absorbed Cape May County in the months following Pearl

Harbor. Raymond M. Burke, Sr., chairman of the Middle Township civil defense council and an aircraft spotter with the Mayville observation post, published a set of air raid instructions. Local civil defense councils circulated these rules and held air raid tests throughout the county. When the Cape May Court House siren on the firehouse proved inadequate to warn residents, the Middle Township committee purchased new sirens for installation around the county seat. Mayor George D. Richards of Ocean City petitioned the board of freeholders to turn off the siren, which sounded when the county drawbridge opened, "in order that the persons in the 34th Street area will not have the idea that an air raid warning is being sounded."[9]

At first, the county required only a dimout of lights along the boardwalks and in beachfront businesses and houses. After the sinking of the *Varanger*, an 8,510-ton Norwegian tanker, by a German submarine off the coast of Cape May County in January 1942, naval authorities ordered a blackout of lights along the New Jersey coast. Blue lights were installed in the Cape May City High School, Convention Hall, and other public buildings. The blackout extended ten miles inland. Not everyone observed the blackouts, and the farmers of Cold Spring protested the drawing of shades in the rural areas during hot summer nights. The Coast Guard and county authorities restricted fishing in local waters, partly to avoid the mines reportedly laid by the Germans at the mouth of the Delaware Bay. The board of freeholders ordered all boats away from county bridges, fearing sabotage. The army forbad telescopes, cameras, or field glasses on the beach anytime, and allowed no one on the county beaches after dark.[10]

The war brought a series of war bond, rubber, and scrap iron drives to Cape May County. Percy H. Jackson, director of the board of freeholders in 1942, called "upon all the people of the county to lend every effort and give their scrap to rap the Japs and the others who have caused the present world turmoil." Charles A. Swain, Jr., a Cape May City merchant and Kiwanis Club leader, headed the scrap iron drive in the county. Swain scavenged iron from inland farms and the old trolley rails in Cape May City along Washington Avenue. Wildwood filled an entire railroad gondola car with tin cans and scrap for the war effort. The war meant rationing. The county established a tire rationing board in January 1942 and issued sugar rationing books in the public schools in March. Gas rationing disrupted county life more than other wartime measures. Mrs. R. E. Wolcott explained that it interrupted religious services. "The hymn sing was held at the Rio Grande Baptist Church on Sunday evening," Wolcott noted, and "this was the last one to be held because of gas rationing."[11]

Gas rationing hurt resort business. T. Millet Hand, the mayor of Cape May City, petitioned the county rationing coordinator, Robert K. Bell, for a larger share of the gas ration because of the increase of war workers and servicemen traveling around his city. County businessmen appealed for increased gas allotments so that war workers could take weekend trips to the beach. Not until 1943 did the Office of Price Administration allow the use of the A-Ration book for one automobile round trip from Camden and Philadelphia to the Cape May County seashore for the July Fourth weekend. Gas rationing prevented a planned extravagant celebration of Cape May County's two hundred fiftieth anniversary. Instead of parades, festivals, dances, and games, the county recognized this landmark event with a quiet Court House gathering. Percy H. Jackson hoped that people would visit the beaches anyway. "You'll be a million miles from care and you'll go back to your jobs, defense or otherwise, worth twice as much to yourself and to Uncle Sam," Jackson proclaimed.[12]

Cape May County promoted the vacation and resort business throughout the war years. Early in the war rumors circulated that enemy submarines and other dangers had closed the county beaches. Local leaders dispelled the rumors. I. Grant Scott declared that Cape May County was less exposed to an attack than most eastern cities, and T. Millet Hand demanded that *Time* magazine retract an article that portrayed the New Jersey beaches as covered with oil, bodies, and barbed wire. "Cape May has not been evacuated," the local journalist continued, and "we are not living in the eternal darkness of blackouts." French B. Loveland, the Cape May County prosecutor, blamed vicious fifth columnists for spreading such damaging rumors. Resort leaders tried to make the war situation more attractive to tourists by claiming that the blue dimout lights along the boardwalks and waterfront added a relaxed and romantic atmosphere for the wartime vacationer.[13]

Natural disasters to the Cape May County beachfront hurt resort business more than the war. The worst fire in Wildwood's history razed three beachfront blocks along the boardwalk in December 1943. The wind-driven fire destroyed twenty-five businesses between Twenty-sixth Street and the North Wildwood line, the Ocean Pier and Surfside Hotels, and the Nixon Theater. A coincidental blast heard out at sea caused some to fear a sneak attack on Wildwood, adding to rumors of the enemy along the waterfront and drawing an FBI investigation of the fire. Less than a year later, one of the most destructive hurricanes ever to hit Cape May County ripped through the resort towns. Much of the damage occurred when ninety-three-mile-per-hour winds blowing into the surf created a great wave that exploded against the beaches. The hurricane of September 1944 tore up the boardwalk and wrecked Convention Hall in Cape May City. It destroyed 50 percent of Strathmere, 20 percent of Sea Isle City, part of Avalon including the municipal pier and boardwalk, and Stone Harbor's fishing pier. The *Gazette* estimated that the storm caused $8 million dollars in damage to Cape May City. The hurricane struck the bayside as well. An eight-foot wall of water inundated Reed's Beach and carried fishing boats from Bidwell's Creek, a man-made ditch just below Goshen Creek on the bayside, to distant inland meadows.[14]

The world war altered Cape May County's landscape in other ways as well. The *Cape May County Times* captured the major man-made change. "It was a dramatic moment, one of the most dramatic in Cape May County's history," the *Times* observed in December 1942, "last Friday afternoon [December 11] when the last earth barrier gave way at Cold Spring Inlet and the Cape May County Canal was virtually completed." The vision of a cross-county canal had captured the imagination of Cape May County leaders at least since the American canal building era of the 1840s, when Nathaniel Holmes envisioned government aid for such a project. The Risley brothers of Stone Harbor had drawn blueprints for a canal from Stone Harbor to Bidwell's Creek and had undertaken some dredging of a channel from Stone Harbor toward Court House. Periodically the U.S. Army Corps of Engineers surveyed canal sites, and in 1933 it drew a route from Cedar Swamp Creek to Dennis Creek, a canal that several county writers worried "would have cut all the resorts of the county off."[15]

The proliferation of public works projects during the New Deal stimulated additional interest in a canal. A meeting called by the Philadelphia office of the Army Corps of Engineers held in the courtroom of the new courthouse building in 1935 heard various proposals for canal routes. Six different routes were outlined at the meeting, including the Great Cedar Swamp and Stone Harbor routes. Another traced a canal from Hereford's Inlet to Dias Creek. The most popular route extended from Cape May harbor (old Cold Spring Inlet) to any one of three creeks on the bayside in Lower Township. The following year, I. Grant Scott introduced legislation for development of the Inland Waterway and construction of a cross-county canal. Scott consulted with officials from the War and Navy departments, seeking their support for a canal. At the moment, the canal was considered a nonessential public works. The war changed this view, and in July 1942 the Navy Department allocated a million dollars for construction of a canal. The New Jersey legislature appropriated $100,000 to purchase rights-of-way from residents and to empower the county to condemn land for national defense.[16]

The pipeline dredge *Baltimore* started digging in the Delaware Bay in July very near the site where the lost whaling town of Portsmouth or New England Town, which once served as the county's first settlement, had fallen into the bay. The government dredge cut through Town Bank Road and headed for the New England Creek meadow. The huge machine cut a hundred-foot-wide, fifteen-foot-deep (twelve feet at low-water mark) channel along New England Creek to Cold Spring Inlet through the oldest, most historic region of the county. As the dredge worked twenty-four hours a day, the U.S. District Court in Trenton directed condemnation proceedings against this land. Cape May County Freeholder Osman Corson claimed that the federal and state governments carried out the condemnations without consulting county administrators. Owners of some of the ancient houses in the path of the canal gave up their property reluctantly and moved several to new locations.[17]

The canal severed major arteries through the lower part of the peninsula, including the Bayshore, New England, and Seashore roads, Route 9, and the Shunpike. It made the tip of the peninsula an island once more, and according to geographer Charles A. Stansfield, Jr., led to the artificial accumulation of sand north of the canal jetties and the terrible erosion of beaches to the south of the canal. It also upset the ecological balance, water table, and other natural features of the Jersey Cape. On the other hand, the canal facilitated pleasure boat traffic to the bayside and access to the Inland Waterway, and allowed craft to avoid the Cape May rips, the dangerous waters around the tip of the Cape. It provided the long-sought protected anchorage for a ferry line across the Delaware Bay.[18]

The other major wartime construction project in Cape May County during the Second World War also had a mixed legacy for the area's future development. The federal government built a giant airfield with three five-thousand-foot runways near Rio Grande in 1942 to supplement the badly overcrowded Naval Air Station, Cape May. The location drew opposition from Freeholder Ralph T. Stevens. He worried about the legality of a resolution that turned nine hundred acres of county and private lands over to the U.S. government and about the contractual and financial arrangements for the county. Stevens "stated that he was of the opinion that the County had no right to adopt any such resolution, nor did it have any right to give the land to the Government." Percy H. Jackson, director of the board of freeholders, defended the decision. Jackson claimed that a government airport would bring $3 million worth of public improvements to Cape May County. "Although no promises are made," Jackson argued, "it is quite probable that after the War these improvements will be turned over to the County and with the modern trend in aviation, will be of great benefit." In the end, the board of freeholders voted 4–1 to acquire the airport land "by gift, grant, purchase or condemnation."[19]

The navy designated the new airfield as Naval Auxiliary Air Facility, Rio Grande, then commissioned it the Naval Air Station, Rio Grande. Apparently the name caused immediate confusion for those who thought the station was located in Texas. Redesignated Naval Air Station, Wildwood, in April 1943, the airfield became a training base for aircraft carrier dive bomber pilots from Carrier Air Group 30 attached to the *Monterey*, a light carrier constructed by the New York Shipbuilding Corporation in Camden. Bad luck plagued the naval air station from the outset. A dynamite expert from Philadelphia was killed in May 1942 while clearing a path for a runway when a huge tree stump blew up and fell on his head. The following month a navy ensign on routine flight became disoriented and plunged into the woods near Coxe Hall Creek. Cape May County newspapers recorded thirteen more pilots from the Naval Air Station, Wildwood, killed in training flights, mostly lost over the Delaware Bay. Two pilots were injured when their dive bomber ditched into the ocean off Sea Isle City's beaches, which were crowded with Sunday afternoon bathers. These crashes disturbed county residents, who complained that carrier pilots approached the peninsula as low as possible along the beachfront, buzzing cottages and bathers. Low flying had became a "menace," the *Star and Wave* complained.[20]

Reports of Cape May County's own war casualties began to reach home during the spring of 1943. The local newspaper announced that a Cape May City Navy radioman had died in the North

Atlantic in April and that the Japanese had captured a Wildwood aircraft spotter stationed in the Philippine Islands. During the next two years of war, 102 Cape May County men died. Nearly every municipality lost at least one, and Wildwood recorded twenty deaths, Ocean City seventeen, and Cape May City sixteen. Despite these personal losses, the rest of the county prospered during the Second World War. "Cape May apparently is nearing the long sought goal of stable off-season income," F. Mervyn Kent, a local newspaper editor, wrote in January 1942.[21]

Woodbine's clothing factories, often in financial trouble during the Depression, revived with war work. Jacob M. Franklin, a Russian-American tailor and clothes designer, moved from Massachusetts to Woodbine in 1940 and opened a clothing factory that contracted with the government to manufacture military service coats. Franklin's factory and the nearby Kravitz Clothing Company produced one hundred thousand military coats during the war and employed over four hundred Woodbine residents. The Holtz Boat Works and Basin Company reincorporated as the Holtz Shipbuilders in 1942 and constructed 28-foot motor launches for the Army Corps of Engineers at its Ocean City yard. In Cape May City, Harry Mogck, I. Grant Scott, and T. Millet Hand organized the Cape May Shipbuilders in October 1942. During World War II the Cape May Shipbuilders yard on Cape Island Creek at the foot of Wilson Street in Cape May City built Navy tugboats, YFBs (sixty-five-foot navy ferryboats), dredges, and fishing craft. The construction of defense housing units and access roads to the navy base in Cape May City also provided local civilian employment.[22]

Work started in early 1942 on the Northwest Magnesite plant, the largest chemical plant built in Cape May County. The plant was located along Sunset Boulevard on the bay near the spot where for two decades world-renowned ornithologist Witmer Stone had observed the birds that he recorded in his *Bird Studies of Old Cape May*. After Stone's death in 1939, the bayshore land had been set aside by Audubon Society members and other conservationists as a bird sanctuary. However, the *Star and Wave* called the sanctuary undeveloped waste land and welcomed the chemical factory. "The once barren lands occupied by the Witmer Stone Wildlife Sanctuary," the paper explained in April 1942, "are now scenes of intense activity as nearly 200 workmen speed construction of the plant, which promises to be the county's largest industry." The Northwest Magnesite plant extracted water from the bay and mixed it with dolomite shipped from Chester County, Pennsylvania, on a railroad spur between Cape May City and the plant, to produce special refractory bricks used in steel production.[23]

Ralph Townsend Stevens, president of the Cape May Sand Washing Company located near the new chemical plant, hoped that the magnesite facility would be the beginning of a huge bayside industrial complex. Stevens, a member of the Board of Freeholders between 1925 and 1951, insisted that bayside industrial development meant an end to the county's perennial seasonal economic slump and winter unemployment. "We would have the best summer resorts on the Atlantic Coast," Stevens explained, and "the best farms inland to feed the resorts and industries on the bayshore." Catching the spirit of bayside development, Harry Errickson of Reed's Beach offered five acres on the bay free to any manufacturing concern that would build a factory and hire Cape May County residents.[24]

World War II boosted Cape May County's tourist and amusement business, adding to the income and population of the area. Wildwood actively sought servicemen's business. While Ocean City restricted shirtless bathing for men, banned liquor, and frowned upon noisy amusements, Wildwood became a wide-open resort. Black and white entertainers filled Wildwood's lounges and cabarets. The Surf Room at the Manor Hotel on Twenty-fifth Street advertised the Three Aces and a Queen, the "sing-sational Sepia Stars of Radio and Stage," and Sir Evans Brown, the master of the swing harp. Wildwood Convention Hall entertained servicemen with wrestling bouts between the Turkish Angel and Gino Garibaldi. Joy Gaylor and her All-Girl Band sang at the Starlight Ballroom. Wildwood's wartime movie theaters packed in crowds to see Abbott and Costello at Hunt's Casino, William Bendix at the Strand, and Van Johnson in *Two Girls and a Sailor* at the Regent. Charles Kerr's Orchestra provided dance music at Convention Hall in Cape May City each summer during the war. Ann Dupont, "Queen of the Clarinet and her Rhythmen," drew large crowds at Congress Hall, and Arnold's Cafe Club on Beach Avenue featured Vito Lamonica and Russ Cortese with the Baldwin Twins.[25]

An easing of wartime controls in Cape May County accompanied the Allied drive against Nazi Germany that led to V-E Day in April 1945. The Office of Price Administration permitted gas for pleasure boaters on weekends, and the navy lifted restrictions against fishing. The midnight curfews and brownouts ended in May 1945. Patience Ludlam, chairperson of the Cape May County Chapter of the Red

Cross who had recently learned about her son's death in the war, reminded the county that the war had not ended with defeat of Germany. Ludlam appealed to residents to increase their Red Cross volunteer work and not to let down until Japan had been subdued. Decorated war veterans held a rally at the Colonial Theater in Woodbine urging factory workers to continue war production. Two hundred German prisoners of war arrived at the Dias Creek Civilian Conservation Corps camp from Fort Dupont in Delaware in May 1945. Guards put the prisoners to work digging mosquito control drainage ditches around the Naval Air Station, Wildwood. Finally in August 1945, Japan surrendered, unleashing wild V-J Day celebrations throughout the United States. "Joy was unconfined in Cape May County," the *Gazette* observed. Thousands of sailors swarmed Wildwood's boardwalk, hugging and kissing everyone. Auto horns blew all day. The county's church bells rang and fire sirens sounded. Bus loads of weekend tourists sang "God Bless America" as they passed through Cape May Court House on their way to the seashore beaches.[26]

The postwar period brought a welter of problems to the United States, including inflation, housing shortages, and difficult adjustment of returning veterans to civilian life. At the same time, deteriorating conditions between the United States and the Soviet Union led to a Cold War. FDR died in April 1945, and Vice President Harry S. Truman, a former Missouri senator, took the nation into this troubled postwar era. Cape May County confronted many of the same problems that existed on the national level. A severe housing shortage plagued the county, and landlords evicted families to make room for the flood of tourists expected to accompany the return of peace. "Hundreds of year-round residents of resort communities have been given notice either to move out or pay exorbitant rents," observed Emil J. McCall, the regional director of the Office of Rent Control. Shortage of building materials prevented the construction of desperately needed new housing on the Jersey Cape, even after the War Production Board lifted the ban on new house construction in September 1945.[27]

Roads and bridges had been neglected during the war, and important county routes such as the Corson's Inlet drawbridge had to be condemned as too dangerous for travel. The condition of local roads became most critical after an end to gas rationing had freed hundreds of thousands of automobiles to rush to the shore. The *Cape May County Gazette* estimated that during the weekend of 4 July 1947,

600,000 people visited Cape May County resort beaches in their automobiles. At the same time, the Pennsylvania-Reading-Seashore Railroad threatened to abandon rail service between Philadelphia and Wildwood and to eliminate the stops at Belleplain, Woodbine, Dennisville, South Dennis, Goshen, and Whitesboro.[28]

The county had also neglected mosquito control during the Second World War, and now the tiny creatures were back to discourage summer vacationers. The county's mosquito extermination commission determined in 1945 to eliminate the insect once and for all by applying a new wonder pesticide. "DDT, the sledgehammer insecticide that walloped the mosquitoes in the Pacific," the commission told the board of freeholders, "was turned on their pestiferous cousins in Cape May County." The mosquito commission sprayed the South Seaville Camp Meeting grounds and soaked the Cape May County Park with DDT just before a big clambake in July 1945. The mosquito control group sprayed the salt meadows with DDT. Still, the insect disrupted tourism. "Your present commissioners have already taken steps to spray the town with DDT," Mayor Edith M. Greenan of Avalon told the Regular Republican Club, "but we cannot promise complete elimination of mosquitoes, as these little pests have a most annoying habit of flying in from the meadows with the first strong land breeze."[29]

Cape May County's military facilities demobilized as rapidly as those located around the United States at the end of the Second World War. The navy surrendered the Admiral Hotel to Cape May City officials in December 1945 and transferred the Naval Air Station, Cape May to the Coast Guard in 1946. Several years later, the U.S. Coast Guard commissioned the Cape May station as one of its two recruit receiving centers and training stations. Most military facilities in the county simply closed. The government abandoned the Naval Auxiliary Airfield, Ocean City (now the Ocean City airport), and the Woodbine Outlying Airfield, and placed the Naval Air Station, Wildwood, on a caretaker, or inactive, status. The War Assets Administration and the Surplus Property Administration took charge of the facility in order to dispose of materials, buildings, and runways. A private syndicate incorporated the Bellanca Vocational and Flying School in 1946 to develop the Naval Air Station, Wildwood, as a commercial airport and aircraft manufacturing facility. This syndicate included a prominent group of postwar county developers such as Bayard L. England, Atlantic City Electric Company executive, Benjamin

F. Lee of Wildwood, manager of the Cape May County Bridge Commission, Robert K. Bell, Ocean City attorney and Cape May County counsel, and Frank Bellanca, president of the Blue Star Airlines of Delaware.[30]

Harry Feit, the mayor of Woodbine, promoted the development of his borough's airfield to offset the economic crisis that he expected would accompany the loss of government contracts by Woodbine's factories after the war. For a time, Feit tried to locate a proposed air force academy in Woodbine. Feit met with U.S. Air Force officers and civilian officials, taking them on an inspection tour of the wartime outlying flying field's three 2,500-foot runways. Probably the Air Force never considered Woodbine seriously as a site and planned from the beginning to locate its academy in Colorado. Woodbine officials continued to search for occupants for their largely undeveloped airport. A lease was signed in 1953 with private contractors working on construction of the Garden State Parkway to store and repair heavy road-building equipment at the Woodbine airfield.[31]

The New Jersey legislature passed a parkway bond in 1952 to build a four-lane toll road from Fort Lee near the George Washington Bridge in Bergen County all the way to Cape May City on the tip of the Jersey Cape. Only the last twenty-seven miles lying in Cape May County remained to be completed by the summer of 1953. The Parkway Authority established a land office in the county in August to purchase rights-of-way on the surveyed route lying east of the present Route 9 along the first dry mainland strip encountered after crossing the salt meadows from the barrier islands. Engineers had selected this route at least partly to avoid cutting through the county's farmlands. Nevertheless, a number of Upper Township farmers opposed the route. One Palermo farmer claimed that the parkway went through the center of his piggery. Superior Court Judge Elmer B. Woods appointed a commission of county legal, real estate, and landowning officials, including Palmer M. Way, Jr., Frank Hoffman, and W. Carroll Koeneke, to settle disputes between farmers and the parkway commission. Bayard L. England, the parkway commissioner and county airport developer, assured Cape May County landowners that they would receive a fair price for their properties. The disputes delayed construction for several months, and the last sections, between Wildwood and Cape May City and between Beesley's Point and Route 50 in Upper Township, opened to automobile traffic in September 1954.[32]

The Garden State Parkway fundamentally altered Cape May County life, accelerating seasonal travel and the growth of permanent population. It brought hundreds of thousands of newcomers, many from northern New Jersey and New York, into the county for vacations. The county felt the impact at once as the weekend of 4 July 1955 brought "all-time record crowds" to the Jersey Cape resort. Every barrier island street was filled with bumper-to-bumper traffic. A mile-long bottleneck developed at the end of the parkway as tourists waited to cross the narrow bridge over the canal to Cape May City. The resort opened public school playgrounds to provide additional parking for the flood of visitors.[33]

Less spectacular, but equally important to the county's postwar development, the Garden State Parkway contributed to a continued growth of Cape May County's permanent population. After the loss of residents during the Depression, the county recovered during the war years, and the year-round population increased between 1940 and 1950 from 28,919 to 37,131, an increase twice that of New Jersey overall during the same period. During the next decade, the rate of county growth was more phenomenal, increasing 30 percent to 48,555 permanent residents by 1960. Rapid growth occurred in Lower Township, Wildwood Crest, Cape May Point, and Cape May City. The Garden State Parkway improved transportation to Atlantic County and connections to Camden and Philadelphia, stimulating an increase in Ocean City's population between 1950 and 1960.[34]

The most notable population increase in the postwar era occurred along the bayshore north of the Cape May Canal to Fishing Creek, where Joseph Millman, Ellery M. Bowman, and other Philadelphia and Cape May County developers built North Cape May, Wildwood Villas, Highland Beach, Miami Beach, and other housing developments. All these developments had begun during the county-wide real estate boom of the 1920s. At that time, streets, lots, sidewalks, and waterlines had been laid out. Most property remained unsold. The Depression interrupted the ambitious North Cape May development, and by 1940 only three houses and four people were located there. George A. Redding introduced legislation in 1945 to dissolve both the borough of North Cape May, incorporated in March 1929, and the borough of South Cape May, the latter largely washed away over the years by the ocean. In 1951 the North Cape May Development Company, headed by realtors Carl T. Mitnick and Harry T. Kalish, purchased the land, and Fred C. Barthelmess, a

former naval intelligence officer, served as the company's sales manager. Barthelmess sold hundreds of lots in North Cape May to Philadelphia, Gloucester County, and Camden County buyers, many of
them retired persons.[35]

North Cape May had one thousand houses by 1956. Bayshore
developers attracted light industry to the area, including a hosiery
mill and a button factory. With the increase in permanent population,
the bayshore communities exerted more influence in county affairs.
The *Star and Wave* published a "Bayshore" edition, and WCMC, the
Wildwood radio station, broadcast a Villas Home Town hour. Bayshore political leaders such as Fred C. Barthelmess and Leslie P. Bate,
a Villas turkey farmer, became influential in Lower Township and
county politics.[36]

Rising population placed new demands on postwar county institutions. Middle Township added over one hundred new students in
1945 to its already badly overcrowded and outdated schools. The
township lacked recreational fields for its schools, and in 1946 the
Middle Township Recreation Association and Middle Township Committee developed Memorial Field on Pacific Avenue, Cape May Court
House, for football, baseball, and track. The athletic field opened in
time for township football fans to watch one of the most exciting
high school football teams in county history, led by powerful running
back John Roberson, member of a prominent Stone Harbor African-
American family. Meanwhile, Dennis Township met overcrowded
conditions in its schools by building a consolidated school in 1952
on Academy Road in Dennisville.[37]

The worst overcrowding occurred at the Cape May City High
School, built in 1917 to serve the city but now drawing students from
the rapidly expanding areas of Lower Township. The communities of
Cape May Point, Cape May City, West Cape May, and Lower Township
organized a consolidated school commission in 1952 headed by Richard M. Teitelman, a Cape May City restaurateur and longtime school
board member, to select a site for a new regional high school. Years of
feuding ensued as the three Lower Township members consistently
outvoted the Cape May City and West Cape May representatives to
block proposed school sites along Lafayette Street on the old Cape
May Golf Club course in Cape May City and another at Sixth Street and
Landis Avenue in West Cape May. After three public votes and dozens
of meetings, voters finally selected the Bennett Farm in Erma. The
Lower Township regional high school opened at last in January 1961.[38]

Cape May County's growing postwar population was marked by a dramatic increase in older residents. County people over the age of sixty-five rose from 6 percent of the population during World War II to 17.8 percent in 1960. The aging population accelerated the demand for hospital and welfare institutions on the Jersey Cape. The board of freeholders built the Crest Haven county welfare complex in 1953 on the old almshouse grounds adjacent to the Cape May County Park just above Court House. At the same time, a hospital committee made up of William C. Hunt, Dr. James S. D. Eisenhower, Jr., Burton J. Smith, editor of the *Gazette*, and other county leaders revived prewar plans for a county hospital. Just before the war, Burdette Tomlin, a wealthy Upper Township native who had amassed a fortune with a Millville sand company, donated $25,000 toward a county hospital on the condition that the county would raise matching funds. War delayed fund-raising, and Dr. Eisenhower, president of the Cape May County Medical Society, resumed the fund drive after the war. "The Burdette Tomlin Memorial Hospital is a must," Eisenhower announced. "We must have it without delay." The successful fund drive led to the construction of Burdette Tomlin Hospital, a sixty-five-bed facility, which opened on the Shore Road in Cape May Court House in October 1950. Almost at once the hospital proved too small, and trustees planned another fund-raising campaign to construct an addition.[39]

The greatly increased number of summer visitors and permanent residents strained aging county garbage and refuse disposal services. New Jersey state government ordered Cape May City, West Cape May, and Cape May Point to build a waste disposal plant and to stop pouring their waste into the Delaware Bay. The state fined West Wildwood after it delayed construction of a waste disposal facility. The state ordered Cape May City to move its dump site in 1958 from along Cape Island Creek to West Cape May near the site of the old racetrack and grandstand. Pollution of drinking water became a major concern as well, and Cold Spring, long known as a fountain of pure healthful water, closed because of pollution. When salt water fouled Cape May City's wells, Mayor Carl R. Youngberg decided to pump 100,000 gallons of fresh water into the wells and "recharge" them.[40]

Nearly unregulated and unplanned postwar economic expansion added to the growing burdens on local social services and public works. Motel construction proceeded at a rapid pace between 1950 and 1960 with gaudy, gimmicky overnight tourist accommodations such as the Fantasy Motel on Rio Grande Boulevard appearing in nearly every resort town. Cape May City built its first motel in 1952 and Stone Harbor in 1956. North Wildwood developed an entire motel row, and though Ocean City prohibited the construction of garish motels, new buildings resembled motels more than they did the traditional rooming house or hotel. Developers bought farmlands along the Shore Road and almost indiscriminately put up cheap motels and eating places. More carefully planned but equally disturbing to the traditional rural landscape, between 1950 and 1958 the Marlyn Manor development at the junction of Routes 47 and 9 in Rio Grande transformed pastures and farms into a shopping center, motels, restaurants, housing developments, and the county's first drive-in movie theater, the Wildwood Drive-In.[41]

Development of an industrial park at the former Naval Air Station, Wildwood, proceeded in an erratic fashion. The U.S. government turned the airport over to the county in June 1947, but after Bellanca pulled out, only a flying service run by M. Curtis Young, an Army Air Force veteran, operated on the field. One visitor noted that vandals had destroyed property at the former naval station, and that almost no other activity could be found at the airport. Young, William C. Hunt, president of the Cape May County Chamber of Commerce, and others called for an investigation of the county's conduct of airport business. Gradually the county filled some of the empty buildings, transferring welfare offices and a National Guard unit to the former base, and renting space to several small concerns. Allegheny Airlines instituted a summer airline service, and in one flight Vice President Richard M. Nixon got off the plane at the county airport in 1953, shook hands with several residents, and then departed. By the end of the decade five larger tenants—Young's Flying Service, United States Overseas Airlines, F. H. Snow Canning Company, Resdel Plastics Company, and A. C. Anderson, Inc., a manufacturer of hydraulic equipment—rented space at the county airport industrial park.[42]

A county grand jury found the airport in a rundown condition in 1960 and suggested that Walter H. Treen of Wildwood, the freeholder in charge of the county airport, held no particular competence in managing airport affairs. The criticism of Treen's direction of the county airport was the culmination of years of postwar political turmoil in Cape May County. Postwar conditions convulsed local politics. The state senatorial election of 1945 was one of the dirtiest in county history. Democratic party leaders accused Republican party candidate George A. Redding, the mayor of North Wildwood, of once consorting with prostitutes and gangsters. The county Democrats brought Frank Hague, Jersey City boss, to Cape May Court House to campaign for Robert Bright of Wildwood. Hague's attack on Cape May County Republicans backfired, and Redding defeated Bright for the state senate seat. Meantime, a citizens group tried to oust Mayor Edith M. Greenan, a former Camden County Democratic party committeewoman who had held office in Avalon since 1931. Feuding, indictments, and investigations ensued until finally an irate insurgent punched Mayor Greenan in the face when one of her supporters ducked the blow aimed at him. "I never struck a woman before," the incredulous assailant explained after he had socked the female mayor of Avalon.[43]

Avalon's political turmoil led to another county grand jury probe. The investigators claimed that 14 percent of Avalon's voters lived outside Cape May County, and demanded reorganization of the county election board, introduction of voting machines, and the purge of outsiders from registration lists. New Jersey Governor Robert B. Meyner and Attorney General Grover C. Richman, Jr., intervened in the Avalon election probe of 1955. "There are instances in other counties where election boards have not carried out their duties in publishing the names of ineligible voters," Meyner said, "but I consider the lack of action in Cape May to be a flagrant abuse of our election laws." County Republican party leaders accused Meyner, a Democrat, of using the voting case to destroy their organization, and according to F. Mervyn Kent, editor of the *Star and Wave*, of injecting "top level state officials into the affairs of a local community or even a county."[44]

The turmoil surrounding county politics in the postwar era arose in part from the changing nature of local political alliances. The New Deal and Second World War had brought new elements to the center of county politics, including women, Jewish-Americans, and Italian-Americans. The latter had developed an extensive political and social network in the county. Stanley Pontiere, Harry Sannino, and Anthony Adelizzi of Ocean City had formed the Italian Independent Club "to assist Italians either native or foreign born to take an active part in all matters of a civic nature." Dominick Loscalzo, Ralph Battendieri, and other Court House residents formed the Italian-American Citizens Beneficial Society of Cape May County in 1926 to "promote better and more patriotic citizens." Other clubs followed, most notably the Italian American Citizens of Cape May County, formed in 1932 by Ocean City and Wildwood Italian-Americans. This organization helped to bring Anthony J. Cafiero to the center of county politics.[45]

Born in Philadelphia and educated in Catholic schools, Anthony J. Cafiero came to Wildwood in 1920. Cafiero attended New Jersey Law School in Newark in 1931 and the following year became the first Italian-American in Cape May County to hold the posts of clerk of the board of freeholders, county prosecutor (1944), and state senator (1948). Cafiero joined Clyde W. Struble, the mayor of Ocean City and state assemblyman from Cape May County, as the Jersey Cape's representatives to the New Jersey state constitutional convention in New Brunswick, where the delegates approved a sweeping reform of the outdated New Jersey constitution. Cafiero vigorously promoted constitutional revision throughout the county, undoubtedly contributing to the large barrier island vote in favor of the constitution of 1947 that offset opposition from the mainland townships.[46]

Charles W. Sandman, Jr., also reflected the changing political fabric in postwar Cape May County. A Lower Township attorney and developer of the Erma Park community, Sandman found that this most rapidly growing region of the county had lost political influence to the barrier island "bosses," including John Boswell of Ocean City, Walter H. Treen of Wildwood, and Edith Greenan of Avalon. These bosses represented their barrier island communities and not the interests of the lima bean farmers and other mainland residents who needed new roads and bridges, particularly a new span over the Cape May Canal. The barrier island politicians neglected issues that were of importance to the lower portion of the county such as the development of a Cape May-Lewes ferry. Sandman, who spent seven months in a Nazi prisoner-of-war camp after his bomber was shot down over Pilsen during World War II, also thought that county politicians did not represent the interests of returning veterans. Sandman agreed with his friend, Dr. Leon H. Schuck of Clermont, a freeholder and retired Philadelphia dentist, that the county needed to develop social welfare programs without outside federal government interference. Sandman began to challenge the barrier island bosses in 1954. Sol Needles, Jr., the local Republican party chairman, insisted that Sandman stood behind the investigation of the Avalon voting list in order to oust Edith Greenan from office. After an unsuccessful bid for the state senate seat in 1954, Sandman defeated John Boswell, former state assemblymen and then president of the state public utilities commission, for the senate in one of the major election upsets in Cape May County history. Sandman carried every mainland township.[47]

Sandman battled the regular county Republican party organization for the next five years, and in 1959 won a difficult reelection. During the campaign a so-called Truth Group represented by F. Mervyn Kent hounded the incumbent state senator. Sandman sued Kent for libel but eventually dropped the lawsuit. Sandman advanced a number of county projects, including the ferry to Delaware, Cape Island marina development, and a high-level bridge across the Cape May Canal dubbed the "Sandman Skyway." Sandman represented veteran's interests. He formed an alliance with Anthony J. Volpe of Ocean City, recipient of a Purple Heart in World War II and the director of the Cape May County Veteran's Bureau. Sandman helped Volpe win an assembly seat, and Volpe tried to gain legislative support in 1960 for Sandman's bill to reduce the Cape May County Board of Freeholders from five to three members, a move generally viewed as an attempt to purge Walter Treen of Wildwood from the board. Though Sandman failed to reduce the board of freeholders, his candidates Edwin Zaberer, a North Wildwood restaurant owner, and Kenneth Holmstrup, president of the Cape May Chamber of Commerce and owner of an ornamental ironware company at the County Airport, defeated Treen and John Sudak of Cape May City for seats on the board of freeholders. During this campaign, Sandman debated Treen in front of six hundred people at the courthouse and a large radio audience.[48]

Sandman's political insurgency generated other movements to change the form of local government in Cape May County. Walter C. Wright, Jr., who held degrees from Duke University, Temple Law School, and the University of Pennsylvania graduate school, led a citizen's movement in Cape May City in 1960 to change the city commission to a council and municipal manager format. Begun as a protest against Mayor Carl R. Youngberg, boss of the entrenched old-line Republican party city machine, who attempted to raise mercantile license and luxury taxes in the resort, Wright's movement blossomed into a major political reform. Wright won a stunning victory in October 1960, in a referendum that supported the change in government, and then in the ensuing election in which he polled the highest vote for the council.[49]

Taxes formed the catalyst for the change in Cape May City government, but the issue of urban decay lay at the root of support for Walter C. Wright, Jr. Sections of downtown Cape May City resembled on a small scale the urban blight found in most large American cities in the 1960s. Stores, cottages, and the older hotels had fallen into disrepair. The city lacked parking space, modern waste disposal, or water service. The huge seven-story Admiral Hotel stood vacant, and Wright proposed to renovate it as low-cost housing for the elderly. The old commission lacked a redevelopment plan, and when Howard Tenenbaum, a city businessman and real estate agent, recommended the creation of a municipal planning board, Mayor Carl R. Youngberg disregarded it as too expensive. The new council and municipal manager promised to develop a Victorian-era gaslight district in the downtown section.[50]

Cape May County adopted community planning during the 1950s. The idea of urban and regional planning had gained support during the New Deal, and New Jersey had passed a County and Regional Planning Enabling Act in 1935 that directed county planning boards to develop master plans and to advise boards of freeholders on the development of county programs and budgets. The Cape May County Board of Freeholders formed a committee on postwar planning in February 1942. This committee included Rolland Sharp, the county engineer, Percy H. Jackson, director of the board, and Osman Corson, zoning expert, city engineer, and head of a planning board for Cape May Court House. The board of freeholders resolved "to encourage and assist non-Federal public agencies, such as State, County, Municipal and other governments in assembling data and in preparing long range public improvement programs based upon actual need." Editorials advocating postwar planning appeared from time to time in all the county's newspapers, but nothing concrete developed until 1952, when Lawrence M. Lear, director of the board of freeholders, introduced the concept of a county planning commission to the League of Municipalities of Cape May County. "If we want Cape May county to become the county beautiful tomorrow," Lear explained, "we must begin to plan today to make it so."[51]

The board of freeholders appointed a Cape May County planning board in February 1954. Mayor William A. Haffert of Sea Isle City, the only official before 1950 to develop a master plan for the community, became director of the county board. The newly organized board met during its first year with local township committees to advise on zoning and planning. Some resisted planning board advice. "The development of a sound building code, the establishment of a major street plan, the revision of the township zoning ordinance in accordance with a well worked out master plan," the board observed, "is urgently needed if Lower Township is to avoid growing into a confused, blight producing, inefficient urbanized complex." The planning board also studied the probable impact of the Garden State Parkway on county land use, transportation, and the tourist trade. The board hired as its first planning expert John J. Holland, former senior planner for Saginaw, Michigan, and submitted its first progress report in December 1954. "We feel that the report transmitted herewith," Haffert told Lawrence Lear, "will indicate that we are well on our way toward becoming an effective force for assisting you in the problems of development facing Cape May County."[52]

Professor Edward Wilkens, a Rutgers University regional planning expert, advised the board of freeholders in 1956 that the county needed to construct land use maps, draw zoning regions, and formulate a master plan. In response, the board named Henry H. White of Swainton, a retired county agricultural agent and member of the planning board, to head a master plan committee. White's committee started collecting data on population, resources, transportation, and recreational development. Planning board studies between 1956 and 1962 revealed postwar trends that affected the county's future developments. The studies showed an aging population: the percentage of people over the age of sixty-five had increased from 8.5 in 1930 to 17.8 by 1960. Entire new communities centered around retired residents. Villas advertised as "retirement haven," and North Cape May as "the St. Petersburg of the North." For county planners, this meant a lower ratio of available labor to the total population, and an increased demand on the county for old age assistance, welfare services, and hospitals. Indeed, by 1958, welfare services accounted for one half of the county's $2.2 million annual budget.[53]

Planning studies in the 1950s suggested that Cape May County was growing increasingly white and native born. The white population on the Jersey Cape had risen between 1930 and 1950 from 79.9 percent to 85 percent of the total. African-Americans comprised 9.4 percent of the total Cape May County population in 1930 but only 7.8 percent in 1950, although the concentrations of blacks had increased in Wildwood to 21.4 percent and in Woodbine to 11.1 percent of the municipality's population. Similarly, foreign-born residents made up

10.7 percent of the Jersey Cape in 1930 but only 7.5 percent in 1950. The largest foreign-born populations resided in Wildwood, Ocean City, and North Wildwood, with 50 percent of these of Italian birth. Woodbine's foreign-born population had steadily decreased until in 1950 only 10.7 percent of this once entirely foreign-born community had been born overseas.[54]

The first Cape May County planners in the 1950s recorded how dominant the tourist and resort business had become by mid-century. Once farming, fishing, lumbering, and shipbuilding had provided far more income to the county than the resort business, which until the 1880s had been limited to Cape Island. County planning studies indicated that by 1950 eight out of ten people in the county worked on some phase of the resort, tourist, and service support sectors of the Cape May County economy. A small but significant economic sector, roughly 1,900 people, worked in the shellfish and menhaden fishing industry. The resort industry provided mostly seasonal work and was based upon the tremendous influx of summer residents and visitors. Consequently, the county planning board sought to enumerate the summer population. "These people are as important to Cape May County as good seed is to the Mid-western farmer," the planning board noted in 1958, "and yet very little is known about them."[55]

The planners measured the differences between year-round and tourist populations by comparing bread sales, store receipts, telephone calls, and water consumption. The county sent teams on door-to-door census surveys in July to Stone Harbor, a family-type resort, and to Wildwood, which attracted entertainment-oriented weekend visitors. They discovered that the permanent population of 800 in Stone Harbor increased to 10,000 on a summer weekend day, and that Greater Wildwood (North Wildwood, Wildwood, Wildwood Crest, and West Wildwood) had a permanent population of 13,000 that swelled to nearly 150,000 on a busy resort weekend. The latter led to concentrations of 34,000 people per square mile in the blocks closest to the Wildwood boardwalk. Estimating these increases on a countywide basis, the planning board determined that in 1960 the 48,552 permanent residents increased to 354,973 summer residents, which translated to a 67.7 percent jump in seasonal employment. This huge increase compared to the 9.7 percent increase in Salem County or the 7.1 percent seasonal adjustment in Camden County, the most industrialized section in Cape May County's neighboring South Jersey economic region. "Cape May County appears as a playground on the periphery of an expanding area," the county planners concluded.[56]

The county planning board declared that Cape May County's future development and prosperity centered on the expansion of the tourist and resort business. The county needed to establish a partnership with private enterprise in guiding an orderly growth of this business. "The construction of one or more historical villages and the eventual scheduling of the Old Home Tour during the off season," the board recommended, "should also be considered as specific attractions to lengthen the resort season." The opportunity to expand the resort business occurred in 1959, as the planners completed their assessment, with the celebration of the three hundred fiftieth anniversary of the discovery of Cape May County by Henry Hudson in 1609. County business and government leaders prepared a summer-long series of events, partly to compensate for the inability to celebrate the county government's two hundred fiftieth anniversary because of the Second World War.[57]

The board of freeholders set the tone for the celebration by securing a special die from the U.S. Post Office Service to cancel all mail sent from the county: "350th Anniversary, Cape May County, 1609–1959." At the same time, the Cape May County Art League (founded in 1929) and other organizations, sponsored the Tenth Annual Old House Tour, which included visits to the Jonathan Hand house in Court House, the Nathaniel Holmes house in Dennisville, and the Calvary Baptist Church in Ocean View, among others. Cape May City held an inaugural ball, beard-growing contest, and parade. The city welcomed the annual meeting of the National Trust for Historic Preservation in the hope of attracting support for its restoration of the historic district as a Victorian village. The historic preservation conference met at Congress Hall to hear addresses by Richard P. McCormick, Rutgers University scholar of New Jersey history, and Harold F. Wilson, Glassboro State College historian and author of *The Jersey Shore*. The city's celebration culminated with the arrival of a life-size replica of the *Half Moon*, the ship in which Hudson had explored the Cape May coastline in 1609.[58]

The 350th anniversary celebration became as much a statement of the county's history as of the event it represented. Dr. Bailey Pepper, a Rutgers University entomologist, reported that the summer of 1959, during the peak of the celebration, was the wettest in memory, with unusually heavy rains and high tides. The wet season in turn created the worst salt marsh mosquito invasion since before the Second World War, discouraging the expected flood of tourists. A severe squall broke the masts and bowsprit of the *Half Moon II*, which had anchored in front of the old Stockton Hotel beach. No sooner had the masts been repaired with cedar from the Dennisville woods than high tides and gale-force winds dragged the historic replica's anchor and drove the tiny vessel onto Twelve-Mile Shoal, where the Coast Guard rescued it and towed it back to Cape May City. The damaged *Half Moon II* added to the celebration's growing financial problems and to the shortage of volunteers. Cape May City residents held a town meeting in the auditorium of Cape May High School and voted to cut back on programs for the celebration.[59]

Nevertheless, the three hundred fiftieth anniversary celebration of Hudson's voyage defined Cape May County's postwar identity as a summer tourist and vacation resort. During the celebration the Cape May County Chamber of Commerce produced a film for screening in Fox theaters around the Delaware Valley. This two-and-a-half-minute motion picture promoted the county as the nation's oldest and healthiest seashore resort community. It pictured the county as an historic region, showing excerpts from the Old House Tour. The movie portrayed the county as an ideal retirement community for older citizens. In the end, the three hundred fiftieth anniversary drew national attention to New Jersey's southernmost resort community. President Dwight D. Eisenhower sent his best wishes, and Governor Robert B. Meyner extended the state's official greetings. "New Jersey is proud of the part Cape May plays in its important tourist-recreational industry," Meyner announced.[60]

Some county leaders felt that the tourist industry alone could not sustain the county's economy, and in 1959 they welcomed news that the Atomic Energy Commission (AEC), created to develop the peaceful use of the atom, had selected Cape May County as one of the possible sites along the Delaware Bay for an atomic industrial park. F. Mervyn Kent, editor of the *Star and Wave* in 1959, wrote that the county needed to acquire this atomic park because it would bring millions of dollars during the off season. He reminded his readers that in the past Cape May County had lost such opportunities, particularly Henry Ford's automobile and marine engine project. "A glance back over the history of years gone by," Kent said, "shows that time and again we have had an 'inside track' in many things that could have changed our destiny completely and time after time we have lost out because of a lack of cohesive action to carry through to a successful conclusion."[61]

The Cape May County Chamber of Commerce and the board of freeholders petitioned the AEC to locate the atomic industrial park in Cape May County. They took officials on a tour of the bayshore, presenting it as the ideal site. Mayors and representatives from Cape May County's sixteen municipalities met at Zaberer's Anglesea Inn in North Wildwood in October 1959 and agreed unanimously to promote the atomic park. Edwin Zaberer, the inn's owner, served as the chairman of the Chamber of Commerce's atomic industrial park committee.[62]

Several county residents questioned the impact of an atomic industrial park on Cape May County. One letter to the editor of the *Star and Wave* asked what an atomic industrial park meant. F. Mervyn Kent assured readers that the park would be located on the bayshore far from the oceanfront resort beaches. He stressed the economic benefit to the county. Already the AEC had granted $98.5 million in contracts to New Jersey, including $64.9 million for the James Forrestal Research Center in Princeton. AEC officials met finally with state representatives in February 1960 to explain the proposed atomic industrial park along the Delaware. The full extent of the plan stunned local officials. It included a docking and refueling port for atomic-powered ships such as the *Savannah*, just launched up the river at the New York Shipbuilding Corporation yard in Camden. It also included an atomic reactor, a hospital for radiation burns, a research center, and an atomic-waste-processing plant. The AEC wanted to make Cape May County an "atomic dump," New Jersey Congressman Milton W. Glenn cried.[63]

F. Mervyn Kent recognized the implications of the atomic park as well. "The proposed Atomic Industrial Park would, in the conception of some, be a disposal area for highly radioactive atomic waste," Kent explained. The *Star and Wave* concluded that the atomic industrial park posed a serious threat to the tourist and resort industry. The county would not tolerate anything that undercut the image of cool, healthful Cape May County. The Cape May County community escaped the atomic industrial park but in the years ahead confronted equally dangerous threats to its resort industry from a combination of offshore dumping, water and air pollution, and diminishing natural resources. The board of freeholders recognized a growing threat to Cape May County's environment from pollution by the late 1950s, passing a resolution to stop Philadelphia from dumping trash and garbage into the Delaware Bay. George J. Carter, executive secretary of the Cape May Chamber of Commerce, wrote Mayor Richardson Dilworth of Philadelphia in January 1960, protesting against the city's fouling of Cape May County waters. The subsequent thirty years of Cape May County government, until its three hundredth anniversary in 1992, would tell the story of how the county confronted these threats to its resort industry.[64]

CHAPTER TEN

A Resort Community in Transition, 1962–1992

The worst storm in Cape May County history struck the peninsula in early March 1962. Twenty-foot-high waves smashed Cape May City's boardwalk, pier, and Convention Hall. Two feet of water flooded East Cape May, swirled through the downtown as far as Corgie Street, and raced up Cape Island Creek into West Cape May. The South Cape May meadow disappeared under water. Cape May Point, already badly eroded over the years, flooded all the way to Lake Lily, cutting off 150 residents. Houses fell into the sea, including the former Lankenau Villa, weakened by earlier storms. Parts of Town Bank, close to where the ancient whaling town had disappeared into the bay centuries before, crumbled and toppled into the water.

On the ocean side of Cape May County, huge waves, high winds, and a record flood tide surged across Five Mile Beach, severing Wildwood from the mainland. U.S. Coast Guard helicopters evacuated stranded patients and nurses from the Sea Isle City Mercy Hospital (founded as Surf Hospital in 1946 and sold in 1953 to the Sisters of Mercy of Merion, Pennsylvania). The sea crossed Avalon, Stone Harbor, and Ocean City, uniting with the waters of the back bays and sounds. Flooding caused electrical fires. Leland Stanford, Cape May County civil defense and disaster control coordinator, reported that forty-five fires burned simultaneously from Cape May City to Ocean City during the height of the storm.[1]

The storm of March 1962 revealed once again the fragile nature of the Cape May County resort economy. Cape May County suffered more property damage than any other New Jersey coastal community and double the damage recorded by neighboring Atlantic County. Millions of dollars of destruction to boardwalks, amusements, cottages,

249

houses, and hotels threatened the upcoming summer tourist season. Flooding polluted local water supplies, a problem confronted centuries before when early settlers suffered from the "bloody flux" caused by drinking water fouled by the sea. "Cape May County is in an extremely vulnerable position with respect to salt contamination, being almost completely surrounded by salt water bodies," the county planning board observed in 1962. The storm also eroded hundreds of feet of beachfront, forcing the U.S. Navy to abandon an antisubmarine surveillance station near the lighthouse at Cape May Point.[2]

The storm of 1962 reminded Cape May County that it had become tied inextricably to state and federal governments for its continued survival. New Jersey Governor Richard J. Hughes declared the coastal region a disaster area and requested emergency relief funds. State assistance arrived within months of the storm. Town Bank received funds to repair the bayfront. State aid arrived to erect seawalls and jetties in Ocean City and North Wildwood and to build bulkheads on Reed's Beach and at Pierce's Point on the bayside. Federal monies rehabilitated the jetties at Cold Spring Inlet. Cape May County officials applied for more funds and loans from state and federal government to rebuild beaches and develop erosion-prevention measures. These applications continued the trend toward using state and federal assistance to develop Cape May County that had begun prior to the storm. County officials had created an Economic Development Commission in 1961 to coordinate applications for financial assistance and grants under an area redevelopment program promoted by the John F. Kennedy administration. The Cape May County Board of Freeholders and the county planning board studied ways to obtain state and federal grants that became available in 1961 to assist areas with high rates of unemployment such as that experienced in Cape May County.[3]

Cape May City government employed the period after the storm of 1962 to develop programs of state and federal aid to revive the city's languishing resort business. "Cape May was at the point of losing its identity as a resort and becoming little more in the summer than it was in the winter—a ghost town, a military base, and a fishing village," wrote George E. Thomas and Carl Doebley, authors of an architectural history of Cape May City. The storm had damaged the city so severely that it provided an opportunity to rebuild and renew the area around the concept of a Victorian Village, an idea advanced by Dr. Irving Tenenbaum and members of the Cape May County Art League, which had moved into the Emlen Physick estate's carriage house in 1961. City planners received the first federal grant from the Urban Renewal Administration, a forerunner of the Department of Housing and Urban Development (HUD), in December 1963. Meantime, the state provided funds to build a concrete and asphalt "promenade" on the city's beachfront to protect the resort from future high tides and storms.[4]

Rev. Carl McIntire, a fundamentalist minister and radio evangelist, arrived in Cape May City in 1963 and started purchasing property. Over the next five years he bought the vacant Admiral Hotel, Congress Hall, and lots along Jackson and Ocean streets and Stockton Avenue. During the summer of 1964 McIntire moved Shelton College, a four-year Christian liberal arts school located in Ringwood, New Jersey, near the New York state line, to Cape May City. McIntire revealed plans to develop a twenty-four-acre campus behind the Admiral Hotel, which he had renamed the Christian Admiral Conference Center. Operating from the hotel and several neighboring houses, the college prospered briefly, with two hundred students and twenty faculty members. McIntire planned a gymnasium and other college buildings. Students from Shelton College marched in Washington to support the United States war in Vietnam. The college's soccer team won the North Atlantic Christian Conference title and played against a team from Rutgers University's South Jersey campus in Camden. Some county leaders suggested that Shelton College might become the base for the development of a badly needed Cape May County Community College.[5]

Shelton College became entangled in extended controversy with Cape May City officials over taxes, zoning, and the moving of an historic building (the Star Villa) to the campus from another part of town. The college lost state accreditation as a degree-granting institution when it failed to meet New Jersey Department of Education guidelines and academic standards. Eventually, Rev. Carl McIntire moved the college to Florida. McIntire retained the Christian Admiral Hotel and other Cape May City properties and crusaded to obtain tax-free status for his holdings as part of a religious institution. Once the fundamentalist minister and his followers seized the beach in front of the Christian Admiral Hotel to protest against his treatment by the city government. McIntire also led a protest against the presence of Russian trawlers just off the Cape May County coast, particularly after a 250-foot Soviet ship had cut the anchor cable of a Cape May County party boat while passing too close to it in 1969.[6]

During his confrontation with city government, McIntire negotiated with Charles W. Sandman, Jr., Cape May City solicitor and New Jersey state senator. Sandman continued to be an important political figure in the county and the state, serving as state senate president from 1963 to 1965 and running unsuccessfully for governor three times between 1965 and 1973. Sandman served as the congressman from the Second Congressional District between 1966 and 1974, becoming President Richard M. Nixon's staunchest defender on the House Judiciary Committee during the Watergate scandal and impeachment hearings. Eventually Sandman voted for impeachment after release of the Watergate tapes revealed Nixon's attempt to cover up illegal activities. However, Cape May County voters rejected Sandman in 1974 in favor of William J. Hughes, an Ocean City marina, real estate, and hotel entrepreneur and Rutgers Law School graduate.

Charles Sandman controlled, and sometimes convulsed, Cape May County's powerful Republican party organization throughout the 1960s. He cut off old allies such as Dr. Leon H. Schuck and formed new alliances, for example with Philip R. Matalucci, a Burleigh businessman. Sandman's major contributions lay in his successful campaign to obtain the Cape May-Lewes ferry service, which opened at last on 1 July 1964. Sandman had been the "spearhead and guiding force behind the successful effort," the *Star and Wave* observed, adding that "Cape May County will no longer be a dead end area." Sandman became a leading advocate of legislation to protect the New Jersey shore. He introduced a bill against ocean dumping and defended it before the House Merchant Marine and Fisheries Committee. Sandman opposed the construction of an underwater pipeline terminal and pumping facility off the Jersey Cape. He initiated a lawsuit enjoining a huge Delaware Valley company from dumping chemical waste off the Jersey Cape, and established the Advisors on the Coastal Environment (ACE) in 1971.[7]

Most Cape May County political and civic leaders, like Sandman, adopted the politics of preserving the coastal environment during the late 1960s. Cape May County's continued existence as a major seashore resort depended upon clean air, pure water, and pristine beaches. An awareness of threats to the coastal environment from polluters appeared in Cape May County before conservation and antipollution crusades had become a national movement in the 1960s. The Cape May County Board of Freeholders had fought against oil pollution of their beaches as early as 1922, when they passed a resolution that "deplored [the] practice of oil burning and carrying boats dumping their oil refuse near the coast line of Cape May County resorts because it floats ashore and spoils our bathing beaches and it also covers the wings and feathers of the birds causing them death." The board of freeholders sought state and federal assistance in 1922 to stop the dumping of oil off the New Jersey coast. At the same time, William A. Haffert, editor of the *Cape May County Times*, attacked the Atlantic Ocean oil polluters in his newspaper.[8]

Wilbur J. Ostrander, a Wildwood city commissioner in 1970, thought that toxic waste and sludge from Philadelphia and New York City dumped off the New Jersey coast, rather than oil pollution from ships, posed the greatest threat to Cape May County. Ostrander formed the Stop Ocean Dumping Association (SODA) to publicize the threat to New Jersey fishermen and beaches posed by ocean dumping. Ostrander discovered that Philadelphia dumped millions of gallons of sludge and waste only five and one half miles off Five Mile Beach and Cold Spring Inlet. He directed photographers to the site to document that it had become a "dead sea" devoid of fish. Through contacts with New Jersey Senator Harrison Williams, Jr., and Congressman Charles Sandman, Jr., who received a retainer from SODA for giving antipollution speeches, Ostrander moved the Richard M. Nixon administration to send officials from the newly created Environmental Protection Agency (EPA) to visit the "dead sea" site off the Cape May County coast. SODA activity contributed to efforts by the Nixon administration, Senator Williams, Representative Sandman, State Assemblyman James S. Cafiero, and others to pass legislation to control offshore dumping of toxic waste.[9]

Wilbur Ostrander battled to save Cape May County beaches from pollution by offshore sludge dumps but doubted that his city's own waste contributed to pollution along the seashore. Ostrander bristled at a newspaper allegation that Wildwood city sewage threatened the beaches. "This assertion that the City of Wildwood is bypassing its sewage into the inland waters is totally incorrect," Ostrander told a reporter. Nevertheless, the county's own waste, particularly runoff from storm sewers, posed a hazard both to the health of residents and to the tourist trade and resort business. Local disposal of waste and garbage had long been a problem in Cape May County. Cape May City had polluted Cape Island Creek and the bay since the late nineteenth century, and barrier islanders dumped their refuse in Whitesboro and other mainland locations. Waste disposal had become a more serious problem in the postwar period, and federal and state officials ordered Cape May County municipalities to develop new waste disposal plants.[10]

The great increase in year-round and summer population on the ecologically fragile Cape May peninsula, with its limited areas of dry land was the single most important factor in the county's development since 1945. County population increased at a startling rate, far outstripping the percentage of increase in the state of New Jersey. Cape May County grew from 37,131 residents in 1950 to 48,555 by 1960, a 30.7 percent increase in population. Growth between 1970 and 1980 was more spectacular, increasing from 59,554 to 82,266, a 38.1 percent rise in year-round residents. County planners estimated that there would be over 100,000 permanent residents on the Jersey Cape by the early part of the 1990s. At the same time, summer residents had increased from 300,000 at the end of the Second World War to over 500,000 by 1980. Developers scrambled to keep up with the increase in population, creating an unprecedented building boom on the barrier islands and parts of the mainland during the 1960s. Federal and state fish and wildlife officials expressed concern about the impact on the seashore environment in the early 1960s. "Unless building development activities can be curtailed in New Jersey's salt marshes," a fish and wildlife officer told the Cape May County Planning Board in 1964, "the virtual elimination of the natural habitat of these fish and wildlife is assured."[11]

Forces to conserve the Jersey Cape gathered strength during the late 1960s, reflecting a national movement toward conservationism. The World Wildlife Fund, an international nonprofit group, met in Stone Harbor in July 1969 to discuss methods to save the endangered Cape May County saltwater marshes and tidelands from developers of hotels, motels, and housing projects. Speakers at the conference included Charles Lindbergh, world-famous aviator, and Arthur Godfrey, television star and leading conservationist. After the conference, Herbert Mills and Marion Glaspey, members of the organization, purchased marshlands between Sea Isle City and the Wildwoods to establish a Wetlands Institute. The Wetlands Research Center, funded by the World Wildlife Fund, opened in Stone Harbor in December 1971. Lehigh University marine biologists and scientists staffed the center. The following year, Prince Bernhard of the Netherlands, president of the World Wildlife Fund, officially dedicated the Wetlands Institute.[12]

The state joined private conservationists in the early 1970s in trying to protect Cape May County natural resources with the passage of the Wetlands Act (1970), Coastal Area Facility Review Act of 1973 (CAFRA), and other measures to protect the seashore. At the same time the state Department of Environmental Protection (DEP) monitored developments on the Cape, and in November 1971 banned the installation of septic tanks (and hence the construction of new houses until sewers were installed) in low coastal areas. Gradually state and federal governments constructed a layer of laws, regulations, and organizations between private developers and the land. Builders needed to meet the many guidelines established under these laws, such as obtaining a CAFRA permit in order to build a housing development of more than twenty-five units in Cape May County.

An Ocean City case illustrates the development process. A developer found a sixty-acre tract of open land on Ocean City's back bay, barren except for phragmites, weeds that choke out wetlands, and applied for a CAFRA permit to build a hundred-home development. The developer claimed that the tract had been created from the spoils dredged up during the 1950s to form a nearby lagoon, but state and federal officials insisted that the tract was wetland, protected under the Wetlands Act. The Army Corps of Engineers gained a court order to stop construction on the land and turned the case over to the state DEP. For three years, the courts heard testimony from Ocean City officials, civic associations, county agents, the DEP, the Army Corps of Engineers, and the private developers. Many other developers skirted the review process by building fewer than twenty-five units on a number of subdivisions, thus avoiding CAFRA review. William J. Watson and Michael Diamond, investigative newspaper reporters, argued that CAFRA had created "the myth of coastal protection." They found that only 467 of the 3,493 dwelling units constructed in Cape May County between 1984 and 1991 had been reviewed by CAFRA.[13]

Some Cape May County municipalities remained uncomfortable with all the state and federal intrusions. They resisted efforts to establish a countywide or regional waste disposal system. The mainland towns opposed the barrier islands dumping solid waste in landfills or disposal plants on the mainland as proposed under a regional system, and the barrier island communities opposed the mainland getting rid of their liquid waste through outfalls across their beaches. The pollution problem continued to grow. Richard Sullivan, commissioner of the state Department of Environmental Protection in 1972, observed that Cape May County municipalities had not dealt with the waste disposal problem. "These cities are presently using inadequate treatment," Sullivan said, "and more important, they are discharging their waste into inland waters, damaging shellfish areas." Wilbur Ostrander also recognized that the individual towns had failed to meet the waste crisis. "It is our hope that our county Board of Freeholders," he wrote a Wildwood resident, "will eventually find an answer for all our Municipalities, in the foreseeable future, they are all experiencing the same problem."[14]

State DEP pressure for a regional sewage plan led the Cape May County Board of Freeholders to form a Municipal Utilities Authority (MUA) in August 1972. They created MUA, the freeholders explained, because "the waters of Cape May County are subject to pollution to such a degree that in the judgment of the Board of Freeholders, the pollution of said water is, or is likely to become, a threat to the public health of the communities with this county unless an authority is created." MUA organized in September 1972 and embarked on the most difficult course of operations confronted by any local agency in Cape May County history. Years of frustration, resignations, conflicts of interest, and corruption plagued the authority. A scandal surrounding MUA activities led to the indictment and conviction of one of the county's most popular freeholder directors. Municipalities resisted contracts with the authority. Middle Township hired an environmental lawyer to force MUA to eliminate odors from its innovative sludge-composting plant. Conservationists such as the Citizens Association for the Protection of the Environment (CAPE) opposed the appointment to the MUA of a developer who had once operated a polluted landfill and had been denied a CAFRA building permit.[15]

The Cape May County MUA operated as a forum where developers, local officials, state and federal bureaucrats, waste management engineers, environmentalists, and citizens fought for their interests. In a way, all Cape May County became an environmental battleground. "It is under severe stress and the costs of not making major commitment for its protection and preservation are high," wrote Elwood R. Jarmer, director of the Cape May County planning staff. The political cost of protecting the county's environment was high, too. Freeholders Leon H. Schuck and Joseph W. Rixey, two mainlanders, lost a reelection bid in November 1971 after they had accepted a master plan that would have poured mainland waste through offshoot pipes across the barrier islands and then had fought over the plan during tumultuous meetings of the board of freeholders. Later Schuck quit his post as chairman of a county environmental council when he complained that the freeholders displayed little understanding of the "impact of industrialization upon our recreationally oriented economy."[16]

County waters grew increasingly polluted during the 1970s. Dennisville Lake was too dirty for swimming. Dangerously high bacteria counts appeared at Stockton Beach in Cape May City, in Wildwood, and on the Tuckahoe River. A *Gazette* reporter discovered the reason for the pollution of the latter in August 1975 when he spied a Pennsylvania trucking firm dumping Wildwood sewage sludge into the Tuckahoe River. Pollution closed some Cape May County beaches in July 1975 for the first time in the resort's history. High fecal coliform bacteria counts affected the county's beaches over most of the following decade, causing adverse publicity and affecting the summer beachgoing tourist trade so vital to Cape May County's economy. Beach closings in 1985 created an aftershock throughout the following winter when television and newspaper coverage drew a bleak picture of beach pollution. One Wildwood official insisted that the county hire a "crisis public relations firm" to restore confidence in the county resort business. Pollution from runoff caused by heavy rains and medical waste, probably from New York City ocean dumping, fouled Cape May County beaches in July 1989. Wildwood Crest merchants reportedly dumped chlorine into stagnant pools near the rainwater runoff pipes in an attempt to bring down the bacteria count.[17]

Despite reports of beach pollution, the tourist business steadily expanded in Cape May County. The resort's attractions were not limited to the seashore. Thousands of campers and their trailers arrived on the peninsula each summer season and settled into one of the fourteen thousand campsites in Cape May County's forty-six campgrounds, which were located mostly in Dennis and Middle townships. The county planning board considered the campgrounds beneficial to mainland tourism since they supplemented the barrier island resort business. County businessmen estimated that campers brought millions of dollars to the county each summer. However, some residents complained that the "trailerites" added to pollution and defiled the land. Clare Campbell, an Ocean View resident, explained that the campers caused traffic jams, polluted inland lakes

and streams, and destroyed vegetation. Others suspected that campers contributed to the forest fires that from time to time raged
through the pine forests in Upper and Dennis townships.[18]

As the permanent population and numbers of summer visitors
grew, the concept of developing open space in the county competed
with the rush to develop living space. State acquisition of the
Belleplain forest in 1928 and Tuckahoe wildlife preserve before the
Second World War introduced the open space idea to Cape May
County. Stone Harbor had secured 21 acres for a permanent heronry
and bird sanctuary in 1947, and in 1965 the National Park Service
registered the Stone Harbor Bird Sanctuary as a national landmark.
The U.S. Navy abandoned its facility on Cape May Point in 1962 and
in 1963 turned it over to the state for development as a park and for
use by the New Jersey Marine Science Consortium. Between 1972
and 1992, 30,000 acres were declared state or federal open space
under the Wetlands Law and part of the Wetlands Institute. The state
purchased over 500 acres along Higbee's Beach with Green Acres
Funds in 1976 and developed the area as a state park. A private firm
donated the South Cape May meadows in 1981 to the Nature
Conservancy for a bird sanctuary. The first phase of a Cape May
National Wildlife Refuge that will extend some 7,500 acres along the
bayshore and another 8,000 acres into the Great Cedar Swamp was
dedicated in May 1989.[19]

The Cape May County Farmland and Open Space Trust Fund
Plan, adopted by the board of freeholders in April 1990, revealed that
by the end of the 1980s over 93,000 of Cape May County's total
170,000 acres had become officially protected open space under the
control of state, federal, or local governments. Another 15,000 acres
were slated to become part of the Cape May National Wildlife Refuge.
This meant that 64 percent of all Cape May County would be open
space, and the rest was subject to CAFRA review or Pineland
Conservancy regulations. In 1990 the county's major goal became
the preservation of farmland, which had dropped from 29,212 acres
in 1950 to 13,992 acres by 1982.[20]

While governmental agencies placed more and more of the
county under open space management, other agencies rebuilt and
developed the county's living space. President Lyndon B. Johnson
envisioned the creation of a "Great Society" and introduced the largest
federal spending program in American history to combat poverty,
urban decay, and inadequate public services. Johnson created a

cabinet-level Department of Housing and Urban Development (HUD) in 1965 with which to construct this Great Society. Though seen as a program for urban renewal in larger cities, HUD became an important part of the development of smaller urban centers and rural communities such as those in Cape May County.

In Cape May City, John S. Needles, the city planner, David Teel, the city manager, and Mayor Frank A. Gauvry recognized the opportunities provided by HUD to rebuild their small resort city. The trio met in Washington with HUD officials in March 1966, paving the way for federal assistance in the city's program to develop a Victorian-style town. HUD funds for the Victorian District Urban Renewal Project in 1967 helped tear down dilapidated sections, build public housing, and complete a center-city shopping village. The Victorian Village Plaza shopping mall featured three walkways named after local heroes: Dr. Edgar Arthur Draper, Cape May County's first African-American physician; Edwin J. Hill, Congressional Medal of Honor winner, killed in the Japanese attack on Pearl Harbor; and Col. Henry W. Sawyer, the Civil War prisoner who narrowly escaped execution by Confederate authorities.[21]

Urban renewal in Cape May City ran into controversy, which centered on the preservation of the Emlen Physick Estate, built in 1879 by famous Philadelphia architect, Frank Furness. One of the few structures in the city to actually embody Victorian architectural style, the Physick Estate became neglected and rundown in the late 1950s. The Cape May County Art League rented the estate's carriage house and tried unsuccessfully to raise the $15,000 needed to buy and renovate the house. City government promised to save it with HUD monies but turned its back on the Emlen Physick Estate. City administrators argued that the house, which stood on Washington Street north of the downtown section, was not part of the Victorian Village renewal project. A group of concerned architectural preservationists, including Bruce Minnix, Gregory Ogden, and Ray Schultz, organized the Mid-Atlantic Center for the Arts (MAC) in 1970 to raise the then-necessary $90,000 to save the estate. After efforts to obtain support from the city failed, Minnix ran for city government and was elected Cape May City mayor in May 1972. The new administration helped MAC save the Physick Estate, which became the cornerstone for the Victorian historic district, museum, and resort business.[22]

Housing and Urban Development grants came to a number of other Cape May County communities during the late 1960s and

1970s. Wilbur J. Ostrander wrote his friend Harrison A. Williams, Jr., U.S. senator from New Jersey and frequent Cape May County visitor, that Wildwood had benefited greatly from HUD in the development of low-cost housing projects and community centers. HUD funds also built a recreation center on Main Street in Whitesboro in 1969, and a community center in Cape May City. HUD funding and other public works programs increased during the late 1970s. Congress passed a $3.9 billion public works employment law in July 1976, over President Gerald Ford's veto, and almost at once Cape May County officials applied for money under the new act. "Just about every municipality in the county is preparing an application for something," said Donald Kelly, executive director of the Cape May County Economic Development Commission.[23]

Senator Harrison Williams, Jr., thought that Cape May County stood a good chance of receiving federal grants under this program because local unemployment in 1976 stood at 9.9 percent, well above the 7.3 percent national average. Off-season unemployment in Cape May County reached 28.6 percent of the work force, one of the highest rates in the United States. Year-round employment had been devastated by the closing of three major county industries, causing the loss of 1,800 jobs. The Bradstone Rubber and Adhesive Company, founded in Woodbine in 1919, closed its factories in 1969, citing a shortage of skilled workers as the reason. Shortly thereafter, the Cape May Foundry, a Tuckahoe firm that produced gray iron ductile alloy castings, closed because the state required the installation of expensive pollution-control equipment. Then the R. B. Mason and Son basket factory in Belleplain closed down after five years of labor shortages.[24]

Federal money began to arrive in Cape May County under the new legislation in 1976. Woodbine, the most depressed area in the county, with the highest unemployment, smallest per capita income, and highest concentration of persons in dwelling units, received federal grants for a recreation field and park and a community development block grant under the Small Cities Program to rehabilitate houses, buy a new ambulance, and expand community services. North Wildwood received a grant to build a community center. Lower and Middle townships secured several grants but only after the federal government had first given the money to Wildwood and Ocean City, unaware that they were not sections of the Lower and Middle townships.[25]

The Comprehensive Employment Training Act (CETA) dispatched $400,000 to a Woodbine bookbinding firm in 1972 to train low-income and minority workers. The company failed to use the federal funds for such training, however. In a more successful project, CETA workers built a children's zoo at the Cape May County Park, a park started by WPA workers during the New Deal. CETA labor also repaired public buildings in Sea Isle City and rebuilt the Franklin Street School in Cape May City. Meanwhile, Whitesboro obtained a community development discretionary block grant to pave its dirt roads, Swainton to renew houses on Sigtown Road, and Mayville for low-cost housing.[26]

The massive federal social welfare programs of the 1960s coincided with and undoubtedly stimulated the civil rights movement. The Johnson administration passed a landmark Civil Rights Act in 1964, antipoverty legislation, and other acts to curb discrimination. Meantime, Martin Luther King, Jr., led civil rights marches throughout the nation. The civil rights movement made a quiet impression on Cape May County. The main vehicle for civil rights in the county remained the local chapter of the National Association for the Advancement of Colored People (NAACP), headed for the better part of the era by Dorothy Mack, a Cape May Court House schoolteacher and secretary of the Cape Human Resources organization. A moderate organization that opposed violent confrontation, the NAACP first intervened to protect the civil rights of African-Americans in Cape May County in 1960 when the local chapter protested the firing of a black teacher by the Woodbine Board of Education. The local NAACP leaders met at the Asbury A.M.E. Church in Wildwood and voted to take the case to the New Jersey state commissioner of education. State officials upheld the firing, however, agreeing with Woodbine Borough's contention that the teacher filled a temporary position created when the school system had been overcrowded with the influx of Hispanic and African-American residents during the 1950s. When many students left Woodbine to attend new schools, the need for additional staff had ended.[27]

Gradually African-Americans, who comprised 8 percent of the total county population, received recognition for their contributions to Cape May County history. William J. Moore, a former West Cape May schoolteacher, clubhouse attendant, and tennis instructor at the Cape May Golf Club, was honored at the age of ninety-one as the outstanding "New Jersey Negro of 1963." Cape May City had memorialized African-American physician Dr. Edgar Arthur Draper by naming a walkway after him in the new Victorian downtown shopping center. Several African-Americans became political leaders in their communities. Charles Payne, Sr., was elected to the Woodbine borough council in 1968, and Adrian Capehart served as a Cape May City councilman between 1976 and 1988. Jack Vasser, Jr., served as a committeeman and mayor of West Cape May, the first African-American mayor in county history. Despite his years of loyal organization work and campaigning for the county Republican party, party leaders passed over Vasser in 1976 to fill the unexpired term of Freeholder Bernard A. Berk. Vasser "did not get it," he insisted, "only because I'm black." In the same vein, Dorothy Mack, president of the county NAACP, charged in 1976 that subtle discrimination against blacks existed in county hiring practices and treatment of employees. The board of freeholders defended the county's minority hiring practice, noting that large numbers of blacks worked on the county roads, as social workers, and at the Crest Haven complex.[28]

County planners revealed in 1980 that 21.2 percent of Cape May County's African-American population lived below the poverty level, compared to 7.8 percent of the white residents. The glittering motels, condominiums, and new homes along the seashore contrasted sharply with the dilapidated houses and projects of Wildwood's West Side, where most of the city's nonwhite population, which made up 23 percent of Wildwood's year-round residents, lived. In 1980 Lorraine Bowers, an investigative reporter for the *Cape May County Gazette-Leader*, toured the West Side and revealed the depth of poverty, frustration, and neglect found there. Bowers asserted that federal funds had created new pockets of poverty in the low-cost housing project known as the Commissioner's Court. Another journalist contended that the Civil Rights Act of 1964 had actually created poverty and neglect on Wildwood's West Side. African-Americans now patronized the formerly whites-only clubs and entertainment centers nearer the boardwalk and abandoned the once-bustling largely black-owned West Side clubs, where in former days they had seen the Platters at Old Blue Heaven, Redd Foxx at the High Steppin' Club, and Dizzy Gillespie at the Esquire Club.[29]

Signs of frustration with poverty and neglect appeared in Cape May County. The rash of fires and vandalism around Cape May Court House in 1968 that burned an abandoned glass factory on Hereford Avenue may have been related to anger over the assassination of

Martin Luther King, Jr. Hispanic-American youths rioted in Woodbine in 1977, and Mayor Daniel Guida had to declare a state of emergency. Angry African-American residents met at the Eureka Baptist Church in Wildwood to hear Leroy Brown, president of the Mainland branch of the county NAACP, demand that Wildwood hire a black housing authority official and that Whitesboro seek autonomy and break away from Middle Township. Dorothy Mack advised moderate political organization. "You could have a black freeholder if blacks would register and vote," Mack told the African-American clergymen and community representatives gathered at the Eureka Baptist Church.[30]

The women's rights movement that swept the nation during the 1960s also found some support in Cape May County. Cape May County had a tradition of strong, politically active women, including the Baker and Bright women in Wildwood. Doris W. Bradway and Edith Greenan had become important political figures in the county during the 1930s, serving as mayors of their barrier island communities. Bradway continued to speak out on public issues well into the 1960s. In one impassioned speech before the Wildwood City Commission in 1966, Bradway deplored the "human trash" of teenage drunks and gangs who cluttered the boardwalk on the barrier island resort. The barrier islands continued to be a source of female political leadership in Cape May County. Mary Kalbach of Wildwood, a licensed practical nurse and vice chairman of the county Democratic Executive Committee, ran for election to the board of freeholders in 1968, only to be buried in the Republican party landslide that elected President Richard M. Nixon, Congressman Charles Sandman, and Cape May County Freeholder Dr. Leon H. Schuck. More successful, Ocean City resident Angela F. Pulvino, a Republican party candidate, in 1972 became the first elected female Cape May County clerk (although in 1791 Elizabeth Holmes had been the first woman to serve as county clerk).[31]

Political progress for women developed more slowly on the mainland. Margaret M. Bieberbach became a Lower Township committeewoman in 1977 and was elected as the township's first female mayor in 1982. Dennis Township elected Margaret Westhoven in 1990 as its first female mayor. Countywide, though, no dominant leader emerged to make a serious bid for election to the board of freeholders or other major offices. Partly to fill this gap, the Cape May County Commission on the Status of Women organized in 1984 to advise the board of freeholders on child care, domestic abuse, rape, and other issues, and to recognize the contributions of women in Cape May County.[32]

The Cape May County Board of Freeholders, without minority or female representatives, reflected the character and nature of the Jersey Cape on the eve of the three hundredth anniversary of its formation as a county government. The membership of the board of freeholders in 1990 came from the five primary political-economic regions of Cape May County. Their occupations represented the socioeconomic dynamics that had shaped the county's development since the opening of the barrier islands to settlement over one hundred years ago. Ralph W. Evans of Stone Harbor was a builder of custom houses. Herbert C. Frederick, former mayor of West Wildwood, taught in the public schools. James S. Kilpatrick, Jr., of Ocean City was an attorney and student of county history and traditions. Daniel Beyel, mayor of Upper Township, ran a Marmora business. William E. Sturm, Jr., a Rio Grande resident, was a public utilities manager. These freeholders all belonged to the long-dominant county Republican party organization.

The Cape May County Board of Freeholders actively promoted the county's traditional culture and historic heritage. To this end, the freeholders accepted the donation of Historic Cold Spring Village from Dr. and Mrs. Joseph Salvatore and provided ongoing support for its operation. The village is a nineteenth-century replica of a county town filled with historic buildings that have been salvaged from destruction and moved to this popular tourist attraction. Likewise, the Cape May County Board of Freeholders financed as part of the tercentennial celebration of the founding of county government the research and writing of the first comprehensive history of the resort community since Lewis Townsend Stevens published his collection of data in 1897.

What the Cape May County leaders and people have received in 1992 is this story of the evolution of an American maritime community from its founding by those who hunted whales and farmed their own land to those who use the Jersey Cape for recreation, relaxation, or retirement. From the beginning of formal county government in 1692, the few hundred Cape May County settlers created a community of clusters of houses separated from each other by geography and religion but coming together on court day to reaffirm their common identity as Cape May men and women. Three hundred years later, over ninety thousand Cape May County residents retain that intensely local character. In 1977 James Barthold, editor of the *Ga-*

zette Leader, claimed that the county had lost its own identity in the rapidly changing modern American society. Viewed in a larger histori- cal perspective, however, county residents, today reaffirm their com- munity's traditional identity as a unique maritime peninsular region.[33]

The clusters of houses and villages are larger and more concen- trated than they once were, and the technology of life and the ethnic composition of the Cape May County community have changed, but the patterns of existence would seem familiar to the earlier commu- nity. As they did hundreds of years ago, Cape May County residents live along a bayshore road (now Route 47 or the Delsea Drive) that wanders past scattered rural villages, small houses, and over tidal creeks down the Delaware Bay side of the peninsula. Crossing from Cumberland County into Cape May County over West Creek on the Delsea Drive, the present-day traveler enters Eldora, once a remote collection of millponds and farmhouses that formed the three com- munities of Stipson's Island, West Creek, and East Creek, and is still an isolated corner of the county. Going east on the Delsea Drive, the visitor passes the intersection of the East Creek Mill Road, probably the original stagecoach route, and then skirts the sparsely populated stretch of pineland that forms the southern boundary of the Belle- plain State Forest. Reaching the cluster of houses known as North Dennis, the visitor might turn off on Jakes Landing Road, which runs down to Dennis Creek. The tiny Ludlam burial ground and remains of stone foundations nearly buried in the thick woods on either side of this narrow road attest to the community of farmhouses, a tavern, and shiplanding that once existed there.

Returning to the Delsea Drive and going east, the visitor enters Dennisville. The former shipbuilding and commercial center of Den- nis Creek, Dennisville today retains some of the charm of the once- prosperous village, with its historic houses built by Nathaniel Holmes, Jesse Diverty, and other shipbuilders and merchants. Just to the south the road crosses Dennis Creek near the spot where once stood a covered bridge, torn down over eighty years ago, and past the site where several busy shipyards long ago constructed coastal schooners. Today there is no sign of the former shipyards in the salt marshes. Below the creek on the Delsea Drive stands a cluster of houses known as South Dennis, a large cemetery containing family plots of original whaler yeoman families, an old Methodist church, and the Falkinburg house, one of the few brick houses built in Cape May County before the twentieth century.

Continuing down the bayside on Delsea Drive the traveler enters still-quaint Goshen, a town that was built up around the great shipyard and steam sawmill once located at the end of Goshen Landing Road toward the creek and bay. South of Goshen the road passes Bucks Avenue where, deep in the underbrush and woods, is hidden the Smith family cemetery, filled with eighteenth century headstones. Delsea Drive continues over Bidwell's Ditch, the former Wills Creek, dug out in the 1890s by Richard Bidwell, a South Vineland, Cumberland County, salt hay entrepreneur. The wide artificial creek fundamentally altered the marshes in the region, nearly drying up the once-deep Goshen Creek. Delsea Drive wanders past the County Mosquito Commission and fire tower, the former site of a Civilian Conservation Corps camp that housed German POWs during the Second World War. The road passes through Dias Creek and probably near where Springer's windmill once stood. The motorist passes trailer parks and family campgrounds, entrances to Pierce's Beach and other small bayside fishing communities, and some farmlands, finally entering a concentration of houses, several churches, and a country store at Green Creek.

The bayside route splits at Green Creek, with the Delsea Drive continuing on through Nummytown, past the Wildwood Pumping Station (supposed site of an ancient Indian burial ground), through Rio Grande, close to the location of the old sugar factory, and across the Cape to the barrier island community of Wildwood. Turning right off Delsea Drive at Green Creek takes the visitor toward Fishing Creek through some lovely farmlands and then south along the bay through Del Haven, Sunray Beach, Miami Beach, Villas, North Highlands Beach, and Wildwood Highlands Beach. The land on which these housing projects stand was subdivided in the late 1920s but not settled until after the Second World War. The bayshore road along these developments is filled with restaurants, motels, small stores, and tiny houses. A sign in Villas points the visitor toward the bay and Town Bank, where a stone monument claims the community as "our earliest settlement 1640."

The bayshore road continues south through North Cape May, another development surveyed and laid out in the late 1920s but not settled until after World War II. The old bayshore road meets a newer route, called the Sandman Parkway after the Erma political leader who helped bring the Lewes—Cape May Ferry to the county. The Sandman Parkway connects the bayside ferry terminal with Route 9 and the Garden State Parkway to the east. Continuing south, now on a section of the old Seashore Road, the visitor passes the Jacob Spicer house, once the center of county life in the lower part of the peninsula, and then follows the road up and over the more western of the two automobile bridges that cross the Cape May Canal.

After crossing the canal the traveler enters West Cape May, and a turn right on Fourth Avenue brings the visitor along the northern boundary of a site where a large oval racetrack and grandstand once stood. The road rejoins the Bayshore Road, which had been interrupted by the canal, and runs down into Sunset Boulevard, the old Cape Island Turnpike. Sunset Boulevard leads west to Sunset Beach and the Delaware Bay, where the iron skeleton and some concrete hull of the broken *Atlantus* can be seen just off the beach. The *Atlantus* is disintegrating after sixty-five years of incessant pounding by the surf and will soon disappear entirely into the bay waters. Also gone is the huge Magnesite plant that once stood along Sunset Beach. Weeds, rubble, and an old water tower are all that remain on the spot; it is hoped that shorebirds will return to their natural habitat along the bayshore.

A short trip south of Sunset Beach takes the visitor to the center of the former Presbyterian retreat of Sea Grove, now Cape May Point. One can reconstruct the original layout of streets radiating from the center of town, where once stood a religious meeting pavilion. A few original cottages, an older hotel now used as a Catholic retreat house, and newer cottages fill Cape May Point. Lake Lily, once a popular ice-skating and boating pond, still attracts swans, geese, and ducks. Each year, however, the ocean takes away more of the community's beachfront around the point and to the east, where the historic Cape May lighthouse stands in a state park and bird sanctuary.

Returning to Sunset Boulevard and going east, the motorist skirts the South Cape May meadows, now a bird sanctuary where once stood the Neptune Land Company's wooden-and-tin elephant along the tiny railroad tracks that took tourists from the steamboat landing on the bayside along the beachfront to Cape May City. Sunset Boulevard leads into the city of Cape May, the Jersey Cape's original resort community and reputedly the oldest seaside resort in the United States. Narrow streets, older houses and hotels, and quaint bed-and-breakfast inns give this unique town an historic charm that is disrupted slightly by incongruous modern architecture, a small midtown shopping mall, and the erratic layout of streets.

Traveling through the center of town along Washington Street brings the tourist to the Emlen Physick Estate, a marvelously restored Victorian mansion that reminds us that Cape May City was once a summer playground for the wealthy nineteenth-century gentry elite. East of the Physick Estate lie portions of Cape May City that still contain empty, undeveloped lots, reminiscent of the turn of the century, when Peter Shields and other real estate speculators tried unsuccessfully to develop this part of Cape Island. A massive brick hotel, the Christian Admiral, stands stark and somewhat neglected along the beachfront. Built in 1908, it is an intriguing old structure that has seen better days as a luxury hotel, naval hospital, officer's quarters, and religious conference center.

Leaving Cape May City by the eastern bridge over the Cape May Canal, the motorist can see the U.S. Coast Guard Training Center and receiving station on the right across the Cape May harbor, which is filled with fishing and pleasure craft. The bridge crosses Schellenger's Creek, near the site of the original route into Cape May City, and brings the visitor back to Lower Township and to the entrance for three possible routes up the peninsula.

Straight ahead, the Garden State Parkway allows the traveler to race up the Jersey Cape to Beesley's Point, where a bridge takes the motorist across Great Egg Harbor and into Atlantic County. By choosing the Garden State Parkway, however, the visitor misses the two essential sections that define Cape May County, the historic middle of the cape and the barrier islands.

Access to the historic region along the center of the peninsula can be obtained by turning onto the old Seashore Road that for a short time parallels Route 9. This route goes through Cold Spring, past the old brick church and cemetery, Historic Cold Spring Village, and the Hildreth mansion. Rejoining Route 9, the visitor travels through Erma, Rio Grande, Whitesboro, Burleigh, and Mayville, and enters Cape May Court House. Somewhere between Erma and Whitesboro in Middle Township, possibly where the Garden State Parkway intersects with the former Pennsylvania Reading Seashore Railroad tracks from Wildwood Junction to Wildwood, was the site of Aaron Leaming's plantation, tavern, and the Baptist church that served as the county seat of government until the county court session of 1764. The current county seat is situated four miles to the north in Cape May Court House, where the white, gold-domed old courthouse (built in 1850) and newer government offices stand along Route 9.

Moving north above Cape May Court House, the clusters of houses approximate the locations of early settlements. The names of these settlements have changed, but old houses on Route 9, such as the John Holmes house in Swainton, now used as the Cape May County Historical Society Museum, the Thomas Leaming house, now part of Leaming's Run Gardens, and the John Townsend house, still sitting across from Magnolia Lake, the oldest remaining house in Cape May County, remind the visitor of the original plantations and settlements along this historic route. Unfortunately, older structures such as Aaron Townsend's windmill in Ocean View have long since disappeared, but the tiny Friends meetinghouse in Seaville, the Rising Sun Tavern, and other historic buildings along Route 9 through Dennis and Upper townships to Beesley's Point recapture some of the county's past.

Just north of the Middle Township-Dennis Township border in Clermont where Route 83 from South Dennis intersects Route 9 is the site of the entrance to the Old Cape Road. Today the route goes north through South Seaville, a onetime bustling railroad center, fairground, and Methodist camp meeting place. Traveling north along approximately the route of the county's oldest road the visitor goes through Mt. Pleasant, site of the Tiffareth Israel Cemetery and a onetime railroad stop. The Woodbine Municipal Airport lies off to the left in the woods. There are well-maintained runways, but the rusting Quonset hut and handful of rundown buildings suggest little activity at this airport. The road crosses the old Pennsylvania Seashore Reading Railroad bed where off to the right the Woodbine Junction railroad stop is now overgrown with weeds and brush. There is nothing left except abandoned wooden structures. The road enters Woodbine, the former Jewish community founded by the de Hirsch Fund in 1891. Once a bustling factory, shopping, and cultural center, Woodbine now contains a few older brick buildings from the original de Hirsch Agricultural School and more modern facilities that comprise the Woodbine State Colony for Feeble-Minded Males. The unused Brotherhood Synagogue stands as a lonely reminder of this once-booming town.

Farther west, the town of Belleplain along the now-empty railroad bed also shows evidence of earlier prosperity. Sprawling wooden buildings of the old Mason basket factory and other local businesses are used for storage or stand empty. Steelmantown just northeast of Belleplain is a cluster of houses in the woodland. The once-active cranberry bogs are filled in, and there is no sign of the sawmills that once brought employment to the region. Farther north, tucked in the northwest corner of Cape May County along the Tuckahoe River, stands Marshallville, once a busy glassmaking and shipbuilding town on the river but today an attractive, sleepy cluster of older and modern houses out of sight from the main road. Returning east along the river the traveler enters Tuckahoe, another shipbuilding town of former days, and then passes Middletown and Petersburg, crossing the Cedar Swamp Creek where a shipyard has existed for over two hundred years. Just up the road hidden in a clump of wild cherry trees lies the Young burial ground with headstones dating back to the eighteenth century. The road then enters Marmora on Route 9, and the visitor takes the Roosevelt Boulevard across the salt marsh to the northern-most Cape May County seaside resort of Ocean City, entering the world of the barrier islands.

The barrier island resorts of Ocean City, Strathmere, Sea Isle City, Avalon, Stone Harbor, and the Wildwoods fill the once-wooded wilderness islands with condominiums, motels, houses, and stores laid out along wide central streets that run parallel to the ocean and narrow streets that cut across the islands, connecting beaches with back bays and sounds. Each barrier island town is tied by a bridge to the mainland; the islands are linked together by the Ocean Drive, a toll road that extends all the way to Cape May City at the tip of the peninsula. Though they share a similarity in settlement patterns and physical landscape, the oceanfront resorts have their own distinctive traits and personalities.

The largest towns, Ocean City and Wildwood, have boardwalks filled with stores and amusements. But Ocean City is quieter and in some ways less vigorous than Wildwood, with its amusement parks, nightclubs, and bars. Avalon and Wildwood Crest contain sections of more expensive houses than the other resorts, while Stone Harbor has a distinctive section of small shops, a heronry, and the Wetlands Institute. These barrier island resorts seem to share little with the mainland or bayshore communities of Cape May County, but the founders of these oceanfront resorts came from the same southern New Jersey, Pennsylvania, and mainland stock as the settlers of the inland region. They developed similar traditions. They left the same unique Cape May County characteristic of intense individualism and desire for autonomy and separation from the next island and from each other on the same island that existed between the mainland towns. Just as the mainlanders gathered on court days, the barrier islanders cross their bridges to the mainland courthouse town to conduct politics and business, reaffirming that even the most remote barrier island community is an integral part of Cape May County, America's oldest seashore resort community.

APPENDIX A

The Thirty-Five Whaler Yeoman Families

Family name	Founder	Land title	Acreage of farm	Precinct (Township) location, 1723
Corson	John	1695	300	Upper, seaside
Corson	Peter	1695	400	Upper, seaside
Crawford	John	1694 or 1695	380	Lower, bayside
Cresse	Arthur	1692	350	Middle, seaside
Crowell	Samuel	1695	226	Lower, bayside
Eldredge	Ezekiel	169(5)?	200?	Lower, bayside
Forman	Jonathan	1694	250	Lower-Middle
Foster	Samuel	1696?	100	Lower, bayside
Gandy	Thomas	1694	50	Middle, seaside
Garretson	Remgar	1693	400	Upper, seaside
Godfrey	Benjamin	169?	210	Upper, seaside
Goldin	William	1693	600	Upper, seaside
Hand	Shamgar	1695	700	Middle, seaside
Hand	Thomas	1695	300	Lower, seaside and Cape Island
Hewitt	Randall	1695	340	Lower, Cape Island
Holdin	Joseph	1692	200	Middle, seaside
Hughes	Humphrey	1695	206	Lower, Cape Island
Johnson	William	1695	435	Middle, seaside
Leaming	Christopher	1694	204	Middle, seaside
Leonard	Henry	1700	150	Middle, seaside
Ludlam	Joseph	1692	500	Upper-Middle, seaside
Matthews	Samuel	1695	175	Lower, bayside
Osborn	Jonathan	1694?	285	Middle, seaside
Page	John	1699	125	Lower, bayside
Parsons	John (?)	1697	315	Lower, bayside
Reeves	John	1695	200	Middle, seaside
Richardson	John	1695	124	Middle, seaside
Shaw	John	1696	315	Lower, seaside
Shaw	William	1695	200	Middle, seaside

Schellenger	Cornelius	1695	134	Lower, seaside and Cape Island
Smith	William	1695?	130?	Middle, seaside
Spicer	Jacob	1694 or 1695	400	Lower and Middle, bayside
Stillwell	John	1694	?	Lower, bayside
Stites	Henry	1695	200	Middle, seaside
Taylor	George	1691 or 1692	200	Lower and Middle, seaside
Townsend	John	1695	640	Upper and Middle, seaside
Whilldin	Joseph	1695	150	Lower, Cape Island

APPENDIX B

Intermarriage among the Whaler Yeoman Families
1700–1799

Family name	Number of marriages Total	Whaler yeoman	Percentage within 35 families
Corson	16	11	68.75
Cresse	9	6	66.67
Crowell	9	5	55.56
Eldredge	10	9	90.00
Forman	1	1	100.00
Gandy	4	0	00.00
Garretson	6	5	83.33
Godfrey	9	8	88.89
Goldin	3	1	33.33
Hand	48	31	64.58
Hewitt	2	2	100.00
Holdin	4	3	75.00
Hughes	13	8	61.54
Johnson	5	2	40.00
Leaming	8	7	87.50
Leonard	2	1	50.00
Ludlam	12	7	58.33
Matthews	6	6	100.00
Osborn	2	1	50.00
Page	2	1	50.00
Reeves	3	1	33.33
Richardson	7	3	42.86
Shaw	9	6	66.67
Schellenger	7	4	57.14
Smith	18	11	61.11
Spicer	2	2	100.00
Taylor	10	5	50.00
Townsend	24	16	66.67
Whilldin	7	3	42.86
Totals	258	166	64.34

<u>APPENDIX C</u>

Manumissions of Slaves, 1802–1834

Slave name	Slave-owning family	Location	Date
Nancy Coachman	John Stites	Lower Township	1802
Selance	Christopher Ludlam	Middle Township	1803
Eace	Seth Hand	Middle Township	1803
Ishamal Armour	Levi Smith	Middle Township	1803
Viney Armour	John Hand	Middle Township	1803
Edward Cox	Parsons Leaming	Middle Township	1804
Susan	Joseph Hughes	Lower Township	1805
James Lively	Elizabeth and Jesse Hughes	Lower Township	1805
Judith Sommers	Elizabeth Ludlam	Upper Township	1806
Benjamin Coachman, Jr.	Jeremiah Hand	Upper Township	1806
Abel Cox	Parsons Leaming	Middle Township	1806
Rheuma Scott	Humphrey Stites	Middle Township	1806
Scene Turner	Parsons Leaming	Middle Township	1807
Bethula Mingo	Elijah Townsend	Middle Township	1807
Dina	Ann Edmunds	Lower Township	1808
Pricilla Anderson	Joseph Mulford	Middle Township	1808
Audrey (Alindey?)	Nathaniel Holmes	Middle Township	1808
Ame Coachman	Aaron and Furman Leaming	Middle Township	1808
Robert Smith	John Van Gilder	Upper Township	1809
Francis Coachman	Jacob Godfrey	Upper Township	1810
Elizabeth Jacock	Elijah Townsend	Middle Township	1811
Negro Ceasar	Memucan Hughes	Lower Township	1812
Flower (Flora) Cox (wife of Abel Cox)	Phillip Stites	Middle Township	1812
James Green	Abigail Townsend	Middle Township	1812
Harmon Lively	Nathaniel Holmes	Middle Township	1815
Simeion Taylor	Christopher Smith	Middle Township	1815

Marshael Peterson	Robert M. Holmes	Middle Township	1815
Dempcey Collins	Jacob Willets	Upper Township	1816
Anthony Wanton	James R. Hughes	Lower Township	1817
Bethany Seagraves	Reuhamah Cresse	Upper Township	1817
Peter Murkin	Aaron Hughes	Lower Township	1818
Susan Turner	Robert M. Holmes	Middle Township	1819
Dericks Turner	Furman Leaming	Middle Township	1819
Julius Caesar	James R. Hughes	Lower Township	1819
Prudence Seagraves	James R. Hughes	Lower Township	1819
Betty Jacocks	Judith Townsend	Middle Township	1823
Ruhma Squirrel	John Bennett	Lower Township	1825
Ishmael Armour	John Townsend	Middle Township	1826
Job Moor	Thomas H. Hughes	Lower Township	1828
Darick Smith	Lewis Corson	Upper Township	1831
Orris Cox (mulatto)	Robert Cox	Lower Township	1832
Briant Marshall	Thomas Beesley	Upper Township	1833
Jethro Alingo	Nathaniel Holmes, Jr.	Dennis Township	1834

Notes

Abbreviations Used in Notes

BCFMB   Minute Books of the Cape May County Board of Chosen Freeholders, Board Clerk's Office, Cape May County Library, Cape May Court House (Board of Chosen Freeholders Minute Book)

CMCCA   Cape May County Clerk's Archives, Record Room and Safe Vault, Cape May Court House

CMCHS   Cape May County Historical (and Genealogical) Society, Swainton

CMCL   Cape May County Library, Cape May Court House

CMCMHG   *Cape May County Magazine of History and Geneaology*

CMGS   Cape May Geographic Society, Cape May

GSCL   Glassboro State College Library (Frank Stewart Room, Savitz Learning Center), Glassboro

HSP   Historical Society of Pennsylvania, Philadelphia

NJSA   New Jersey State Archives, Trenton

NJA   Archives of the State of New Jersey (published series)

NJH   *New Jersey History* (magazine)

OCHSM   Ocean City Historical Society Museum, Ocean City

PMHB   *Pennsylvania Magazine of History and Biography*

PNJHS   *Proceedings of the New Jersey Historical Society*

RUL   Alexander Library, Special Collections, Rutgers University Library, New Brunswick

VF, CMCL   Vertical File, Cape May County Library, Cape May Court House

VHS   Vineland Historical Society, Vineland

WHS   Wildwood Historical Society, Wildwood

Chapter 1. Founding a Community of Whaler Yeomen

1. Robert Juet, *Juet's Journal: The Voyages of the "Half Moon" from 4 April to 7 November 1609* (Newark: New Jersey Historical Society, 1959), 24–25; Robert C. Alexander, "Henry Hudson and the Delaware Bay," CMGS, *13th Annual Bulletin* (1959): 1–5.

2. C. A. Weslager, *Dutch Explorers, Traders and Settlers in the Delaware Valley, 1609–1664* (Philadelphia: University of Pennsylvania Press, 1961), 33ff; possibly Mey cruised in the Delaware Bay as early as 1614 (see William McMahon, *South Jersey Towns: History and Legend* (New Brunswick, N.J.: Rutgers University Press, 1973), 3–4.

3. Weslager, *Dutch Explorers,* 88–89; Roger T. Trindell, "Historical Geography of Southern New Jersey as Related to its Colonial Ports" (Ph.D. diss., Louisiana State University, 1966), 28–31; McMahon, *South Jersey Towns,* 137–38.

4. John E. Pomfret, *The Province of West New Jersey, 1609–1702: A History of the Origins of an American Colony* (Princeton: Princeton University Press, 1956), 6–9; Weslager, *Dutch Explorers,* 84–85, 88–89; "DeVries Journal," in Albert Cook Myers, ed., *Narratives of Early Pennsylvania, West New Jersey, and Delaware, 1630–1707* (New York: Barnes & Noble, 1953; reprint of 1912 edition), 7–25.

5. "Patent to Samuel Godyn and Samuel Bloemmaert for the East Side of Delaware River, now Cape May County, New Jersey, 3 June 1631," NJA, *Documents Relating to the Colonial History of the State of New Jersey,* first series, 1:1–2, and in Weslager, *Dutch Explorers,* 271–272.

6. Entry, 11 September 1609, Juet, *Journal,* 30; Weslager, *Dutch Explorers,* 98–99; 111.

7. Harry B. Weiss, Howard R. Kemble, and Millicent T. Carre, *Whaling in New Jersey* (Trenton: New Jersey Agricultural Society, 1974), 13; Pomfret, *West New Jersey,* 9–10; Weslager, *Dutch Explorers,* 98–100.

8. Folklore has become part of the tradition of Delaware Valley river communities (see Sharon F. Fitzpatrick, "Buried Pirate Treasure in Burling-

ton, New Jersey," *New Jersey Folklore* 1 (Spring 1978): 3–7). Old traditions can lead to extended discussions over Cape May County history. Cape May County tradition claims that Abraham Lincoln came to Cape Island (Cape May City) on 31 July 1849 and supposedly signed a hotel register page now in the possession of the Cape May County Historical Society. Each year on Lincoln's birthday the local newspapers repeat the story of Lincoln's visit. The county's historical society published an article treating Lincoln's visit as historical fact (see Stanley Williamson, "When Lincoln Came to Cape May," *CMCMHG* 2 (1945); 291–292. However, Lincoln's correspondence indicates that he was in Springfield, Illinois, between 13 July and 15 December 1849 and could not have been in Cape May County. See Roy P. Basler, ed., *The Collected Works of Abraham Lincoln* (New Brunswick, N.J.: Rutgers University Press, 1953), 2: 59–69.

9. Ratzer Map, 1977, in Horace G. Richards, *A Book of Maps of Cape May, 1610–1878* (Cape May: Cape May Geographic Society, 1954), 18.

10. Charles J. Hoadly, *Records of the Colony and Plantation of New Haven from 1638 to 1649* (Hartford: Case, Tiffany, 1857), 56–57, 80, 106, 280; Pomfret, *West New Jersey*, 20–21; Cape May County resident Samuel Johnson held "New Haven lands" in 1724–1725 (NJA, *Calendar of New Jersey Wills*, 1:264; Weslager, *Dutch Explorers*, 137–138). Cape May County's first historian doubted that New Haven colonists came to the Jersey Cape in the 1640s (see Maurice Beesley, "Sketch of the Early History of the County of Cape May," in George H. Cook, *Geology of the County of Cape May, State of New Jersey* [Trenton: True American, 1857], 160).

11. G. D. Scull, ed., *The Evelyns in America: Compiled from Family Papers and Other Sources, 1608–1805* (Oxford: Parker, 1881), 131; Edward S. Wheeler, *Scheyichbi and the Strand, or Early Days Along the Delaware with an Account of Recent Events at Sea Grove* (Philadelphia: Lippincott, 1876), 28; Lewis Townsend Stevens, *The History of Cape May County, New Jersey: From the Aboriginal Times to the Present Day* (Cape May City: Lewis T. Stevens, publisher, 1897), 23–24.

12. Beesley, "Sketch of Cape May," 165–166; Weslager, *Dutch Explorers*, 106; Wheeler, *Scheyichbi*, 8.

13. Alanson Skinner and Max Schrabisch, "A Preliminary Report of the Archaeological Survey of the State of New Jersey made by the Department of Anthropology in the American Museum of Natural History," *Geological Survey of New Jersey*, Bulletin No. 9 (Trenton: MacCrellish & Quigley, 1913), 41–46; Charles Tomlin, *Cape May Spray* (Philadelphia: Bradley Bros., 1913), 41, 53; Cresse discovery in *Cape May County Gazette*, 8 July 1932, 19 May 1933; Julius Way in *Star and Wave*, 7 July 1927.

Dr. Maurice Beesley examined Native American remains on the Joshua Garretson Farm in Upper Township in 1857, concluding that "it cannot be denied by any one who will view the seaboard of our county, that they

[Lenape] were very numerous at one time here, which is evidenced by town plats, extensive and numberless shell banks, arrow heads, stone hatchets, burying grounds, and other remains existing with us" (Beesley, "Sketch of Cape May," 187–188).

14. Skinner and Schrabisch, "Archaeological Survey," 41–66; telephone interview with Dr. Lorraine Williams, archaeologist, New Jersey State Museum, Trenton, 17 April 1989; Weslager, *Dutch Explorers,* 106–119; Frank H. Stewart, *Indians of Southern New Jersey* (Woodbury, N.J.: Gloucester County Historical Society, 1932), 68–70; H. Clay Reed and George J. Miller, eds., *The Burlington Court Book: A record of Quaker Jurisprudence in West New Jersey, 1680–1709* (Washington, D.C.: American Historical Association, 1944), 47 (hereafter cited as *Burlington Court Book*).

15. See Adlord Bowde deed with Sakamoy and other "Sackimackers" for Governor Coxe, 30 April 1688, Liber of Deeds B, part 1:202, New Jersey State Archives; NJA, *Colonial Documents,* 21:424; Beesley, "Sketch of Cape May," 188; "Nummys or Nummies" lands are mentioned in NJA, *Calendar of Wills,* 3:142; 4:177; 5:299–302. Edgar Page Stites, Sr., author of the hymn "Beulahland," also wrote "An Ode to King Nummy" in 1888 (see Indian File, CMCHS). Clare Campbell, "Princess Snow Flower," *CMCMHG* 9 (1987): 22–26, is folklore based on Thompson-Stites family tradition found in Mary Thompson Cresse correspondence with Edward Post, 1 July 1932, 11 and 23 November 1936, Cresse-Post Letters, CMCHS. For Delaware Valley and New Jersey chiefs, see Dorothy Cross, *Indians of New Jersey* (Trenton: Archaeological Society of New Jersey, 1955), 14.

16. NJA, *Colonial Documents,* 21:559.

17. John P. Snyder, *The Story of New Jersey's Civil Boundaries, 1606–1968* (Trenton: Bureau of Geology and Topography, 1969), 4–9; Trindell, "Historical Geography," 77–81; Richard P. McCormick, *New Jersey from Colony to State, 1609–1789* (Newark: New Jersey Historical Society, 1981), 20–30.

18. Franklin Ellis, *History of Monmouth County, New Jersey* (Cottonport, La.: Polyanthos, for the Shrewsbury Historical Society, 1974; reprint of 1885 edition), 82ff; NJA, *Colonial Documents,* 21:42.

19. Pomfret, *West New Jersey,* 65–69; *Burlington Court Book,* xvi; see also Robert W. Harper, *John Fenwick and Salem County in the Province of West Jersey 1609–1700 including Burlington, Cape May, Cumberland and Gloucester Counties* (Salem, N.J.: Salem County Cultural and Heritage Commission, 1978).

20. Pomfret, *West New Jersey,* 92–93.

21. Rev. Daniel L. Hughes claimed that William Penn visited Jacob Spicer on the Jersey Cape ("Cape May County Records," typescript compiled by Karl Dickinson, CMCHS); McMahon, *South Jersey Towns,* 6; Weslager, *Dutch Explorers,* 100, 104; Weiss et al., *Whaling,* 14.

22. Thomas Budd, *Good Order Established in Pennsilvania & New-Jersey* (Ann Arbor: University Microfilms, 1966; copy of 1685 edition), 5–6; Budd's role in Cape May County, Liber of Deeds B, 30, CMCCA.

23. *Burlington Court Book,* 11, 26; Pomfret, *West New Jersey,* 102–126.

24. *Burlington Court Book,* 47, 49, 54, 87–88.

25. Ibid., 46–47, 49, 82–83.

26. There are several versions and copies of what is called variously the First Minute Book, Cape May Town Book, First Book of Court Records, and Liber A. The original is deposited in the Safe Vault in the Cape May County Clerk's Office, Court House. Accurate transcription of the original appears as Lewis T. Stevens, ed., "First Public Records of Cape May County," *CMCMHG* 1 (1937):269–285, and "First Official Records of Cape May County," *CMCMHG* 1 (1938):316–337. References will be to the *CMCMHG* transcripts. "First Public Records," *CMCMHG* 1:269; *Burlington Court Book,* 2, 11.

27. G. D. Scull, "Biographical Notice of Doctor Daniel Coxe of London," *PMHB* 7 (1883):317; for the view that Coxe was little more than a real estate speculator, see John E. Pomfret, *Colonial New Jersey: A History* (New York: Scribner's, 1973), 40, and Pomfret, *West New Jersey,* 61.

28. Pomfret, *West New Jersey,* 91–92, 132; "Dr. Daniel Coxe, His Account of New Jersey," in Scull, "Biographical Notice," 327. For an account of the abandonment of feudal remnants in West Jersey, see Frederick R. Black, "The Last Lords Proprietors of West Jersey: The West Jersey Society, 1692–1702," (Ph.D. diss., Rutgers University, 1964), 199–200.

29. NJA, *Colonial Documents,* 21:421–422, 424; Black, "Last Lords," 23, 195; Stewart, *Indians,* 68–69; Ralph L. Goff, "Surveys and Surveyors," *CMCMHG* 4 (1957):107–108.

30. Panktoe deed in Stewart, *Indians,* 79; John Dennis in *Burlington Court Book,* 84, 87, and in Pomfret, *West New Jersey,* 90; "Ludlam Marriages," *CMCMHG* 6 (1970):419; Kathryn Eisenberg, "The Northwest Area of Dennis Township," *Dennis Township Historical Society "Archives"* (1988):6–9, in VF, CMCL; Paul Sturtevant Howe, *Mayflower Pilgrim Descendants in Cape May County, New Jersey, 1620–1920* (Cape May: Albert R. Hand, 1921).

31. These early leases are recorded in Liber of Deeds B, CMCCA; see also Black, "Last Lords," 445–462; "Dr. Daniel Coxe Account," in Scull, "Biographical Notice," 327.

32. Pomfret, *West New Jersey,* 165; "Dr. Daniel Coxe Account," 327; Weiss et al., *Whaling,* 16–25; Humphrey Huse (Hughes) Whale Company, 1667, in Henry P. Hedges, et al., *The First Book of Records of the Town of Southampton with Other Ancient Documents of Historical Value* (Sag Harbor, N.Y.: John H. Hunt, 1877), 2:49: Huet (Hewitt) Whalefishing Company, 1678–1679, and Johnson Whalefishery, 1668, in NJA, *Colonial Documents,*

21:30, 42; "Huntington Mills, Long Island," map, and "Sagaponack Whalers," in *CMCMHG* 6 (1968): 271–272.

33. H. C. Campion, Jr., "Caleb Carmen [Carman], Whaler, Millwright, and Miller," *CMCMHG* 2 (1945):283–290; Carmen (Carman) Family Genealogy, H. Clifford Campion Memorial Collection, CMCHS; Carman deeds, in Liber of Deeds C, 14, 30, CMCCA.

34. *Burlington Court Book,* 103–110; Coxe appointment of Taylor, 26 August 1689, and grant of lands, 20 May 1691, in Liber of Deeds A, 21, 30, CMCCA; NJA, *Colonial Documents,* 21:431.

35. *Burlington Court Book,* 109; "Dr. Daniel Coxe Account," 321, 327–329.

36. "Dr. Daniel Coxe Account," 329; marriage 20 July 1697, "First Official Records," *CMCMHG* 1:322, 329–330.

37. *Burlington Court Book,* 48, 107–110, 174–175.

38. "Dr. Daniel Coxe Account," 328; *Burlington Court Book,* 107–111.

39. For the view that Cape May was a county government in 1685, see Snyder, *Civil Boundaries,* 12; NJA, *Colonial Documents,* 2:74; Aaron Leaming and Jacob Spicer, *The Grants, Concessions, and Original Constitutions of the Province of New Jersey* (Philadelphia: W. Bradford, 1758), 507–508; slightly different version in Stevens, *Cape May County History,* 46–47.

40. Leaming and Spicer, *Grants, Concessions,* 530–535; boundary changes in 1822, 1844, 1845, 1878, and 1891 between Cape May and Cumberland Counties in Synder, *Civil Boundaries,* 30–32, 113.

41. Leaming and Spicer, *Grants, Concessions,* 508, 514–515, 533–534, 553–554; NJA, *Colonial Documents,* 2:145–146.

42. Leaming and Spicer, *Grants, Concessions,* 556; Stevens, *Cape May County History,* 56.

43. Richard S. and Mary Maples Dunn, *The Papers of William Penn* (Philadelphia: University of Pennsylvania Press, 1986), 3:547, 626.

44. NJA, *Colonial Documents,* 2:91–92; Pomfret, *West New Jersey,* 174–178; Stevens, "First Public Records," *CMCMHG* 1: 227.

45. Stevens, "First Public Records," in *CMCMHG* 1: 278–279.

46. Ibid., 279–280.

47. Robert Hackshaw, Instructions to Basse, 25 December 1692, NJA, *Colonial Documents,* 2:98–99.

48. Edmund Burley developed the concept of a "windjammer farmer" in 1948 to describe the nineteenth-century Cape May County truckboat captains who sailed from Tuckahoe to Atlantic City with farm products (*Cape May County Gazette,* 25 March 1948). Leaming quoted in John E. Stillwell, *Historical and Genealogical Miscellany, Early Settlers of New Jersey and Their Descendants* (New York: privately printed, 1914), 3:429.

Chapter 2. Whaler Yeoman Ascendancy

1. John E. Pomfret, *The Province of West New Jersey, 1609–1702: A History of the Origins of an American Colony* (Princeton: Princeton University Press, 1956), 207–215; Lewis Townsend Stevens, *The History of Cape May County, New Jersey from Aboriginal Times to the Present Day* (Cape May City: Lewis T. Stevens, publisher, 1897), 60.

2. John E. Pomfret, *Colonial New Jersey: A History* (N.Y.: Scribner's, 1973), 77–91; Pomfret, *West New Jersey,* 202–224.

3. Court session, 18 June 1700, Cape May County Court Minute Book, 1698–1715, CMCCA (hereafter cited as Minute Book).

4. Stevens, *Cape May County History,* 59; NJA, *Colonial Documents,* 2:164–166; "Captain Kidd's Tree Destroyed," *Cape May Wave,* 23 February 1901; also see Sharon F. Fitzpatrick, "Buried Pirate Treasure in Burlington, New Jersey," *New Jersey Folklore* 1: (Spring 1978): 3–7.

5. Undated entry, Aaron Leaming's Survey, Deeds, and Miscellaneous Record Book, CMCCA.

6. Percentage of ownership derived from Frank H. Stewart, "Cape May County Ratables," *CMCMHG* 2 (1940):74–84. In the Lower Precinct, the whaler yeoman families owned 9,138 of the 10,942 taxable acres, or 83.5 percent. List of public officials in Stevens, *Cape May County History,* appendices, 450–464. Whaler yeomen held 19 of 27 assembly seats, 18 of 25 sheriff's posts, 6 of 7 clerkships, 4 of 4 surrogates, 24 of 28 overseers of roads, 12 of 17 tax assessors, 11 of 15 overseers of the poor, and 24 of 28 top militia posts.

7. Statistics on intermarriage are based upon H. Stanley Craig and Julius Way, *Cape May County Marriage Records* (Merchantville, N.J.: H. Stanley Craig, 1931); Cresse to Post, 12 and 18 May 1937, Cresse-Post Correspondence, CMCHS.

8. Whaler yeomen land purchases between 1700 and 1720 in Liber of Deeds B, CMCCA; Peter O. Wacker, *Land and People: A Cultural Geography of Preindustrial New Jersey: Origins and Settlement Patterns* (New Brunswick, N.J.: Rutgers Univesity Press, 1975), 131–137. Estimated population "in excess of 300," H. C. Campion, Jr., "A Partial Census of Cape May County, 1704," *CMCMHG* 2 (1942):164–165; seventy freeholders listed in "Account of Inhabitants of West New Jersey, 1699," NJA, *Colonial Documents,* 2:305.

9. For these family names see Lewis T. Stevens, ed., "First Public Records," *CMCMHG* 1 (1937): 269–285, and "First Official Records," *CMCMHG* 1 (1938):316–337.

10. Aaron Leaming's list of deaths in John E. Stillwell, *Historical and Genealogical Miscellany: Early Settlers of New Jersey and their Descendants* (N.Y.: privately printed, 1914), 3:433. Arthur Cresse, Jr., Reman

Garretson, Samuel Goldin, Abraham Hand, Jedidiah Hughes, Sarah Mason, William Mason, John Mathew (Matthews), Samuel Matthews, John Reaves (Reeves), John Townsend, Daniel Wells, David Wells, wills inventoried 1714 and 1715, in NJA, *Calendar of Wills,* 1: 118, 180, 192, 207, 245, 309–311, 378, 498.

11. Funeral expenses in Elijah Hughes Papers, CMCHS; supplement to Inventory of John Crawford Estate, 1731, Inventory 33E, Esther Huits (Hewitt) to Basse, 13 February 1714/15, Inventory 25E, New Jersey, Probate Records, Cape May County, Records of Wills, Surrogate's Court of Cape May County, New Jersey State Archives (hereafter Records of Wills); Joseph Hewitt, 10 December 1714, NJA, *Calendar of Wills,* 1:245–246.

12. The county court minutes of 1705 locate the jail east of Gravelly Run on the Queens Highway, and in 1706 at the seat of William Shaw's plantation, court sessions, 21 September 1705 and 25 June 1706, Minute Book, CMCCA. "Town Lots" of thirty to thirty-one acres are recorded for early-seventeenth-century landowners in Liber of Deeds B, CMCCA. "Town" residents included Eldredge, Page, Matthews, Stillwell, Crowell, Brandreth, and Carman. For the rectilinear versus irregular pattern, see Peter O. Wacker, *Land and People: A Cultural Geography of Preindustrial New Jersey: Origins and Settlement Patterns* (New Brunswick, N.J.: Rutgers University Press, 1975), 288–289, 388.

13. In commenting on the visit in 1772 of John Fothergill, a traveling preacher, Isaac Mickle captured the religious character of Cape May County. "Whether the Capemen held out encouragement for the worthy preacher to stay longer with them than he did in Egg Harbor, we do not know, but certain it is the sturdy inhabitants of the latter region have never been fond of long sermons of any kind" (Isaac Mickle, *Reminiscences of Old Gloucester or Incidents in the History of the Counties of Gloucester, Atlantic, and Camden* [Philadelphia: Townsend Ward, 1845; reprinted by Gloucester County Historical Society, 1968], 106).

14. Lila M. Gandy and Norman Harvey Vanaman, "Records From the Great Egg Harbor and Maurice River Meeting of Friends," typescript, CMCHS; Vanaman, "The Early Religious Trends in Cape May County," *CMCMHG* 2 (1943):227–228; Florence Leeds Block, "Seaville Meeting," *CMCMHG* 6 (1965):122–129.

15. Edwin P. Tanner, *The Province of New Jersey, 1664–1738* (New York: AMS Press, 1967; reprint of Columbia University 1908 edition), 566; Stillwell, *Historical Miscellany,* 3:433ff; Thomas Leaming refused to serve and fined in Coleman F. Leaming Draft Book, CMCHS. Eldredge file, Post Collection, CMCHS; NJA, *Journal of the Governor of Council,* 1:415; H. C. Campion, Jr., "Timothy Brandreth," *CMCMHG* 2 (1943): 191–200.

16. Thomas Chalkley, *The Journal of Thomas Chalkley* (Philadelphia: privately printed, 1749), 75, 230–231.

17. Block, "Seaville Meeting," 122–131; Joyce Van Vorst, *Cedar Swamp Creek: Stories and Sketches of the Area* (Cape May: Cape May County Historical and Genealogical Society, 1977), 61–73; for the view that the Quaker meetinghouse was built in 1702 and moved to Seaville in 1716, see Florence Speck, "Early History of Upper Precinct," in *A History of Upper Township and Its Villages* (Marmora, N.J.: Historical Preservation Society of Upper Township, 1989), 7. Quakers in Cape May County made up 4.7 percent of the population compared to 50.8 percent in Burlington County and 43.4 percent in Gloucester County in 1745 (see Wacker, *Land and People,* 183; also see Mary Jane Corson, comp., "Henry Young and His Descendants," *CMCMHG* 7 (1973): 36–41).

18. Richard P. McCormick, *New Jersey from Colony to State, 1609–1789* (Newark: New Jersey Historical Society, 1981), 94–95; M. Catherine Stauffer, "The First Baptist Church of Cape May County," *CMCMHG* 3 (1952): 189–190; Stevens, *Cape May County History,* 70–71. Female Baptist leaders in the county included Lydia Parsons Shaw, Ruth and Mary Swain, Hannah Stites, Mary Cresse, Abagail Buck, Margery Smith, Elizabeth and Hannah Taylor, and Elizabeth and Jeruthy Hand.

19. Penuel deed, 7 July 1719, Liber of Deeds B, 45, CMCCA; Grace C. Gallaher, "The Jenkins Family of Cape May County, New Jersey," *CMCMHG* 5 (1963):369–380; M. Catherine Stauffer, "Penuel—Baptist Meeting House County Courthouse," *CMCMHG* 3 (1953):239–244.

20. Bradner File, Post Collection, CMCHS; Rev. Daniel Lawrence Hughes, "First 175 Years of Cold Spring Church," *CMCMHG* 2 (1943): 203–224; Stevens, *Cape May County History,* 98; Bradner deed, 7 June 1719, Liber of Deeds B, 146, CMCCA.

21. Court session, 2 April 1723, Minute Book, 1715–1723, CMCCA; Stevens, *Cape May County History,* 92. The six county representatives in 1723 were essentially the board of justices and freeholders for Cape May County provided for by the New Jersey colonial assembly act of 28 February 1713–1714, by which each town or precinct chose two freeholders and a justice to conduct county business (see Mickle, *Reminiscences,* 55, and Thos. Cushing and Charles E. Sheppard, *History of the Counties of Gloucester, Salem, and Cumberland, New Jersey with Biographical Sketches of their Prominent Citizens* [Philadelphia: Everts & Peck, 1883], 524.

22. Harry B. Weiss, *The Personal Estates of Early Farmers and Tradesmen of Colonial New Jersey, 1670–1750* (Trenton: New Jersey Agricultural Society, 1971), 23; Stevens, *Cape May County History,* 90; Thomas L. Purvis, *Proprietors, Patronage, and Paper Money: Legislative Politics in New Jersey, 1703–1776* (New Brunswick, N.J.: Rutgers University Press, 1986), 145–154.

23. Stevens, *Cape May County History,* 88, 101–102.

24. Entries, 21–22 October, 24 April, and 1 May 1734, 24 April 1740,

Leaming diary, CMCHS; this diary fragment is transcribed in two parts in Karl A. Dickinson, "Comments on Aaron Leaming, Jr. Diary—1737," *CMCMHG* 7 (1979): 541–553 and (1980): 620–635; entry, 17 October 1743, Aaron Leaming, Jr., diary fragment, GSCL; court session, 25 June 1706, Minute Book, CMCCA.

25. These cases appear in court sessions of 1 February 1731, 4 October 1720, 4 April 1721, and 20 May 1707, Minute Books, CMCCA.

26. Court sessions, 26–27 March 1706, 20 May 1707, 5 July 1720, 5 November 1724, Minute Books, CMCCA.

27. Court sessions, 19 May 1724, 3 October 1721, Minute Books, CMCCA; "a stranger" received "25 strikes on bare back," entry, 12 April 1756, Lewis Cresse, "The Whaler's Diary," *CMCMHG* 6 (1968): 279 (hereafter cited as Cresse diary).

28. "Ye bloody fever" in entry, 12 January 1761, Lewis T. Stevens, ed., "Diaries of Aaron Leaming," *CMCMHG* 1 (1932): 71. This is an accurate copy of the original deposited in the Historical Society of Pennsylvania. Also Leaming to Henderson, 13 February 1759, Leaming Papers, RUL; entry, 16 July 1756, William A. Ellis, ed., "Diary of Jacob Spicer, 1755–6," *PNJHS* 63 (1945): 193 (the original is in the New Jersey Historical Society, Newark); Stevens, *Cape May County History*, 119. The colonists recognized that contaminated water spawned the "Bloody Flux" (see Carville V. Earle, "Environment, Disease, and Mortality in Early Virginia," in Thad W. Tate and David L. Ammerman, eds., *The Chesapeake in the Seventeenth Century: Essays on Anglo-American Society* [New York: Norton, 1979], 96–125).

29. Ministers drunk in Stevens, *Cape May County History*, 72, 98; entry, 18 February 1775, Elijah Hughes diary, CMCHS; entry 9 April 1741, Leaming diary, CMCCA; Schellenger in entry, 1774(?), Thomas Leaming, Jr., Memorandum Book, HSP; Goldin case in court sessions, 4 August 1736, 17 August 1737, Minute Book, 1736–1739, CMCCA. Eventually the supreme court in Burlington acquitted Goldin, but court costs bankrupted him and he sold his lands in the Upper Precinct to the Stillwell family (Jacob Goldin in NJA, *Calendar of Wills*, 3:131).

30. Charles S. Boyer, *Rambles Through Old Highways and Byways of West Jersey* (Camden: Camden County Historical Society, 1967), 57; court sessions, 3rd Tuesday 1698, 20 September 1699, 20 May 1707, Minute Books, CMCCA; Henry A. Scribner, "The Old Cape Road," Roads file, VF, CMCL; Egbert L. Viele Map of 1856 to accompany George H. Cook, *Geology of the County of Cape May, State of New Jersey* (Trenton: Office of the True American, 1857), in Map File, CMCL.

31. Court sessions, 26–27 March 1706, 18 July 1710, Minute Books, CMCCA.

32. Maurice Beesley, "Sketch of the Early History of the County of Cape

May" in Cook, *Geology,* 171; court session, 26–27 March 1706, Minute Book, CMCCA.

33. Entry, 25 May 1740, Dickinson, "Leaming Diary," *CMCMHG* 7 (1980): 624; Roger T. Trindell, "Historical Geography of Southern New Jersey as Related to its Colonial Ports (Ph.D. diss.: Louisiana State University, 1966), 149; Purvis, *Propietors, Patronage, and Paper Money,* 32; Weiss, *Personal Estates,* 3–4.

34. Entry, 25–26 November 1736, Dickinson, "Leaming Diary," *CMCMHG* 7 (1979): 550; entry, 20 June 1755, Ellis, "Spicer Diary," *PNJHS,* 63: 87; bounties in court sessions, 25 June 1706, 1 January 1711, Minute Books, CMCCA.

35. Cape May County Mortgages, Ear Marks, Miscellaneous Record Book A, CMCCA; court session, 22 May 1734, Minute Book, CMCCA. Gloucester County drew large ears in its earmark book, while Cape May County showed entire cattle or sheep's faces with ears (see Frank H. Stewart, ed., *The Organization and Minutes of the Gloucester County Court, 1686–7 and Gloucester County Ear Mark Book, 1686–1728* [Woodbury, N.J.: Gloucester County Historical Society, 1930]).

36. Entry, 16 July 1755, Ellis, "Spicer Diary," *PNJHS,* 63: 94; entry 17 October 1743, Leaming diary, GSCL; entry, 7 December 1739, Dickinson, "Leaming Diary," *CMCHGS,* 7:543.

37. Entry 13 February 175[3], "Cresse Diary," *CMCMHG,* 6:277; entries, 20 June 1740, 3 and 11 September 1737/8, 28 April 1741, Dickinson, "Leaming Diary," *CMCMHG,* 7:546, 625–629; Lewis T. Stevens, "Memorandum Book of Jacob Spicer, 1757–1764," *CMCMHG,* 1 (1933):113, (1934): 164. Cedar trees exhausted in Trindell, "Historical Geography," 144–145. Mid-eighteenth-century Cape May County mills included Mackey's Mill on Cedar Swamp Creek; two Ludlam Mills on Dennis Creek; Townsend's Mill, seaside Middle Precinct; Hand's Mill on Green Creek; Springer's Mill on Dyer's Creek; Skellinger (Schellenger) Mill on Cold Spring Creek; Swain's Mill on Cold Spring Creek; and Crowell's Mill, location unknown, (NJA, *Calendar of Wills,* 2:217, 309, 486, 418; 3: 315).

38. Entry 14–17 February 1734, Dickinson, "Leaming Diary," *CMCMHG,* 7: 623; entry, 28 February 1775, Stevens, "Leaming Diaries," *CMCMHG,* 1: 78; entries, 7 March 1755, 24 February 1756, 27 February 1754, "Cresse Diary," *CMCMHG,* 6: 278–279.

39. Entry for 27 February–9 April 1754, "Cresse Diary," *CMCMHG,* 6: 278; average whale kill calculated from reports in colonial press, NJA, *Some Account of American Newspaper Extracts from American Newspapers, relating to New Jersey,* volumes 1–4, and from the Cresse and Leaming diaries. Aaron Leaming, Jr., "An Interesting Document Concerning the Whaling Industry and Its Decline," 11 July 1772, *CMCMHG,* 7 (1978): 487–490. The tradition that Cape May County produced "prodigious nay vast quantities" of

whalebone and oil and contained a "great fishery" that took "great numbers of whales," was established by Gabriel Thomas in *An Historical and Geographical account of the Province and County of Pennsylvania and of West New Jersey, in America*, published in 1698, quoted in Mickle, *Reminiscences,* 116. Thomas paraphrased Dr. Daniel Coxe's promotional account designed to attract whalers to the Cape May peninsula as settlers.

40. Entry 21 April 1741, Dickinson, "Leaming Diary," *CMCMHG,* 7: 547; entry, 5 April 1755, Ellis, "Spicer Diary," *PNJHS,* 63: 48; entry, 17 February 1757, Stevens, "Spicer Memorandum Book, *CMCMHG,* 1:109; Stevens, *Cape May County History,* 122–124.

41. Shipbuilding or repair most likely took place on Townsend Inlet, Tuckahoe River, Cold Spring and Dennis creeks in the mid-eighteenth century (see entries, 1 March 1760, July 1758, Stevens, "Spicer Memorandum Book," *CMCMHG,* 1:118, 182). Capt. Alonzo T. Bacon and Edward M. Post, "Vessels That Have Been Built in Cape May County," *CMCMHG,* 1 (1937): 298, listed *Adventurer* (1705), *Necessity* (1706), and *Dolphin* (1708), but no other ship until 1800.

42. Entries, 15 February, 12 March, 4 April 1755, Ellis, "Spicer Diary," *PNJHS,* 63: 39, 42, 48; entry, 26 August 1747, Dickinson, "Leaming Diary," *CMCMHG,* 7:622; 31 March 1761, Stevens, "Leaming Diaries," *CMCMHG,* 1:76; NJA, *Newspaper Extracts,* 4: 195–197.

43. There were fourteen slaves in Cape May County in 1726 and fifty-two by 1745 (see Stevens, *Cape May County History,* 101, 105; Deborah Hand inventory, 27 August 1767, Inventory 268E, and Hannah Young inventory, 25 August 1766, 265E, both in Records of Wills, NJSA; "Red Negroe" in entry, 8 February 1756, Ellis, "Spicer Diary," *PNJHS,* 68: 188; NJA, *Calendar of Wills,* 5:457.

44. Entry, 29 January 1794, Thomas Leaming, Jr., Memo Book, HSP; entries 2 and 10–14 January 1737, Dickinson, "Leaming Diary," *CMCMHG,* 7:549; NJA, *Calendar of Wills,* 1:287; McCormick, *New Jersey,* 95; entry 29 November 1753, "Cresse Diary," *CMCMHG,* 6:278.

45. Only 29 percent of the Jersey Cape was arable land (Wacker, "Land Use in New Jersey," lecture, Historic Cold Spring Village, 20 April 1989); boundary disputes in Leaming to John Lawrence, 17 October 1763, Leaming Papers, GSCL; Resurvey Map, 18 December 1764, Cape May County Maps, GSCL; A. Leaming, Jr., to his brother [Jeremiah] Leaming, 23 March 174[?], Spicer Leaming Papers, HSP.

46. Entry, 13 February 1755, Ellis, "Spicer Diary," *PNJHS,* 63: 38; Hand's petition, 22 January 1755, Inventory 197E, Records of Wills, NJSA.

47. Stevens, *Cape May County History,* 113; Spicer statement, 6 May 1762, Inventory 253E, 14, Records of Wills, NJSA.

48. Entries, 8 April, 15 July 1755, Ellis, "Spicer Diary," *PNJHS,* 63: 48, 94; entry, 29 January 1759, Stevens, "Spicer Memo Book," *CMCMHG,* 1:164;

Spicer statement, 6 May 1762, inventory 253E, Records of Wills, NJSA; entry, n.d., Thomas Leaming Jr., Memo Book, 1774, HSP.

49. Entries 23 March 1761, Stevens, "Leaming Diaries,"*CMCMHG,* 1:72; John Clement, *Notes and Memoranda Relating to the West New Jersey Society of West New Jersey* (Camden, privately printed, 1880), 31; Spicer statement, 6 May 1762.

50. Purvis, *Proprietors, Patronage, and Paper Money,* 30–35.

51. For intermarriage and kinship ties, see Paul Sturtevant Howe, *Mayflower Pilgrim Descendants in Cape May County, New Jersey, 1620–1920* (Cape May: Albert R. Hand, 1921); entry, n.d., Thomas Leaming, Jr., Memo Book, 1774, HSP; Spicer statement, 6 May 1762.

52. Entries 21–22 October 1747, Dickinson, "Leaming diary," *CMCMHG,* 7:622; Stevens, "Spicer Memo Book," 1755," *CMCMHG,* 1:164; Stevens, *Cape May County History,* 122–123; inventories of thirty-five whaler yeomen families, Records of Wills, NJSA.

53. See Frank H. Stewart, "Cape May County Ratables," *CMCMHG* 2 (1940):78–84; inventories of Wills in Records of Wills, listed boats for the Corson, Cresse, Eldredge, Godfrey, Golden, Hand, Leaming, Foster, Hewitt, Richardson, Schellenger, Hughes, and Townsend families, and slaves for the Crawford, Crowell, Eldredge, Godfrey, Hand, Hewitt, Holden, Hughes, Leaming, Spicer, Smith, Stillwell, Stites, Swain, Taylor, Townsend, and Whilldin families; entry, 26 February 1761, Leaming diary, *CMCMHG,* 1:72.

54. Zelopheard Hand, "Naming Cape May Court House," in *Gazette,* 25 November 1910; Robert C. Alexander, "The Principal Settlements," *CMCMHG,* 6 (1964): 25; entry, 29 October 1744, Leaming diary fragment, Leaming Papers, GSCL; entry, 16 July 1750, Stevens, "Leaming diary," *CMCMHG,* 1:70; Stevens, *Cape May County History,* 103, 55, 137, incorrectly referred to Cape May Court House as the county seat in 1745. A courthouse was not erected there until 1764. The Leaming plantation and Baptist meetinghouse was the county seat. Court sessions, 19 September and fourth Tuesday of October 1741, third Tuesday of May 1745, Minute Book, 1740–1762, CMCCA.

55. Purvis, *Proprietors, Patronage, and Paper Money,* 181–182; court sessions, 23 October 1764, 5 February 1765, 21 May 1765, Minute Books, 1763–1770, CMCCA.

56. Mid-eighteenth-century tavern and inn owners included Ludlam, Stillwell, Spicer, Leaming, Hand, Hughes, Ross, and Whilldin (see Robert C. Alexander, "Tavern Keepers of Cape May County, 1741–1801," *CMCMHG,* 7 (1976):223–237; licensing of "publick houses" in court sessions, third Tuesday of May 1743, fourth Tuesday of October 1748, Minute Books, 1740–1762, CMCCA; NJA, *Newspaper Extracts,* 2:320; Stevens, *Cape May County History,* 104.

57. Entries, 30 November, 23 and 25 December 1755, Ellis, "Spicer

Diary," *PNJHS,* 63: 103–117, 177–178, 181–182; Capt. Nicholas Stillwell, Jacob Hand, and Silas Swain drafted seventy militia men in the county for the French and Indian War (diary entry, 15 August 1757, "Cresse diary," *CMCMHG,* 6:280; Stevens, *Cape May County History,* 118; Anthony Nicolosi, "Colonial Particularism and Political Rights: Jacob Spicer II on Aid to Virginia, 1754," *NJH* 88 [Summer 1970]: 77).

Chapter 3. Revolution and the New Nation

1. James H. Levitt, *For Want of Trade: Shipping and the New Jersey Ports, 1680–1783* (Newark: New Jersey Historical Society, 1981), 139–142; Larry R. Gerlach, "Customs and Contentions: John Hatton of Salem and Cohansey, 1764–1766," *NJH* 89 (Summer 1971): 69–72.

2. Spicer, quoted in Larry R. Gerlach, ed., *New Jersey in the American Revolution, 1763–1783: A Documentary History* (Trenton: New Jersey Historical Commission, 1975), 8; Anthony Nicolosi, "Colonial Particularism and Political Rights: Jacob Spicer II on Aid to Virginia, 1754," *NJH* 88 (Summer 1970): 77, 69–88.

3. Entry, n.d., Thomas Leaming, Jr., Memo Book, 1774, HSP; Mary Cresse to Edward Post, 18 May 1937, Cresse-Post Correspondence, CMCHS; see also John E. Stillwell, *Historical and Genealogical Miscellany: Early Settlers of New Jersey and their Descendants* (N.Y.: privately printed, 1914), 3:438.

4. Lewis Townsend Stevens, *The History of Cape May County, New Jersey, from the Aboriginal Times to the Present Day* (Cape May City: Lewis T. Stevens, publisher, 1897), 143–170; Larry R. Gerlach, *Prologue to Independence: New Jersey in the Coming of the Revolution* (New Brunswick, N.J.: Rutgers University Press, 1976), 53–61; court sessions, 5, 6, and 12 February and 9 November 1771, Minute Book, 1771–1773, CMCCA. Copy of Hatton's indictment in Leaming Family Papers, GSCL.

5. Gerlach, *Prologue to Independence,* 54–55, 398–399; Stevens, *Cape May County History,* 143–170.

6. Entry 3 October 1774, Elijah Hughes diary, CMCHS (also transcript in *CMCMHG,* 6 (1976): 89; "Letter of Thomas Leaming, Jr., to Hon. William Paterson, 1789," *PMHB* 38 (1914): 115–119, quote 116; Robert W. Harper, *Old Gloucester County and the American Revolution, 1763–1778, Including Atlantic, Burlington, Cape May, Cumberland, and Salem Counties* (Woodbury, N.J.: Gloucester County Cultural and Heritage Commission, 1986), 14–18.

7. Aaron Leaming, Jr., "Notes to Constituents," 26 May 1771, original draft, Leaming Family Papers, GSCL.

8. John Hatton, Jr., quoted in, Gerlach, *Documentary History,* 121–123.

9. "Hard-core royalists" in Gerlach, *Prologue to Independence,* 300, 483n19; entry 17 February 177[6], Hughes diary, CMCHS; Thomas Leaming, Jr., Richard Townsend, Henry Young Townsend, James Whilldin, Hugh Hathorne, Jesse Hand, Jeremiah Eldredge, and Eli Eldredge, county leaders, were all ardent Whig supporters of the Revolution.

10. Entries, 3 October 1774, 27 January–3 February 177[6], Hughes diary, CMCHS.

11. Entries 21 September 1775, 14 October 1777, Aaron Leaming, Jr., diary, HSP; Committee of Thirty membership in Stevens, *Cape May County History,* 179–180, and in Gerlach, *Prologue to Independence,* 467n24; the Committee of Thirty contained the county's largest landowners (see Carlos E. Godfrey, comp., "Cape May Land Owners in Revolutionary Times," *CMCMHG* 1 (1933):91–107.

12. Godfrey, "Cape May Land Owners," 91–107; Stevens, *Cape May County History,* 172, 195–198; Stevens, "Soldiers from Cape May in the Revolutionary War," *CMCMHG* 1 (1932):46–52; entry 14 October 1777, Leaming diary, HSP.

13. Samuel Steele Smith, *Fight for the Delaware, 1777* (Monmouth Beach, N.J.: Philip Freneau Press, 1970), 6–18; Martin I. J. Griffin, *Commodore John Barry* (Philadelphia: privately printed, 1903), 36–37; *Nancy* incident in George F. Boyer and J. Pearson Cunningham, *Cape May County Story* (Egg Harbor City, N.J.: Laureate Press, 1975), 46–48; Hamond to Lt. John Graves, Hamond to Captain Phipps, 25 May 1777, Hamond Naval Papers, Microfilm reel 2, University of Virginia Library, Charlottesville.

14. Entries 3 May, 23 June 1777, Leaming diary, HSP; Stevens, *Cape May County History,* 183–193; James Parker, in NJA, *Calendar of Wills,* 5:377.

15. Entry 19 September 1777, Leaming diary, HSP.

16. Entries 1 July 1777, 19 and 22 September 1777, ibid.; Seth Whillden to his wife, 25 December 1776, Revolutionary War Letters, CMCHS; Elijah Hughes to his wife, 2 June 177[?], Hughes Papers, CMCHS; court session, February 1777, Minute Book, 1774–1790, CMCCA.

17. Smith, *Fight for the Delaware,* 6–18; entries, 19 and 22 September 1777, Leaming diary, HSP.

18. Smith, *Fight for the Delaware,* 17–18; see also Harper, *Old Gloucester and Revolution.*

19. Gerlach, *Documentary History,* 378; David A. Bernstein, ed., *Minutes of the Governor's Privy Council, 1777–1789* (Trenton: New Jersey State Library Archives and History Bureau, 1974), 1:71, 75, 116.

20. Harry B. Weiss and Grace M. Weiss, *The Revolutionary Saltworks of the New Jersey Coast* (Trenton: The Past Times Press, 1959), 34–35;

Arthur D. Pierce, *Smugglers' Woods: Jaunts and Journeys in Colonial and Revolutionary New Jersey* (New Brunswick, N.J.: Rutgers University Press, 1960), 230, 249–250; Stevens, *Cape May County History,* 201, 213–214; 16d per bushel of salt in diary entry, 17 February 177[?], Hughes diary, CMCHS; entries, 23 May, 18 and 27 July 1777, Leaming diary, HSP.

21. Privateering in diary entry, 10 November 1775, Leaming diary, HSP; entries, November 1778–19 January 1779, Thomas Leaming, Jr., Receipt Book, HSP; Nesbitt to Conyngham, 20 April 1779, in NJA, *Colonial Documents,* 3:334–336.

22. William Evans Price, "The Stillwells—A Patriotic Family, and Their Descendants," *CMCMHG* 2 (1940): 51–55; NJA, *Colonial Documents* 3: 593, 606, 613.

23. For list of Philadelphia merchant owners and bondsmen of Cape May County privateers see Lewis T. Stevens, "Cape May Naval Activities in the Revolution," *CMCMHG* 2 (1944): 244–254; Thomas Leaming, Jr., to Rev. Jeremiah Leaming, 4 April 1781, Leaming Papers, HSP.

24. Stevens, "Cape May Naval Activities," 244–254; Aaron Leaming, Jr., to Thomas Leaming, Jr., 17 September 1779, 15 March 1780, Leaming Papers, HSP; also see Pierce, *Smugglers' Woods,* 69–70.

25. Entry, n.d., Reuben Willets Journal, CMCHS; Stevens, *Cape May County History,* 198–199, 212. In comparing the Cape May County revolutionary war militia rolls against British War Department records of the prisonship *Jersey,* the following Cape May County names appear: Pomeus (Parmenas) Corson, Hiram Chester, John Crawford, Amos Cresse, Thomas Day, Moses Griffing, Richard Matthews, John Newton, James Plumer, Thomas Scott, Enoch Stillwell, Joseph Wheaton, and James Willets (Danske Dandridge, *American Prisoners of the Revolution* [Baltimore: Genealogical Publishing Company, 1967; reprint of 1911 edition], 457–474); Nathaniel Holmes may have been a prisoner on the *Jersey* (see Holmes File, Post Collection, CMCHS).

26. Gerlach, *Documentary History,* 343, 348–349; Stevens, *Cape May County History,* 198–199.

27. Boyer and Cunningham, *Cape May Story,* 44–45; also see David J. Fowler, "Egregious Villains, Wood Rangers, and London Traders" (Ph.D. diss. Rutgers University, 1987).

28. Gerlach, *Documentary History,* 395–396; Stevens, *Cape May County History,* 218; see also Richard P. McCormick, *Experiment in Independence: New Jersey in the Critical Period, 1781–1789* (New Brunswick, N.J.: Rutgers University Press, 1950).

29. Order of the Board of Justices and Freeholders, Petitions, 2 November 1784, CMCCA.

30. Sheriff's sales in NJA, *Calendar of Wills,* 8:121–122; 12:163–164; 13:221; entry, n.d., Reuben Willetts Journal, CMCHS; debtor problem dis-

cussed in court session, February 1798, Minute Book, 1798–1799, CMCCA; tax lists, 1774 and 1784, in Godfrey, "Cape May Land Owners," 1:91–103; 146–161: Maurice Beesley, "Sketch of the Early History of the County of Cape May," in George H. Cook, *Geology of the County of Cape May, State of New Jersey* (Trenton: Office of the True American, 1857), 197.

31. Slaves listed in Godfrey, "Cape May Land Owners," 1:146–161.

32. Entry, n.d., Reuben Willets, Journal, CMCHS; Jean Gordon Lee, *Philadelphians and the China Trade, 1784–1844* (Philadelphia: Philadelphia Museum of Art, 1984), 92, 166; J. Bennett Hill and Margaret Howe Hill, "William Fisher, Early Philadelphia Quaker," in *Genealogies of Pennsylvania Families From the Pennsylvania Genealogical Magazine* (Baltimore: Genealogical Publishing Company, 1982), 1:594; entries, 1816–1818, J. Fisher Leaming Account Books, Leaming Papers, HSP.

33. Aaron Leaming to Daniel Elmer, 13 February 1759, Edward M. Morier et al., "The East Creek Mill Site: Archaeological Date Recovery, Dennis Township, March 1988" (Paper in Gloucester County Historical Society).

34. Roy Hand, "The Mills of East and West Creek," *CMCMHG* 4 (1957): 117–129; Hand, "Early West Creek Settlers," *CMCMHG* 4 (1958): 142–148; Charles S. Hartman, "Cape May County Mills," *South Jersey Magazine* (Winter 1984): 15–21.

35. Entry, 1795, "Notes from the Account Book of Rev. John Goff," *CMCMHG* 5 (1962): 363–364; Goff File, Post Collection, CMCHS; Roy Hand, "The Goff and Bishop Families," *CMCMHG* 6 (1964): 45–57; also see Hand, "Mills," 117–129.

36. "Ludlam Marriages," *CMCMHG* 6 (1970): 436–439; NJA, *Calendar of Wills,* 12:267.

37. Elizabeth Holmes, in County Collectors Book of Cape May, 1790–1803 (reverse side of Parsons Leaming Day Book, 1790–1803, which is essentially the first volume of the Cape May County Board of Chosen Freeholders Minute Books, in CMCHS; Winfield Scott Weer, "Hannah Holmes: A Study in Identification," *CMCMHG* 7 (1978): 469–471; see Diverty File, Post Collection, CMCHS.

38. Road applications and surveys, 21 April, 7 May 1781, 17 October 1782, 25–26 February 1783, 20 January 1789, 16 March 1790, Cape May County Road Book A, CMCCA; road applications, 21 June 1798, 13 November 1799, Road Book B, CMCCA; bridges in entries, 11 November 1789, 26 May 1792, Miscellaneous Book B, 50–53, 301–302, CMCCA; Stevens, *Cape May County History,* 219–220.

39. *Pennsylvania Gazette,* 26 July 1766.

40. Road surveys, 6 June 1783, 7 April 1785, Road Book A, CMCCA; court session, 28 May 1799, Minute Book, 1797–1811, CMCCA; Robert C. Alexander, "Tavern Keepers of Cape May County," *CMCMHG* 7 (1976): 231–236.

41. Surveyors' report, 25–26 February 1783, Road Book A, CMCCA.

42. See McCormick, *Experiment in Independence,* 284.

43. Ibid., 266–268; Stevens, *Cape May County History,* 219, lists Jacob Eldredge as constitutional delegate. This seems unlikely since in 1787 he was a young, propertyless nephew of county leader Jeremiah Eldredge.

44. Carl E. Prince, *New Jersey's Jeffersonian Republicans: The Genesis of an Early Party Machine, 1789–1817* (Chapel Hill: University of North Carolina Press, 1967), 31, 52, 59, 92, 225, 227.

45. Lucius Q. C. Elmer, *A Digest of the Laws of New Jersey* (Bridgeton, N.J.: James M. Newell, 1838), 66–72, 571–579; freeholder meeting, 25 August 1798, Minutes of the Board of Chosen Freeholders Cape May County (reverse side Parsons Leaming Day Book), CMCHS (hereafter cited as P. Leaming Day Book).

46. Freeholder meetings, 8 May 1799, 13–14 May 1800, 9 June 1801, P. Leaming Day Book.

47. Fifty percent of the criminal cases heard by the Grand Jury in 1799 dealt with African-Americans (court session 28 May 1799, Minute Book, 1797–1811, CMCCA).

Chapter 4. Cape Island and Dennis Creek

1. Philadelphia *Aurora and General Advertiser,* 1 July 1801, 3.

2. Ibid.; Robert Crozer Alexander, *Ho! For Cape Island* (Cape May, N.J.: privately printed, 1956), 14–16.

3. *Philadelphia Gazette,* 26 July 1766; Alexander, *Cape Island,* 10–11.

4. Alexander, *Cape Island,* 27–30; Alexander, "John F. Watson at Cape Island," CMGS, *20th Annual Bulletin* (1966): 6–7; Alexander, "The Cape May Boats," *CMCMHG* 4 (1956): 55–62.

5. Philip English Mackey, ed., *A Gentleman of Much Promise: The Diary of Isaac Mickle, 1837–1845* (Philadelphia: University of Pennsylvania Press, 1977), 2:460, 384.

6. Freeholder meeting, 11 May 1803, Minutes of the Board of Chosen Freeholders Cape May County, reverse side Parsons Leaming Day Book, CMCHS.

7. Craig Mathewson, "Cape May County Post Offices," *CMCMHG* 6 (1969): 391–392; Mathewson, "Postal Highlights," *CMCMHG* 7 (1978): 491–498.

8. Entries, 1816–1823, J. Fisher Leaming Invoice Book, Leaming Papers, HSP; entry, 1821, James Smith Memorandum Book, CMCHS; entry, 1862, Coleman F. Leaming Draft Book, CMCHS.

9. "An act to establish a new township in the county of Cape May, to be called the township of Dennis," passed 9 November 1826, *Acts of the Fifty-First General Assembly of the State of New Jersey* (Trenton: Joseph Justice, printer, 1826), 6–7.

10. Alexander, *Cape Island,* 23, 61; George E. Thomas and Carl Doebley, *Cape May, Queen of the Seaside Resorts: Its History and Architecture* (Philadelphia: Art Alliance Press, 1976), 22.

11. Thomas F. Gordon, *Gazetteer of the State of New Jersey* (Cottonport, La.: Plyanthos reprint of 1834 edition, 1973), 150; Memorandum of Agreement to keep Goshen Creek Landing Road Open, 26 February 1805, Liber of Deeds C, 25, CMCCA; notes on history of Goshen, Charles Tomlin Papers, CMCHS.

12. Dias Creek School House, Record Book, 1811–1910, Tomlin Papers, CMCHS; Roland Ellis, "Windmills: The Ugly Duckling of Cape May County," *CMCMHG* 4 (1959): 191–201; Dyer's Creek (Meadow) Banking Company, 27 September 1814, Cape May County Road Book B, 79–81, CMCCA. See also Thos. Cushing and Charles E. Sheppard, *History of the Counties of Gloucester, Salem and Cumberland,* (Philadelphia: Everts Peck, 1883), 331–332. For an article that confused the meadow banking company with a financial banking institution, see Emily A. Clark, "Paper Money Issued in Cape May County," *CMCMHG* 7 (1980): 616–619.

13. Camp meeting, in *Cape May County Gazette,* 6 July 1906.

14. Fishing Creek Banking Company, 16 October 1806, Road Book B, 22–23, CMCCA; freeholder meeting, 16 January 1817, P. Leaming Day Book, CMCHS; Ellis, "Windmills," 191–201.

15. Harvey Strum, "South Jersey and the War of 1812," *CMCMHG* 9 (1987): 4–21; Lewis Townsend Stevens, *The History of Cape May County, New Jersey from Aboriginal Times to the Present Day* (Cape May City: Lewis T. Stevens, publisher, 1897), 237–240.

16. Freeholder meetings 25 July 1812, 20 March, 25 May 1813, all in P. Leaming Day Book, CMCHS.

17. Charles Tomlin, *Cape May Spray* (Philadelphia: Bradley Bros., 1913), 83; Stevens, *Cape May County History,* 237–238; Strum, "War of 1812," 4; Robert C. Alexander, "Lake Lily," CMGS, *Bulletin* (1950): 6–7.

18. New Jersey Adjutant-General's Office, *Records of Officers and Men of New Jersey in Wars, 1791–1815* (Baltimore: Genealogical Publishing Company 1970; reprint of 1909 edition), 141–142, 146; Lewis T. Stevens, "Cape May Soldiers in the War of 1812," *CMCMHG* 1 (1935): 179–181; Stevens, *Cape May County History,* 233–237.

19. Strum, "War of 1812," 5–7, 10–12; entry, 4 August 1813, Lucius Q. C. Elmer diaries, RUL; Karl A. Dickinson, "County History Records British Landings on Cape In War of 1812," *Cape May County Gazette,* 5 May 1955.

20. Strum, "War of 1812," 15–16; Tomlin, *Cape May Spray,* 52; Harold

Fisher Wilson, *The Jersey Shore; A Social and Economic History of the Counties of Atlantic, Cape May, Monmouth and Ocean* (New York: Lewis Historical Publishing Company, 1953), 1: 371, 391–392; Gandy's Mill supplied wood for the furnace (see Deed Book 1: 554, CMCCA).

21. Joyce Van Vorst, "Cedar Swamp Creek Meadow Company," *CMCMHG* 9 (1989):211–220; and Van Vorst, *Cedar Swamp Creek: Stories and Sketches of the Area* (Cape May: Cape May County Historical and Genealogical Society, 1977), 41–45; saltworks, in NJA, *Calendar of Wills,* 13:495; Upper Township Census, 1850, CMCCA; Van Vorst, "Day Book No. 1, October 1809, Stephen Young, His Book of Sundries," *CMCMHG* 8 (1985): 399–405.

22. Mackey, *A Gentleman of Much Promise,* 2:382; entry, 4 July 1843, Zerulia Stillwell Edmunds diary, CMCHS.

23. Maurice Beesley, "Sketch of the Early History of the County of Cape May," in George H. Cook, *Geology of the County of Cape May, State of New Jersey* (Trenton: Office of the True American, 1857), 199; Mary Van Gilder McCafferty and Terry W. Van Gilder, "Van Gilders from Cape May County," *CMCMHG* 8 (1985): 387–388; Hildreth File, Post Collection, CMCHS; Thos. and Phebe Yates to Jonathan Leaming, n.d., *CMCMHG* 2 (1940): 71–72.

24. Obituary of Esther Leaming Foster, *Ocean Wave,* 15 July 1858; Lewis Ludlam to Henry Ludlam, 15 March 1816, Ludlam Letters, CMCHS; Raymond E. Giron, Jr., "The Nickelson Family," *CMCMHG* 8 (1984): 303–305; Charles A. Nicholson, "Residents of Sangamon County, Illinois in 1850 Who were Born in New Jersey," *CMCMHG* 7 (1977): 441–442.

25. Lewis Godfrey to John Price, 25 October 1826, Price, Ledger of John Price, 1819–1826 quoted in Paul Sturtevant Howe, "Romance in Old Account Books," *CMCMHG* 1 (1936): 245–254, quote 249.

26. Freeholder meetings, 9 January 1808, 20 February 1821, 20 March 1826, all in P. Leaming Day Book, CMCHS; entry 20 February 1821, Alms House Minute Book, Board of Chosen Freeholders' Clerk's Office, hereafter AHMB; Freeholder meeting, 26 May 1829, BCFMB. See David J. Russo, *Families and Communities: A New View of American History* (Nashville, Tenn.: American Association for State and Local History, 1974), 204–205; Edward Byers, *The "Nation of Nantucket": Society and Politics in an Early American Commercial Center, 1660–1820* (Boston: Northeastern University Press, 1987), 300–301.

27. Entries, 20 February, 9 May, 24 December and 28 December, 1821, all in AHMB.

28. Entries, 2, 4, and 27 April 1821, all in AHMB; freeholder meeting, 24 March 1821, P. Leaming Day Book, CMCHS; entries, 24 August, 29 November 1821, 12, 16, and 28 January 1822, 19 February 1823, all in AHMB.

29. Freeholder meeting, 12 May 1824, P. Leaming Day Book, CMCHS; entries, 12 and 16 January 1822, 14 February 1823, 28 January 1828, 14 and 17 February 1828, 28 March 1835, all in AHMB.

30. Freeholder meetings, 5 December 1848, 30 May 1843, both in BCFMB; Middle Township Census of 1850; entry, 27 October 1812, Miscellaneous Book A, Liber of Deeds C, CMCCA; Rumy, in M. Catherine Stauffer, "The First Baptist Church of Cape May County," *CMCMHG* 3 (1952): 188.

31. Record of Manumissions, Miscellaneous Book A Liber of Deeds C, CMCCA; Clement Alexander Price, ed., *Freedom Not Far Distant: A Documentary History of Afro-Americans in New Jersey* (Newark: New Jersey Historical Society, 1980), 73–75, 79.

32. Upper Township Census, 1860, CMCCA; NJA, *Calendar of Wills,* 13:109; freeholder meeting, 27 May 1834, BCFMB.

33. "Negro Slavery and Settlers" file, CMCHS; William J. Moore, "Early Negro Settlers of Cape May County," *CMCMHG* 4 (1955): 20–22; Hughes to Armer, 4 June 1831, Deed Book O, 367, CMCCA; Hughes to Turner, 14 September 1847, Deed Book W, 160–161, CMCCA; "Jarena Lee," in Joan N. Burstyn, ed., *Past and Promise: Lives of New Jersey Women* (Metuchen, N.J.: Scarecrow Press, 1990), 77–79.

34. For African-American intermarriage, see Stanley Craig and Julius Way, *Cape May County Marriage Records* (Merchantville, N.J.: H. Stanley Craig, 1931); a survey of grave markers in Tabernacle Cemetery and Mt. Zion Cemetery also helped to reconstruct African American community intermarriage; F. W. Beers, *Topographical Map of Cape May Co. New Jersey from Recent and Actual Surveys* (New York: Beers, Comstock & Cline, 1872), shows Mt. Zion chapel location, Map File, CMCL.

35. Lower Township Tax List, 8 November 1842, CMCCA; Lower Township Census of 1850, CMCCA.

36. Lower Township Census of 1850, CMCCA; Moore, "Early Negro Settlers," 21; Craig and Way, *Cape May Records;* Price, *Freedom Not Far,* 92.

37. "Negro Slavery and Settlers" file, CMCHS; Middle Township Census of 1850, CMCCA; Tomlin, *Cape May Spray,* 9. Sarah Hand to Abel Cox, April 28, 1819, Deed Book K, 493–494, CMCCA.

38. Entries, 14 April, 14 July, 2 August 1832, all in part of a Record Book, 1831–1834, no cover but most surely Nathaniel Holmes Record Book, in a file with Jeremiah Leaming's Dennis Creek Meadow Company Day Book, CMCHS.

39. See Dennis Creek Meadow Company Day Book, 1815–1823, CMCHS.

40. Freeholder meetings, 20 March 1826, 16 January 1817, both in P. Leaming Day Book, CMCHS; entry, 18 November 1818, Road Book B, CMCCA; meetings 25 September 1830, 25 April 1831, both in BCFMB.

41. Dr. Thomas Rolph's observations in Oral S. Coad, *New Jersey in Traveler's Accounts, 1524–1971: A Descriptive Bibliography* (Metuchen, N.J.: Scarecrow Press, 1972), 103; freeholder meetings, 8 August 1825, 20

March 1826, P. Leaming Day Book, CMCHS; meeting 8 May 1833, both in BCFMB.

42. See Thomas L. Purvis, *Proprietors, Patronage, and Paper Money: Legislative Politics in New Jersey, 1703–1776* (New Brunswick, N.J.: Rutgers University Press, 1986), 181–82.

43. Freeholder meetings, 14 July 1827, 25 July 1828, 19 March 1831, all in BCFMB; entries, 1831, [Nathaniel Holmes] Record Book, 1831–1834, CMCHS.

44. Freeholder meeting, 9 May 1832, BCFMB; Road to Ludlam's "Big House," 25 June 1833, Road Book B, CMCCA; Alexander, *Cape Island,* 27–34.

45. Freeholder meetings, 14 and 24 May 1845, 7 and 26 August 1844, 27 May 1845, all in BCFMB.

46. Freeholder meetings, 31 May 1845, 2 June 1846, 7 December 1847, all in BCFMB.

47. Thomas Fleming, *New Jersey: A Bicentennial History* (New York: W. W. Norton, 1977), 94–95; Herbert Ershkowitz, *The Origin of the Whig and Democratic Parties: New Jersey Politics, 1820–1837* (Washington, D.C.: University Press of America, 1982), 15; Horace E. Wood II, "John Wiley, M.D.," *CMCMHG* 4 (1955): 2–5.

48. John Wiley, "To the Independent Voters of Cape May," handbill, CMCHS; Wiley was probably the single most effective political organizer in nineteenth-century Cape May County, forming both the local Whig and later the Republican party organizations. New Jersey Whig leader J. Wilson, wrote Wiley after the election victory of 1846 that "all parts of the State have done well, yet none better than Cape May—and among the leading Whigs those you have yourself borne a most useful and honorable part" (Wilson to Wiley, 14 November 1846, Wiley Letters, CMCHS.

49. C. E. Godfrey, "When Cape May Court House Was Made the County Seat," *CMCMHG* 2 (1939): 3–24; freeholder meeting, 10 May 1848, BCFMB; Cape May County voted 115 to 14 for the constitution of 1844 (*Proceedings of the New Jersey State Constitutional Convention of 1844* [Trenton, New Jersey State House Commission, 1942], 636).

50. Freeholder meetings, 13 May 1848, 6 June 1848, 7 May 1850, BCFMB.

51. Freeholder meeting, 10 June 1851, BCFMB.

52. Borough meetings, 2, 23 May 1848, Cape Island Record Book, 1848–1885 CMCHS.

53. Entry, 27 July 1844, Mackey, *A Gentleman of Much Promise,* 2: 462–463; Robert C. Alexander, "Frederika Bremer at Cape Island in 1850," CMGS, *Bulletin* (1965): 2:4–11; Alexander, *Cape Island,* 65–67; James Matlack Scovel, "The 'Blue Pig', Summer 1902," *Star and Wave,* 23 June 1932; Albert Hand, *A Book of Cape May, New Jersey* (Cape May: Albert Hand

Co., 1937), 70 (Hand's staff probably wrote the book, but Hand is cited in this study as the author).

54. Cape May County Census of 1850, CMCCA; freeholder meeting, 11 May 1849, BCFMB.

Chapter 5. The Railroad and the Civil War

1. Charles Elmer to Richard C. Holmes, 20 May 1859, Holmes Family Papers, CMCHS; Thomas Fleming, *New Jersey: A Bicentennial History* (New York: W. W. Norton, 1977), 103–107.

2. Sarah W. R. Ewing and Robert McMullin, *Along Absecon Creek: A History of Early Absecon, New Jersey* (Bridgeton, N.J.: privately published, 1965), 136–139; Charles E. Funnell, *by the Beautiful Sea: The Rise and High Times of That Great American Resort, Atlantic City* (New York: Alfred A. Knopf, 1975), 3.

3. Articles of incorporation of Cape May County Banks, 1851–1853, in Miscellaneous Book B, 159, 167, 201–202, 212–214, CMCCA; Cape May County merchants reliance on Cumberland Bank, see entry, 1 November 1833, Silas Church Account Book, 1796–c.1833, CMCHS.

4. Thos. Cushing and Charles E. Sheppard, *History of the Counties of Gloucester, Salem, and Cumberland, New Jersey* (Philadelphia: Everts Peck, 1883), 592, 627–628, 674; the Cape May County Board of Freeholders consulted the Nixon and Elmer law firm of Bridgeton over lawsuits against Joseph Higbee and Daniel Hughes, Lower Township businessmen, for destroying a county bridge (freeholder meeting, 11 January 1860, BCFMB); Elmer to Holmes, 20 May 1859, Holmes to W. G. Nixon, n.d., Holmes Papers, CMCHS; Elmer properties in Coleman F. Leaming Draft Book, CMCHS; cranberry bog in Aaron Leaming to Daniel Elmer, 13 February 1759, Leaming Papers, RUL.

5. Whilldin to Holmes, 28 May 1857, Holmes Papers, CMCHS; [Wilmon Whilldin], "To the People of Cape May County, NJ," n.d. (c. 1857), pamphlets, RUL.

6. Henry Swain to Richard C. Holmes, 15 April 185[7], Wheaton to Holmes, 19 March 1857, Holmes Papers, CMCHS; "The Shunpike," *CMCMHG* 7 (1975): 215.

7. Entries, 21 March, 19 June 1857, Journal of Minutes of the "Cape May Turnpike Company," 1854–1865, CMCHS; John Wheaton, 19 March 1857, Wiley to Holmes, April 1858, Holmes Papers, CMCHS Gentry in Cape May County Census, 1860, CMCCA.

8. The Turnpike Company collected $1,016 in tolls and expended $1,600 in repairs, in 1859 ("Annual Statement, November 5, 1859," *Ocean*

Wave, 29 December 1859); meeting, 6 November 1858, Turnpike Company Journal, CMCHS; Report of the Engineer, Camden and Cape Island Railroad, 1 November 1852, CMCHS.

9. Report of the Engineer, 1852, CMCHS.

10. Elmer to Holmes, 20 May 1850, [Ware, Wales, or Wiley?] to Holmes, 25 December 1853, Holmes Papers, CMCHS; Funnell, *By the Sea,* 139.

11. Isaac Townsend to his son, William S. Townsend, 5 December 1851, Townsend Family Papers, CMCHS; [Ware, Wales, or Wiley?] to Holmes, 25 December 1853, Holmes Papers, CMCHS; for glass industry problems, see Cushing and Sheppard, *Gloucester, Salem, and Cumberland,* 716.

12. William Baird to Richard C. Holmes, c. 1857–1859, Holmes Papers, CMCHS; for rival syndicates, see *Ocean Wave,* 23 February, 5 April 1860.

13. *Ocean Wave,* 14 May 1857, 29 March 1860; probably the oldest copy of the newspaper can be found in the Cape May County Clerk's Office safe vault; for R. D. Wood, see Cushing and Sheppard, *Gloucester, Salem and Cumberland,* 643–644.

14. *Compendium of Charters of the West Jersey Railroad and other Railroads in West Jersey, South of Camden,* [1869], pamphlet, Gloucester County Historical Society, Woodbury, New Jersey.

15. Lewis Townsend Stevens, *The History of Cape May County, New Jersey, From the Aboriginal Times to the Present Day* (Cape May City: Lewis T. Stevens, publisher, 1897), 299–300, 289–290; Coleman F. Leaming Survey and Letterbook, CMCHS.

16. *Ocean Wave,* 1 December 1859, 15 November 1860, 5 January 1861.

17. Entry, 10 March 1862, Henry Swain diary, CMCHS; *Ocean Wave,* 15 December 1859, 5 January 1861.

18. "Washington friend" to Holmes, 3 December 1860, Holmes Papers, CMCHS.

19. Richard C. Holmes to Judge Holmes, 20 June 1857, Holmes Papers; freeholder meetings, 10 May 1854, 22 November 1858, BCFMB.

20. Albert Hand, et al. *A Book of Cape May New Jersey,* (Cape May: Albert Hand, 1937), 65; *Ocean Wave,* 4 June 1857, 2 May 1861.

21. Cape May County Census, 1860, CMCCA.

22. H. H. White, "The Old and New in Cape May County Agriculture," *CMCMHG* 3 (1952): 193–198; H. C. Woolman, T. F. Rose, and T. T. Price, *Historical and Biographical Atlas of the New Jersey Coast* (Philadelphia: Woolman and Rose, 1878; Ocean County Historical Society reprint, 1985), 10–12; Maurice Beesley, "Sketch of the Early History of the County of Cape May," in George H. Cook, *Geology of the County of Cape May* (Trenton: Office of the True American, 1857), 198.

23. List of mills in Cape May Census of 1860, CMCCA; see Charles S. Hartman, "Cape May County Mills," *South Jersey Magazine* (Winter 1984):

15–21; Roy Hand, "Mills of East and West Creek," *CMCMHG* 4 (1957): 117–123, and 5 (1961): 273–295; Roland Ellis, "Windmills," *CMCMHG* 4 (1959): 191–201; Marian C. Robertson, "Steelman Family," Steelman File, Post Collection, CMCHS.

24. Margaret A. Folger, "The Story of the Marshalls and Their Town of Marshallville," *CMCMHG* 7 (1973): 44–48; Richard V. Anderson, "Goshen Shipbuilding," *CMCMHG* 4 (1956): 47–51; Stevens, *Cape May County History*, 229–232.

25. Hannah K. Swain, "The Country Stores of Cape May County," *CMCMHG* 7 (1977): 451–459 John Townsend General Store Day Book, "Dennistown," 1822–1823, CMCCA; Hand Day Books, John Gandy Day Book, 1842–1846, Ocean View-Gandyville Country Store Day Books, CMCHS; *Ocean Wave*, 16 May 1861.

26. List of milliners in Cape May County Census, 1860, CMCCA; price quoted in *Ocean Wave*, 8 May 1862.

27. *Star of the Cape*, 17 April 1897; Frances D. Benckert, "A Little Look at Old Cape May," *CMCMHG* 7 (1973): 4.

28. Eleven Methodist, five Baptist, two Presbyterian, and one Catholic church listed in Cape May County Census, 1860, CMCCA; Walter Measday, "Our Lady Star of the Sea Church Cape May," *CMCMHG* 7 (1977): 425–432; James and Martha Ludlam to trustees Methodist Meeting House, Dennis Creek, 17 July 1802, Deed Book B: 344–347; J. W. Presby, "Tabernacle M. E. Church," *CMCMHG* 2 (1944): 258–273 and 2 (1945): 294–313; A. Atwood, "History of Methodism in Cape Island," *CMCMHG* 1 (1935): 199–221; Joyce Van Vorst, *Cedar Swamp Creek* (Cape May: Cape May County Historical and Genealogical Society, 1977), 63–67; Bethel M. E. Church, Green Creek, 15 February 1850, First M. E. Church, Cape Island, 8 April 1843, Mt. Zion M. E. Church, all in Miscellaneous Book B: 20, 123, 316; Wendeline Moore, "Recollections of Old Swainton," *CMCMHG* 8 (1981): 44.

29. Alwina D. Bailey, "The Restoration of the Friendship School, Palermo," *CMCMHG* 8 (1985): 376–380; see William Garrison Hunter II, "A History of Education in Dennis Township" (M.A. thesis, Glassboro State College, 1965), VF, CMCL; R. Cordelia Taylor, "History of Education in Lower Township," *CMCMHG* 5 (1963):389–408.

30. J. R. Wilson, "Old Time School Conditions," *CMCMHG* 8 (1985): 381–383; Reuben Willets Journal, 1852, CMCHS; Albert Matthews, "Autobiography of Rev. A. Mathews," *CMCMHG* 6 (1972): 544–546.

31. Census of Cape Island, 1860, CMCCA.

32. George E. Thomas and Carl Doebley, *Cape May: Queen of the Seaside Resorts* (Philadelphia: Art Alliance Press, 1976), 19–20, 50; Robert C. Alexander, "Cape Island, New Jersey," *CMCMHG* 6 (1968): 289–298, and *Ho! For Cape Island* (Cape May: privately printed, 1956), 121–129; Stevens, *Cape May County History*, 272–276, 284. Henry Clay visited in 1847

and President Franklin Pierce in 1855; Lincoln reputedly visited in 1849, but his correspondence suggests that he never visited Cape May County. Presidents Grant and Benjamin Harrison visited the county after the Civil War.

33. *Ocean Wave,* 26 July 1860; Alexander, *Cape Island,* 117–118, 124.

34. *Ocean Wave,* 17 May 1860; Stevens, *Cape May County History,* 284–287; Craig C. Mathewson, Jr., "Joseph S. Leach—Public Servant and Citizen Extraordinary," *CMCMHG* 7 (1974): 67–73.

35. Mathewson, "Joseph S. Leach," 67–69; *Ocean Wave,* 23 May 1861.

36. *Ocean Wave,* 16, quote 23, 30 May, 11 June 1861, 19, 27 April 1861.

37. *Ocean Wave,* 17 October 1861; Stevens, *Cape May County History,* 301–343.

38. Horace E. Wood II, "John Wiley, M.D.," *CMCMHG* 4 (1955): 2–5; Stevens, *Cape May County History,* 316–324; Earl Schenck Miers, ed., *New Jersey and the Civil War: An Album of Contemporary Accounts* (Princeton: D. Van Nostrand, 1964), 93–100; Tomlin obituary in *Cape May Wave,* 4 November 1905.

39. Emily Clark, "The Wheaton Brothers," *CMCMHG* 8 (1983): 182; "History of the 25th New Jersey Volunteers," *CMCMHG* 7 (1974): 92–125; freeholder meeting, 11 June 1862, BCFMB; entry, 1 September 1862, Amelia Hand diary, CMCHS; Cresse to Post, 1 July 1932, Mary Thompson Cresse-Edward Post Correspondence, CMCHS.

40. *Ocean Wave,* 14 July, 18 August 1862; Reports on Soldiers, CMCCA. The local enrollment board rejected 86.5 percent of the draftees and volunteers from Middle Township, 76.9 percent from Dennis Township, and 84.6 percent for Lower Township and Cape Island.

41. Entry, 18 December 1862, Amelia Hand diary, CMCHS; Richard Thompson to Richard Townsend, 4 July 1863, Townsend Family Papers, CMCHS.

42. Entries for 1863, Amelia Hand diary, CMCHS; *Ocean Wave,* 17 October 1861, 17 September 1863.

43. Albert H. Ludlam to Richard Leaming, 27 March 1862, Ephraim Sayre to Richard Leaming, 28 March 1862, Leaming Papers, GSCL.

44. *Ocean Wave,* 19 April 1865; entries 26 August, 27 October 1863, January–June 1864, April 1865, Amelia Hand diary, CMCHS.

45. Cresse to Post, 18 May 1837, Cresse-Post Correspondence, CMCHS; entry, 1865, Amelia Hand diary, CMCHS; *Ocean Wave,* 19 April 1865; see also Harold Fisher Wilson, *The Jersey Shore: A Social and Economic History of the Counties of Atlantic, Cape May, Monmouth, and Ocean* (New York: Lewis Historical Publishing Co., 1953), 2:674.

46. The committee to condemn President Johnson was made up of Thomas Williams of Upper Township, Maurice Beesley of Dennis Township, Alexander Young of Middle Township, Downs Edmunds of Lower Township, and W. W. Ware of Cape Island (*Ocean Wave,* 31 October 1866).

47. Entry, 9 November 1868, Amelia Hand diary, CMCHS; entries, 26, 30 October 1868, F. Sidney Townsend daily journal, CMCHS.

48. *Star of the Cape,* 28 May 1873; freeholder meeting 18 September 1874, BCFMB.

49. *Ocean Wave,* 17 September 1863.

50. George F. Boyer and J. Pearson Cunningham, *Cape May County Story* (Egg Harbor City, N.J.: Laureate Press, 1975), 65; Hand, "Mills," 4: 213.

51. See *Beers Map,* 1872, Map File, CMCL; J. Fleming Van Rensselaer, map of Woodbine, advertisement, CMCHS.

52. Karen Collins Swain, "Highlights of the History of South Seaville," typescript, Dennis Township file, VF, CMCL. Another railroad stop was founded c. 1863 just below South Seaville station on lands donated by the Swain family; hence the station was called Swainton.

53. Cape May County Census of 1870, CMCCA; see also Wilson, *Jersey Shore,* 2:679–682.

54. Glass Company, 1 July 1865, Miscellaneous Book B, 377–378, CMCCA; *Star of the Cape,* 17 April 1878.

55. *Ocean Wave,* 19 April 1865; Cape May Provision Co., 1 November 1871, Miscellaneous Book B, 514.

56. Alonzo Bacon and Edward Post, "Vessels that Have been Built in Cape May County," *CMCMHG* 1 (1937): 289–293; David T. Shannon, "The Wreck of the *Mair and Cranmer,* March 31, 1887," *CMCMHG* 8 (1985): 361–369; James M. McLaughlin, "Maritime History of Cape May County: Part II, Shipbuilding and Trade in the County," *CMCMHG* 7 (1980): 650–662. Joseph R. Wilson, "A Lost Industry: Reminiscence of Ship Building and Builders in Cape May County," in *Cape May County Gazette,* 8 March 1912; *Star of the Cape,* 28 May 1873.

57. Launching of *William E. Lee* in *Star of the Cape,* 7 March 1877, and *Ocean Wave,* 3 March 1877; freeholder meeting, 18 September 1874, BCFMB.

58. *Star of the Cape,* 21 May 1873, announced Beesley's crab business in Goshen; Ingham and Beesley Cancerine in Cape May County Census of 1870, CMCCA; Robert C. Alexander, "Shingle Miners," *CMCMHG* 4 (1957): 99–104; C. F. Leaming to R. S. Leaming, 6 November 1865, Leaming Papers, GSCL.

59. *Ocean Wave,* 26 July 1865.

60. West Jersey Railroad Company takeover and merger with Cape May and Millville Railroad Company, 16 May 1868, 12 November 1869, Miscellaneous Book B, 462–464; Hand, *Book of Cape May,* 86–105; *Star of the Cape,* 7 March 1877; also see "The Cape Island Trolleys," *Star and Wave,* 9 May 1963.

61. Hand, *Book of Cape May,* 89–107; Thomas and Doebley, *Cape May,* 52–61; Cape May Saving Fund and Building Association, 21 February 1867, Cooperative Building Association of Cape May County, 13 November

1869, Miscellaneous Book B, 406, 465, CMCCA; H. C. Woolman, T. F. Rose, and T. T. Price, *Historical and Biographical Atlas of the New Jersey Coast* (Philadelphia: Woolman and Rose, 1878), 97–98.

62. *Ocean Wave,* 26 July 1865.

63. *Ocean Wave,* 31 October 1866.

64. Robert C. Alexander, "A Picnic at Diamond Beach," CMGS, *9th Annual Bulletin* (1955): 6–10; Hand, *Book of Cape May,* 88–89, 96–98; Diamond Beach Park and Hotel Association, 7 January 1867, 13 April 1868, Deed Book 33, 350, and Deed Book 34, 43–47.

65. Cape May & Millville Railroad Company Report, 1865, in *Ocean Wave,* 18 April 1866; freeholder meeting, 13 June 1867, BCFMB.

66. Freeholder meeting, 14 April 1877, also 27 January, 20 April 1877, BCFMB; *Star of the Cape,* 23 August 1876, 14 November 1878; *Ocean Wave,* 16 November 1878; see also Thomas and Doebley, *Cape May,* 28, 31–32, 61–67.

67. *Star of the Cape,* 17 April 1878; see Stevens, *Cape May County History,* 354.

68. *Star of the Cape,* 29 August, 26 September 1878.

69. *Ocean Wave,* 18 April 1866; *Star of the Cape,* 21, 28 May 1873; freeholder meetings 25 August 1871, 13 May 1873, 11 May 1875, BCFMB.

70. Freeholder meetings, 5 April, 15 June 1871, 1 February 1872, 31 December 1873, BCFMB.

71. *Ocean Wave,* 19 April 1865, 31 January 1866; freeholder meeting, 7 May 1867, BCFMB; Rules of the Swaintown School, 1866, CMCHS; see also "Higher Education in the Cape Area," *Bayshore Star and Wave,* 12 June 1962; David J. Russo, *Families and Communities: A New View of American History* (Nashville, Tenn.: American Association for State and Local History, 1974), 207–209.

72. *Ocean Wave,* 31 January, April 18, 1866.

73. Whilldin deed to Sea Grove Association, 15 March 1875; See Grove Building Association, 30 December 1875; Union Hall Association, 27 November 1875, all in Miscellaneous Book C, 133–134, 143, 446–447; Edward S. Wheeler, *Scheyichbi and the Strand, or Early Days Along the Delaware with an Account of Recent Events at Sea Grove* (Philadelphia: J.B. Lippincott, 1876), 83–91; Thomas and Doebley, *Cape May,* 30–31; Stevens, *Cape May County History,* 364; see also *Cape May Herald Dispatch,* 29 October 1986; *Star of the Cape,* 14, 21 April, 30 June, 1 July 1875.

Chapter 6. Settlement of the Barrier Islands

1. Karl Dickinson, "Five Mile Beach," and George F. Boyer, "Brown Cows of Five Mile Beach," both in *CMCMHG* 6 (1971):495–499, 478–483,

respectively; *History of Stone Harbor* (pamphlet assembled by Stone Harbor school pupils, 1925–1926), 8, CMCL; Tatham in Gilbert S. Smith to J. M. Canfield, 27 March 1905, letter in Avalon file, VF, CMCL; Parker Miller in Bertram M. Darby, "Ocean City Story," part 2, *CMCMHG* 3 (1953):199–201; Darby, "Notes on History of Ocean City," OCHSM.

2. List of Cape May County lifesaving stations and lighthouses in Sumner Kimball (General Superintendent of U.S. Light House Service) to Francis Bazley Lee, 19 January 1892, F. B. Lee Papers, RUL; see also David J. Seibold and Charles J. Adams III, *Shipwrecks and Legends' round Cape May* (Wyomissing Hills, Pa.: D. J. Seibold, 1987).

3. Mary Townsend Rush, *Ocean City Guide Book and Directory, Ocean City, New Jersey, 1892* (Camden, N.J.: Gazette Printing House, 1892), 16; Lewis Townsend Stevens, *The History of Cape May County, New Jersey, from the Aboriginal Times to the Present Day* (Cape May City: Lewis T. Stevens, publisher, 1897), 446.

4. Rush, *Ocean City Guide Book, 1895:* 17–18; see Charles Funnell, *By the Beautiful Sea* (New York: Alfred A. Knopf, 1975), Thomas Fleming, *New Jersey: A Bicentennial History* (New York: W. W. Norton, 1977), 137–138, contends that the drive to escape the industrial city gave rise to New Jersey seashore resorts such as Long Branch in Monmouth County.

5. Association meetings, 20, 21, 27 October 1879, all in First Minute Books, Ocean City Association File, OCHSM; see also Darby, "Ocean City Story," parts 1–5, *CMCMHG* 3–6, (1953–1958).

6. Rush, *Ocean City Guide Book, 1895;* entry, February 1880, William Lake diary, 1879–1887, OCHSM; also quoted in Darby, "Ocean City Story," part 5, *CMCMHG* 4 (1958): 15.

7. Wood quoted in Darby, "Ocean City Story," part 7, *CMCMHG* 5 (1963): 443; Jesse Somers Deed to Parker Miller, 25 October 1873, Parker Miller Papers, OCHSM; Peck's Beach Land Company, 13 December 1881, and Peck's Beach Turnpike Company, 13 December 1881, both in Miscellaneous Book D, 151–154, CMCCA; see also Darby, "Notes."

8. *Star of the Cape,* 24 July 1897; see Rush, *Ocean City Guide Books, 1892–1895.*

9. Rush, *Ocean City Guide Book, 1894,* 27; Lake's death in Darby, "Ocean City Story," part 5, *CMCMHG* 4: 173; Ocean City Electric Railroad Company, 2 February 1893, Ocean City Electric Light and Heat Company, 26 January 1893, Ocean City Sewer Company, 1 June 1893, all in Corporation Book No. 1, 186–188, 182–183, 193–194.

10. Entry, 31 July 1878, Charles K. Landis diaries, VHS (hereafter Landis diaries); Thos. Cushing and Charles E. Sheppard, *History of the Counties of Gloucester, Salem, and Cumberland, New Jersey with Biographical Sketches of their Prominent Citizens* (Philadelphia: Everts Peck, 1883), 705.

11. Narrow gauge in *Cape May Wave,* 23 April, 30 May 1877;

Landis-Sewell meeting in *Star of the Cape,* 10 July 1879; entries 11, 18 May 1880, Landis diaries.

12. Entries, 25 February 1880, 29 August 1878, 2 November 1881, Landis diaries; Charles K. Landis, "Plan of Protection for Small Boats upon the Ocean front at Sea Isle City," with sketch, Charles K. Landis Papers, VHS.

13. Entries, 31 July 1878, 29 December 1879, 25, 26 February, 6 March, 6 May 1880, 13, 16 April 1880, Landis diaries.

14. Entries, 12 March, 11 May, 23 February, 3 August 1880, 29 December 1879, Landis diaries; see also H. Gerald McDonald, "A Brief History of Railroads on Ludlam's Beach," *CMCMHG* 8 (1982): 129–137.

15. Sea Isle City Improvement Company, 15 February 1881, Cape May Miscellaneous Book D, 113–114, 138–139; entry, 28 May 1880, Landis diaries; freeholder meeting, 8 June 1882, BCFMB; *Cape May Wave,* 1 April 1882; see also Walter M. Sawn, *Sea Isle City New Jersey: A History* (Sea Isle City, N.J.: Sea Isle City Tercentenary Committee, 1964), 14.

16. Entries, 27 September, 10, 19 October, 11 November 1882, Landis diaries.

17. Entries, 10 December, 5, 13 November 1882, Landis diaries; Matilda Landis to John Burk, 7 April 1881, Landis Papers; Holly Beach Improvement Company, 12 April 1882, Miscellaneous Book D, 166–169, CMCCA; Burk folder, Map file, WHS.

18. Cecil T. Ober's testimony, *William Goldstein* v. *Holly Beach City Improvement Company,* 20 May 1926, Law and Court Cases file, WHS; Eloise Bright to Glenn W. Dye (*Wildwood News*), 9 July 1975, Eloise Bright Papers, WHS; Measy Resolution in freeholder meeting, 18 June 1885, BCFMB.

19. Eloise Bright to John P. Sparrow (editor, *Wildwood News*), 13 June 1975, Bright Papers; Horace Richardson testimony, Law and Court Cases file, WHS; see George Boyer, "Five Mile Beach Newspapers," *CMCMHG* 7 (1974): 55–57; Boyer, *Wildwood: Middle of the Island* (Egg Harbor City, N.J.: Laureate Press, 1976), 3–25; Boyer, "Jeanette DuBois Meech of Holly Beach," *CMCMHG* 6 (1969): 393–398.

20. Apparently a group of Philadelphia and Brooklyn, New York, investors founded the Hereford Island Company, 10 December 1878, to develop the area (Miscellaneous Book C, 415–416, CMCCA); Frederick E. Swope, James H. Lafferty, and Dr. William L. Robinson of Philadelphia organized the Five Mile Beach Improvement Company, 22 August 1879 (Miscellaneous Book C, 446–447, CMCCA); Anglesea Land Company, 1 February 1882, Miscellaneous Book D, 161–163, CMCCA.

21. H. Gerald MacDonald, "History of Railroads on Five Mile Beach," part 1, *CMCMHG* 7 (1975): 202–214; Eleanor Gross, "The Shivers Family on Five Mile Beach," *CMCMHG* 9 (1987): 1–3; Dr. Julius Way, "Medical Men of Early Times in Cape May County," *CMCMHG* 1 (1935): 190–191; *Cape May*

County Gazette, 15 September 1883; for J. J. Burleigh see Jeffery M. Dorwart and Philip English Mackey, *Camden County, New Jersey 1616–1976: A Narrative History* (Camden N.J.: Camden County Cultural & Heritage Commission, 1976), 70–71, 73–74, 79–81.

22. Boyer, *Wildwood,* 16–17; "Florida City," in *Wave,* 26 July 1884; *Star of the Cape,* quote 15 May 1891, 23 August 1890; see also Boyer, "Philip Pontius Baker," *CMCMHG* 6 (1972): 614–616.

23. Seven Mile Beach Company, 1 April 1887, Avalon Beach Improvement Company, 6 August 1888, Avalon Beach Hotel Company, March 1889, Peermont Land Company, 22 October 1894, all in Corporation Book No. 1, 57–59, 90–91, 106–107, 222, CMCCA. See also Gilbert Smith, "My First Experience in Avalon," *CMCMHG* 7 (1978): 482–486; Peermont founding in Gilbert S. Smith (mayor of Avalon) to J. M. Canfield (president Avalon Improvement Company), 27 March 1905, letter in Avalon file, VF, CMCL.

24. *Star of the Cape,* 30 May 1890; entries, 4 February, 3 May 1888, F. Sidney Townsend diaries, CMCHS; Smith, "My First Experience in Avalon"; *Wave,* 30 May 1891. The railroad and bridge work to Avalon resulted in ethnic violence and antiforeign commentary by the *Cape May Daily Wave,* 18 October 1888, which noted "the party of Dagoes working on the road or bridge got into an altercation and soon began fighting furiously, as only Italians can."

25. Cape May County Census, 1895, microfilm, CMCL; *Star of the Cape,* 9 October 1891, 12 September 1890, for pounds of fish shipped from Anglesea on the West Jersey Railroad; recollections of Anglesea in 1890, Coleberg folder, biographical files, WHS; George F. Boyer, "Gustave Anderson: Pioneer Swede," *CMCMHG* 6 (1971): 503–505.

26. Cape May County Census, 1895; John Burk to John Vance, 29 August 1885, Bullitt to John Vance, 3 January 1882, Deed Book 70, 399–401; John M. Vance was elected constable in Holly Beach in 1889, possibly the first African-American elected official in Cape May County (John M. Vance folder, biographical files, WHS); Mt. Pisgah Church trustees in 1883 included Joseph Vance, Mark Williams, Henry Wilkins, Lewis Major, and William White (22 May 1883, Corporation Book No. 1, 1); *Cape May Wave,* 9 May 1891.

27. See Samuel Joseph, *History of the Baron DeHirsch Fund* (New York: Baron de Hirsch Fund, 1935).

28. Olive S. Barry, "Woodbine, New Jersey: Land Use and Social History" (undergraduate paper, Stockton State College, 1975), 4, Woodbine file, VF, CMCL; Rensselaer's Woodbine Map, CMCHS; entry, 5 March 1891, Landis diaries. Sulzberger (called Mayer Sulzbach in Landis's diaries) was one of the seven major stockholders in the Organization of the Jewish Agricultural Aid Society, which cooperated with the Baron de Hirsch Fund and Jewish Colonization Association in Cape May County (17 November 1892, Corporation

Book No. 1, 177–179). See also Joseph Brandes, *Immigrants to Freedom: Jewish Communities in Rural New Jersey Since 1882* (Philadelphia: University of Pennsylvania Press, 1971).

29. Barry, "Woodbine," 8–11; Leo Shpall, ed., "Korolenko's Letters on the Woodbine Colony," *PNJHS* 83 (April 1965): 93–106, quote 97; Katharine Sabsovich, *Adventures in Idealism: A Personal Record of the Life of Professor Sabsovich* (New York: Arno Press, 1975; reprint of 1922 edition), 21–28. Jacob Feldman, Hirsh L. Sabsovich, and Herman Rosenfeld organized the Woodbine Brotherhood (7 December 1893, Corporation Book No. 1, 204–205).

30. Dennis Township attitude toward Woodbine, *Star of the Cape,* 9 October 1891, and Sabsovich, *Adventures in Idealism,* 77–80, 134; Kotinsky and Lipman at Rutgers Agricultural College, *Cape May Wave,* 5 January 1895; Census of the "Russian Jewish Community" at Woodbine, 1895, New Jersey State Census, 1895; see also Barry, "Woodbine"; Lipman obituary, *Cape May County Gazette,* 5 July 1951.

31. Woodbine Manufacturing Company, 26 March 1894, Corporation Book No. 1, 209–211.

32. Lake Manufacturing Company, 20 January 1885, Corporation Book No. 1, 25; see also Darby, "Ocean City Story," part 7, 432–433; Roy Hand, "Mills of East and West Creek," *CMCMHG* 4: 126, 294; Recollections of D. W. Dawson, typescript, Dennis Township file, VF, CMCL; Springer Manufacturing Company, 6 June 1893, Eldora Paper Company, 14 April 1894, both in Corporation Book No. 1, 195–197, 216.

33. John D. Christine, "West Cape May Gold Beaters," *CMCMHG* 8 (1984): 264–267; William J. Moore, "The Goldbeating Industry in West Cape May," *CMCMHG* 4 (1957): 105–106.

34. Rio Grande Sugar Company, 29 November 1881, Miscellaneous Book D, 149–151; the sugar company owned twenty tracts of land totaling 1,965½ acres (11 August 1890, Deed Book 93, 406–426, CMCCA); *Cape May County Gazette,* 15 September 1883, for sugar cane harvest; entry 13 November 1882, Landis diaries; Harold J. Abrahams, "The Sorghum Sugar Experiment at Rio Grande," *PNJHS* 83 (April 1965): 118–136; John D. Christine, "South Jersey Sugar," *South Jersey Magazine* (Summer 1983): 6–11.

35. *Cape May County Gazette,* 21 October 1882; *Star of the Cape,* 15 May 1891; "The Gatzmer House," *CMCMHG* 7 (1976):275; see Alonzo Bacon and Edward M. Post, "Vessels That Have Been Built in Cape May County," *CMCMHG* 1 (1937): 289–293.

36. *Star of the Cape,* 15 May 1891; Bacon and Post, "Vessels," 289–293.

37. Entry, 18 February 1891, Landis diaries; *Star of the Cape,* 16 June 1893, quote 2 March 1894.

38. George E. Thomas and Carl Doebley, *Cape May, Queen of the Seaside Resorts* (Philadelphia: The Art Alliance Press, 1976), 33–34, 62–63.

39. Delaware Bay and Cape May Railroad Map, 1879, N. C. Price Survey Book, CMCCA; Cape May and Sewell Point Railroad, 10 March 1882, East Cape May Beach Company, 26 February 1883, both in Miscellaneous Book D, 163–164, 176–177, CMCCA; *Cape May Wave,* 28 June 1879; see also Howard Carrow, comp., *Charters and Ordinances, and Decisions & Relating to the Cape May, Delaware Bay and Sewell's Point Railroad Co.* (1901), pamphlet, RUL.

40. Neptune Land Company, 9 October 1882, Miscellaneous Book D, 173–174; Robert C. Alexander, "Light of Asia," *CMCMHG* 9 (1990): 288–292; Light of Asia blueprints, CMCHS; Hand, *Book of Cape May,* 115–116; *Cape May Wave,* 11 July 1896; "Borough of South Cape May," typescript, South Cape May File, VF, CMCL.

41. West Cape May Improvement Company, 21 May 1884, Corporation Book No. 1, 16–17; Stevens, *Cape May County History,* 404; Edmunds's traction interests in *Cape May Herald,* 16 March 1901; Edmunds's feud with Republican city council in *Wave* v. *Star* editorial war and in Lewis T. Stevens diaries, 1888–1894, in the possession of Mary Ann Stevens Nyblade, Cape May City; Cape May Driving Park Co., 11 May 1887, Deed Book 76, 464, CMCCA; Edwin V. Machette's Cape May Driving Park Company, 14 September 1887, Deed Book 78, 41, CMCCA.

42. *Cape May Wave,* 26 July 1881; entries, 28 July, 1, 7, 11 August 1888, all in F. Sidney Townsend diaries, CMCHS; for a comparison of racetrack politics surrounding the growth of Long Branch, Monmouth County, as an oceanfront resort, see Harold Fisher Wilson, *The Jersey Shore: A Social and Economic History of the Counties of Atlantic, Cape May, Monmouth, and Ocean* (New York: Lewis Historical Publishing Co., 1953), 1: 561, 566–567.

43. Entry 22 June 1889, F. Sidney Townsend diaries; *Star,* 22 August, 5 September 1890, 5 July 1892; John Edgar Reyburn obituary, *Star and Wave,* 17 January 1914. See also "Big League Baseball Training in Cape May," *Star and Wave,* 26 March 1964, for an account of the Philadelphia Phillies spring training camp in Cape May City, March–April, 1898.

44. Cape May Driving Park at sheriff's sale, 1888, Deed Book 83, 55, CMCCA; *Cape May Wave,* 23 May 1891; *Star of the Cape,* 20 June 1890; Thomas and Doebley, *Cape May,* 35–36.

45. Entries, 11, 12 March 1889, F. Sidney Townsend diaries; *Wave,* 23 October 1897; *Star of the Cape,* 30 October 1897; Alfred Cooper, *My Traditions and Memories, 1859–1938* (Cape May Court House, N.J.: Gazette Print Shop, 1938), portrayed Robert Hand as a ruthless political boss; Sewell's extensive personal intervention in Cape May County politics in Sewell to R. S. Leaming, 30 July, 8 November 1894, Richard S. Leaming file, 1826–1895, Leaming Papers, GSCL; see also William E. Sackett, *Modern Battles of Trenton from Werts to Wilson* (New York: Neale Publishing, 1914), 2: 19–20.

46. Entries, 14, 16 June 1889, 30 August 1890, F. Sidney Townsend diaries; *Star,* 30 May 1890, 22 May 1891, quote 14 July 1893; local reporters such as Lewis T. Stevens hounded the Harrisons for interviews (entry, 14 June 1889, Stevens diary); President Grant's impact on Long Branch in Fleming, *New Jersey,* 139–141.

47. *Star of the Cape,* 31 August 1894; *Cape May Wave,* 12 January 1895; Morris Bernheim to J. B. Weber, 20 February 1894, Bernheim to Isaac, 20 February 1894, both in Woodbine Hotel Correspondence, CMCHS; North Highland Land and Improvement Company, 18 September 1890, Corporation Book No. 1, 126; Highland City-on-the-Bay, Map, 1890, N.C. Price Survey Book, CMCCA; railroad violence in Cooper, *Traditions and Memories,* 159–161.

48. *Cape May Wave,* 12 January 1895; *Star of the Cape,* 21 December, 26 October 1894; see also Lower Township Ledger, Overseer of the Poor, Account Book for Relief of Poor, 1883–1886, CMCHS.

49. *Cape May Wave,* 22 July 1893; *Star of the Cape,* 26 October, 9 November 1894, Populist candidates Townsend and Van Gilder won 41 and 44 votes respectively in Dennis Township.

50. *Cape May Wave,* 18 July 1896; *Star of the Cape,* 24 July 1897; what became the Reading Seashore Railroad line in Cape May County opened in 1894 and operated until its merger with the Pennsylvania Railroad in 1933 ("A 2nd Railroad for the Cape," *Star and Wave,* 28 November 1963); bicycle racetrack in *Cape May County Gazette,* 10 May 1895.

51. Cooper, *Traditions and Memories,* 141–142; *Cape May Wave,* 9 October 1897.

52. *Daily Star,* 8 November 1895, 27 March 1897; entry, 20 February 1894, Stevens diary; see also entry, 11 March 1890, F. Sidney Townsend diaries; Stevens, *Cape May County History,* 389.

53. Entry, 11 March 1890, quote 20 March 1888, F. Sidney Townsend diaries; Stevens, *Cape May County History,* 397; *Star of the Cape,* 19 September, 21 December 1894.

54. Indictment for murder, 25 April 1894, Trial minutes, May 8–9, 1894, Appointment of Jury to Witness Execution of Richard Pierce, 9 May 1894, Cape May County Oyer and Terminer Court Records, CMCCA; Pierce was executed in an enclosed yard next to the Cape May County court house on 13 July 1894 (Cooper, *Traditions and Memories,* 178–179).

55. *Star of the Cape,* 17, 24 July 1897; possibly the International Telephone Company of Philadelphia established a Cape May City line in 1894 (*Star of the Cape,* 13 July 1894).

56. *Star of the Cape,* 1 November, 25 December 1897; *Cape May Wave,* 25 December 1897.

57. *Star of the Cape,* 23, 28 April, 7 May 1898.

58. *Star of the Cape,* 17 April 1897; Douglass Glass Company, 1 Decem-

ber 1896, Corporation Book No. 1, 270–271; "Citizen's Local Telephone Company," *CMCMHG* 7 (1976): 300–301.

59. Board of Trade, 24 March 1897, Corporation Book No. 1, 284.

Chapter 7. Progress and World War

1. *Cape May Wave,* 5 January 1901; *Star of the Cape,* 5 January 1901.

2. *Star of the Cape,* 5 January 1901; "Queen Anne's Connection," CMGS, *Magazine* (1964): 7–13.

3. *Star of the Cape,* 9 June 1900; *Cape May Herald,* 19 October 1901. The third newspaper in the city actually was the short-lived *Cape May Buzz,* published in 1886 by L. T. Stevens.

4. *Star of the Cape,* 23 March, 18 May, 24 August 1901; *Cape May Herald,* 5 October 1901; *Cape May Wave,* 24 August 1901; freeholder meeting, 21 August 1902, BCFMB.

5. *Star of the Cape,* 9 March, 23 November 1901, 3 May 1902, 9 March 1903; *Cape May Herald,* 16 March, 13 April, 19 October 1901, 31 January 1903; *Cape May Wave,* 3 May 1902, 7 March 1903.

6. *Cape May Herald,* 19 October, 23 November 1901, 20 December 1902; *Cape May Wave,* 6 December 1902.

7. George E. Thomas and Carl Doebley, *Cape May, Queen of the Seaside Resorts* (Philadelphia: Art Alliance Press, 1976), 71–75; *Star of the Cape,* 28 April 1906, 29 November 1902, 24 October 1903.

8. *Cape May County Gazette,* 10 April 1903, *Cape May Wave,* 3 November 1906; *Star and Wave,* 28 March, 25 July 1908; William E. Sackett, *Modern Battles of Trenton from Werts to Wilson* (New York: Neale Publishing, 1914), 2: 293.

9. *Cape May Wave,* 20 January, 24 March 1906; *Star of the Cape,* 10 November 1906.

10. Cape May Automobile Club, 18 July 1905, Corporation Book No. 2, 94, CMCCA; Robert C. Alexander, "The Cape May Automobile Races," *CMCMHG* 6 (1966):165–175.

11. Henry Ford purchases, 28 October 1908, Deed Book 232, 447–454, CMCCA, 11 October 1911, Deed Book 277, 1–3, CMCCA; Ford's properties were leased by the U.S. government during World War I and sold after the war. *Star and Wave,* 14 November 1908; William McMahon, *South Jersey Towns* (New Brunswick, N.J.: Rutgers University Press, 1973), 39–42.

12. Cape May City Census, 1905, New Jersey State Census, microfilm, CMCL; trustees of the Colored American Equitable Industrial Association included James W. Fishburn, Joseph G. Vance, William L. Selvy, Thomas J. Griffin, and Charles H. Finaman (26 March 1901, Corporation Book No. 1,

356, CMCCA); *Star of the Cape,* 22 June 1901; *Cape May Wave,* 21 September 1901.

13. Scull owned properties on the southeast side of Lafayette Street near Schellenger's Landing (Deed Book 182, 132–133, CMCCA); *Cape May Herald,* 31 May 1902; the *Herald* changed its antiblack policy under Lewis T. Steven's editorship, 1903–1912.

14. Cape May City Census, 1900, U.S. Census, microfilm, CMCL; meeting in James W. Fishburn's house, *Cape May Herald,* 15 June 1901; see Robert Hand to James Fishburn, 22 August 1901, Deed Book 162, 358–371, CMCCA; see also "George Henry White," in Bruce A. Ragsdale and Joel D. Treese, *Black Americans in Congress, 1870–1989* (Washington, D.C.: U. S. Government Printing Office, 1990), 159–161.

15. Whitesboro file, VF, CMCL; see Louis R. Harlan and Raymond W. Smock, eds., *Booker T. Washington Papers* (Urbana: University of Illinois Press, 1977)), 6: 557–558.

16. *Star,* 21 June 1902; *Star and Wave,* 12 September 1914; for the view that Booker T. Washington visited Woodbine, see Olive S. Barry, "Woodbine, New Jersey" (undergraduate paper: Stockton State College, 1975), 15.

17. Whitesboro Census, 1905, Middle Township Census, New Jersey Census of 1905, microfilm, CMCL, listed eleven African-American families in Whitesboro, including Askew, Artice, Blanks, Cherry, Beaman, Stanford, Mitchel, Spaulding, Land, and Moore all from North Carolina, and the Colbert family from Virginia; George White et al. to General Scott Askew, 20 January 1902, Deed Book 166, 405; Whiteboro Baptist Church fiftieth anniversary reported in *Gazette,* 30 September 1954; Mt. Olive Church of "Whiteboro," 12 May 1913, Corporation Book No. 3, 182–183; Recollections of Daniel W. Spaulding, Whitesboro file, VF, CMCL; *Wave,* 22 November 1902.

18. Risley property transfers, 4, 12 September 1907, Deed Book 218, 290, 300, 304, 340, CMCCA; Cathy Johnson, "The History and Establishment of Stone Harbor," *CMCMHG* 8 (1985): 353–357.

19. Stone Harbor, Middle Township Census, 1910, U.S. Census of 1910, microfilm, CMCL lists 104 residents, 23 born in Pennsylvania, 28 in Italy, 19 in New Jersey, 5 in Norway, 8 in Germany, and 7 of African-American heritage.

20. *Star and Wave,* 1 July 1911; *Map of Cross County Canal* (South Jersey Realty Company, 1911), CMCHS; Risley obituary, *Cape May County Times,* 17 August 1934.

21. The *Star and Wave,* explained that "a president of a great university like Princeton who consents to run for any political office whatever needs to have his head examined" (24 September 1910). Wilson lost Cape May County 2,356 to 2,171. Wilson's Court House and Wildwood speeches of October 1910, in Arthur Stanley Link, ed., *The Papers of Woodrow Wilson*

(Princeton: Princeton University Press, 1966–), 21: 281–287 (hereafter *Wilson Papers*).

22. Stone Harbor Address, 5 July 1911, August visit 1911, both in *Wilson Papers,* 23:185–186, 272–275.

23. Appointment of Baker, *Wilson Papers,* 22: 516; *Star and Wave,* 9 November 1912; Jefferson later went to jail for taking money from slot machine operations (*Cape May County Times,* 14 May 1915); Wilson's 1912 visit, *Wilson Papers,* 25: 474–478, 481.

24. *Wilson Papers,* 25: 477; *Star,* 23 July 1904.

25. Freeholder meetings, 21 March, 13 May, 13 November 1902, BCFMB; *Herald,* 19 October 1901, 23 May 1903; *Star,* 30 November 1901.

26. E. C. Hutchinson to Anthony B. Smith, 19 March 1907, letter tucked in hidden pocket in Freeholder Minute Book, 1893–1907, BCFMB; see freeholder meetings, 5 October, 6 November, 3, 24 December 1907; for the view that the Dennisville covered bridge was torn down in 1893, see Norman F. Brydon, "The Covered Bridges of New Jersey," *NJH* 85 (Summer 1967): 100–122.

27. *Cape May County Gazette,* 27 January, 7 April 1911.

28. Progressive League, 8 December 1911, Corporation Book No. 3, 74–75.

29. *Cape May County Times,* 5 October 1915, 1 December 1922; *Star and Wave,* 2, 9 September 1911, 14 October 1922.

30. *Cape May County Times,* 17 September, 5, 22 October 1915; *Cape May County Gazette,* 24 July, 13 November 1914, and *Star and Wave,* 18 September 1915, supported by the Cape May County suffragettes.

31. *Cape May County Gazette,* 15 September 1915; *Cape May County Times,* 11 June 1915.

32. New Jersey State Census Supervisor's Reports, 1905, New Jersey Census, 1905, microfilm, CMCL; Cape May County Census, 1900, 1910, U.S. Census, microfilm, CMCL.

33. *Cape May Wave,* 19 October 1901; Alfred Cresse obituary, *Cape May County Gazette,* 25 December 1942.

34. *Cape May Wave,* 19 October 1901; *Cape May County Gazette,* 10 April 1903; *Cape May County Times,* 21 September 1917.

35. Rev. Hallowell to Dr. Margaret Mace, 8 January 1928, Margaret Mace Scrapbook, WHS; Samaritan Hospital, 4 April 1911, Corporation Book No. 3, 29–30; "Dr. Margaret Mace, Humanitarian," *CMCMHG* 7 (1974): 49–52; Mace obituary, *Cape May County Gazette,* 20 December 1951.

36. *Star and Wave,* 19 October 1912; Katharine Baker, "Entertaining the Candidate," *Atlantic* 111 (February 1913): 280, probably based on Woodrow Wilson's visit with her family; the Wildwood barrier island setting figured prominently in Baker, "The Rover," *McClure's* 36 (January 1911): 278–288, which was filled with "cold-eyed silent Swedes" and "melancholy

Italians" who inhabited the Jersey coastal islands; a shrewd businesswoman outwits a greedy male speculator in Baker, "The Property Qualification," *Hampton Magazine* 28 (April 1912): 198–200, 232–233; see also Katharine Baker folder, biographical files, WHS.

37. *Star and Wave,* 29 March 1909, 13 August 1910, 11 July 1914; Thomas and Doebley, *Cape May,* 38, 77.

38. Whitesboro File, VF, CMCL; *Star and Wave,* 19 July 1913; *Cape May County Times,* 5 January, 16 March 1917. The Court House fire of February 1905 started in Theodore Yourison's Hardware Store on Mechanic Street and eventually destroyed twenty-eight buildings in the center of the town (*Cape May Wave,* 25 February 1905).

39. *Star and Wave,* 2 August 1913, 15 August 1914, 25 March 1916, 13 May 1916, 16 March 1917.

40. H. R. Whitcraft to James E. Whitesell, 4 March 1914, Advertising folder, WHS; Porter quoted in *Cape May Wave,* 9 September 1905.

41. Thomas Brady to P. P. Baker, 28 March 1916, Charles A. Norton to Wildwood Board of Trade, 6 February 1917, both in Advertising folder, WHS.

42. Ephraim Sloan quoted *Philadelphia Press,* 6 June 1885, in *CMCMHG* 7 (1976): 372; entry, 15 July 1888, F. Sidney Townsend diary, CMCHS; *Wave,* 26 October 1901; *Star,* 28 April 1906; *Star and Wave,* 20 May 1916; freeholder meeting, 21 March 1916, BCFMB; Wilson, *Jersey Shore,* 2: 889–893.

43. McMahon, *South Jersey Towns,* 32; Bethlehem Steel purchases in 15 June 1915, Deed Book 310, 331–333; 31 August 1916, Book 317, 477; 19 October 1916, Book 318, 329; J. I. Merritt, "The Guns of Cape May," *Sunday Press* (Atlantic City), 11 May 1975, 5–8, clipping, Higbee's Beach File, VF, CMCL; Adella Reed, "Dias Creek," *CMCMHG* 8 (1986): 439–440 this might also be Higbee's Beach; Belcoville in Harold Fisher Wilson, *The Jersey Shore: A Social and Economic History of the Counties of Atlantic, Cape May, Monmouth, and Ocean* (New York: Lewis Historical Publishing Co., 1953), 2: 987–988; McMahon, *South Jersey Towns,* 219.

44. Bethlehem Steel Upper Township land purchases, 24 May 1917, Deed Book 324, 310–311; 2 November 1917, Deed Book 327, 490–492; *Cape May County Times,* 26 January, 18 May 1917; freeholders meeting, 6 March 1917, BCFMB.

45. *Star and Wave,* 21 June 1913.

46. *Star and Wave,* 8 July, 19, 26 August 1916.

47. Jos. G. Champion, "Call For War Preparedness," 10 April 1917, Ocean City Organizations file, OCHSM; freeholder meetings, 3 April, 17 July 1917, BCFMB.

48. *Star and Wave,* 7, 14 April 1917, *Cape May County Times,* 2 February, 23 March, 13, 30 April, 8 June, 17 July 1917.

49. Freeholder meetings, 11, 19 June 1917, BCFMB; *Star and Wave,* 21

July, 4 August 1917; Harry Merz, "Camp Wissahickon in Cape May," *South Jersey History* 9 (Fall 1980): 15–19; see also "History of Cape May, N.J., Section Base, U.S. Navy, World War I," typescript, H. Gerald MacDonald private collection of Cape May Coast Guard Training Station papers, Wildwood Crest (hereafter MacDonald Collection).

50. *Camden-Post Telegram* quoted in *Star and Wave,* 14 July 1917; Albert Hand, *A Book of Cape May New Jersey* (Cape May: Albert Hand Co., 1937), 163; Cooper, *My Traditions and Memories, 1859–1938* (Cape May Court House: Gazette Print Shop, 1938), 191; *Gazette,* 5 July 1918; Joe Diemer, "This Land of Ours: A History of the Training Center," part 2, copy from *The Cape May Eagle,* U.S. Coast Guard Training Station, 1974, pamphlet in MacDonald Collection.

51. Freeholder meeting, 27 January 1916, BCFMB; Whale Beach Realty Company, 16 October 1913, Corporation Book No. 3, 191–193; *Cape May County Times,* 7 September 1917, 29 March, 19 July 1918, Brick quoted 5 October 1917.

52. *Cape May County Times,* 4, 25 January 1918; *Cape May County Gazette,* 16 November 1917, 25 October 1918.

53. Cooper, *Traditions and Memories,* 188–190; *Cape May County Times,* 30 August, 6 September 1918.

54. W. M. Hanlsee, comp., *Soldiers of the Great War* (Washington, D.C.: Soldiers Record Publishing Association, 1920), 2: 253–262; *Cape May County Gazette,* 21 August, 27 December 1918, 20 May 1921; *Cape May County Times,* 8, 15 November 1918, 28 May 1920; Croker Memorial, *Cape May County Gazette-Leader,* 29 January 1986.

55. *Cape May County Times,* 18 October, 28 December 1918; John T. Cunningham, *New Jersey: America's Main Road* (Garden City, N.Y.: Doubleday, 1966), 279–280.

56. Katharine Baker to Bess, 1 January 1919, Baker folder, biographical file, WHS. Baker was named by the Red Cross as one of the four most outstanding nurses in the First World War.

Chapter 8. Prohibition, Depression, and the New Deal

1. *Star and Wave,* 2 October 1920; Albert Hand *A Book of Cape May, New Jersey* (Cape May: Albert Hand Co., 1937), 158.

2. *Star and Wave,* 31 July 1920, 17, 24 July 1924, 26 April 1928; *Gazette,* 1 March 1935.

3. *Star and Wave,* 31 July, 6 November 1920.

4. *Gazette,* 7 November 1924; election returns were broadcast over the radio to the county for the first time at the M. E. Social Hall, Court

House, through loudspeakers installed by Charles Hoffman; *Cape May County Times,* 9 November 1928.

5. *Star and Wave,* 13 September 1924; *Cape May County Times,* 2 November 1928; see New Jersey Legislature, Joint Legislative Survey Committee, *Reports of the Joint Legislative Survey Committee of New Jersey* (Trenton, 1925).

6. *Star and Wave,* 14 May 1924, 17 April 1926, 8 August 1929; freeholder meeting, 7 August 1929, BCFMB; Jeffery M. Dorwart and Philip English Mackey, *Camden County, New Jersey: A Narrative History* (Camden, N.J.: Camden County Cultural & Heritage Commission, 1976), 207–227.

7. *Star and Wave,* 7 March, 15 August 1929; *Cape May County Times,* 5 July 1929; Erwin Schwatt to Joseph G. Champion, 30 November 1936, discuss their visit to Ocean City airport site in 1929, Airport Box, OCHSM; freeholder meeting, 3 July 1929, BCFMB; see also Airport file, VF, CMCL.

8. Joy Bright Hancock, *Lady in the Navy: A Personal Reminiscence* (Annapolis: Naval Institute Press, 1972), 36–37.

9. *Star and Wave,* 1 November 1924, 5 July 1928, 7 August 1926, 15 November 1931; Hand, *Book of Cape May,* 165, 179–181.

10. *Star and Wave,* 21 May 1921, 12 June, 7 August 1926; *Cape May County Gazette,* 29 December 1922; *Atlantus* file, VF, CMCL.

11. *Star and Wave,* 13 March, 7 August 1926.

12. Hand, *Book of Cape May,* 176; *Cape May County Gazette,* 16 July 1926.

13. New Jersey and Delaware Transportation Company, 24 July 1930, Corporation Book No. 7, 136–139; Hand, *Book of Cape May,* 173–174, 178–179.

14. *Cape May County Gazette,* 14 August 1925, 2 April 1926; freeholder meeting, 1 April 1925, BCFMB; *Star and Wave,* 7 July 1927.

15. Hand, *Book of Cape May,* 164, 170; *Star and Wave,* 3 February 1923.

16. *Cape May County Gazette,* 2 March 1923; *Cape May County Times,* 13 October 1922, 29 September 1923; see also Eloise Bright folder, Biographical File, WHS.

17. *Star and Wave,* 17 March 1927; Beach Estates deed, 25 June, 1926, Deed Book 436, 20, CMCCA; Miami Beach subdivision map, 5 February 1931, CMCCA; North Wildwood Villas Company, 21 February 1929, Corporation Book No. 7, 40–43, CMCCA.

18. *Star and Wave,* November 1920; *Cape May County Times,* 11 November 1921; Wildwood Crest Improvement Company and MacKissic, Deed Book 279: 56, 59.

19. *Star and Wave,* 13 November 1920; voting patterns and alliance, freeholder meetings, 1911–1921, BCFMB.

20. *Star and Wave,* 28 August 1920.

21. *Gazette,* 7 April 1911; *Star and Wave,* 5 April 1913; *Cape May County Times,* 23 March 1917.

22. *Cape May County Times,* 24 December 1920, 21 January 1921; MacKissic was the only freeholder not voting for a resolution to pay for the investigation of county affairs (Freeholder meeting, 19 April 1921, BCFMB).

23. Minutes, April 1921 court session, Cape May County Court of Oyer and Terminer and General Jail Delivery Book No. 2 (1895–1924), CMCCA; Jerrell obituary, *Star and Wave,* 28 March 1946.

24. *Star and Wave,* 21 May 1921.

25. Minutes, 14 June 1921 court session, Oyer and Terminer and Jail Delivery Book No. 2; *Cape May County Times,* 17 June 1921; *Gazette,* 17 June 1921; N. A. Cohen to Charles Black, 13 June 1921, Cape May Court of Quarter Session Records, Criminal Case File, 1921, CMCCA; H. H. Eldredge obituary, *Star and Wave,* 19 April 1934.

26. *Cape May County Times,* 14, 28 October, 11, 25 November 1921.

27. Freeholder meetings, 1 January 1923, 2 January 1925, BCFMB; *Star and Wave,* 30 July 1921, 2 September 1922, 10 February 1923; "Board of Commissioners of Cape May County," listed as the form of county government in *Boyd's City of Wildwood Directory,* 1922; William H. Bright of Wildwood pushed for creation of a five-member board of commissioners for Cape May County in Trenton (*Cape May County Times,* 26 October 1923).

28. See Andrew Sinclair, *The Era of Excess: A Social History of the Prohibition Movement* (New York: Harper and Row, 1964).

29. *Star and Wave,* 24 September 1921, 4 November 1922; Frank Hilton obituary, *Cape May County Times,* 30 June 1933; also 22 July 1921, 28 September 1929, 5 July 1929; *Cape May County Gazette,* 19 September 1924; Max Hoff purchased 2,409 acres, 21 May 1926, Deed Book 441, 468; Hand, *Book of Cape May,* 166–177; Kenneth C. Hollemon, "From Whence We Came: A History of the Coast Guard in Southern New Jersey and Delaware," Typescript, 30 March 1987, 66, H. Gerald MacDonald private collection, Wildwood Crest.

30. *Star and Wave,* 8 April 1922, 15 October 1931.

31. Hand, *Book of Cape May,* 175; *Star and Wave,* 23 August 1924; *Cape May County Times,* 22 July 1921; *Gazette,* 20 March 1925; Alfred Cooper, *My Traditions and Memories, 1859–1938* (Cape May Court House: Gazette Printing Shop, 1938), 186.

32. *Star and Wave,* 4 November 1922, 23 February 1924; *Cape May County Gazette,* 4 April, 4 July 1924; Dorwart and Mackey, *Camden County History,* 240–241; see also Kenneth T. Jackson, *The Ku Klux Klan in the City, 1915–1930* (New York: Oxford University Press, 1967).

33. Lewis T. Stevens, "Inception and History of the Society," *CMCMHG* 1 (1931): 3.

34. *Star and Wave,* 27 September 1924, 17 March 1927; Stevens, "Inception and History of the Society," 3.

35. *Cape May County Times,* 31 October 1930.

36. *Star and Wave,* 22 March, 9 May, 8, 15 August 1929.

37. Joseph G. Champion to Ocean City Commissioners, 18 March 1929, Ocean City Scrapbook, OCHSM.

38. Champion obituary, *Cape May County Gazette,* 18 November 1948; *Star and Wave,* 15 August 1929; *Cape May County Times,* 27 February, 5 November 1931; this political struggle was carried onto the 1950s by John E. Boswell, the product of Champion's Ocean City organization, against Charles Sandman of Lower Township (see Scrapbook of Ocean City Biographies, OCHSM).

39. *Cape May County Gazette,* 9, 16 October 1931; *Ocean City Sentinel,* n.d., Clipping Ocean City Scrapbook, OCHSM; *Cape May County Times,* 28 June 1929.

40. *Cape May County Times,* 1 March, 4 January 1929; Headley to Board of Chosen Freeholders, 28 December 1928; freeholder meetings, 6 February, 6 March 1929, BCFMB; *Cape May County Gazette,* 8 July 1932.

41. *Cape May County Times,* 15 November 1929, 16 January, 6 March 1931, *Star and Wave,* 19 June 1930; *Cape May County Gazette,* 25 September, 10 July 1931.

42. *Star and Wave,* 26 November, 22 October 1931; *Cape May County Times,* 27 February 1931.

43. *Star and Wave,* 15 October, 26 November, 17, 31 December 1931, 27 October 1932; Cooper, *Traditions and Memories,* 202.

44. *Star and Wave,* 5 November 1931; *Cape May County Times,* 28 July 1932; Erwin Schwatt to Wynn, 13 October 1935, Airport Box, OCHSM.

45. *Cape May County Gazette,* 5 August 1932; some Bonus Marchers may have settled on woodlands located in Cumberland County between Head-of-the-River and Millville (*Star and Wave,* 25 August 1932).

46. *Cape May County Times,* 11 November 1932; Evans G. Slaughter obituary, *Cape May County Gazette,* 19 January 1950.

47. Cooper, *Traditions and Memories,* 203; *Star and Wave,* 27 October 1932; *Cape May County Times,* 11 November 1932.

48. E. T. Bradway, Inc., 5 November 1930, Corporation Book No. 7, 176–179; Robert Bright, interview with author, 11 November 1990; *Cape May County Gazette,* 10 June, 22 July, 12 August 1932; *Cape May County Times,* 25 August 1933.

49. Bradway Republican Club of Wildwood, 19 October 1934, Corporation Book No. 8, 147; trustees included Grace McGonigle, Josephine Bright, Frances Elsey, Ina Neill, Florence Livezey; *Cape May County Times,* 11 November 1932; *Gazette,* 21 October 1932, 12 May 1933.

50. *Cape May County Gazette,* 14, 21 October 1932, 31 August 1934.

51. *Cape May County Gazette,* 1 June 1934, 10 November 1939; 12 May 1944; *Star and Wave,* 24 February 1938.

52. See *Wildwood City Directories,* 1937–1938, WHS; Sara R. Way to the People of North Wildwood, 1 March 1938, Bills, Letters and Deeds file, WHS; Helen O. Bristol, "Sarah A. Thomas—A Personal Appreciation," *CMCMHG* 6 (1968): 318.

53. Roosevelt Democratic Club of Wildwood, 31 January 1933, Corporation Book No. 8, 56–57; Colored Regular Republican Organization Circle, 7 December 1933, Corporation Book No. 7, 484–485.

54. *Star and Wave,* 24 November, 1, 8 December 1932.

55. Freeholder meetings, 2 March 1932, 17 May, 7 June, 5 July, 20 September 1933, BCFMB; *Cape May County Times,* 23 December 1932, 13, 20 January 1933; *Cape May County Gazette,* 13 January 1933.

56. *Star and Wave,* 1 December 1932; *Cape May County Times,* 20 January, 3 February, 17 March 1933.

57. *Cape May County Times,* 10, 17 March 1933; the vote was 9,208 to 2,531 for repeal of Prohibition (*Cape May County Gazette,* 19 May 1933; see also 7 July 1933).

58. Freeholder meeting, 19 July 1933, BCFMB; *Cape May County Times,* 7 April, 4 August 1933.

59. *Cape May County Gazette,* 26 May, 24 November, 8 December 1933; *Cape May County Times,* 13, 20, 27 1933, 26 April 1935; Thomas Champion, "Belleplain State Forest," *CMCMHG* 8 (1984): 288–291.

60. *Cape May County Gazette,* 4 August 1933; *Star and Wave,* 17 August 1933.

61. *Star and Wave,* 5 October 1933; *Cape May County Times,* 6 October 1933; *Cape May County Gazette,* 8 September 1933.

62. *Cape May County Gazette,* 23 June 1933, 6 May 1938.

63. *Cape May County Times,* 5 April, 20, 27 September 1935; *Cape May County Gazette,* 21 October, 18 November 1938; Cape May County Egg Producers Association, 10 October 1931, Corporation Book No. 7, 317.

64. The WPA expended $547,000 in Cape May County by 1937 compared to $6.7 million for neighboring Atlantic County, which supported FDR's administration (*Cape May County Gazette,* 30 July 1937, also 2 December, 24 June 1938); *Cape May County Times,* 27 September, 1, 7, 15 November 1935; *Star and Wave,* 11 January 1934; Hand, *Book of Cape May,* 185.

65. *Cape May County Gazette,* 6 March, 7 October 1938, 24 July 1926.

66. *Star and Wave,* 6 April 1933; Hand, *Book of Cape May,* 181; *Cape May County Times,* 10 July, 14 August 1936; *Cape May County Gazette,* 9 December 1938.

67. Henry C. Lapidus, "There's Work to be Done! Watchword of Cape May County's Fabulous 'Bill' Hunt," *New Jersey County Government* (June

1952): 25; Hunt folder, biographical file, WHS; *Cape May County Times,* 22 May 1936. Hunt's theater chain included the Nixon, Plaza, Blaker, Regent, and Casino in Wildwood; the Grand in Court House; the Liberty, Palace, and City Pier in Cape May City; and the Avalon Pier in Avalon; Hunt employed three hundred summer workers (*Cape May County Gazette,* 6 August 1934).

68. *Cape May County Times,* 13, 20 November 1936.

69. *Cape May County Times,* 18 December 1936; *Star and Wave,* 10 December 1936, 14 January 1937.

9. A Wartime and Postwar Resort Community

1. Woodbine protest meeting led by Mayor Nathaniel Rosenman and Councilman Louis Feldman, *Cape May County Gazette,* 2 December 1938; "Billions for Defense, But Not One Cent for Europe," editorial, *Cape May County Gazette,* 6 October 1939; Burke in *Star and Wave,* 7 September 1939.

2. *Cape May County Gazette,* 26 April, 23 May, 10 November 1939, 23 February 1940; *Cape May County Times,* 20 June 1941; *Star and Wave,* 13 April, 13 June 1940; South Dennis overpass project can be followed in freeholder meetings, 1939–1940, BCFMB.

3. *Cape May County Times,* 31 January, 28 February, 26 December 1941; *Star and Wave,* 2 January 1941; Redding moved to Anglesea in 1895 after his father, a Philadelphia policeman, had been killed. Redding became a major political and economic figure, developing fisheries and serving as mayor of North Wildwood, county sheriff (1922–1924), and state senator (1945–1949) (obituary, *Star and Wave,* 11 February 1960).

4. I. Grant Scott came to Cape May City in 1928 and established a marine engineering business. John E. Boswell was an Ocean City attorney. Durell received his B.A. at Princeton in 1902, moved to Belleplain in 1912 to manage the family's cranberry bogs, and served during the Depression as the county superintendent of public schools; *Cape May County Gazette,* 10 November 1939, 15 November 1940, 2 January 1942; *Star and Wave,* 8 January 1942; *Cape May County Times,* 10 January 1941, 7 May 1942.

5. *Star and Wave,* May 1938, 26 October, 9 November 1939, 15 August 1940; *Cape May County Gazette,* 23 February 1940.

6. *Cape May County Gazette,* 21 June, 20 September, 17 October 1940; *Star and Wave,* 13 June, 17 October, 26 December 1940; *Cape May County Times,* 18 October, 27 December 1940; Cape May County "fisherman" interview with the author, 27 November 1990; Kenneth C. Hollemon, "From Whence We Came: A History of the Coast Guard in Southern New Jersey and Delaware," typescript, 30 March 1987, 83. Charles A. Swain, Jr.,

Floyd Hoffman, and T. Millet Hand composed the local draft board in October 1940.

7. *Cape May County Times,* 10 January, 4 July, 26 December 1941; *Cape May County Gazette,* 18 April, 4 July 1941; freeholder meetings, 20 August, 3 September, 19 November 1941, BCFMB; see also Hollemon, "From Whence We Came," 143–144.

8. For aircraft observation post organization, see Mrs. Ernest H. Corson, chief aircraft observer, correspondence, War Records file, CMCHS; *Cape May County Times,* 26 December 1941.

9. Freeholder meeting, 18 December 1941, BCFMB; *Cape May County Gazette,* 12 December 1941, 29 January 1943.

10. Freeholder meeting, 17 June 1942, BCFMB; *Cape May County Times,* 30 January 1942; *Star and Wave,* 16 April, 25 June 1942; *Cape May County Gazette,* 27 March, 16 April 1942; see also Hollemon, "From Whence We Came," 149.

11. Jackson quoted in freeholder meeting, 7 October 1942, BCFMB; the war bond drive was headed by Stuart R. Trottman, F. Mervyn Kent, Mary (Mrs. Luther) Ogden, F. Mulford Stevens (*Star and Wave,* 8 January, 5 March, 16 April, 21, Wolcott quote 28 May, 8 July, 29 October 1942).

12. *Star and Wave,* 16 April, 28 May, 15 October, 12 November 1942.

13. *Star and Wave,* 5 February, 5 March, 28 May, 11 June 1942.

14. *Star and Wave,* 30 December 1943; *Gazette,* 31 December 1943, 22 September 1944.

15. Hand, *Book of Cape May,* 183; *Cape May County Times,* 18 December 1942.

16. Map of the six canal routes in *Cape May County Times,* 29 November 1935; *Star and Wave,* 28 November 1935, 2 May 1940, 29 January, 5, 12 February, 21 May 1942; Risley Brothers Map of proposed Stone Harbor canal route, CMCHS.

17. Mark Blasko, "A Brief History of the Cape May Canal" (undergraduate paper, Trenton State College, 1975), 8, typescript, CMCL.

18. *Star and Wave,* 30 July, 6 August 1942; Charles A. Stansfield, Jr., *New Jersey: A Geography* (Boulder, Colo.: Westview Press, 1983), 35; the Army's Corps of Engineers still blames the erosion on the southern part of the Jersey Cape partly on the canal (*The Press* [Atlantic City], 15 December 1990).

19. Stevens's opposition to county airport deed, freeholder meetings, 9 February, 2, 16 September 1942, BCFMB; *Star and Wave,* 29 January 1942; Hollemon, "From Whence We Came," 152–154.

20. "History of U.S. Naval Air Station, Wildwood, N.J.," in Milo F. Draemel, "War History of the 4th Naval District from December 7, 1941," original in Naval Historical Division, Operational Archives, Washington Navy Yard; *Star and Wave,* 21 May 1942, 12 August 1943, 8, 29 June 1944; *Cape*

May County Gazette, 10 December 1943; *Cape May County Times,* 18 February 1944; Hollemon, "From Whence We Came," 153–154.

21. *Star and Wave,* quote 11 January 1942, 1, 29 April 1943; the Adjutant General's Office, Department of Defense, New Jersey, recorded seventy-six U.S. Army deaths and twenty-six U.S. Navy and Marine Corps deaths among Cape May County service personnel during the Second World War. The complete list is Harold Fisher Wilson, *The Jersey Shore: A Social and Economic History of the Counties of Atlantic, Cape May, Monmouth, and Ocean* (New York: Lewis Historical Publishing Co., 1953), 2, appendix A: 1119–1124; casualty reports in *Cape May County Gazette,* 20 October, 22 December 1944, 16 February 1945, 10 May 1946; *Star and Wave,* 11 January 1942, 29 June 1944, 4 July 1946.

22. *Cape May County Times,* 26 December 1941; *Star and Wave,* 20 January 1944; Holtz Shipbuilding, 28 December 1942, Cape May Shipbuilders, 8 October 1942, both in Corporation Book No. 9, 154, 398–401, CMCCA.

23. Witmer Stone, *Bird Studies at Old Cape May: An Ornithology of Coastal New Jersey,* 2 vols. (Philadelphia: Delaware Valley Ornithological Club, 1937); *Star and Wave,* 2, 16 April, 12 November 1942; *Cape May County Times,* 10 April 1942.

24. *Star and Wave,* 21 May 1942; Ralph Townsend Stevens obituary, *Star and Wave,* 25 February 1954.

25. *Cape May County Gazette,* 14 July 1944; *Star and Wave,* 20 July, 10 August 1944.

26. *Cape May County Gazette,* 11, 18, 25 May, 29 June, 20 July 1945.

27. *Cape May County Gazette,* 1 August 1947; WPB ban lifted, *Cape May County Times,* 21 September 1945.

28. *Star and Wave,* 28 February 1946; *Gazette,* 11 July 1947, 12 February 1948.

29. *Cape May County Gazette,* 20 July 1945, Greenan quote 21 March 1947; *Star and Wave,* 7 November 1946; for county decision to use DDT against the mosquito see freeholder meetings, 1945–1946, BCFMB.

30. Bellanca Vocational and Flying School, 25 November 1946, Corporation Book No. 10, 58; *Gazette,* 23 August 1946, 7 March 1947 (Bellanca withdrew from the syndicate); B. F. Lee and Bayard L. England were part of an Atlantic City Electric Company group that sought to develop postwar Cape May County utilities, turnpikes, bridges, and airports (see Lee obituary, *Star and Wave,* 8 June 1961; see also Hollemon, "From Whence We Came," 158–162).

31. *Cape May County Gazette,* 13 July 1953.

32. *Cape May County Gazette,* 12 November 1953, 25 March, 16 September 1954; *Star and Wave,* 11 March 1954.

33. *Star and Wave,* 7 July 1955.

34. Cape May County Planning Board (hereafter CMCPB), *Population* (Court House: Cape May County Planning Board, 1958); between 1950 and 1960 Lower Township grew from 2,737 to 6,332; Wildwood Crest population increased between 1940 and 1950 from 661 to 1,788, and between 1950 and 1960 from 1,772 to 3,011; Ocean City grew from 4,672 to 7,618 between 1940 and 1960, and Cape May City from 2,583 in 1940 to 3,585 in 1950 and from 3,607 to 4,477 between 1950 and 1960.

35. Of the bayshore property transfers in 1952, 51.5 percent went to Philadelphia buyers (*Star and Wave*, 12 June 1952), also *Star and Wave*, 12 April 1945, 26 January 1956 for history of North Cape May.

36. *Cape May County Gazette*, 11 November 1948, 24 September 1953; *Star and Wave*, 20 July 1961; the *Bayshore Star and Wave* became a regular supplement in 1952; CMCPB, *Population*, 17.

37. *Cape May County Gazette*, 23 August 1946, 4 December 1947; for intensity of postwar football rivalries between county high schools see *Star and Wave*, sports pages, 1945–1949; for Dennisville schools see William Garrison Hunter, "A History of Education in Dennis Township" (M.A. thesis, Glassboro State College, 1965), VF, CMCL.

38. *Star and Wave*, 8 May, 11 December 1958, 5 January 1961.

39. Cora E. Chambers, "A Brief Deed History of Crest Haven Farm and Adjacent Farms," *CMCMHG* 4 (1958): 149–150; " 'A Caring Place' Crest Haven," *CMCMHG* 9 (1990): 279–285; *Cape May County Times*, 9 May 1941, 7 May 1942; *Star and Wave*, 7 May 1942; 20 June 1946; *Cape May County Gazette*, 12 July 1946, 21 September 1950.

40. *Star and Wave*, 12 December 1929, first reported closed because of pollution, see also 15 January, 23 October 1958; see also Robert C. Alexander, "The Cold Spring," *CMCMHG* 7 (1975): 165–174.

41. CMCPB, *Population*, 87–88; motel boom in *Cape May County Gazette*, 5 April 1956. The Drive-In Theater Corporation purchased the tract in Rio Grande from the Cape May County Land Company in October 1950 and transferred it to the Rio Grande Drive-In Theater Company in 1951, which transferred it to Fox Theaters, Inc., in 1952. Fox Theaters sold it to the Rio Grande Association in 1986 to develop a shopping mall and apartments; see Deed Book 757, 47; Deed Book 767, 22; Deed Book 1621, 341, all in CMCCA. The original deed to the Drive-In property in 1928 from the Wildwood Manor Developing Company to Joseph Weinstein was "subject to the condition that no building or buildings to be erected shall at any time hereafter forever be occupied or permitted to be occupied by any person or persons others than those of the Caucasian race" (Deed Book 482, 22–23, CMCCA).

42. *Cape May County Gazette*, 7 March, 27 June, 20 November 1947, 4 November 1948; *Star and Wave*, Nixon visit 13 August 1953, list of airport tenants 7 April 1960.

43. *Cape May County Gazette,* 21 May 1943, 2, 9 November 1945, 11 November 1954, 24 May 1956, 14, 21 July 1960; *Cape May County Times,* 26 October 1945; *Star and Wave,* 24 May 1956; see also M. Spencer Young, "Avalon, Only N.J. Resort with Woman Mayor," *New Jersey County Government* (June 1952): 34.

44. *Star and Wave,* 3, 24 March, 7 April 1955.

45. Italian Independent Club, 17 October 1921, Corporation Book No. 4, 82; Beneficial Society, 14 June 1926, Corporation Book No. 5, 292–293; Italo-American Civil Club of Wildwood, 18 February 1932; Citizens Club, 1932, both in Corporation Book No. 7, 346, 425–426.

46. James F. Fowler, "Senator Cafiero works Hard at Solving Cape May County Problems," *New Jersey County Government* (June 1952): 17, 40–42; *Cape May County Gazette,* 16 October, 6 November 1947; *Star and Wave,* 30 October 1947.

47. Sandman's early career can be traced in *Star and Wave,* 12 July 1945, 22 April 1954, 7, 14, 21 April 1955; *Cape May County Gazette,* 5 May 1955.

48. *Cape May County Gazette,* 14, 21 April, 30 June 1960; Volpe also organized a committee to study construction of Cape May County Vocational and Business School; *Star and Wave,* 28 January, 11, 18 February, 3 March 1960.

49. *Star and Wave,* 30 June, 11 August, 6 October, 3 November 1960.

50. *Star and Wave,* 15 January, 2 July 1959, 16 June 1960, 13 April 1961; see also George E. Thomas and Carl Doebley, *Cape May, Queen of the Seaside Resorts* (Philadelphia: Art Alliance Press, 1976).

51. CMCPB, *Comprehensive Plan for Cape May County* (Cape May Court House: Cape May County Planning Board, 1962), 14; freeholder meeting, 18 February 1942, BCFMB; *Cape May County Gazette,* 16 February, 20 April 1945, quote 21 February 1952.

52. CMCPB, *Planning Progress, 1960* (Cape May Court House: CMCPB, 1961), 10; CMCPB, *Progress Report for 1954* (Princeton: Community Planning Association, 1954), cover letter; *Star and Wave,* 25 February 1954.

53. *Star and Wave,* 21 July 1955, 29 October 1959; *Cape May County Gazette,* 8 March 1956; CMCPB, *Population,* 70–73; CMCPB, *Comprehensive Plan,* 49.

54. CMCPB, *Population,* 70–73; CMCPB, *Comprehensive Plan,* 64.

55. CMCPB, *Population,* 99–108.

56. CMCPB, *Comprehensive Plan,* 37; CMCPB, *Population,* 47.

57. CMCPB, *Comprehensive Plan,* 91; in 1962 county planners proposed the development of a Crest Haven and Cultural Center with an historic village, museum, county library (later constructed on Mechanic Street behind the county courthouse and offices in Court House), vocational school, and county college, see plate 12, p. 109. Only the vocational school was built on this site.

58. *Star and Wave,* 2 April, 11 June, 9, 11 July 1959. Examples of the 350th Anniversary postmark can be found in Safe Vault, CMCHS. See also Richard P. McCormick to Mrs. Arnold C. Nyblade, 1 March 1987, letter in possession of the author.

59. *Star and Wave,* 23 July, 6 August 1959.

60. *Star and Wave,* 21 May, 6 August 1959.

61. *Star and Wave,* 2 July, 29 October 1959.

62. *Cape May County Gazette,* 28 May, 8 October 1959; *Star and Wave,* 4 February 1960; freeholder meetings, 1959–1960, BCFMB, trace the freeholders' interest in an atomic park.

63. Pauline Newcomer letter to the editor, 9 July 1959, *Star and Wave,* see also 11, 18 February 1960.

64. George J. Carter, executive secretary, Cape May County Chamber of Commerce, to Richardson Dilworth, mayor of Philadelphia, 19 January 1960, freeholder meeting, 19 January 1960, BCFMB.

Chapter 10. A Resort Community in Transition

1. A. G. Richards, "The Great Storm of March, 1962," CMGS, *Bulletin* (June 1962): 1–5; *Star and Wave,* 8 March 1962.

2. CMCPB, *Comprehensive Plan, for Cape May County* (Cape May Court House: CMCPB, 1962), 30; *Star and Wave,* 26 July, 2 August 1962.

3. *Star and Wave,* 11 May, 8 June 1961, 9 August 1962.

4. George E. Thomas and Carl Doebley, *Cape May, Queen of the Seaside Resorts* (Philadelphia: Art Alliance Press, 1976), *Gazette,* 6 April 1967; Ann Biddle Pratt, *The Emlen Physick House Museum: A Victorian House Tour* (Fletcher, Ohio: Cam-Tech Publishing Company, 1990), 58.

5. McIntire's property acquisitions, Deed Book 1181, 805; 1190, 74; 1187, 485; 1085, 845; all in CMCCA; *Star and Wave,* 7 September 1967, 31 October 1968.

6. *Star and Wave,* 23 July, 17 September 1964, 28 October 1965; *Gazette,* 15 April 1971. Soviet trawlers in *Gazette,* 17, 24 April 1969; Star Villa moved in *Gazette,* 23 March 1967.

7. Dr. Leon H. Schuck called Sandman a dictator (*Star and Wave,* 16 December 1965; also 25 June 1964, 10 November 1966, 7 January 1971); William J. Miller, Jr., *A Ferry Tale: Crossing the Delaware on the Cape May-Lewes Ferry* (Wilmington, Del.: Delapeake, 1984), ignores Sandman's role; Sandman obituary, *New York Times,* 27 August 1985.

8. *Star and Wave,* 21 August 1968; freeholder meeting, 21 February 1922, BCFMB; *Cape May County Times,* 28 July 1922.

9. Joe Olwell, director of SODA, to Wilbur Ostrander, 25 February, 28

April 1971, Wilbur Ostrander Papers, WHS; *Cape May County Gazette,* 14 January, 11, 25 February, 4 March 1971; *Star and Wave,* 7 January, 4 February 1971.

10. Ostrander to L. G. MacNamara, 25 August 1969, Ostrander Papers; *Cape May County Gazette,* 28 July 1966.

11. CMCPB, *Population Characteristics of Cape May County, New Jersey* (Cape May Court House: CMCPB, 1980); *Star and Wave,* 2 January 1964.

12. *Star and Wave,* 24 July 1969; *Cape May County Gazette,* 21 September 1972, 12 August 1971; see also "Wetlands Champion Marion Glaspey," *Women,* magazine section, *Sunday Press* (Atlantic City), 30 March 1987.

13. *Gazette,* 25 November 1971; *Press* (Atlantic City), 24 December 1990; George A. Clark, "The Wetlands Order," CMGS, *Bulletin* (June 1973): 6–8.

14. Sullivan quoted in *Gazette,* 21 September 1972; Ostrander to Lillian A. Hagen, 19 April 1973, Ostrander Papers.

15. Copy of Freeholder Resolution, 8 August 1972, Cape May County MUA file, VF, CMCL; Mary Jane Briant, "The MUA," *Gazette-Leader, Times Reporter* (hereafter *GLTR*), 27 April 1977, also 25 August 1976; *Gazette Leader,* 9 August 1978, 17 September 1986; *Press* (Atlantic City), 24 March 1990; *Herald-Lantern-Dispatch,* 29 August 1990.

16. Elwood Jarmer, "Coastal Issues," unpublished paper, CMCPB files, CMCL, Cape May Court House; *Gazette,* 14 October, 4 November 1971, 25 September 1974.

17. *Cape May County Gazette,* 6, 13 August, 23 July 1975; *Gazette-Leader,* 28 August, 4 September, 6 November 1985; *Press* (Atlantic City), 20, 23 July 1989.

18. Jarmer, "Coastal Issues," 5; *Gazette-Leader,* 26 June, 28 July 1978; CMCPB, "Campground Study, 1978," CMCPB files.

19. *Cape May County Gazette,* 21 September, 27 April 1972, 26 April 1973, 21 January 1976; *Gazette Leader,* 25 November 1981; *Press* (Atlantic City), 30 April, 14 May 1989; see also Thomas Champion, "Belleplain State Forest," *CMCMHG* 8 (1984): 288–291; George A. Clark, "The Belleplain State Forest," CMGS, *Bulletin* (1968): 2–4.

20. "Farmland and Open Space Trust Fund Plan adopted by the Cape May County Board of Chosen Freeholders, April 24, 1990," typescript in CMCPB files.

21. *Star and Wave,* 31 March, 30 June, 1966, 18 April 1968, 13 August 1970, 22 July 1971; Walter Measday, "Historic Walk-Ways in Cape May," *CMCMHG* 6 (1971): 467–477.

22. Mary E. Stewart, ed., *Mid-Atlantic Center for the Arts, 1970–1990: 20th Anniversary Commemorative Book* (Cape May: Mid-Atlantic Center

for the Arts, 1990), 1–9; *Gazette,* 4 August 1966; Carolyn Tice, *The Cape May County Art League: A History Marking Sixty Years of Service and Creativity, 1929–1989* (Cape May: Cape May County Art League, 1989), 28.

23. Williams-Ostrander friendship, Ostrander to Williams, 14 April 1977, Williams to Ostrander, 14 January, 26 March 1975, 29 November 1976, Bill Bradley to Ostrander, 16 December 1981, all in Ostrander Papers; *Cape May County Gazette,* 1 February 1973; Kelly quoted in *Cape May County Gazette-Times-Reporter,* (hereafter *CMCGTR*), 25 August 1976.

24. *Gazette,* 26 June 1969; CMCPB, *Population Characteristics.*

25. CMCPB, *Population Characteristics,* 23, 27; *Cape May County Gazette,* 18 February 1976; *Gazette-Leader,* 18 July 1977, 27 December 1978.

26. *Cape May County Gazette,* 2 November 1972; *Gazette-Leader,* 25 September 1978, 25 February 1981.

27. *Cape May County Gazette,* 30 June, 7, 14, 21 July 1960.

28. See William James Moore, "William of Cape May," *CMCMHG* 7 (1973): 11–33; Payne obituary, 18 August 1990, Capehart obituary, 3 December 1989, both in *Press* (Atlantic City); Vasser in *CMCGTR,* 25 August 1976, 16 May 1977; Mack in *CMCGTR,* 18, 25 August 1976.

29. CMCPB, *Population Characteristics,* 30; *Gazette-Leader,* 1, 4 August 1980, 23 July 1982; Yvette Craig, "Wildwood Woman Remembers Black Entertainment Scene," *Press* (Atlantic City), section B, 26 February 1991.

30. Adeline Pepper, *The Glass Gaffers of New Jersey and Their Creations from 1739 to the present* (New York: Charles Scribner's Sons, 1971), 273; *GLTR,* 20 May 1977; *Gazette-Leader,* 13 January, 17 February 1982.

31. Bradway in freeholder meeting, 2 February 1960, BCFMB; *Cape May County Gazette,* 17 November 1966 (Bradway), 31 October 1968 (Kalbach), 16 November 1972 (Pulvino); *Gazette-Leader,* 5 November 1980; Elizabeth Holmes, entries 1791, Parsons Leaming Day Book and County Collector's Book of Cape May, 1790–1803, CMCHS.

32. *Press* (Atlantic City), 16 March 1989, 2 January 1990.

33. *Gazette-Leader,* 23 May 1977.

Bibliographic Essay

This essay includes the sources that were most helpful in reconstructing Cape May County's history. Other materials and fuller references can be found in the chapter notes.

Any study of Cape May County should begin with the collection of official records in the County Clerk's Archives and Records Room, Cape May County Clerk's Office, Cape May Court House. These records include ancient Deed Books, Road Books, Minute Books of the Court of Quarter Sessions and Common Pleas, Survey Books, and Cattle Earmark Books. The county archives contain Justice of the Peace Dockets, Military Pension Records, Naturalization Records, Census Records, Maps, and newspaper files. Miscellany Book A Liber of Deeds C includes deeds, powers of attorney, boundary settlements, leases, agreements, articles of association, and the manumission records for Cape May County slaves. The Corporation Books provide extensive information on business, political, and social organizations in the county from the 1870s to the present.

The New Jersey Department of State, Division of Archives and Records Management, New Jersey State Library, Trenton holds deeds and wills that supplement the County Clerk's Archives. Probate Records, Cape May County Records of Wills, Surrogate's Court of Cape May County, State Archives are available on microfilm. Important early documents from the State Archives are published in William A. Whitehead, William Nelson, Frederick W. Ricord, eds., *Archives of the State of New Jersey,* 1st series, *Documents Relating to the Colonial Revolutionary and Post Revolutionary History of the State of New Jersey* (Newark, Trenton, Paterson: New Jersey Historical Society, 1880–1949), 43 vols. The *Calendar of Wills,* volumes 30–42, of the *Archives of the State of New Jersey,* is invaluable for Cape May County families. The source for Cape May County government and organization before

331

1962 is H. Clay Reed and George J. Miller, eds., *The Burlington Court Book: A Record of Quaker Jurisprudence in West New Jersey, 1680– 1709,* American Legal Records, vol. 5 (Washington, D.C.: American Historical Association, 1944). There are important documents relating to Cape May County in Aaron Leaming and Jacob Spicer, *The Grants, Concessions, and Original Constitutions of the Province of New Jersey* (Philadelphia: W. Bradford, printer, 1758).

The Records of the Board of Chosen Freeholders of Cape May County, 1827–present, are located in Minute Books stored in the office of the clerk, Cape May County Board of Chosen Freeholders, Cape May County Library Building, Cape May Court House. The records also include the Cape May County Alms House Records. The Minute Books in the clerk's office are a continuation of the first book of Freeholder Minutes, 1798–1827, found on the reverse side of Parsons Leaming Day Book and County Collector's Book of Cape May, 1790–1803, deposited in the Cape May County Historical (and Genealogical) Society, Route 9, Swainton.

The Cape May County Historical (and Genealogical) Society contains a large number of manuscript collections, journals, diaries, ledger books, store day books, church records, and some private correspondence and letters. The society's library holds pages from the Aaron Leaming Diary, 1737, 1739, 1740–1741, 1746–1748; the Elijah Hughes and Judith Spicer Hughes Papers; and the Townsend Family Papers. F. Sidney Townsend's Journals record life in Seaville in the late 1860s and in Cape May City between 1888 and 1892. The Holmes Family Papers contain extensive correspondence about mid-nineteenth-century Cape May County business, politics, and society. Jeremiah Leaming's Day Book and the Ludlam Family Papers reveal more about early-nineteenth-century county business affairs. Amelia Hand's Civil War Scrapbook and Diaries are important records of Cape May County during and immediately after the Civil War. Lt. Nicholas W. Godfrey's Civil War diary retells a county soldier's wartime experiences. Other collections include the Reuben Willets Journal, the Richard Thompson Memorandum Book, and the Charles Tomlin Papers. The H. Clifford Campion Memorial Collection and Edward Post file house genealogical and some historical records about many original seventeenth- and eighteenth-century Cape May County families.

The Historical Society of Pennsylvania in Philadelphia holds four small volumes of the Aaron Leaming diaries, 1750–1751, 1761, 1775,

1777; Thomas Leaming, Jr.'s, Memorandum Books, 1762–1798; and J. Fisher Leaming's Invoice Books, 1810–1844. Part of the Aaron Leaming diaries in the Historical Society of Pennsylvania have been edited by Lewis T. Stevens and have been published in the *Cape May County Magazine of History and Genealogy* 1 (June 1932): 69–82, but the originals should be consulted for the full text. More pages from Aaron Leaming's diaries, 1743–1744, are in the Leaming Family Papers, Special Collections, Frank Stewart Room, Savitz Library, Glassboro State College. There are three folders of Aaron Leaming's papers, including personal letters, in the Special Collections, Alexander Library, Rutgers University Libraries, New Brunswick. Rutgers University Special Collection manuscripts useful to the history of Cape May County also include the Lucius Q. C. Elmer Diaries and the Francis Bazley Lee Letters. The Jacob Spicer Papers are in the New Jersey Historical Society Library in Newark. The Spicer Diary and Memorandum Book from that collection have been published by William A. Ellis, ed., "Diary of Jacob Spicer, 1755–6," *Proceedings of the New Jersey Historical Society* 63 (1945): 37–50; 82–117; 175–193; and Lewis T. Stevens, ed., "Memorandum Book of Jacob Spicer, 1757–64," *Cape May County Magazine of History and Genealogy* 1 (1933): 109–118; 162–173.

The most important manuscript collection for settlement of the barrier islands is the Charles Kline Landis Journals and Papers, Vineland Historical Society. Other collections are the Lake Family and Joseph G. Champion Papers in the Ocean City Historical Society Museum in Ocean City, and the private family papers in the Wildwood Biographical Files and the Wilbur J. Ostrander Papers, both in the Wildwood Historical Society. Also useful are the Lewis T. Stevens Diary and Papers in the possession of Mary Ann Stevens Nyblade of Cape May City.

Several memoirs and recollections about Cape May County have been published. The best was written by the founder and editor of the *Cape May County Gazette:* Alfred Cooper, *My Traditions and Memories, 1859–1938* (Cape May Court House: Gazette Print Shop, 1938). Charles Tomlin, a Dias Creek schoolteacher, focused on the bayside in his *Cape May Spray* (Philadelphia: Bradley Bros., 1913). Albert Hand's newspaper staff writers discussed Cape May City in Albert Hand's *A Book of Cape May, New Jersey* (Cape May: The Albert Hand Co., 1937). Dr. Julius Way, *An Historical Tour or Cape May County, New Jersey* (Sea Isle City, N.J.: Atlantic Printing and Publishing

Company, 1930), and the Cape May County tours described in the Federal Writers' Project, *New Jersey: A Guide to Its Present and Past* (New Jersey Guild Association, 1939; reprinted New York: Hastings House, 1956) are both largely travel guides around the city.

Katharine Sabsovich, *Adventures in Idealism: A Personal Record of the Life of Professor Sabsovich* (New York: Arno Press, 1975; reprint of 1922 private printing), discusses the founding of the Woodbine Jewish colony. Joy Bright Hancock, *Lady in the Navy: A Personal Reminiscence* (Annapolis: Naval Institute Press, 1972), recalls growing up in Wildwood and Cape May Court House. There are a number of personal recollections of other communities in the *Cape May County Magazine of History and Genealogy, CMCMHG.* These include Everett B. Townsend, Sr., "Some Random thoughts About Clermont, Its Places and People," *CMCMHG* 6 (1969): 358–376; Bessie Bristol Mason, "Recollections of Holly Beach and Wildwood," *CMCMHG* 6 (1970): 446–449; Wendeline Moore, "Recollections of Old Swainton," *CMCMHG* 8 (1981): 42–45; Adella Reed, "Dias Creek," *CMCMHG* 8 (1986): 433–441; and Hannah Kimble Swain, "Hildreth-Rio Grande," *CMCMHG* 9 (1987): 68–75, and (1988): 97–116.

The standard history of Cape May County has long been Lewis Townsend Stevens, *The History of Cape May County, New Jersey, from the Aboriginal Times to the Present Day* (Cape May City: Lewis T. Stevens, publisher, 1897). Steven's eulogistic local history borrowed heavily from Maurice Beesley, "Sketch of the Early History of the County of Cape May," in George H. Cook, *Geology of the County of Cape May, State of New Jersey* (Trenton: Office of the True American, 1857), 159–202, and from Edward S. Wheeler, *Scheyichbi and the Strand, or Early Days Along the Delaware with an Account of Recent Events at Sea Grove* (Philadelphia: J. B. Lippincott, 1876). A Dennisville physician and a founder of the New Jersey Historical Society, Beesley wrote a carefully researched analytical essay on the county's early history that is still a valuable introduction to Cape May County's history. Recent popular surveys of the county are: George F. Boyer and J.[ane Ann] Pearson Cunningham, *Cape May County Story* (Egg Harbor City, N.J.: Laureate Press, 1975); and Herbert M. Beitel and Vance C. Enck, *Cape May County: A Pictorial History* (Norfolk, Va.: The Donning Company, 1988), a book sponsored by the Cape Savings Bank.

Several regional historians discuss Cape May County in some detail. The best is Harold Fisher Wilson, *The Jersey Shore: A Social and Economic History of the Counties of Atlantic, Cape May, Monmouth and Ocean,* 2 vols. (New York: Lewis Historical Publishing Co., 1953). The Jersey Cape receives extensive coverage in William McMahon, *South Jersey Towns: History and Legend* (New Brunswick, N.J.: Rutgers University Press, 1973), and *Historic South Jersey Towns* (Atlantic City: Press Publishing Company, 1964). Isaac Mickle, *Reminiscences of Old Gloucester or Incidents in the History of the Counties of Gloucester, Atlantic, and Camden* (Philadelphia: Townsend Ward, 1845; reprinted by the Gloucester County Historical Society, 1968), is still an important work on southern New Jersey and contains insight into Cape May County's history. Thomas Cushing and Charles E. Sheppard, *History of the Counties of Gloucester, Salem, and Cumberland, New Jersey with Biographical Sketches of their Prominent Citizens* (Philadelphia: Everts Peck, 1883), remains the best history of nearby Cape May County's neighbors. Also useful for ocean resorts in Atlantic County are Sarah W. R. Ewing and Robert McMullin, *Along Absecon Creek: A History of Early Absecon, New Jersey* (Bridgeton, N.J.: private printing, 1965), and Charles Funnell, *By the Beautiful Sea: The Rise and High Times of That Great American Resort, Atlantic City* (New York: Alfred A. Knopf, 1975).

There are several good histories of individual Cape May County communities. George E. Thomas and Carl Doebley, *Cape May, Queen of the Seaside Resorts: Its History and Architecture* (Philadelphia: The Art Alliance Press, 1976), is a model of scholarship and analysis. A competent study of the early history of what became Cape May City can also be found in Robert Crozer Alexander, *Ho! For Cape Island* (Cape May: privately printed, 1956). The best history of Woodbine is Olive S. Barry, "Woodbine, New Jersey: Land Use and Social History," (undergraduate paper, Stockton State College, 1975), typescript in the Cape May County Library. Woodbine is also discussed in Joseph Brandes, *Immigrants to Freedom: Jewish Communities in Rural New Jersey since 1882* (Philadelphia: University of Pennsylvania Press, 1971). The better barrier island histories include George F. Boyer, *Wildwood, Middle of the Island* (Egg Harbor City, N.J.: The Laureate Press, 1976); Harold Lee, *A History of Ocean City, New Jersey* (Ocean City, N.J.: The Friends of the Ocean City Historical Museum, 1965); and Walter M. Sawn, *Sea Isle City, New Jersey: A History* (Sea Isle City, N.J.: Sea Isle City Tercentenary Committee, 1964). The Historical Preservation Society of Upper Township published *A History of Upper Township and Its Villages* (Marmora, N.J.: Historical Preservation

Society of Upper Township, 1989). Other Upper Township studies include H. Stanley Craig, *The History of Petersburg, New Jersey* (Merchantville, N.J.: H. Stanley Craig, 1913), and Joyce Van Vorst, *Cedar Swamp Creek: Stories and Sketches of the Area* (Cape May: Cape May County Historical and Genealogical Society, 1977).

Genealogical research and writing make up an important body of literature about Cape May County. The most important work is Rev. Paul Sturtevant Howe, *Mayflower Pilgrim Descendants in Cape May County, New Jersey, 1620–1920* (Cape May: Albert R. Hand, 1921). Also important for Cape May County genealogical study are John E. Stillwell, *Historical and Genealogical Miscellany: Early Settler of New Jersey and their Descendant's* 3 vols. (New York; privately printed, 1914), and H. Stanley Craig and Julius Way, *Cape May County Marriage Records* (Merchantville, N.J.: H. Stanley Craig, 1931; reprinted Woodbury: The Gloucester County Historical Society, 1978). The search for possible New England and Long Island roots of Cape May County families should begin with Charles J. Hoadly, *Records of the Colony and Plantation of New Haven from 1638 to 1649* (Hartford: Case, Tiffany, 1857), and Henry P. Hedges, William S. Pelletreau, and Edward H. Foster, *The First Book of Records of the Town of Southampton with Other Ancient Documents of Historic Value,* 2 vols. (Sag Harbor, N.Y.: John H. Hunt, 1874, 1877).

The *Cape May County Magazine of History and Genealogy* (*CMCMHG*) is the major forum for the publication of genealogical articles about Cape May County families. These include William Evans Price, "The Stillwells—A Patriotic Family, and Their Descendants," *CMCMHG* 1 (1940): 51–57; H. C. Campion, Jr., "Timothy Brandreth," *CMCMHG* 2 (1943): 191–200; T. L. Derwent Kinton, "Hughes Family, Genealogy," *CMCMHG* 3 (1949): 78–89; Karl A. Dickinson, "The Leamings," *CMCMHG* 4 (1955): 85–92; and George W. Jenkins, "The Wife of John Hand," *CMCMHG* 7 (1974): 78–91. Recent genealogical articles in the *Cape May County Magazine of History and Genealogy* are Isabelle Peel Foster Sakewicz, "The Christopher Foster Family History, 1603–1981, in Cape May County, New Jersey," *CMCMHG* 8 (1981): 35–41; Mary Van Gilder McCafferty and Terry W. Van Gilder, "Van Gilders from Cape May County," *CMCMHG* 8 (1985): 386–392; Elizabeth P. White and Winfield Scott Weer, "The Whilldin Family of Cape May County, New Jersey," *CMCMHG* 9 (1987): 44–67; and Wilmer F. Burns III, "Hewitts of Cape May County, New Jersey," *CMCMHG* 9 (1989): 221–243.

There is little written about Cape May County's Native Americans. Some discussion of the county's Indian roots appear in Frank H. Stewart, *Indians of Southern New Jersey* (Woodbury: Gloucester County Historical Society, 1932; reprinted 1977); and in Alanson Skinner and Max Schrabisch, "A Preliminary Report of the Archaeological Survey of the State of New Jersey Made by the Department of Anthropology in the American Museum of Natural History," in *Geological Survey of New Jersey,* Bulletin 9 (Trenton: MacCrellish & Quigley, 1913). The best study of early Dutch interest in the Jersey Cape is C. A. Weslager, *Dutch Explorers, Traders and Settlers in the Delaware Valley, 1609–1664* (Philadelphia: University of Pennsylvania Press, 1961). The English experience is discussed in John E. Pomfret, *The Province of West New Jersey, 1609–1702: A History of the Origins of an American Colony* (Princeton: Princeton University Press, 1956), and *The New Jersey Proprietors and Their Lands, 1664–1776* (Princeton: D. Van Nostrand, 1964). For a discussion of the Spicer and Leaming families of Cape May County as part of a colonial elite, see Thomas L. Purvis, *Proprietors, Patronage, and Paper Money, Legislative Politics in New Jersey, 1703–1776* (New Brunswick, N.J.: Rutgers University Press, 1986).

The Cape May County whaling industry is surveyed in Harry B. Weiss, Howard R. Kemble, and Millicent T. Carre, *Whaling in New Jersey* (Trenton: New Jersey Agricultural Society, 1974). Cape May County's role in the economic problems leading to Revolution can be found in James H. Levitt, *For Want of Trade: Shipping and the New Jersey Ports, 1680–1783* (Newark: New Jersey Historical Society, 1981), and Larry R. Gerlach, "Customs and Contentions: John Hatton of Salem and Cohansey, 1764–1776," *New Jersey History* 89 (Summer 1971): 69–92. The county's role in the Revolution is surveyed in Robert W. Harper, *Old Gloucester County and the American Revolution, 1763–1778, Including Atlantic, Burlington, Cape May, Cumberland and Salem Counties* (Woodbury, N.J.: Gloucester County Cultural and Heritage Commission, 1986); also Larry R. Gerlach, ed., *New Jersey in the American Revolution, 1763–1783: A Documentary History* (Trenton: New Jersey Historical Commission, 1975). Cape May County saltworks during the Revolution are in Harry B. Weiss and Grace M. Weiss, *The Revolutionary Saltworks of the New Jersey Coast* (Trenton: Past Times Press, 1959). The only study that involves Cape May County's role in early national politics is Herbert Ershkowitz, *The Origin of the Whig and Democratic Parties: New*

Jersey Politics, 1820–1837 (Washington, D.C.: University Press of America, 1982).

An introduction to the geographic factors that influenced the historic development of Cape May County and southern New Jersey can be found in Roger Thomas Trindell, "Historical Geography of Southern New Jersey as Related to its Colonial Ports" (Ph.D. dissertation, Louisiana State University, 1966), and Peter O. Wacker, *Land and People: A Cultural Geography of Preindustrial New Jersey: Origins and Settlement Patterns* (New Brunswick, N.J.: Rutgers University Press, 1975). Horace G. Richards, *A Book of Maps of Cape May, 1610–1878* (Cape May: Cape May Geographic Society, 1954), is invaluable, as are F. W. Beers, *Topographical Map of Cape May Co., New Jersey From Recent and Actual Surveys* (New York: Beers, Comstock & Cline, 1872); Egbert L. Viele, *Cape May, State of New Jersey* (Trenton, 1856); and R. Fendall Smith, *Map of Cape May Co.* (Cape May, 1913). Also useful is H. C. Woolman, T. F. Rose, and T. T. Price, *Historical and Biographical Atlas of the New Jersey Coast* (Philadelphia: Woolman and Rose, 1878; reprinted by the Ocean County Historical Society, 1985); Thomas T. Gordon, *Gazetteer of the State of New Jersey* (Cottonport, La.: Plyanthos reprint of 1834 edition, 1973), and John P. Snyder, *The Story of New Jersey's Civil Boundaries, 1606–1968* (Trenton: Bureau of Geology and Topography, 1969).

Studies of the Jersey Cape's natural environment can be found in George H. Cook, *Geology of the County of Cape May, State of New Jersey* (Trenton: Office of the True American, 1857); Otway H. Brown, *Plants of Cape May County* (bound typescript in Cape May County Library); Robert C. Alexander, *Noteworthy Trees of Cape May County, New Jersey* (Cape May: Cape May Geographic Society, 1948); and Witmer Stone, *Bird Studies at Old Cape May: An Ornithology of Coastal New Jersey,* 2 vols. (Philadelphia: Delaware Valley Ornithological Club, 1937). The Cape May County Geographic Society *Bulletin* (later *Magazine*), 1947–present, contains a wealth of information about the county's history, geography, and natural environment.

This bibliographic essay concludes with Cape May County's newspapers, which in the end became the most important source because of the lack of manuscript or other sources on Cape May County's recent history. There are periods of the county's history, particularly during parts of the twentieth century, when county newspapers provide most of the information that we have about the Jersey

Cape's past. Fortunately there were several good local newspapers. The county's first newspaper, the *Ocean Wave,* was founded in Cape May City in 1854 and began publishing a weekly edition under the editorship of Joseph Leach in 1855. The *Ocean Wave* became the *Cape May Wave* in 1876 and the *Cape May News and Wave* in 1907, when it was purchased by the *Star of the Cape* and became the *Cape May Star and Wave.* The Cape May County Clerk's Archives and Records Room holds bound copies of the newspapers and microfilm editions from 1860 to 1971. *The Star of the Cape* was founded in 1868 at Court House, moved to Cape May City (Island) in 1873, where it competed with the *Wave* until the newspapers merged in 1907 to form the *Star and Wave.*

In 1880 Alfred Cooper arrived at Court House from Millville and began publishing the *Cape May County Gazette.* Eventually the *Gazette* became the voice of the mainland townships and regions, providing better countywide coverage than the Cape May City newspapers. The *Gazette* merged with the *Cape May County Times* and *Wildwood Leader* and published since 1977 as the *Gazette Leader.* The bound copies can be found in the Clerk's Archives and a microfilm edition in the Cape May County Library. A third major county newspaper, the *Cape May County Times,* began publishing in Sea Isle City in 1886. The *Times* became the primary source of barrier island news. There were other barrier island newspapers, some short-lived such as the *Sea Isle Pioneer* (microfilm copy 1882–1884 in the Clerk's Archives), the *Ocean City Sentinel, Wildwood Tribune Journal, Wildwood Leader, Five Mile Beach Journal,* and *Cape May Herald* (Cape May City). There are incomplete runs of most of these local newspapers on microfilm in the County Clerk's Archives and Records Room or in the County Library. A complete inventory of Cape May County newspapers can be found in William C. Wright and Paul A. Stellhorn, *Directory of New Jersey Newspapers, 1765–1970* (Trenton: New Jersey Historical Commission, 1977).

Index